On
Shaky
Ground

Books by John J. Nance:

On Shaky Ground

Blind Trust

Splash of Colors

On Shaky Ground

John J. Nance

WILLIAM MORROW AND COMPANY, Inc.
NEW YORK

Library of Congress Cataloging-in-Publication Data

Nance, John J.
    On shaky ground.

    Includes index.
    1. Earthquakes. I. Title.
QE534.2.N36   1988   363.3'495   88-12800
ISBN 0-688-06648-8

Printed in the United States of America

First Edition

1   2   3   4   5   6   7   8   9   10

BOOK DESIGN BY PANDORA SPELIOS

To Harold Simmons

Author's Note

I've written this book to engage you with the pace of a gripping novel, yet I want you to know that everything you find in these pages is true and scientifically accurate (even though presented in nontechnical, everyday terms). My footnotes are also narrative in form, but in order to keep them from getting in the way of the rapid flow of the story, I've put them in the back of the book (just ahead of the Appendices). Nevertheless, I hope you'll refer to them throughout whenever a footnoted passage raises additional questions in your mind.

Finally, Appendix 1 contains a demystifying explanation of the different types of earthquake magnitude scales we all tend to call generically (and incorrectly) "the Richter Scale." There is, as well, a short but important list of things you can do at home to protect yourself and your family in Appendix 2, and a narrative bibliography (References) placed after the Acknowledgments.

First, however, the dynamic human story itself awaits you.

Contents

Introduction

Living on this planet can be hazardous to our health, because the structures we occupy on its surface are at constant risk from damaging earthquakes.

Only in the last twenty years, however, have we really begun to understand the nature of this risk, and how widespread it is across North America. And only during the last decade have we realized that we do have the ability to minimize that risk, provided we also have the resolve to act quickly.

Major earthquakes have shaken and savaged North America at various points from the East Coast to the West throughout its geologic history. But to protect ourselves from future episodes, we have to know where those previous quakes occurred. The earthquakes that rocked the East Coast from Boston to Charleston during the previous three hundred years are well documented, as are the three great quakes that shook the Midwest at the start of the nineteenth century. But there were uncounted earthquakes that came before the arrival of the colonists—previously unknown seismic convulsions now traceable through tantalizing shreds of telltale evidence left behind in layers of muds and silts and soil. These are records of ancient upheavals in maritime marshes and silent streams—the harbingers of future earth shaking in unsuspecting realms.

We know now that where major earthquakes have occurred before, such quakes will probably occur again, ripping and roiling the surface of the earth where once stood only the prairies and forests of primeval America, landscapes now supporting delicate dwellings and workplaces, the vulnerable dams and marginally protected nuclear power and petroleum storage facilities, and the fragile web of vital utility networks carrying a bewildering variety of

11

water, gas, communications, and transportation lifelines as they weave through the fabric of America.

We have only begun to uncover those seismic histories and decipher their meanings, and the story of that process alone is fascinating. But equally important is the realization that these new discoveries dictate immediate action, from a Saturday afternoon of family earthquake preparation in our homes to the need for a natural hazards insurance program and the funding of much more scientific research along with regional programs to teach hazard mitigation techniques to people and communities alike.

These are unsettling discoveries, focusing us for the first time on just how exposed we are as a people to massive, catastrophic earthquakes. Los Angeles, for example, is almost certain to be hit by a great earthquake in the next few decades, a monstrous repeat of an 1857 quake which this time around may kill ten thousand fellow Americans and cause sixty billion dollars of damage. The financial impact alone of such a cataclysm would affect virtually everyone in the nation.

And by no means is this sort of threat limited to the West. The greatest known quake in the United States occurred along the Mississippi River between St. Louis and Memphis, and another such earthquake may occur again at any time. In fact, thirty-nine states in the United States, including Missouri, South Carolina, New York, Massachusetts, Tennessee, Illinois, Indiana, and even Texas—and all the great cities and citizens within them—live daily in the shadow of sudden destructive earth shaking. They live as well with the possibility of shattered lives and financial ruin which can occur when building codes are inadequate, earthquake insurance is unavailable, and hazard reduction programs at city and state level do not exist. We know, in other words, what steps to apply to live with earthquakes in far greater safety. The question is, Are we willing to take those steps before a great quake proves they are needed?

The progress in the last twenty-five years in understanding earthquakes—the science of seismology and related fields—has been staggering. But progress in the last few years in applying that new knowledge to our buildings and houses and bridges and dams has been far too slow. What has saved Americans repeatedly in past major earthquakes is luck, but luck will not save us indefinitely.

As usual in our vibrant, free society, it is up to us to decide whether to face the reality of the seismic threat and embrace the availability of the solutions or to continue to lie helpless before quakes which can flatten our houses, destroy our employers, damage our national economy and national defense, and wipe out the financial equity of a lifetime in a mere thirty seconds of ground shaking.

What follows, then, is a dynamic human story of the great distance we have come, and the distance we have yet to travel.

Chapter 1

Neah Bay, Washington—1986

He seemed terribly out of place—barely visible in the midst of a wet, verdant meadow—crouching suspiciously at the edge of the small tidal stream which meandered with picturesque abandon toward the waters of the Pacific Ocean less than a mile to the south.

The visual richness around him was startling. The spruce-carpeted ridgeline to the east bordered the short, green valley that ran only a few feet above sea level from the Strait of Juan de Fuca on the north end to the ocean beaches on the south end, almost making an island of the highland mountain to the west. That lone mountain, covered with western red cedar and spruce and standing 1,395 feet above sea level, was the northwesternmost piece of real estate in the continental United States: Cape Flattery.

From the eye of a passing eagle, watching the solitary human through the hanging mists of a Pacific Northwest late afternoon, the meadow seemed a tranquil, peaceful setting. For uncounted afternoons it must have looked the same, the majesty of nature at its finest, accompanied by the gentle sounds of softly flowing stream water in the foreground, riding lightly over the basso profundo thunder of crashing surf and boiling sea-foam in the distance, in concert with the gentle patter of raindrops falling like an afterthought through the foggy air.

The valley and the people of the Makah Indian tribe had coexisted in functional harmony for centuries, the patterns of daily human life molded to the imperatives of the seasons, blending into the backdrop of falling rains and flowing waters. But the actions of the lone figure at streamside were in contrast with those patterns—unusual, audacious, and unfamiliar. With short strokes of a camp shovel chopping into the dirt and sand of the embankment, Brian Atwater was obviously searching for something—a geological detective looking for evidence nature was suspected of hiding.

15

Atwater looked around at the ghostly image of the tree-covered ridge to the west, barely visible through the steady rain which had been dampening his spirits and seeping through his rain gear for much of the day.

He glanced back to the east, conscious of the rise in the landscape on that side—conscious that the area between the two sides had probably once contained the free-flowing waters of the Pacific Ocean, making Cape Flattery, to the west, a true island.

He had expected that. He had expected to find some evidence that this meadow had evolved from an ocean inlet.

But Atwater was not expecting what his shovel had just uncovered on the first series of thrusts: a black line—a flat layer—running horizontally through the sand and silt which formed the wall of the streambed.

What on earth did it mean?

There, several feet down from the top of the bank where the grasses and roots of the meadow above were anchoring a thin layer of humus—below several feet of loosely compacted gray sand with the remains of dead grass roots embedded here and there—the sand suddenly, abruptly rested on a layer of black peat.

Brian stared at the layer at first, struggling to put it into perspective.

"Okay, what do we have here?" The words were spoken to the riverbank, and to himself—a practiced, professional breakpoint between action and analysis.

He began digging into the peat then with a knife, finding the buried stems of grasslike plants killed long ago interlaced in the dark material. It looked, in fact, like the remains of a brackish-water marsh, perhaps from some previous century—a marsh which had been buried so quickly and deeply by sand that its soil had been preserved.

But how could that be?

If a great ocean wave—a tsunami—had overrun the ancient meadow, could giant waves or surging salt water have washed up that much sand to cover the area completely? Or could the entire marsh have suddenly dropped below sea level?

One thing was indisputable: The layer of peat in front of him definitely existed, and that meant something catastrophic had happened in this beautiful place. But when?

16

He poked at the peat some more, satisfied there would be enough material to send for analysis. Once a properly equipped lab had measured the amount of radioactive decay in the carbon, he would have a reasonably close idea of how long ago the marsh had died.

Brian Atwater began digging again in earnest, spading away at an adjacent wall of the streambank, standing on the narrow bank between water and dirt wall, exposing more of the black layer that had surprised him. His feet were protected from the water seeping around his knees by the hip waders he was wearing, while a knitted watch cap diverted much of the drizzle from his head. Even with the protection of a coarse wool sweater (a handwoven gift from his sister), the pervasive cold had distracted him.

No longer, however, was he conscious of the chill in the air. This was far too intriguing.

Atwater knew some of the theories, of course. That was why he had come to Neah Bay and Cape Flattery looking for a record of changes in the level of the land—evidence of how much it had risen or fallen relative to sea level over the centuries. He was aware of the work of a young seismologist in California, Dr. Tom Heaton, who along with several others had found some scary similarities between what was happening to the ocean floor off the coast of the Pacific Northwest, which did not seem to have a history of great, damaging earthquakes, and what was happening off the coasts of southern Japan and southern Chile, which did.

Atwater knew that Heaton had developed a substantial amount of circumstantial, scientific evidence that the Pacific Northwest should be no different from those areas of Chile and Japan that had been rocked by earthquakes so great that they were capable of killing thousands of people and producing unbelievably huge tsunamis. Such quakes were the result of incredible planetary forces shoving the ocean floor (oceanic plates) into and beneath the equally thick plates of rock which formed the major continents. It was a process called subduction in which layers of rock, each one miles thick, were being shoved in opposite directions, snagging against each other for centuries at a time, and building up incredible pressure year by year as a result.

Along the Pacific Northwest coast, the battle line between the tectonic plates was called the Cascadia subduction zone, and Tom Heaton had a growing suspicion that it was dangerous. If he was

17

correct, the immense pressures which would inevitably build up between any snagged crustal plates as they strained to move past each other would eventually overcome the snags and release the energy, causing great, catastrophic earthquakes in the process.

But Tom Heaton was hamstrung without hard evidence. While the last monstrous quake in southern Chile—one of the most powerful earthquakes in recorded history—had rocked the South American coast in 1960 killing fifty-seven hundred people, and southern Japan had been hit by quakes in 1944 and 1946, there was no recorded history of great earthquakes (with magnitudes above 8.0) in the Pacific Northwest from Vancouver, Canada, all the way south to the redwood forests of Northern California. If they had occurred in the Northwest, the last one must have been before white settlers arrived in the late 1700's.

Brian Atwater stopped his digging, momentarily unsure. What if this peat layer was not continuous? What if he couldn't find it elsewhere—couldn't validate what he was sure it had to represent: a suddenly deceased marsh from centuries past? That was always a possibility, but if the next few days of digging did find the same layer at different points, it would be time to head for the local post office in Neah Bay to send a postcard to Tom Heaton. He had never corresponded with Heaton before, but tempered by normal scientific caution, Brian was beginning to get excited.

It was by chance he was there to begin with. In 1985 he had moved his family to Puget Sound to be closer to medical and therapeutic help for his young daughter Sarah, a Down's syndrome child who had suffered brain damage from meningitis.

The family home had been in San Francisco, California, a forty-minute train ride from Menlo Park, the locale of the western headquarters of the U.S. Geological Survey (USGS), for which Brian Atwater had worked as a geologist since 1973.

But the San Francisco Bay area is an expensive place to live, and Sarah's disabilities were proving difficult to combat—problems which did not escape the attention of Dr. Atwater's USGS managers. They encouraged the young geologist to find a place where the best medical care would be available.

That place was Seattle, which held the teaching hospital at the University of Washington, a Down's syndrome specialty center. With great human caring and concern—and no small expense—the

Geological Survey transferred Brian, his wife, Fran, and their daughters Sarah and Patricia to the Pacific Northwest in the fall of 1985, even though no one had any clear idea what projects the thirty-four-year-old geologist would work on once he settled there.

The move helped, and the professional reception was gracious: The chairman of the university's Geology Department gave Brian an office on campus almost immediately (a recognition of the value of having a USGS scientist in residence). It was a gesture that helped keep the workplace, their new home, and the hospital where little Sarah underwent frequent therapy, all within blocks of each other. And it was the best that could be made of a difficult situation.

Even before leaving San Francisco, Brian Atwater had figured he could make himself professionally useful in his new Seattle posting by mapping poorly identified areas of seismic (earthquake) risk and seismic shaking around Puget Sound, a sort of mapping that was sorely needed.

There was, however, an area of research which needed his skills even more—a project which could meld the fields of seismology and geology in search of answers to new and disturbing questions about the exposure of the Pacific Northwest to great earthquakes. It was a scientific need he knew little about—until he heard Tom Heaton address a Seattle seminar in October 1985.

Heaton, a thirty-four-year-old seismologist Ph.D. from the California Institute of Technology, had come to speak to the group because he knew the possibility of great quakes in the Pacific Northwest couldn't be ignored. If the enormous section of the ocean floor off the coasts of Washington and Oregon did produce great earthquakes, they held the frightening potential for damage and destruction and deaths to the people and structures of the Pacific Northwest on a scale never before imagined.

Shaped roughly like a huge triangle with its hypotenuse running parallel to the coastline some eighty miles offshore, that particular part of the planetary crust along the northwest coast had been named the Juan de Fuca plate and it had some unusual characteristics. As all the so-called plates which make up the earth's crust, it too was forever in motion. As seismologists like Heaton had come to understand, new lava was constantly coming up from the depths of the planet's interior at the western boundaries of the plate as it moves approximately 2 centimeters per year toward the east. At the eastern edge, however, the plate meets the rather impressive obstacle of the North American continent—the North American plate—which at the same time is moving westward at the same steady speed of at least 2 centimeters per year, driven by the same sort of mid-ocean lava flows (known as crustal spreading) more than five thousand miles away in the middle of the Atlantic Ocean. The colossal collision between the plates has been going on in very slow motion for literally tens of millions of years, but that motion—as Heaton had patiently explained to so many—is the basic engine which created most mountain ranges, volcanoes, and earthquakes on earth.

Scientists had long assumed that the tectonic plates which meet at the Cascadia subduction zone off the northwestern coast slip past each other without causing great earthquakes. Yet the same type of plate in the same type of subduction zone causes horrendous earthquakes in southern Chile and southern Japan. There, snags develop between the plates as they move past each other, the oceanic plate thrusting at a shallow angle downward beneath the continental plate, but getting stuck temporarily in the process.

The forces that drive them, however, do not stop. When two tectonic plates are coming together at a combined rate of four centimeters per year, the pressure will continue to build whether or not the leading edges are snagged, meaning that snags will eventually break. When such a "locked" section does shatter, great earthquakes of a magnitude of 8.5 to 9.5 are the result. And when the earth is lashed by seismic energy of that level, the ocean floor moves, portions of the land and the seabed are thrust upward sometimes in excess of fifteen to twenty feet, and other areas are suddenly submerged by as much as eight feet, with devastating tsunamis created just offshore by the shifting seafloor. In other words, when such gigantic quakes occur, not only are buildings and dams and highways and all the surface works of man subjected to violent shaking for minutes at a time, but coastal areas (and all things and people on them) can be hit by unbelievably powerful surges of water—sometimes in the form of breaking waves—twenty, thirty, or forty feet high.

History had only kept track of the last two hundred years in the Northwest. A great quake just three hundred years ago would be unknown, but another one might already be lurking in the unseen depths of the subduction zone beneath Puget Sound or Portland or Vancouver, building up pressure that would someday be released catastrophically. The thought of that type of destructive earthquake occurring beneath an unsuspecting populace in the Pacific Northwest was a call to action—which is why Tom Heaton journeyed to Seattle in October 1985 to speak to a three-day U.S. Geological Survey-sponsored conference of concerned civic leaders, law enforcement officials, and scientists about that very possibility.

It was a meeting Brian Atwater decided to attend.

Heaton knew that his audience would rather not believe such speculation, and that without hard proof, his carefully researched theories were just that—theories. The largest earthquake anyone had traditionally expected for the Puget Sound region was in the magnitude 7.0–7.2 range, and Seattle had already had two damaging ones in the previous forty years, one in 1949 (magnitude 7.1), and another in 1965 (magnitude 6.5). The claim that something of magnitude 8 or magnitude 9.5 (similar to the type of quake that struck Chile in 1960) could happen in the Seattle area was rather heretical—not to mention frightening. Few of the buildings, the schools, the roads, or the many defense installations in the region—let alone the people—were prepared to survive the type of massive ground motion that such quakes could produce. There were no organized earthquake preparedness projects, no upgraded building codes or emergency response plans aimed at dealing with destruction on a greater scale than even California's San Andreas Fault could cause. And yet, if he was right, that was exactly the nature of the threat. Bad news of that magnitude is seldom accepted without skepticism.

Heaton, in other words, had an uphill battle, and he needed help from field researchers. He needed evidence—proof—before the general population or his fellow scientists would be sufficiently convinced that the Cascadia subduction zone was anything but tame and benign.[1]

Before moving to Seattle, Brian Atwater had heard Tom Heaton talk about this at Menlo Park, as Heaton wondered aloud why no one had found evidence of sudden rises in coastal terrain in Washington and Oregon if great quakes did occur there. Could it be that great earthquakes on the northwestern coast drop the terrain rather than raise it? Maybe there was evidence in the ground itself of the sudden dropping of entire sections of coastal land. These would be drops of two, or four, or eight feet that might have occurred over the space of only a minute as the incredible amounts of energy stored in the tortured, snagged rocks of the two plates beneath the Pacific Northwest coastline suddenly let go and readjusted themselves.

To Brian at the time the speech was only mildly memorable. He had too many other things on his mind.

Now, during the Seattle meeting, he overheard a delegate make an offhand comment which suddenly put it all in perspective—convincing him in the process that there was a role for him to play. "We can't act," the politician had said, "on conjecture alone."

In other words, no proof, no action. Theory be damned.

Now Atwater was impressed. The evidence Heaton needed would have to come from the Pacific Northwest, and here he was in need of a new project in the same backyard. In addition, Brian knew he had just the type of background in stratigraphic geology needed to poke around in the recently deposited layers of dirt and rock, sand and silt, looking for clues to what was obviously an intriguing and increasingly urgent seismological mystery.

With a casual go-ahead from his "moneylender" (a USGS seismologist based in Denver who monitored his projects), Dr. Brian Atwater prepared to tackle the challenge.

Little Sarah Atwater died suddenly in January 1986. With the demands of Sarah's therapy and the family's intense concern during the previous months, leaving for even a day had been difficult. By February, however, Brian Atwater realized he no longer need be afraid to leave his family occasionally for a few days of fieldwork, and he began the first steps of his probe—a solitary scientist on a quiet, almost invisible investigation into the background of a geophysical phenomenon with the potential to affect the lives of millions.

By March, after some digging into the tidal areas of Whidbey Island north of Seattle, he was ready to look for evidence of sudden rises or subsidence along the Washington coast at the north-westernmost tip of the Olympic Peninsula: Neah Bay, along the Strait of Juan de Fuca.

The area was fascinating to Atwater, as well as varied and beautiful. Even the name of the strait had a convoluted history: Juan de Fuca, it seems, never visited the Pacific Northwest, despite his four-hundred-year-old claims to the contrary.

He was a Greek sea captain who sailed on behalf of Spain in the late sixteenth century under the name Juan de Fuca and who told what is considered a tall tale about finding a great inland sea in 1592 approximately where Puget Sound was discovered 200 years later.[2] Whether or not his claim was true, no other European explorers or settlers arrived until the late 1700's, when Spanish sailors established an outpost for a brief time at Neah Bay.

People had lived at Neah Bay before 1775, of course. The original owners and residents—the Indians of the Pacific Northwest (many of them tranquil tribes in a bountiful land)—had lived in the region for thousands of years.

But theirs was not a written history; it was verbal, and imprecise. Through the twisted sinews of that history there were some tantalizing clues about earthquakes, and one had been documented by an early white settler—an ethnologist and prolific diarist named James Swan, who had wandered from the 1849 gold rush to Puget Sound in the 1850's (abandoning his wife and children back in New England in the process).

As well as Swan knew and respected the Northwest Indians, it was with substantial caution that he related tales of their legends and histories, lest his readers get the impression that he believed them all to be true. That care, however, gave an air of credibility to his diaries (and one book), which dealt in part with the Makah tribe—the Northwest Indian tribe that considered the Neah Bay area on the northeast side of Cape Flattery their ancestral home.

Tom Heaton and USGS geologist Parke D. Snaveley, Jr., had read Swan's writings in an effort to uncover *some* documentation or hint of great earthquakes prior to 1775. What they found was a tale of an incident that resembled a tsunami in some ways, told to Swan by "an intelligent chief; the statement . . . repeated on different occasions by several others with [only] slight variation in detail.

"A long time ago, but not at a very remote period, the water of the Pacific flowed through what is now the swamp and prairie between Waatch Village and Neeah Bay, making an island of Cape Flattery. The water suddenly receded leaving Neeah Bay perfectly dry. It was four days reaching its lowest ebb, and then rose again without any waves, or breakers, till it had submerged the Cape, and in fact the whole country, excepting the tops

23

of the mountains at Clyoquot [on Vancouver Island to the north]."[3]

"Could this be," wrote Heaton and Snaveley in an October 1985 professional paper, ". . . an account of a great tsunami? Although there are many features . . . that seem exaggerated, apparently Swan was convinced a remarkable sea-level disturbance had occurred."

Now in the misty afternoon of March 24, 1986, the swamp and prairie that the long-deceased Makah chief had spoken of surrounded Brian Atwater, the steady rain still giving sound and liquid form to the low, wispy clouds that shrouded the hills and hung in the tops of the fir trees and western red cedars. With the black layer of ancient meadow now fully measured and probed—pieces of it resting in his sample bag—he could move on to another site by the stream.

Brian couldn't help leaping ahead mentally to what it meant. Was this in fact the validation of Heaton's theory? Had this meadow and the surrounding coast for many miles north and south suddenly dropped below high tide level in some prior century during a great earthquake?

The juxtaposition of serendipitous discoveries and scientific discipline has always seemed to crop up in the long history of man's scientific breakthroughs. The thought that any scientist, no matter how obscure or remote his or her area of focus, might stumble over a major discovery—find the missing piece to a complex puzzle—or single-handedly advance science by individual effort, has spurred countless graduate students and senior scientists alike to keep on looking for answers.

He recalled the pivotal work of another USGS geologist, Dr. George Plafker, and how that one scientist had been so influential in advancing seismology and the subscience now known as plate tectonics, which embraces the growing understanding of how the plates of the earth's crust behave when they smash into each other at subduction zones. Without plate tectonics as a working, accepted theory, Tom Heaton's papers and suspicions about the Pacific Northwest would be groundless. The hope of forecasting great earthquakes, in fact, would be far less reasonable or possible a goal.

And what had gotten Dr. Plafker started was simple curiosity:

He had been intrigued with the similarities between the great 1960 Chilean earthquake—the hundreds of miles of dropped seashore and uplifted land, the severe shaking, and the ruinous tsunamis—and what happened in Alaska in 1964.

In fact, that one seminal period—1960 through 1964—was the turning point in modern seismology in many respects. There was so much the geological and seismological community did not know at that time, and so much they have learned since; immense advancements in the science resulted directly from the intensive research and increasing governmental and public awareness spurred by the great earthquake disasters of those years. Plafker and others who had studied the Alaska quake knew that documenting and understanding the details of that event—learning the lessons of what it did to the people and the land, and what could have been done to save lives and property had there been a way to know it was coming—were a vital part of reducing earthquake hazards and lighting the way to eventual earthquake prediction.

Did the dark layer Brian Atwater had uncovered record the same sort of great earthquake as those of the early sixties? If the answer was yes, then somewhere in the next minutes or the next few thousand years the Pacific Northwest was destined to experience the sort of seismic cataclysm that had torn into the Alaskan landmass one mild March afternoon twenty-two years before.

Chapter 2

The dog looked puzzled, almost pained, as he stopped in his tracks once more, the cold salt water of Resurrection Bay dripping from his resilient fur. The young husky looked around behind him at the waterfront, across the tracks of the Alaska Railroad, searching for the source of his uneasiness, and finding nothing. His head whipped back suddenly in the direction of home, eyes looking forward at his master standing in the yard. With an almost imperceptible whine he resumed running, bounding again, toward the young man.

The high school senior—an accomplished dog musher even at the age of eighteen—waited uneasily in front of his family's home, watching the husky galloping toward him, and groping for an explanation of what had been going on for the last hour.

He was proud of this animal, a prime sled dog, and a good pet. And, maybe a future champion in the traces. The pup had possibilities, he was certain.

Pup wasn't the right word, of course. The young husky was into his second year and was robust—so big, in fact, that when he rode around town on his young owner's Honda 50 (sitting on the little platform aft of the driver's saddle), people in cars behind them would almost swear it was the dog that was driving the motorbike all by himself. The boy and his dog were rapidly becoming a vehicular legend in Seward, Alaska.

But the husky's odd behavior this Friday afternoon was a puzzle. He never went to the beach. He never got in the water. But here it was a clear, windless, hauntingly beautiful March day with a thirty-eight-degree temperature, and the dog had already made two or three trips to the bay, coming back dripping wet each time.

The young man reached down to greet the dog, scratching him behind both ears and rubbing his neck, grabbing his muzzle in greeting.

"What on earth's gotten into you, boy? Huh? You okay?"

The young husky merely whined, wagging his tail, breaking free suddenly to bound off in another direction beneath the cobalt blue Alaskan sky, the limitless energy of a young sled dog muted somewhat by his obvious confusion.

Shadows from the ridge of mountains—glacier-capped peaks that form the western wall of the town and the western border of the wild Alaskan fjord—always began to creep over the community well in advance of darkness, like a special blue-sky twilight time reserved specifically for people lucky enough to live in deep valleys between majestic peaks. With the clocks showing nearly half past five in the afternoon, the sun was about to disappear behind Mount Marathon, all 4,603 feet of its highest pinnacle a mere 3,600 yards laterally from the almost sea-level city streets of Seward.

From the air—when viewed from the vantage point of high altitude—the tiny community was little more than the faint hint of a crosshatch of streets, barely discernible straight lines covering a small teardrop of land attached to the upper left-hand corner, the northwest end, of the long twenty-two-mile inlet named Resurrection Bay.

From the ground it was home to a community of friends and strangers nineteen hundred strong who worked at being the rail and highway gateway to the interior of Alaska. It was a community that had just been selected as an All America City by the National Municipal League, a prideful designation which validated to Seward residents their feelings of municipal self-worth and permanancy.

But from the point of view of a geologist, it was a tenuous human development placed on a crescent-shaped fan of loose sand and gravel (known as an alluvial fan), silt and cobbles and boulders washed down from the western wall of mountains on the glacial waters of tiny Lowell Creek and deposited on the northwestern shoulder of the glacier-carved bay over the past ten thousand years (the Holocene Epoch of the Quaternary geologic Period). It was a community built on a mound of water-saturated glacial rubble—nature's landfill—clinging like a geological afterthought to the entrance of the majestic inlet.

Even to a pragmatic mind, though, this place was evocative of poetically rich images of man and nature in slightly uneasy coexistence.

28

Which was, in fact, what had attracted Dan Seavey to the area.

Seavey had longed for time in the wild North, time for hunting and fishing and living beneath clean skies in a stand of timber, devoid of phones and the crush of urban life. His wife had finally given up trying to resist the dream. They had come to an agreement on the subject. The Seavey family, equipped with three toddlers, would move to the wilds of Alaska for two years so Dan could get it all out of his system. Then, according to the plan, the Minnesota native would take the family back to the Midwest and begin a long high school teaching career in some comfortable farming community. That, at least, was the stated intention.

The Seaveys rolled into Seward in August 1963, renting a house near Third and Adams, four blocks from the waterfront on high ground near the high school, where he had been hired sight unseen as a new faculty member. It was a small high school, with a fascinating cross section of students, many as self-sufficient as the young musher with the motorbike-riding husky.

And it was closed for this holiday, Good Friday, which gave Dan Seavey an opportunity along with another teacher to do some snowshoeing north of town, taking advantage of the snowpack in the upper valleys before the spring melt got under way in earnest.

Seavey was back now, climbing the steps of a friend's house a half block from his own, the borrowed snowshoes in his hand, having accepted the man's invitation to come in for a cup of coffee. The bracing, sweet, and dusky aroma of woodsmoke wafting on the crisp, still air blended with the smell of coffee as he stood in the open door, stomping the remaining snow off his boots, glancing around at the bay spread out four blocks below.

A coastal tanker Seavey recognized as the *Alaska Standard* was moored at the Standard Oil dock on-loading volatile aviation fuel to the whine of generators and pumps, and a switch engine could be heard rumbling and groaning dutifully around the railyards which spanned the eastern waterfront. The familiar sounds were as sharp and clear as the air—which was very still.

In fact, there was no breeze at all, and Seavey had been here long enough to know that was unusual. Normally a stiff wind would be flowing over them from the north on a clear, spring day. But today there was nothing. Not a breath, which made the thirty-eight-degree temperature seem almost warm and comfortable by contrast. Without wind, there can be no wind chill.

Dan Seavey took note of that small fact the way most observant people take note of slight incongruities: pushed away to the back of his mind—a small memory which would shortly take on great significance.

As the switch engine six blocks away started moving again, Dan Seavey swung the door closed behind him and accepted a chair at the kitchen table, the panorama of Seward in late afternoon playing just outside the picture window to his right.

To the Alaska Railroad engineer, not even the noise and vibration of the 125-ton diesel-electric switch engine could completely mask the special feel of the Seward waterfront. The tracks here were, well, mushy. Well built and solid, to be sure. Thousands of tons rolled over them daily, and the ties and 125-pound steel rails all were in good shape.

But the ground beneath the tracks and ties seemed to echo the vibrations of the locomotive's passage. There was a secondary vibration—almost as if the rails had been placed on an enormous layer of hard rubber. To those familiar with it, that was just Seward.

On the south end of the town one of the three giant gantry cranes on the Alaska Railroad docks resumed its movements alongside berth one, rumbling slowly back and forth on steel legs and wheels, looming over the south shoreline of Seward, which was the south portion of the Seward alluvial fan formed by the glacially eroded gravel and silt pulverized from the nearby mountain slopes. The Alaska Railroad docks were a long series of concrete and steel platforms which formed the southern terminus of the Alaska Railroad—and the longshoremen who populated them in 'round-the-clock shifts were the underpinning of the town's economy. The owner of the docks was the Alaska Railroad, which in turn was owned by the U.S. government, which meant that employment was fairly steady.

The Alaska Steamship Company's venerable old Liberty ship, the *Chena,* had vacated the dock in the early hours of the morning, sailing on its regular run for Valdez (pronounced Val-deez'), more than 150 sea miles to the northeast. The Seward men who had loaded the *Chena* the night before knew the ship would be approaching the Valdez narrows by now, casting a familiar profile against the fir-covered mountain slopes as she churned northward.

30

They also knew that the days were numbered for such World War II-vintage, loose-cargo vessels. The reality that containerships eventually would replace freighters like the *Chena*—and thus replace many a longshoreman's job—was not lost on the Seward dockworkers. But they expected the transition to take a decade, and there would be time to adjust. Meanwhile, it was a good life in Seward, even if the work was physical, occasionally backbreaking, and dangerous.

And there would always be jobs at the head of Resurrection Bay as long as Anchorage stayed healthy, and Seward remained its deepwater port. The cost of digging a channel deep enough to bring oceangoing vessels into Anchorage year-round would be horrendous, and though there was some talk in government circles about doing just that, with the financial momentum of the tremendous investment in Seward's dock facilities and the Alaska Railroad, Seward would probably be safe from sudden change.

The previous sixty years of human presence had altered drastically the appearance and the function of this relatively small teardrop of land at the head of Resurrection Bay. Where the cold waters had lapped at an empty and silty shoreline and gulls had once landed unmolested at the edge of a thin forest of spruce, hemlock, and cottonwood trees, industrial rolling stock and cargo now covered the terrain. It was the spot from which dog sled trails were first blazed to the rich gold fields of Nome—the beginnings of a trail later known as the Iditarod.

The gantry crane was back in motion now, lifting another sling of crates from one spot to another—rearranging the outbound loads for the next ship. Two blocks away up Fourth Avenue to the north, the whining of the electric motors on the crane blended with the rumbling sounds of the switch engine in the marshaling yard to the east and vibrated gently through the interior of a false-fronted two-story building labeled "Brown and Hawkins."

In a small apartment over the expansive Brown and Hawkins sales floor of clothing racks and dry goods, the diminutive figure of an elderly woman moved quietly through a small kitchen and entered her bedroom. Slowly, carefully she lay down on the bed, taking note of the fading daylight through her window and listening to the slow, steady ticking of her clock, knowing without looking that it was around five-thirty in the afternoon. Emma Justice Hawkins, the widow of the man who founded this store and commissioned the building in 1903, had remained right here in Seward since those distant days. A merchant's wife, a mother, one of the founding families—now eighty-eight years of age, down to ninety pounds, and in tenuous health—she was one of a remaining few of the original pioneers. Her husband, T. W. "Bill" Hawkins, had died sixteen years before. Her daughter and son-in-law both were one story below now, finishing the business day.

Emma had come to the outpost of Seward three years after a small group of engineers arrived on the alluvial delta, determined to make it the southern terminus of a railroad for Alaska. By 1905 the railroad company had gone bankrupt, but the outpost—named Seward in honor of Lincoln's secretary of state who bought the territory—remained.

The muffled sounds of people moving around in the store below intruded on her thoughts for a moment. The building was too well built to allow much noise through the walls, so they were only distant murmurings, accompanied by the occasional squeak of a hardwood board in the sturdy old building. They were sounds she knew so very well.

She had always been proud of this building and its quality. It was far more than just a backwater frame structure; it was a frontier craftsman's masterpiece. Part of the decor were such contemporary features as a skylight and spotlight fixtures, rather than old-time drop lamps. The beautiful handworked wooden ceiling beams in the living room of what was now her daughter's apartment were a model of fine workmanship. And the old building was sturdy, standing unaffected through good times and hard times, earth tremors and high winds, and even torrential rains and nearby floods from Lowell Creek (which ran periodically through the middle of town before the city built a concrete diversion tunnel around the south end).

Earthquakes were frequent in Alaska, and her experience with them was lengthy. She and her daughter, Virginia, had survived the 1933 quake in the Los Angeles area—the infamous Long Beach quake which collapsed many schools at a moment that Providence had dictated classes not be in session. Literally thousands of schoolchildren would have been killed and injured if it had happened at any other time, she knew. California had required higher standards after that, but she knew the Californians needed those higher stan-

32

dards because they didn't favor wooden structures; their buildings were too often brick and mortar and other brittle materials. Wooden frame structures like Brown and Hawkins could bend and sway, rattle, shake, and tilt with a quake and seldom do more than pop a nail or two. Masonry buildings, like those in Long Beach, would shatter and fall, crushing those inside.

Many small earthquakes had rattled Seward over the years, but their building had always come through. She had no reason to assume it would ever be otherwise. After all, weren't great quakes reserved for California alone?

The engineer moved the throttle of the big diesel engine forward a bit, listening for the expected sequential report of eighty cars taking up the slack in their couplings one by one, a series of heavy-metal clunks that would blend into a deep-throated metallic shudder. When the sound reached him, he would add more power, increasing the speed of the northbound freight to that of a man's walking pace, lumbering slowly toward the Texaco tank farm on the northeast corner of the shoreline. The last forty cars of the freight were tank cars, filled with highly inflammable aviation gasoline. The caboose was south of the Standard Oil tanks on the southeast corner of the shoreline, the engine nearly a mile north, a few yards from the southernmost Texaco tank.

Slowly the experienced Alaska Railroad veteran inched the throttle lever forward—a rolling high-explosives depot between two dangerous tank farms. It was a rather tenuous means of transporting such materials, he realized. The safety of such a train was always dependent on the stability of the roadbed, which in turn was always subject to landslides, floods, earthquakes, and erosion. His train would proceed safely to Anchorage only so long as nature gave its permission.

And, of course, that permission would always be subject to change without notice.

Valdez, Alaska

Basil "Red" Ferrier and his son Delbert stood at the wheel of their 34-foot fishing boat, the *Falcon,* and watched the 441-foot

33

freighter heading toward them as it steamed out of the Valdez narrows just ahead, on a course to the northeast, moving abeam the unmanned lighthouse which marked the northern entrance to the channel. The rumble of the *Falcon*'s engine joined with the audible rush of the seven knots of wind flowing past their ears, masking the sounds of the oncoming behemoth which was moving steadily against the backdrop of the snow-covered peaks of the Chugach Mountains. It would be several minutes before the low rumble of her powerful reciprocating steam engine would roll over the cold waters of the bay and mark her almost silent passage—a familiar and friendly throbbing bathing both sides of the narrows like a murmured reassurance that human machinery and human ingenuity dominated things even here in the Alaskan wilderness.

The image of the big ship was looming in their perspective as the two dissimilar craft prepared to pass a half mile apart. The steamship had already sailed past the *Falcon*'s destination, the snow-covered slopes of the western side of the narrows, less than three miles south of them now. There would be a beach there and large spruce trees, one of which they would cut down, buck up, and tow back home behind their boat. Red and Delbert Ferrier had their chain saw and a commission to deliver one large log to a friend with an idle sawmill.

"Well, Del, there goes ten hours of work."

For the two commercial fishermen and part-time longshoremen, the S. S. *Chena* was a passing bird in the hand to the lumber they intended to cut in the bush. Father and son could have been standing among the longshoremen waiting for the ship on the Valdez dock. Instead of the better but uncertain pay they were to receive for delivering a log, they could be pulling at least ten hours of wages working the cargo into the night.

The *Falcon* was past the *Chena* now, rolling gently over the swells from the big ship's wake. Behind them the *Chena*'s bow began swinging to the east, the ship running against the current from a mean low tide as she pushed toward the tiny community of Valdez and their waterfront house some ten miles distant at the east end of the bay. Marion Ferrier, Red's wife, would be getting home from her job as a waitress at the Club Valdez Restaurant and from Good Friday service about the time the ship tied up at the dock. Dinner would have to proceed without the Ferrier men, however. Red and Delbert weren't planning to be home until late evening.

34

On the bridge of the *Chena* veteran Captain Merrill Stewart pulled the binoculars from his eyes and took in the beauty of the fjord ahead of his ship. No matter how many times he had sailed into these waters on an Alaska Steamship Company vessel, it was still awe-inspiring. This little outpost tenaciously clinging to the eastern head of a bay formed by the steep sides of five-thousand-foot mountain walls was one of the important gateways to interior Alaska. It claimed prominence in the natural order of Alaskan life as the state's northernmost year-round ice-free port, but its attributes were measured by more than commercial considerations. Valdez also sat amidst a cornucopia of natural grandeur, a portrait in earth tones and snow of wild and magnificent scenery in the teeth of a perpetual stiff and chilly breeze.

The ship's pilot, whose job it was to guide the *Chena* into and out of the ports and bays and inlets, was giving orders to the helmsman now. Captain Stewart could relax for a few minutes. Docking was a half hour ahead, and the fifteen-hour trip from Seward was almost complete.

Six stories below the bridge the rhythmic clanging of impacted seawater vibrating the steel hull of the venerable old freighter echoed through the darkened cargo holds, the crew quarters, and the engine room, giving sound and substance to their speed of nine knots through the salt water, and rattling the dark shapes of assorted cargo—including the star consignment of this trip: a huge D-8 Caterpiller bulldozer chained down carefully in one corner. The oversize blade of the heavy Cat bounced slightly against the steel floor in sympathetic harmony with the constant clanging, adding its own tattoo to the cacophony within.

Within an hour there would be light once again in the hold as burly men worked with hands in heavy gloves, their minds focused on securing slings and barking orders to unseen companions above. There would then unfold a routine but risky ballet of delicate balance involving tons of barely suspended metal. Moving within the narrowest of margins on the strength of a specially rigged crane, they would haul the cargo, and the dozer, vertically up through the opening before swinging it over to the relative security of the dock—a man-made wooden platform suspended on wooden pilings set, basically, in mud. It was a ballet scheduled for performance within the hour at the Valdez dockside before an appreciative au-

35

dience of townspeople even now gathering there, almost twelve miles east of the approaching ship.

Merrill Stewart had sailed in and out of this bay since the late twenties. He knew its history. In fact, he was part of nearly one-half of its chronological history—as much as a master mariner can be in the ports he frequents. Merrill Stewart had watched Valdez through the good times and the bad, and there had been an abundance of the latter from an ecomomic point of view.

He had known before he first saw it that Valdez had been conceived in haste, grown as an afterthought, and maintained as an accident of geography through the determination of human spirit. The first shaky tents pitched at water's edge just below the Valdez Glacier, which in 1897 and 1898 provided a direct path to the goldfields, somehow evolved into a soggy landscape of tar paper shacks and later to a crosshatch of dirt streets and wooden buildings. By the time reformed prospectors Charles Brown and Bill Hawkins had given up on their tiny Valdez toehold to establish themselves as the pioneer merchants of Seward, Valdez was rapidly becoming a ghost town—a process which never quite reached completion. The few intrepid souls who had come there and found life by the cold waters of the bay harsh but satisfying were not the type to be stampeded to greener pastures by such passing calamities as a collapsing economic base. If the gold mining was over, they would find another way to live.

Captain Stewart paused in mid-thought, long-refined habit patterns dictating a progress check of the ship's heading and speed, the rpm's of the huge single propeller, and the depth showing on the fathometer, which was now at 720 feet and coming up slowly. Ahead of him, three miles to the east, was the town itself, a community established at the foot of the glacier sitting tenuously on an outwash delta of gravel and loosely packed rock debris—a community with a waterlogged foundation devoid of bedrock or security.

But then the town was hardly the product of well-thought-out land use planning. No one had thought to consider which was the best townsite from a geologic point of view because frontier communities did not have the luxury of such esoteric hairsplitting. Economics, survival, and convenience, not geologic niceties, were the arbiters. If the water table was inconveniently high in Valdez, the town would simply forgo basements. If the floor of the waterfront seemed a bit unstable, the builders would simply sink more pilings.

The first tents had been pitched exactly where they were needed, on little more than a mudbank which sloped gently into the water before dropping off at a steep angle to the floor of the bay. That was where the town had begun, and that was where the Valdez which the SS *Chena* was now approaching would stay.

As the years progressed and Valdez painfully, slowly carved out a reason for existence as a port, it never occurred to anyone to drill down through the alluvial mud and silt beneath the town to see if anything worrisome was there, and no one regarded the shallow water table as threatening. Valdez was there because it sat in the path of the shortest distance between two points: the end of the dock and the road to Fairbanks. With seniority as a town approaching sixty-six years, the community of Valdez was quite sure it was in the right place, if not always at the right time.

The *Chena* was now the dominant feature to the west of the Valdez dock, her bulk a semisilhouette in head-on profile cupped by the mountains and the water, an occasional fleck of white foam around the bow the only sign of motion. To the townspeople who enjoyed watching her approach for aesthetic as well as economic reasons, she was like a painting come to life, sailing out of the canvas of blue skies, white mountains, and choppy green water. The venerable old Liberty ship slowed her pace, her engine telegraph moving to "one quarter ahead," the harbor pilot and the captain mentally computing the closing rates and the currents with the benefit of experience measured in decades.

John Kelsey, one of the owners of the Valdez Dock Company and the *Chena*'s agent in Valdez, stood on the end of the pier, the ship and the bay filling his field of vision. He had watched this process countless times. After ten minutes of careful slowing and strategic steering, the twenty-thousand-ton (forty-million-pound) vessel would end up a few feet from the dock dead in the water, ready to be hauled in the last remaining inches by six to eight stout lines made of hemp and thrown from the deck by the contingent of merchant mariners now taking their positions along the port side. Mistakes in such procedures could be very costly. Even at a few knots of closing speed, the impact of a ship the size and weight of the *Chena* could do incredible damage to Kelsey's dock.

John Kelsey's appreciation of such artistry in nautical maneuvering ran deep. He had been a Navy man, a deck officer in the

Pacific theater in World War II—navigator of the attack transport USS *Olmstead,* and later the skipper of a submarine tender (the *PC1079*). Just as professional pilots never tire of watching airplanes land, professional mariners never tire of watching their ships come in, and Kelsey was no exception.

Kelsey and his older brother, Bob, owned the complex of piers and warehouses on the leased city dock, which was one of the dominant employers in Valdez. In fact, the community at times seemed as much a company town for the Valdez dock enterprise as it was a gateway to the interior of the Great Land (as Alaska liked to be called).

Longshoremen were arrayed on both sides of Kelsey now, positioning the forklifts and cargo pallets, pulling on gloves, joking with each other as they, too, watched the wall of seagoing metal slowly fill the horizon. John Kelsey was in effect their employer (through North Star Terminal Stevedoring Company, a union operation under contract to the Valdez Dock Company), but he was also their friend and neighbor. There was a camaraderie that cut across economic lines in a community like Valdez, a feeling of common purpose born of pioneering determination and shared hardships. There wasn't room—literally or figuratively—in such a town for a country club set of standoffish owners and managers. It was, as one successful merchant put it, difficult for anyone to live on the other side of the tracks in a community too small to have a railroad.

The Kelsey family had purchased the dock complex in the early years of Valdez's development. Brothers John and Robert, both born and raised by the cold waters of Port Valdez, took over in the late thirties, doubling the size and length of the facilities, adding warehouses, taking on management of the Standard Oil tank farm on the waterfront, and generally husbanding the family business into a family fortune. As the Kelseys knew well, by 1964 replacing his company's facilities alone would cost over seven million dollars.

At 4:12 P.M. heavy hemp ropes snaked out from the deck of the *Chena* as the ship at last sat motionless alongside the dock, bow pointing south-southeast, her bulk lying parallel to the shoreline. Several families had already gathered, participating in what had become a weekly event: watching the Alaska Steamship Company vessel come in. One week the *Chena,* the next week perhaps the *Talkeetna,* both named for Alaska rivers, which had been named in turn by the original native inhabitants.

Kelsey noticed the little Growden boys, David and Jimmy, with their father. Jim Growden, schoolteacher and the town's basketball coach, stood to one side of the dock with his sons, who were waving at the sailors thirty feet above and pointing to various parts of the ship. Over the next few hours scores of Valdezans would drive up to the dock, rumble down the long expanse of planking in family cars and station wagons, and spend a few minutes marveling at the size of the ship and the meeting of the two dissimilar worlds before them: a huge seagoing vessel and the stability of a stout wooden dock firmly anchored in what was assumed to be the solid material below.

John Kelsey signed the settlement papers and handed them back to Captain Merrill Stewart, the usual formal procedure by which a dock and warehouse company acknowledges how much it owes the shipper for the cargo coming ashore.

Both men stood in the office of the Valdez Dock Company, a block above the shoreline on Alaska Avenue. Kelsey and Stewart were a study in contrasts, the manners of old-school gentlemen worn like a comfortable sweater by men who could quaff a mug of beer with their crewmen as easily as they could take high tea in a formal parlor in San Francisco or Seattle. Both were natural leaders with a concern for those who followed, and though their meetings arose from the usual and regular duties of their respective stations, there was a civility underlying such contacts within which business could be conducted with a handshake—in which a man's word was still his bond. Among such men, signing carefully drawn settlement papers was at once the proper procedure—and completely unnecessary.

As the two of them motored back onto the planking of the dock, Stewart noticed one of his men, the ship's steward, energetically taking pictures with an 8 mm movie camera. The fellow had been filming nearly everything for the past three days. Stewart, amused, wondered when he was going to run out of film.

Kelsey stopped at the foot of the gangplank, the dock now alive with the sounds of winches and cranes, forklifts and busy men, flanked by numerous family members and onlookers watching the show. The captain had emerged from the car, closed the door carefully, and was leaning in through the passenger's window.

"John, would you consider joining me aboard for dinner? We haven't had enough time to talk."

Kelsey pictured his wife with dinner ready at home, and realized he didn't have a choice.

"Thank you for the offer, but I'd better not. I'm expected home for dinner tonight; my in-laws are with us."

Captain Stewart smiled and nodded.

"Of course. Maybe next week. See you later."

The master of the *Chena* started up the gangplank as Kelsey put his car in gear—and just as quickly stopped.

The longshoremen were obviously getting ready to rig the ship's forward deck-mounted crane for the D-8 Cat in the cargo hold by positioning the extra boom normally stowed at the top. The process was called topping down the crane. Kelsey looked at his watch and read 5:15 P.M. If they got that huge Cat suspended in midair by 6:00 P.M., he'd have a problem. Either the men would go into penalty time and he would owe extra wages, or they'd go off to dinner, leaving fifty thousand pounds of bulldozer swinging in the breeze, suspended in midair. Neither prospect was acceptable.

John Kelsey got out of his car to look for the dockworkers' superintendent. That Cat had to stay in place until after dinner.

It was the first time thirteen-year-old Tom Gilson could remember Good Friday's triggering a school holiday. But this time it had, and the banker's son was enjoying the chance to cruise around Valdez with several older friends, occupying the back seat of the car and doing nothing at all productive.

The Gilsons were also pioneers in Valdez. Tom's grandfather had survived the 1906 earthquake in San Francisco and had come north to settle in the wild Alaskan outpost in 1910, starting a general store as the Gilson Mercantile. His son, Tom's father, was born in the tiny community in 1919, and Tom had followed in 1951, the third generation. His father was now prime owner and president of Valdez's only bank.

The group had seen the *Chena* dock an hour earlier, but they had been too busy talking to friends to get down to the dock before now. The bulk of the *Chena* could be seen clearly from almost anywhere in the tiny downtown area, her deck cranes in motion, and signs of activity evident along the dock in the distance.

As the car full of teenagers moved closer, rolling slowly down Alaska Avenue toward the water, the boys watched the activity ahead with practiced interest. On board and unseen, Captain Stewart was finishing a quick dinner while his steward plotted another escape from dining room duties to do more filming with his 8 mm camera. Just up from the waterfront John Kelsey was sitting down with his family at their second-story dinner table, while two blocks away Red Ferrier's wife, Marion, was dropping scallops into a frying pan.

As one family drove off the dock, another drove on. Sammie Marie Stuart headed her Travelall toward the end of the pier, her three children in animated conversation and anxious to see their dad, Smokey, who would be waiting at shipside along with many other local fathers. It was a Valdez ritual, and with the temperature pushing forty degrees, no wind, and a holiday atmosphere, the end of the Valdez dock was a fun place to be.

It was naturally assumed by everyone that it was also a safe place to be.

Chapter 3

Anchorage, Alaska—1964

Bob Reeve was enjoying his birthday, which had taken on the aura of an impromptu party held in the brand-new Anchorage Petroleum Club on the top floor of the Anchorage Westward Hotel. The veteran Alaska bush pilot and founder of Reeve Aleutian Airways had started with a solitary lunch in the breathtaking surroundings of the new facilities, but decided to stay around the rest of the Friday afternoon as friends dropped by from all over the city to wish him well. He was one of the founding members of the club, which had instantly become a showplace for Anchorage, its oversize control tower type of windows providing a sweeping view of Cook Inlet and all of the city.

Scaffolding still hugged one side of the fifteen-story hotel, and one outside construction elevator continued in operation as the crews labored to finish interior floors and guest rooms. But the beautiful new landmark had already opened for business, and the smell of fresh paint, new carpets, and carefully crafted woodwork, which adorned the expansive lobby (along with a few remaining tarps), had greeted Bob Reeve's senses hours before as he pushed through the revolving doors to the lobby, looking around with admiration at a facility built principally with local money and civic pride.

For Anchorage, and indeed for all of Alaska, the Westward was a symbol of legitimacy, further testament in mortar and steel to the fact that the largest of Alaskan communities was now an important American city, not just an outpost or another small town. The hotel was to be the focal point for expanded tourism and international commerce, as well as a magnet for conventions.

It was a confusing time for those with promotional responsibilities. On one hand, the frontier image brought in tourists and kept their links with the pioneering nature of the Alaskan wilderness firmly intact. On the other hand, no one wanted to be thought of as a frontier hick town with dirt streets and Wild West attitudes; big business and industry were seldom attracted by such images. So Anchorage existed with one foot in each province, the consummate modern frontier metropolis, where a New York businessman could leave his first-class room at the Westward in his locally purchased Brooks Brothers suit and catch a taxi to go four blocks through snowy streets to an Alaskan saloon with sawdust floors and moose heads on the wall (a place where sidearms were worn occasionally on Friday nights).

In many ways the Westward was also a confirmation that Anchorage had weathered the bad times and the uncertain times, had come of age, and was here to stay.

Certainly the hotel building itself was here to stay. The architects had been sufficiently worried about the layer of clay beneath the city to excavate a gargantuan hole for the foundation, drilling numerous vertical shafts below that bottom basement level for concrete pilings full of steel rods, all put in place before the basement concrete began to flow. Anchorage, after all, was earthquake country, and though in previous years the city's residents and businessmen seldom had the luxury to worry about careful seismic engineering, a showpiece like this had to be done right. As a result, the Anchorage Westward was designed to stay in one piece right where it was, clay or no clay.

Bob Reeve greeted yet another friend as he sat at the bar, the image of freshly set tables with expensive new silverware and china in the foreground as the club staff began preparing for the dinner hour. The windows from the Petroleum Club took in a magnificent view in the background. It was too cloudy to see Mount McKinley to the northwest, but on a clear day the twenty-thousand-foot mountain the natives knew as Mount Denali would be breathtaking. Even with gray skies and low clouds amidst the mild temperature of thirty-eight degrees, the panorama of Cook Inlet to the west and the Chugach range to the east was very impressive.

To the northeast sat Government Hill with its microwave communications station, which bordered the large, important Elmendorf Air Force Base farther over the ridge. With all the people who worked at the Army's Fort Richardson and at Elmendorf, which was headquarters to the Alaskan Air Command, the military and the U.S. government were the dominant employers in Anchorage.

To the north were the tiny port facilities of the city, principally a handful of docks which served shallow-draft barges brought in from Cook Inlet—a waterway oceangoing ships could not use.

Several blocks to the southwest and nearing completion was the new Four Seasons apartment building, built with a unique concrete lift-slab construction technique. Some of the workers on the Four Seasons project were just knocking off for the day.

And three miles to the southwest was the city's exclusive new residential area known as Turnagain Heights, a development of beautiful new houses nestled up to the edge of a thirty-foot bluff overlooking the part of the bay (or inlet) known as Knik Arm.

From such a vantage point it was obvious Anchorage was coming of age—though still a bit hodgepodge in architectural styles and construction quality.

Anchorage had building codes, of course, along with zoning and planning commissions. Without an adequate building inspection staff, however, plans for commercial and public buildings were routinely sent to an expert engineering firm in San Francisco for examination. There were local experts in city planning, such as longtime Alaska resident Lidia Selkregg, a Ph.D. who spent most of her professional time in Alaska trying to guide the growth of Alaska's largest municipality. But for a young, dynamic, expanding city in a hurry in a harsh environment (that made major construction projects all but impossible six months of each year), there was a premium on getting structures up rapidly.

There were houses to be built, housing developments to be started, and commercial buildings to be erected. There wasn't sufficient time to debate the finer points of the geology of the city's foundation, or to delay construction projects while dithering over the merits or the implications of a U.S. Geological Survey report issued three years before by geologists Ernest Dobrovolny and Robert Miller,[1] which had pointed out the inherent instability of the layer of saturated clay that underlay the entire municipality. Bootlegger Cove Clay, he called it. If saturated with water and shaken, the slimy stuff was capable of doing very fluid and unpredictable things.

But in the face of rapid growth the prevailing attitude was disinterest. Earth tremors occurred all the time in Anchorage, and the land always seemed to remain in the same place. As with the Turnagain Heights area, if there was a prime piece of view property that

45

cried for residential development, residential development would be the inevitable result. "They aren't making any more land" went the saying, and that was rationale enough.

As Bob Reeve held court in the top of the Anchorage Westward with the dinner hour approaching, three miles to the west one of the owners of the hotel stood in the living room of his magnificent Turnagain Heights home, positioning a brass horn to his lips, taking a long, deep breath in the process.

With his wife on a late Friday trip to the store, Bob Atwood could play his trumpet at full volume without bothering anyone.

The panorama of mountains and inlet to the west painted an elegant backdrop for his tunes—the gray sky with its thinly veiled threat of snow flurries merely a confirmation that the great land beneath was Alaska in the spring.

Bob Atwood loved being in this place. He loved the challenges, the successes, the independence, and the feeling of being a sort of modern-day pioneer in a land neither hospitable nor tame—a land which always held a whisper of threat, of sinister intent, just below the surface.

Certainly his city had all the modern conveniences, including the respectable daily newspaper, the Anchorage *Daily Times,* of which he was the publisher and owner. But regardless of Chamber of Commerce hype, this community of strangers now known as the forty-ninth state still held a breed of individualists who stared bitter storms in the teeth and defied everything from periodic earth tremors and mind-numbing cold to overly officious federal bureaucrats. It was a heady mixture of adventure and routine—indeed, a frontier in spirit as well as in fact.

Atwood had become a well-liked and respected Alaskan during his many years in Anchorage. With his distinctive features—his rectangular face a memorable mix of clear brown eyes and a quick smile framed by slightly graying hair—he was the very model of a newspaper publisher, a clear-thinking fellow whose stewardship of his city was as zealous as that of any Chamber of Commerce booster.

Alaska in 1964 was a very personal place—an unusual locale where senators and congressmen and governors were people you could talk to almost at will—people who might come to any constituent's house for dinner if invited. But even if the community were not so close and the politicians so accessible, they would still have been guests in Atwood's home. For decades he had balanced the veteran journalist's eye for unvarnished reality with the empire builder's thirst for progress, worrying about such things as the degree of care with which the city's newest buildings were being designed, while sniping in print at anyone who would stand in the way of development.

Bob Atwood stood in his showplace of a home and started down the same coda again, concentrating even harder on his music. All around him were the furnishings and cherished bric-a-brac from years of world travels carefully arranged throughout the modern log house—the first residence to command the view from this particular spot on the bluff. In such pleasant surroundings, such minor details as the suspicious seepage of water he had noticed years ago at the foot of the embankment below were far from his mind.

Four-year-old Mitzi Hines had gone to her room for a late-afternoon nap while her eighteen-year-old brother, Warren, was enjoying his day off from school. His graduation from West Anchorage High was just two months away. The family home at 3109 Turnagain Boulevard West was a few doors from Bob Atwood's house, but the music from publisher Atwood's trumpet didn't penetrate the solitude of the Hineses' living room as Warren gazed out toward Knik Arm, appreciating the snow-covered scene in the midst of a mild Good Friday. His mother, Margaret Hines, had gone to the store and would be back momentarily. His dad, a successful Anchorage optometrist, was at work several miles to the east.

Turnagain was a serene place to live. The list of residents provided almost a who's who of Anchorage with the ranking movers and shakers and builders and leaders crowding the bluff with their expensive homes to gain a view of the inlet. Though Bob Atwood had been the first, now a major housing area sat behind and to the side of his home, and more were under construction. This was prime real estate, a few minutes' commute from downtown and from most of the facilities the city had to offer.

Convenient proximity had attracted another of Bob Atwood's neighbors, Dr. Perry Mead (the city's only neurosurgeon) and his family. At 5:30 P.M. Dr. Mead was just finishing the day at his clinic on the south side of the downtown area, while his wife did some last-minute shopping and four of their five children remained in their new Turnagain home. Penny, nine, Paul, four, and two-year-old Merrill Mead were under the supervision of their twelve-year-old brother, Perry. According to plan, within the hour the family would be together for a relaxing Friday evening.

Six miles east of Turnagain in a neighborhood tucked up against the foothills of the Chugach Mountains, Baxter Rustigan walked angrily over to his brother's stereo and cranked the volume up to glass-shattering levels. Robert, the twenty-three-year-old senior brother, winced in the next room at the wave of sound. "I Want to Hold Your Hand," the latest release from the new British group the Beatles, blared from the speakers, and Baxter didn't care how loud he got it. An argument with his sister, Bonita, and his mother's intervention had left the teenager in a royal huff. Little sister had been into his things again, and he had overreacted. He was softening already, though. Baxter resolved to apologize when his mom and Bonita got home from shopping.

At the same moment several miles to the west, Mary Louise Rustigan was slowing the family car and looking for a parking space with Bonita sitting beside her. She stubbed out another of her omnipresent cigarettes before choosing a space along the curb near the Rustigans' downtown business, City Cold Storage, a food locker and freezer company they had built up from nearly nothing. Their destination was the new J. C. Penney's store several blocks to the west, but they would check in with Baxter senior first.

Baxter Rustigan, Sr., was a hard worker, and Marie understood both hard work and compulsive behavior. For three years she had been free of a disease which had almost killed her, alcoholism, a by-product of years as a headlining rodeo trick rider on the southwestern circuit. Finally, many years after meeting Baxter in Paris, Texas (where he was stationed in the Army), she had overcome her disease with much help and love from family and friends, and her life was quite different now. She was enthusiastically productive, running a restaurant by day and helping other people lick alcoholism by night.

Mary Louise Rustigan had founded a local group, called Alateen, to help the teenagers of alcoholic parents, and through Alcoholics Anonymous had become one of those people who would get up in the middle of a sub-zero night to spend the next eight hours sitting with someone struggling to stay sober, drinking gallons of coffee until dawn. It had given her renewed purpose, and she felt she had helped, and was helping.

Her husband, the son of a prominent merchant family of Armenian descent in Providence, Rhode Island (the grandfather had changed the name from Rustigian to Rustigan to confuse it with the Irish names in the area), had been destined to follow in the family grocery business when he returned from the Army with his new western wife. Several years of trying to carve out their own existence in Providence had not worked well, however, so Baxter had given up, packed up, and in 1957 had taken his family as far west as he could go, arriving in Anchorage after a jarring five-thousand-mile trip (in part over the primitive Alcan Highway).

Mary Louise and Bonita had left the City Cold Storage office and headed west down Fourth Avenue to J. C. Penney's a few minutes after 5:00 P.M. Now her watch read 5:30 as they browsed through the upper floors of the elegant new store. It was supposed to close in thirty minutes. They would need to hurry.

Five blocks away in All Saints Episcopal Church, Father Norm Elliot reached the twelfth Station of the Cross in the Good Friday services. The last quotation from Matthew was in front of him now as he read the familiar words:

"But Jesus cried with a loud voice, and gave up his spirit. And behold, the curtain of the temple was torn in two from top to bottom; and the earth quaked, and the rocks were rent."

It was exactly thirty-five seconds past 5:36 P.M.

49

Chapter 4

The breaking point had been very near for some time. The tortured layers of rock beneath the landmass of Alaska had been under growing stress for decades, and though no one knew it, the dam that held back that growing reservoir of potential seismic energy was about to shatter.

Massive layers of rock miles thick—layers which years later would be referred to as tectonic plates—were being shoved in opposite directions by continental forces beneath the state as one plate plunged in slow motion beneath the other. Yet those layers, or plates, refused to move past each other easily, and became snagged by friction and uneven areas where they came together.

These were sheets of unnamed and unseen rocks of almost unimaginable height and breadth, thousands of cubic miles of them, hundreds of miles wide, forever hidden from daylight, lying under increasing dynamic tension of incredible magnitude—tension which had been building for untold years against a single snagged area 12.5 miles directly beneath the eastern shore of Unakwik Inlet in northern Prince William Sound. That deserted shoreline, the epicenter of what was about to occur 66,000 feet below ground, was a mere 40 miles west of Valdez, 80 miles east of Anchorage, and 130 miles northeast of Seward.[1]

Though geologists and seismologists had not yet realized it—could not observe what was happening so far down—the 12.5 miles of rocks and mountains and water directly above the snagged area were still being pushed to the south and southeast by a little-understood process of movement basic to the earth's crust. At the same time the 30 or 40 miles of earth's lithosphere below the snag were being shoved northwestward by the same process. One gigantic layer was riding over the top of the other one, both in continuous (if very slow) motion along a meeting place geologists called a fault plane.

However, only the movement had been stopped by the snag, not the forces propelling the plates. These were immense forces of planetary magnitude which embody energy that is difficult to express in ordinary terms, energy that on normal scales would require a staggering array of zeros between the first numbers and the decimal point. Such forces are not stopped; they are merely absorbed to be released later on. The energy continues to build, storing itself in twisted and compressed rock, creating a reservoir of power which will one day, inevitably, unavoidably, be released.[2]

In 1964 no one really understood the planetary engine which propelled such systems. No one fully realized that when the strain in such opposing layers builds to great levels, its release will eventually come in a break or a rapid series of breaks tens or hundreds of miles in length as the snagged rocks finally fracture, releasing the mammoth amounts of stored energy behind them, which in turn causes sudden, rapid movement and creates massive seismic waves. When a great break occurs, millions of tons of rock are suddenly displaced many feet as the plates rumble past each other, seeking some form of equilibrium once again. Equilibrium is not to be found, however. The pressures continue and begin to build again immediately. Where snags have developed before, snags will develop again, starting the cycle all over.[3]

Of course, such movement does not—cannot—go unnoticed. When massive volumes of rock move suddenly beneath the surface of the earth, they cause waves of energy to radiate out in all directions, seismic waves that travel around the planet and undulate every molecule of the earth through which they pass.

And, in certain circumstances, when large areas of rocks snap fairly close to the surface (ten to twenty miles being "fairly close" geologically) and massive tectonic plates move against each other, spending pent-up energy, hundreds of square miles of ground can be raised or lowered permanently in a matter of seconds, and great sea waves (tsunamis), or harbor waves (seiches), can result, pummeling sea-level cities and towns and industrial installations with waves as high as forty feet.[4]

At exactly fourteen seconds past five thirty-six on the peaceful afternoon of March 27, Good Friday, 1964, a very small event miles deep in the earth pulled the trigger on what had become a loaded

52

tectonic gun. An otherwise insignificant increase in the pressure on the snagged rocks beneath Unakwik Inlet went a few pounds too far, and the breaking point was reached. The snag disintegrated in a cataclysmic release of stored energy, suddenly moving rock surfaces which were many miles in length along a northeast to southwest fault plane, unleashing a spherical wave front of compression waves—P waves—to race from the source of the break at more than fourteen thousand miles per hour, followed instantly by the slower-traveling S waves, massive undulations of side-to-side movement which chased the primary waves to the west toward an unsuspecting Anchorage, to the southwest toward an unprepared Seward, and to the east toward their first municipal victim: Valdez.

5:36:25 P.M. Valdez, Alaska

Captain Stewart stopped in mid-sentence. He had been lingering over a cup of coffee in the *Chena*'s dining room with the ship's pilot when a sudden rumble, a shudder, vibrated through the ship. In the space of a few seconds his mind considered and rejected a score of possibilities: They wouldn't be getting under way without him . . . not even the bulldozer in the forward hold if dropped could cause such a shudder . . . and the dock was made of wood; it certainly couldn't have caused that noise, or that feeling. So what in the world?

Just as he and the pilot felt the shuddering increase, the first S waves rippled beneath the waterfront, shaking the timbers in the dock, resonating into the interior of the ship, a banging commotion very much like something the captain had experienced several times before in deep water when he thought they'd run aground. This time around he was not fooled. He recognized it immediately.

Captain Merrill Stewart began pushing himself out of his chair, yelling a single word to anyone who could hear:

"Earthquake!"

In a microsecond he had broken for the nearby port door, pausing to yell at the first mate on the dock below, before heading on instinct to the ladder and the bridge—the place a captain belonged when his ship was in danger.

In the number three hold of the *Chena* the first rumble of the compression waves was confusing to the longshoremen working inside. The shudder felt as if the ship's propeller had started to turn, as if they were getting under way—and that made no sense at all.

Jack King, Howard Krieger, and Paul Gregorioff, all longtime Valdez residents, had been rigging the cargo slings near the huge bulldozer. Now they had paused, looking through the gloom of the hold at each other as the first S waves began slamming the ship back and forth, port to starboard, and feeling the sound of the huge hull striking the wooden structure of the dock.

John Kelsey had driven off his dock ten minutes before, climbed the stairs, and was sitting at the dinner table when he felt the compression waves enter Valdez. The vibrations were short and intense, the familiar kickoff to another one of the earthquakes Valdez had always experienced. As the first of the S waves undulated beneath the Valdez Dock Company's two-story building, which was also his home, Kelsey noticed the startled expressions on the faces of his wife's father and mother, who were not familiar with such things.

"Don't worry," he said to them, "it'll be over soon." However, there was a rumbling now, a roaring, frightening sound which began as a low-frequency vibration rising second by second into a thunderous noise. As the side-to-side shaking of the building increased in intensity and amplitude, so did the noise. It was not a slow increase. It was sudden, insistent, and like nothing he had experienced there before.

Kelsey had been through naval battles and had survived a plane crash in which four others died. He was trained and disciplined and experienced at handling emergencies. But this was completely unexpected. Gathering his wits about him as he realized that what he was seeing on the faces of his family was growing panic, Kelsey pushed away from the table, fighting to stay balanced, motioning to them in the process.

"Let's get into a doorway!"

In the back seat of his friend's car Tom Gilson felt the first jolts and wondered why the driver was putting up with it. The car with Gilson and four other boys had stopped in front of Alaska Governor Bill Egan's old house one block from the waterfront, the boys intent on talking to a friend they had seen strolling down the street. Now the car was lurching back and forth, side to side. Gilson figured the other youth was shaking the car, but if so, he couldn't figure out how he could put so much power into it; the shaking was becoming severe.

Ed Irish, the driver, finally figured it out. With eyes wide he turned to the others and, half in amazement, half in fear, stated what was rapidly becoming obvious to the citizens of Valdez:

"It's an earthquake!"

Almost simultaneously the five boys began grasping for door handles, only to find the doors blocked by the road. The car was rolling back and forth so severely with the north-south motion of the ground they couldn't get the doors in sync at first. Finally, one by one, the boys managed to swing a door open at the top of a cycle on each side and leap out, scattering in several directions up the street toward what they thought was safer ground.

Of course, there wasn't any safe ground. Tom Gilson realized that somewhere in the back of his mind as he tried to keep his footing on the surface of the street, which was now rolling visibly like waves on the ocean.

"There must be a truck going by."

Marion Ferrier's son Larry was wrong, and she knew it instantly.

"No, it's a quake." Nothing more. Earthquakes were common, and all this one was doing was jiggling the grease in her deep fryer. The scallops she was putting in would have to wait a minute while it calmed down. Marion and two of the kids, Hazel and Larry, were planning on a quiet evening. Now it was getting interesting—and intense.

The shaking began to increase in amplitude, jerking the house back and forth with growing force until she silently went into motion, grabbing the two of them and getting under the doorframe for protection.

Dishes and silverware rattling and moving around in the cabinets joined with the rising noise level as the house came alive, the smell of disturbed dust joining the cooking aromas.

Earthquakes just weren't like this. They usually ended.

Marion's blood ran cold at the thought, but a sudden, very logical explanation shot through her mind, gathering credence with every new jolt of the house, dovetailing with the tension everyone felt in the shadow of America's northern defense zone amidst the cold war and scares like the Cuban missile crisis.

Oh, my God, they've dropped an atom bomb on Anchorage!

Captain Stewart had reached the bridge in fewer than twenty seconds, climbing like a scalded monkey straight up a three-story ladder, mentally recording in vivid detail sights he wasn't aware of seeing at the time: the image of people streaming from the warehouses onto the dock looking confused, several children looking terrified several stories below his position on the ladder, and the buildings themselves beginning to jump and undulate in the growing intensity of the seismic waves.

Stewart entered the bridge at the same time the third mate came through the opposite door.

"Get the alarm bells going, now!" It was the sharpest order he had barked in weeks, and the sailor to whom it was addressed lunged for the switch. The bells would be the equivalent of general quarters, alerting everyone on board that something was wrong.

What was worrying Stewart with every passing second was the sound of his ship striking the dock. It was unmistakable, and it was getting louder, more insistent, along with a worrisome new development which seemed to be happening in slow motion as Stewart turned back to the port side and headed back to the door: The ship was rising, or the dock was sinking—or both.

He wasn't sure. The increasing roar, the clanging of metal, and the ship's bells made it difficult to sort out what was happening, but the tops of the buildings on the dock were going down in relation to the ship. He reached the side just as several loud snaps reached his ears—the sound of large hemp ropes breaking under tension, unable to restrain the rising mass of twenty thousand tons of freighter.

On the dock below the *Chena* all hell was breaking loose, confusion filling the minds of panicked parents, kids, and workers. The shaking had started innocently enough, building rapidly to a violent lurching back and forth, a north to south motion oriented to, then from the shore, a motion that if continued too long could shatter the causeway and the dock.

Basketball coach Jim Growden and his two sons had been talking to the first mate when the shaking started. Growden and his boys stood back from the ship, waiting it out for a minute, looking puzzled as people began spilling onto the dock from the warehouses and the first mate jumped onto the gangplank. The sounds of the *Chena* assaulting the dock were adding to the inherent roar of the earthquake, which was rising exponentially, and finally, the realization seemed to reach Growden that they had better run.

At that moment one of the boys broke away and ran for the gangplank, which had lifted off the dock and was hanging there, tantalizingly close, a safe passage away from the shaking, gyrating dock. But Jim Growden was in motion instantly after his son, grabbing the boy a few feet from the ramp and spinning him around, taking the other boy by the hand and trying to get them all running in the opposite direction toward the shoreline.

Ahead of him the Stuart family was also in motion, their Travelall parked down the dock. Smokey Stuart swept his youngest daughter up with his right arm as he pulled his other daughter along, Sammie Marie right beside him, holding on to son Larry. They were mere feet away from the ship now, headed toward the perceived safety of the shore hundreds of feet in the distance over the wildly bucking dock, unaware of the motion of the *Chena* as she rose on a swell of water and snapped her lines, at the exact moment that the underwater shelf of loosely compacted silts and muds and glacial debris on which the Valdez waterfront had been constructed turned to a liquid mass and began collapsing toward the five-hundred-foot depths of the bay—the same mud and silt and gravel which provided the foundation for the Valdez dock, and all its warehouses, and all the people standing on its surface.

Something was sucking the water out of Valdez Harbor. Captain Merrill Stewart, his first mate, and numerous other horrified members of the *Chena*'s crew could feel the ship rising slowly before all of them simultaneously realized that the water was retreating in torrents to the port side—the dock side—of the ship and from the small-boat harbor in the distance as well.

The shaking and lurching seemed to increase with each of the sixty seconds that had passed since the first P waves had shuddered beneath the dock and the ship.

Captain Stewart realized what was happening before his mind could embrace it: The docks were collapsing. The warehouse roofs were descending even as he watched from the port wing of the bridge. The families and the dockworkers who had been streaming out of the warehouse entrances all were running in ragged disorder up the causeway, toward the distant shore, away from what was becoming a sloping dock surface that had begun to tilt toward the ship as it descended in slow motion.

The ship's steward had stumbled out to the port rail with his movie camera and pressed the button, pointing the lens in the direction of the warehouses while almost losing his footing, the camera aiming skyward for a second before the frantic crewman could get it back under control and pointed toward the unbelievable scene below.

Captain Stewart saw Jim Growden grab his younger son and head away from the gangplank with both his boys, away from the safety of the ship. He could see them trying to run on the undulating surface of the dock's planking even as it began to give way. Not thirty minutes before, Stewart had patted the youngest boy on the head and had given him an apple.

And there was something else. Ahead of those tiny figures running futilely against time and against the seismic waves in the wooden structure toward the causeway, a black chasm had appeared, growing wider in seconds as the causeway split open, a huge, ugly, gaping line with turbulent water and mud underneath. The running figures saw it at last, braking themselves, stumbling to a halt, confused and unsure what to do, the realization of what it meant not quite hitting them yet.

The men on the ship watched in horror as a number of the longshoremen who had passed the break in the causeway and had turned back to help the others were unable to stop their momentum. In a flurry the men plunged headlong into the widening gap at the same moment that those they were seeking to reach wheeled and began running back toward the dock and the ship, children in tow or under arms, several wives trying to keep their footing, none of them realizing that there was nowhere left to run.

A deafening report—a bang—louder than all the roaring and screeching, the ship's bells, or the deep-throated horn which had begun to blow in staccato bursts at the hand of the terrified third mate, filled the air around the *Chena* as one of the largest warehouses on the dock suddenly collapsed downward, the muddy, turbulent water below washing into the entrance while waves simultaneously began devouring the disintegrating timbers.

Several people lunged at the gangplank hanging over the port side of the *Chena;* but they were too far away, and the ship was too far up, the ramp hanging uselessly twenty feet above them as they descended helplessly with the dock. The Growdens, father and sons, pitched headlong into the water as the Stuart family, having reached their Travelall, were catapulted into the waves along with the dozens of others who tried to turn and head once more for shore, losing their footing and being tumbled backward toward the fragmenting edge of the planking and the rising hulk of the *Chena.*

The ship had rolled to fifteen degrees before Captain Stewart realized fully what was happening. Wherever the water was going, it was rising in the form of a huge surge on the other side of the ship, and the *Chena* was rising and rolling violently to port at the same time. It was heeling inexorably toward the disintegrating dock in slow motion: twenty degrees . . . twenty-five degrees . . . thirty degrees and still going, still rolling over.

Captain Stewart lost his footing and smashed against the left wing of the bridge, trying to hang on to something as the roll increased. On top of the noise and the shaking and the screeching— and the sounds of people screaming in the distance below him—he knew in an instant that they wouldn't make it. The *Chena* was too old to take this kind of abuse. They were on their way to capsizing, and he was powerless to stop it.

In the number three hold the world was beginning to come apart. The ship had been shaking for nearly a minute, the startled longshoremen finally realizing they were facing an earthquake and hoping that like all such quakes, it would be over soon.

Now the walls were moving, tilting, farther and farther, and the steel vault, full of heavy cargo, including the twenty-five-ton bulldozer, was in motion, as was the cargo. Barrels began falling and rolling, the D-8 Cat was threatening to move, pallets of boxes and nets and chains began slithering, falling, clanging, and sliding to the port side as the tilt increased.

The men on the starboard side tried to hang on, those on the port side tried to dodge; but within seconds the *Chena* had rolled over thirty-five degrees to port, toward the disintegrating dock, and the cargo was in rapid motion, tons of material shifting toward the port wall of the hold, where a handful of men had been trapped. Longshoremen such as Jack King and Howard Krieger saw the mass of material in the artificial light of the hold, saw it accelerating, felt themselves pinned by gravity and circumstance, and felt the entire process shift to slow motion as adrenaline coursed into their bloodstreams, quickening their heartbeats, readying the primal human capabilities for using every available ounce of strength and instinct to escape from a mortal threat.

But their backs were quite literally to the wall that formed the port side of the hold. There was nowhere to run.

Clambering over crates and boxes, loose boards, and anything else that might provide a handhold, scores of frightened men and women and several children struggled to find a way out of the maelstrom as the water reached them, inundating the disintegrating dock, which was being dragged along with the supporting mudbank in its quickening slide down the underwater slope, itself now in full collapse. The struggling people in the churning waters looked up at the faces of the *Chena*'s crew as they looked back with horrified expressions of abject helplessness. The *Chena* had become a wall of metal and barnacles rising above the shattered dock, offering no hope of deliverance, heeled so far over toward them that the sailors hanging on to the bridge and the various decks of the ship seemed close enough to touch.

But not close enough.

As Carson Dorney, the ship's second engineer, watched with a death grip on the main deck railing, three men in the water below labored to hang on to some floating debris while being swept into a whirlpool. It was a piece of roofing from the warehouse which had been behind them, a warehouse which was now below the waterline, sucked into the bay, creating the vortex of swirling water that had captured the three longshoremen, two of whom disappeared as the engineer watched.

To his right other heads could be seen in the water, disappearing one by one, some seeming to be yanked beneath the hull of the ship as she continued over, now at least forty degrees to port. With sickening clarity Dorney realized his ship was doomed, too. Obviously they were going to capsize right here.

The last man in the whirlpool was still holding on to his piece of roofing, his face upturned toward the engineer as he made a last cycle, helplessly making eye contact, not realizing what had happened below, what was happening to the entire underwater slope.

60

It seemed an eternity filled with mental desperation as Dorney watched the man rotate in the whirlpool before the wooden debris and its passenger were yanked suddenly from the engineer's view. Within seconds he was gone.

Finally, the *Chena* stopped rolling. But she was heeled over now to forty-five or fifty degrees and rising rapidly, her bow down, her stern coming out of the water, rising over the point where the roofs of the dock warehouses had been just sixty seconds before. The buildings onshore bounced and lurched while the roaring and squealing of protesting timbers and nails and metal, the slamming of the hull, and the sound of unbelievable volumes of moving, foaming water remained constant. But the sounds of agonized voices—the yells and screams and other human noises Captain Stewart and his crew had heard with such shattering clarity—had been there one second, and gone the next.

The ship seemed to stop for a moment, caught in midair with what Stewart was sure would be a fatal list to port, its stern high up, as a gigantic wave created by the upwelling of thousands of tons of water displaced by the collapse of the underwater slope of the harbor (along with the dock) came rushing back in, beneath the ship, beginning to shove it toward shore a thousand feet in the distance.

Tom Gilson was near panic. He had run—wobbled, really—up Broadway to its intersection with McKinley Street after leaving Ed Irish's car. He didn't know what he was running from. Maybe the water. Maybe not. The thirteen-year-old simply knew he had to get away, and as the shaking increased and his legs turned to rubber, he could hardly stand up, let alone run.

There was ice on the road, and he was hitting patches of it, trying to put one foot in front of the other. Power lines overhead were snapping back and forth, and people were yelling to look out for them. He could hear the voices, but he didn't know where they were coming from or what they wanted *him* to do.

And finally, the middle of an intersection was beneath his feet. It was moving and bucking and lurching, but he was as far away as he could get from the buildings all around and the wires overhead.

Tom Gilson stood there feeling completely cornered, not even realizing he was almost yelling the same phrase over and over again:

"We're trapped! We're trapped!"

It was quite obviously the end of the world.

For some reason Tom looked back at the bay, taking in a sight which at once made no sense and confirmed his worst fears.

The huge freighter, which had been at the end of the dock, was in midair. That was what it looked like. The giant ship was above the bay, above the place where the warehouses should have been, her stern high in the air, canted over at a crazy angle in his direction.

But he could still see beneath her. He could see the single propeller and the huge rudder and look right down on the forward deck at the flailing cargo booms.

The ship seemed to hang there for a second. It was moving on the crest of a gigantic wave which was approaching what seemed to be a perfectly dry harbor with a missing dock. None of it made any sense, but even at age thirteen he knew the ship he had seen was doomed. Thirty feet out of the water and leaning at such an angle meant it would go straight in and sink. That was, quite simply, the end of that.

Tom Gilson turned around and looked up Broadway, a port of refuge now in his mind as he tried to figure out how to reach his father in the bank about one block away. The realization that the street before him was undulating and cracking as it rolled over a storm sea of ground waves did not deter him. He might not know from what he was running, but he now knew where he needed to run.

It wasn't a bomb; it was an earthquake. Marion Ferrier was sure of that now. With the house gyrating and rolling, the rattling and crashing sounds blending with the incessant chiming of an old mantel clock which had fallen over with the first great undulations of the quake, she knew no bomb attack could create such shaking.

But why hadn't it stopped? She had never heard of earthquakes lasting so long. It seemed forever since it began, and here they still were, she and her son and daughter, braced in an interior doorway with Red's shotgun hanging precariously overhead, her other daughter at work in another part of town, her husband and older son out on the bay somewhere.

The thought of Red and Delbert on the water brought an instant flash of cold fear.

"Do you suppose we're going to get a tidal wave?"

62

Her son and daughter considered that for a moment, and in unison broke away from the door, moving over the bucking floor to the window that looked out on the harbor.

The *Chena*, stern in the air, propeller and rudder visible thirty feet above the waterline, was starting to descend, the giant wave now breaking toward the town.

Hazel turned back toward Marion, her face ashen, her voice unsteady and constrained.

"Mother, let's get out of here!"

Inside the headquarters building of the Valdez Dock Company, sitting on top of pilings a block above the waterfront, the world had gone quite mad. John Kelsey was as worried about his mother-in-law as anyone else. As he and his wife and daughter stayed braced in the doorway of the violently shaking, tilting two-story building, she was trying to get through the lurching kitchen to catch the coffeepot, which had been dancing a violent mazurka on the top of the vibrating kitchen stove. Like some sort of film clip from a Keystone Kops movie, she had been thrown down, trying to wobble across the floor. If it had not been so frightening, it would have been funny. Her preoccupation with that one item was a typical reaction for someone caught in a nightmarish emergency, but he was afraid she was going to get hurt.

The building itself was apparently going to fall over. The floor had been tilting more with each lurch, and between such worries and the horrendous noise, the repeated sound of the *Chena*'s horn blasting incessant short pulses from the direction of the water did not register.

The ship was settling fast, an ungodly back roll to starboard beginning to lessen the horrible deck angle that Captain Stewart was sure would result in capsize. The docks below them were gone, with only a doomed head or two still visible abovewater when the back roll started. Stewart could feel the big ship shoved sideways, coming down relatively fast, the bow beginning to come up at the same time, gaining speed in her descent as the wave, now past, left them with no water beneath.

Suddenly, sickeningly, he realized that they were over the spot where the docks and warehouses had sat moments before. As the forty million pounds of double-bottomed freighter came through the neutral roll point on its back roll to starboard, she hit bottom with unbelievable impact, the hull smashing into something below. They had sat down hard either on the remains of the dock and the disintegrating slope or just on the edge of the bay. Whatever his ship had hit, he expected her to come up in pieces. No oceangoing vessel could take such an impact and not break up. It was a jarring, horrendous, soul-crushing impact, not the least of which was the knowledge in every mind of those above deck that whatever human life might have been sucked down with the disintegrating docks had just been pulverized by twenty thousand tons of ship. The images of the men and women and children going down, clambering over debris, and trying to escape from an inescapable nightmare burned in their minds and their memories. They were obviously doomed, too, but those poor people never had a chance.

The big ship shuddered again and began to float once more. Captain Stewart had expected to come up in pieces, but with another wave gathering to the starboard side the ship had refloated in one piece, rising slowly at first, then beginning to move forward— to surge forward—farther into the small-boat harbor area.

Third Mate Ralph Thompson had been yanking at the horn, sounding the distress signal. Now he was ashen-faced and addressing the captain, who had regained his feet.

"May I be excused, Captain? I don't feel well."

Here in the midst of the ship's worst crisis he was getting formal and was obviously in distress. As Stewart replied in the affirmative, Thompson slumped to the deck of the bridge.

Stewart had the ship's telephone to his ear, talking to the engine room, telling the engineer to get up steam as fast as possible, that he needed power. If she stayed together—if she could get water under her keel—maybe they could make it.

"We can't give you any steam until we get warmed up." The voice was as shrill as his, filled with barely controlled worry and stress and emotion.

"Okay," Stewart said into the receiver, still holding on to the railing, "I'm going to put the [engine] telegraph on full speed ahead. Give me whatever you can as soon as you can!"

There was still a chance—a slim chance—they might get out of this.

Chapter 5

Anchorage, Alaska

No one saw the ominous movement, but at thirty-two seconds after 5:36 P.M. the backdrop of snowcapped peaks standing along the eastern edge of Anchorage were suddenly in motion. Within the space of a few seconds, every molecule of the mountain range had relaxed slightly, then compressed in turn from the eastern edge to the western foothills as the first seismic wave raced through the bedrock like a shiver, bearing down on the largest of unsuspecting Alaskan communities.

The wave front moved as a silent intruder—arriving without warning—covering the eighty miles in less than twenty-one seconds.

The first undulation shuddered through the last mountain summit between Prince William Sound and Anchorage and across the remaining distance to the Rustigan home. It flickered like a shadow beneath the den where Robert Rustigan was engaged in a phone call, and shot westward at its inexorable, lightning pace, still undetected—a fleeting messenger of what was to come.

Racing behind the first one, the rest of the wave train of push-pull vibrations closed on the target at fourteen thousand miles per hour, vibrating the frozen dirt beneath the foundation of the Rustigan house, transmitting the east-west jiggling motion to the footings and the mudsills, the wall studs and nails, transferring the shaking to the wallboard and doorframes, the furniture and fixtures, and fireplace bricks and ceiling tiles. Robert turned to look at Baxter, distant thunder beginning to roll through the interior of the den as the gentle sound of dishes and glasses clinking and dancing in the kitchen cabinets pushed into their field of awareness, vying for attention.

Baxter looked up in what seemed like slow motion as Robert

formed the word "earthquake" in his mind and spoke the word to his friend in downtown Anchorage five miles to the west who had felt nothing as yet.

As the telephone wires transmitted Robert's voice at nearly the speed of light toward downtown Anchorage, the primary wave front chased behind, passing beneath the steel tracks of the Alaska Railroad and the concrete of the Seward Highway, rippling beneath the main runways at Elmendorf Air Force Base and Merrill Field, shivering the Anchorage Westward, where Bob Reeve was just sitting down with a martini in his hand.

Simultaneously the wave front began to rattle the fancy new J. C. Penney's store, where Mary Louise Rustigan and her daughter, Bonita, were shopping, flashing past the nearly completed Four Seasons apartment building ten blocks distant, shooting on westward, where it began to vibrate the polished hardwood floor beneath Bob Atwood's feet in Turnagain Heights and to rattle the kitchen window of the Hines house next door—while some fifteen feet below, the long-ignored layer of waterlogged sand and clay underlying Turnagain began to shake, and quiver.

Robert Rustigan's friend in downtown Anchorage had felt something now, a vibration, a movement, probably an earthquake. He didn't have time to form the words before the senior Rustigan brother yelled half in excitement and half in concern, and replaced the receiver. The Rustigan residence was beginning to make noise as the vibrations increased, then quieted a little, then increased again—all in the space of a few seconds.

Baxter had a nervous grin of amazement on his face, the sounds of a low rumble, almost a deep-throated roaring noise beginning to drown out the strains of the Beatles' song on the stereo, the jangling and clanking of plates and dishes, figurines and lamps from the kitchen to the living room filling their ears.

It was exciting—almost a break in an otherwise ho-hum afternoon out of school—but these things were always unsettling, too, even though they were usually over in a few seconds.

The volume of the noises from the area of the kitchen increased as the boys realized simultaneously that they were hearing dishes hitting the floor.

Eighteen seconds after the first wave had flashed beneath them, the first of the massive secondary waves—the side-to-side, up-and-down motions which had chased the P waves through the eighty miles' distance—took hold of the Rustigan house, now groaning and straining, trying to keep up with its foundation, which was being yanked north, then south, then seemingly in all directions at once.

The fun was over. Robert and Baxter realized the walls were moving in on them. The front door seemed miles distant, their legs were rubbery, but somehow they were in motion almost simultaneously—scrambling, feet falling on moving wooden floors, shoulders banging against the hallway surfaces as the roar and rumble from beneath them reached incredible levels, like some malevolent monster giving voice to a rising growl of warning. What they had to do was clear: They had to get out. How to do it was becoming the question.

One second after arriving at the Rustigan household, the secondary waves yanked the foundation of downtown Anchorage to the north, then to the south, the rather gentle shaking of the first waves giving way to startling gyrations of concrete and masonry, linoleum and steel.

Mary Louise Rustigan and other shoppers in Penney's had been surrounded by the sounds of jiggling merchandise on glass countertops. Now the entire counters were in motion as the proud new store began to move sickeningly, dancing out from under the feet of the customers and salespeople, the airspace filling with rumbles and roars, tinkling and cracking sounds.

Mary Louise, with Bonita firmly in hand, began to follow others toward the exit, trying with increasing difficulty to keep her footing. These things were not unusual, but they were unsettling. She had tamed a hundred horses as a rodeo rider, but bucking buildings were something else.

On the street in front of his office Dr. Perry Mead realized what was happening as he paused with the key in the door of his Land-Rover. He was still standing, but the Rover was beginning to bounce and lurch as if possessed. The neurosurgeon watched in fascination, wondering what to do if it didn't stop.

At the top of the Westward Hotel, Bob Reeve decided to hit the deck as soon as the building started to roll and bounce. Reeve lay down on the floor and hooked his arm around the brass rail at the base of the wooden bar to hang on, watching as the Petroleum Club came alive with moving tables and chairs and cascading dinnerware.

Father Norm Elliot had felt the first waves shudder through his church as he read the line "and the rocks were rent." Now All Saints was in motion, the chandeliers overhead swinging wildly from side to side, being watched by the wide eyes of a hundred members of his congregation as they almost in unison began lurching for the door.

Margaret Hines had turned off Northern Lights Boulevard onto Turnagain Boulevard North when the car began acting very strangely. She was almost to the driveway; but the vehicle was rocking and bucking, and she was beginning to think the engine was coming apart. A hundred yards ahead of her, unseen in the Hines family kitchen, son Warren was running through a quick mental checklist of what to do if the undulations of the house continued to build, as seemed to be the case. Every time he thought it was ending the shaking began again more strongly. It seemed only a few seconds since the first jiggles began and the noise started. The noise! It was incredible—similar to the distant rumble of a freight train, the vibrations tumbling for miles like rolling thunder, a range of sound he could feel as well as hear. Now the foundation had begun jerking in different directions with increasing vengeance, the house trying with increasing difficulty to follow.

Warren moved toward the hallway, remembering the safety instructions about riding out quakes inside a building.

If this gets any worse, he said to himself, *I'll go down the hall and watch Mitzi.* He began edging in the direction of his four-year-old sister's room as the new, urgent, unsettling noises from the sunken living room reached his ears. The large, expensive Sidney Lawrence painting on the living-room wall, his father's pride and joy, was slapping the wall. The rumble from beneath his feet was becoming overpowering, a chorus of startling vibrations from protesting wood and frozen ground, squeaking construction joints and screaming fixtures. It seemed as if the house were being picked up a few millimeters and slammed back down on the concrete foundation every few seconds, the bone-jarring shudders ripping through his entire body.

68

The fact that this was no ordinary quake was becoming all too obvious. So was the fact that the entire house was beginning to move in wholly unnatural ways.

Not just shake, but *move!*

He couldn't believe it at first, but Warren was watching the north wall of the living room begin to undulate in and out, the front doorframe forming a periodic parallelogram, and the painting increasing its arc, punctuated by the sound of breaking dishes and glasses cascading from kitchen cabinets.

Suddenly a voice rang through his thoughts, whether self-generated or not wasn't important.

Get Mitzi! Get out!

That was all he needed. Warren was suddenly aware of the panicked screams now coming from her room.

The same thought had finally occurred to young Perry Mead, Dr. Mead's twelve-year-old son, standing in the middle of the family home several houses away from the Hineses and the Atwoods.

Whatever was happening, it was clear to Perry that it was getting worse and they had better get out. With neither their mother nor their father present to help, young Perry Mead III yelled to his brother and sister to run ahead, out the door, as he turned and raced deeper into the house, trying to stand up on the wildly whipping floor, struggling to get to his two-year-old brother, Merrill.

Fifty yards from Warren Hines's house, Bob Atwood had abruptly ended his trumpet practice and abandoned his initial intention to stand in place and do what a seasoned reporter is trained to do: observe. The walls were in motion, and this was no usual tremor. Some forty-five seconds had ticked by since the first wave had passed.

Atwood headed for the front door of his beautiful house, the sounds of family possessions hurling themselves to the floor ringing in his ears. Nails were screeching inside the walls and wooden beams, his huge ship's wheel chandelier was swinging wildly, threatening to pull itself loose from the ceiling, and he was having trouble standing.

Bob Atwood gripped his trumpet tightly in his right hand and grabbed for the doorknob with his left—at approximately the same moment that the formation known as Bootlegger Cove Clay, which

69

underlay the entire Turnagain Heights area, suddenly reached the limit of its endurance. With water molecules combining with the molecular structure of the clay in what a chemist would describe as a type of colloidal suspension, the clay changed character, no longer able to support the weight of the landscape above it. In less than sixty seconds it had turned to a liquid, and the instant that happened, Turnagain Heights began to travel.

Prince William Sound

As the layers of subterranean rocks (the opposing plates) rumbled into new positions under Prince William Sound, adjacent sections of the two great plates to the southwest were suddenly placed under new pressures—greater pressures than the snags which had been holding back their movement could handle. Snags which under ordinary circumstances would not have reached their breaking point for decades could no longer contain the stored energy. Within seconds another snag to the southwest of the first one shattered, causing additional massive movement of millions of tons of rocks more than twelve miles deep. Several seconds after that, still another snag failed, and the layers lurched forward again. With each movement the focus of what was becoming a massive tear in the fault system beneath Alaska moved farther to the southwest, each additional snap of the layers sending massive pulses of compression waves out in all directions along with the damaging S waves, which chased the compression waves at a slightly slower rate, but at a speed still measured in thousands of miles per hour.

There were no strong motion seismographs in Alaska capable of staying on scale long enough to track the increasingly complex wave arrivals, but as the wave fronts jiggled distant seismograph needles all over the globe, they left the jumbled and confused signature of what was becoming one of the most amazing earthquakes ever recorded. A series of massive breaks and sudden readjustments were occurring over hundreds of miles of buried fault plane and creating a confusing cascade of P and S waves, reflecting, refracting, canceling, and reinforcing each other in odd ways, seemingly coming from different places as the hypocenters—the foci—of the breakages migrated southwest in the course of several minutes, maintaining a seemingly endless chain of elastic waves of seismic energy coursing through a dozen Alaska communities that were suddenly in shock with the horrifying realization: this was not stopping!

In fact, it was just beginning.

Anchorage, 5:38 P.M.

The two Rustigan brothers had run as fast as they could from the house, threading themselves in a dive through the moving target of the front door with high-pitched cries of alarm, their feet moving far too slowly, the goal of safety unattainable even outside with the whole world in motion. A fleeting glimpse of the den as he moved out to the front yard confirmed to Baxter Rustigan that the heavy metallic art piece hanging on the den wall had been making some of the noise; it was swinging out far enough with each wave for them to see the underside.

The complex seismic waves had been buffeting Robert and Baxter for nearly two minutes by the time they reached the yard, half stumbling, half crawling the short but seemingly impossible distance to the fence, where the plan was to grab on and cling for dear life. The front yard, though, was hardly better than the house. In the driveway Robert's car was bouncing and bucking all over the place, moving back and forth, acting like an angry wild animal snarling to slip its chains. Their neighbor's house was in a weird frenzy of motion, bulging, bouncing, moving left and then right, the walls seeming to stretch, the awful sound of tortured wood and cracking masonry joining the rumbling beneath their feet, the sharp report of frozen ground cracking punctuated by the staccato sounds of the tall fir trees overhead slapping together as one grove was whipped to the left while the other whipped to the right. The feeling of inescapable power gripped them both as the whole world rumbled around them and time became an elastic thing, stretching the nightmare out, seemingly forever.

In the heart of Anchorage, J. C. Penney's new store was starting to come apart. Ceiling tiles and shards of glass from exploding display cases were raining down on the small group of people trying to make their way over the lurching floor to the main exit on Fifth Avenue. Just when the noise had reached deafening proportions, the electricity went out, plunging the bucking, screeching interior of the multistory department store into gloomy blackness, the filtered gray light from the ground-floor windows the only beacon left to guide them outside.

Mary Louise and Bonita Rustigan had managed to avoid injury so far, but it was like dodging live ammunition on an obstacle course—like the nightmare that everyone has at one time or another in which you try to run from something awful, but your feet won't move.

Now the light from outside was in front of them as mother and daughter struggled toward it, feet crunching broken glass every inch of the way, survival instinct suppressing the terror in the pits of their stomachs.

It was beginning to seem as if the world were ending. The shaking had gone on and on for more than two minutes now, the sickening waves and swaying walls like nothing they had ever seen or experienced before.

In the middle of Fifth Avenue in front of Penney's, the managing editor of Bob Atwood's newspaper was clinging to a woman he had never met, trying to help her stand up.

Two minutes before, Bill Tobin had counted himself lucky to find a parking place in front of the store on an after-work errand for his wife. He had backed in carefully, only to feel a large bump—a lurch—as the secondary waves took hold of Anchorage. Puzzled, Tobin looked around, thinking he had been rear-ended by some dolt. The car was bouncing, and now to his left a woman appeared in his field of vision midway across the street, wobbling around and staggering. Tobin couldn't figure out what was wrong with her. He watched for what seemed like a long time, but in fact was only seconds, his attention divided by the strange jerking his car was doing, not really comprehending what was happening. What *was* becoming obvious, however, was that the lady was going to fall and get hurt. Whatever was wrong with her, she was losing her battle to stay vertical.

Bill Tobin jumped out of his car to go to her aid, his coat snagging the turn signal lever on the idling Buick in the process. When his feet touched the vibrating, jerking pavement, his mind served up

72

the explanation for what was happening in a flash of understanding: This was a major earthquake!

Now the two of them were like helpless drunks, holding on tightly to each other while trying to stay upright, as Tobin noticed something happening to the new tile facade of the Penney's store: The walls were moving. Of course, everything was moving as the street undulated in continuous motion, glass breaking everywhere and the rattling and rumbling reaching unbelievable noise levels, but something else was happening: The front of the store was coming loose. As the veteran reporter watched in detached fascination, a four-story-high decorative slab of concrete and metal covered with little blue tiles broke free from the brackets tenuously bonding its several tons of weight to the outside of the building, and began a descent toward the sidewalk below, slowly at first, down a mere foot it seemed in the time it took for his mind to catch up and tell him what had happened—what was happening—what was about to happen.

From inside the store Mary Louise and Bonita Rustigan could see the main exit. They were close now. A few more yards over the pitching floor. The plan was to get out of there as fast as possible— the building was sure to collapse, so violent were the sounds and the vibrations. The noise in the store was deafening.

A young man ran out the door just ahead of them, then stopped on the sidewalk for some reason, losing his balance momentarily, crouching just on the other side of the glass doors. The blur of motion from above the door outside may not have registered at first. The daylight was being blocked only in one area, but something was coming down—fast. As Bill Tobin watched from the street, the huge concrete panel descended the last few yards to the sidewalk in a horrendous crash, the full force landing on top of the crouching young man, obliterating him from view, killing him instantly.

At that same moment, unaware of what had happened, Mary Louise and Bonita covered the last few feet to the main door of J. C. Penney's like a pair of Olympic runners.

Bill Tobin could hardly believe the waves—gigantic waves of concrete, in the street! The pavement was undulating in waves so high he simply could not see over them, and the sound continued to grow, an unbelievable screeching, breaking, tearing, and roaring sound, deep, physical vibrations shaking his very soul. *My God,* Tobin thought, *this—this is the end. This has to be the end of the world!*

Never in all his years had he experienced the terror, the helplessness, the feeling of being powerless in the shadow of such mammoth energy. Everything he looked to for physical stability was in motion—suddenly there was no such thing as "solid ground" or "terra firma." For all he knew, the whole world was dying in this same cataclysmic convulsion. Who knew how far it went? Time is meaningless in such a situation, but before three minutes of the waves had passed, Tobin knew that logic dictated it must be the end of the world.

Bill Tobin noticed the next slab on the side of the store, noticed that it, too, was in downward motion, picking up speed, heading for the sidewalk below. This one was closer to the western end of the five-story building. It crashed into the sidewalk like the first one with a terrible noise and vibration that he could feel even among the constant rumbling and rolling of the street.

The impact cracked the slab at about the five-foot level, and with that the top portion began breaking over toward the street.

It seemed to fall in slow motion, like the first one, but at the moment Bill Tobin realized the concrete and tile would not reach him, he also realized that his Buick was disappearing beneath the huge piece, crushed like a tin can as it folded over the top of the car like a concrete tent, reducing it to little more than eighteen inches in height.

If he had not rushed to the aid of this lady . . . if he had still been inside . . .

At last they were out the door, Mary Louise Rustigan keeping a death grip on her daughter's hand as they jumped over the rubble, cleared the inside of the sidewalk, and turned to the east, running as fast as their legs could carry them on the bucking surface, running with every ounce of energy possible alongside the store and up Fifth Avenue, back toward the family's business location, staggering and stumbling but making headway, running from the horror of the store, running for safety, far enough out now to avoid the fate of the young man back at the entrance. From the drugstore across the street a handful of other traumatized Alaskans watched the drama at Penney's as they hung on. The woman and little girl were directly across from them now, straining to get up the street, being thrown around like everyone else by the heaving pavement. It looked as if they would make it. The two were less than fifty feet from the eastern edge of the store, where they would be out of harm's way from the falling concrete slabs, clear of the mortar and steel and whatever else was in the structural heart of the walls of the store, walls that were beginning to crack near the northeast corner as the multistory corner itself began to fail, suddenly descending alongside the fleeing mother and daughter, dropping toward the sidewalk just to their right, tons of material in downward motion, propelling another of the concrete slabs down with it, mere feet away from Mary Louise and Bonita, who couldn't see what was happening above and to their right, as the people in the drugstore watched, transfixed and helpless.

In his Turnagain Heights home, the walls in front of Warren Hines were undulating in and out as if a platoon of D-8 bulldozers had tied lines on them and were alternately pushing and pulling. This looked like some sort of horror flick. It couldn't be real!

The drapes were now airborne, too, in the living room, giving a macabre air to the scene as a thirty-pound stagecoach lamp flew off the coffee table, sailing through the air. Warren didn't see where it landed. He didn't have time.

Responding to the voice in his head, he broke out of his shock and wobbled to his sister's room. He tucked the screaming four-year-old under his arm like a football and actually bounced off the hallway walls as he tried to get to the front door. The Sidney Lawrence painting in the living room was flying out at a ninety-degree angle when he came within view of it. As he watched, the painting slammed back against the wall, and the canvas slid down and out of the frame. And that, coupled with the realization that his dad's fireplace of solid Mount McKinley stone was coming apart, convinced him that they were in real trouble.

Warren began pawing at the front door; but the frame was distorted, and the door was stuck. Every time he pulled on it, it was locked in and crunching against its frame, which had become a right parallelogram, then a left one, back and forth, daring him to yank at the right second.

Finally, timing his movements, he jerked with all his strength as the wall came through the vertical once again, and the door swung open, almost knocking him down.

The scene outside looked like something out of *Alice in Wonderland.* The concrete patio had broken into jagged chunks which were moving around drunkenly, grinding against one another like some sort of jigsaw puzzle in motion. The slabs were huge, and they were dropping. Warren was completely stunned. He was dwarfed by the Brobdingnagian nightmare, but he knew he and Mitzi had no choice but to dive headlong into it. He launched the two of them out the door and onto the heaving surface.

The trees were in weird motion, tilting seemingly in every direction, and his neighbor's house was actually sailing toward them! The structure was tilted at a thirty-degree angle like a sinking ship and moving at the two of them, inexorably, and there was nowhere to run.

Warren Hines decided they were undoubtedly going to die. A cold chill, a sort of maturity beyond his years, took over. It was a realization that quite possibly he was out of options, but it carried with it a determination to make very sure there wasn't another way out.

One of the jagged slabs just in front of him had begun to rise. It was, perhaps, ten feet across. Without a second's hesitation, Warren jumped over to it, still clutching his sister, the two of them brushing for a second a few jagged pieces of their fragmented concrete patio, which were now being consumed by some sort of gigantic pit. Still standing, Warren and Mitzi Hines spent the next few minutes watching an impossible sight as Turnagain Heights rose and fell, tilted and undulated all around them, all of it moving quite madly out to sea, and not a bit of it making any sense. As they rode it, their chunk of ground rose some thirty feet in the air while the rest of the jumbled remains of the neighborhood fell around them in ruins. He had picked the right spot.

He could hear other people screaming now, not just Mitzi. Amidst the crashing and roaring and tearing sounds—the noises made by rending wood and screaming nails—were the sounds of other humans yelling in panic.

Still holding Mitzi close, keeping her safe, Warren saw their house in its final agony, tearing apart laterally as if seismic bulldozers were crushing it. To his right a last glimpse of Bob Atwood's magnificent home met his eyes as the last of the rubble it had become more or less submerged and disappeared.

And in front of him, about twenty yards away, Warren thought he saw his mother, somehow caught in the midst of what had to be the end of the planet.

Bob Reeve couldn't find his pocket watch. He never wore a wristwatch. He used an ornate pocket watch, which was now missing. As he fumbled in his pocket for it, lying on the floor alongside the bar in the wildly rocking building, a pocket watch roughly matching the description of his slid by as the hotel dipped to the west once again. Reeve watched, fascinated, as the watch retraced its path when the floor tilted the other way, sailing past him toward the other end of the bar. Holding on for dear life to his brass footrail with one arm, Reeve calculated with airmanlike precision the possible return trajectory of the watch and its potential speed of passage, reaching out at exactly the right second to snatch the timepiece as it slithered by once again over the floor of the gyrating Petroleum Club. Sure enough, it was his, and according to its hands, the time was 5:38 P.M.

Dr. Perry Mead was still clinging to the side of his Land-Rover when something caught his eye in the distance to the west. The new Four Seasons apartment building—just weeks away from opening—seemed to slump. Then, in what seemed like a heartbeat, it was simply not there anymore. All six stories had collapsed in a heap, falling down vertically in a thunderous explosion of concrete dust and rubble in the grip of the heaving and rolling surface of Anchorage. Mead looked again. That was unbelievable. The question which chilled him was simple: Had there been anyone left inside?

Two miles away from where Dr. Mead stood, his children were struggling for their lives. Paul and Penny had managed to get out first, but what they were plunging into was a nightmare. Penny looked back at one point, relieved to see Perry, her twelve-year-old brother, emerge from the disintegrating house with two-year-old Merrill. But as she watched, a huge crevasse opened up in front of them, a yawning gash, opening wider and wider, blocking their way, and eroding the ground under Perry's feet as he struggled to get back, teetering, then falling with his brother into the crack. Before Penny could move, she saw the crevasse begin to close, her brothers still out of view, still inside somewhere in that gyrating, grating mass.

*   *   *

Bob Atwood had also fallen into a huge crevasse within a minute after escaping from his disintegrating house, tumbling to the bottom some twenty feet down and fortunately landing in soft sand. Atwood was instantly aware that he had to get out. Dirt and sand, plants, fence posts, and every other imaginable sort of debris were falling in on him as the shaking and jerking continued.

But he couldn't move his arm. Bob Atwood pulled and pulled, yanking hard before his confused senses allowed his mind to provide an answer. His right hand, buried along with his arm all the way to his chest, was still gripping something.

His trumpet! He still had his hand tightly around the trumpet, and with the entire world caving in on him and the crevasse about to close, he was trapped because he couldn't get it out.

Atwood felt his hand release its grip on the instrument, his fingers relaxing and pulling out of the fingerholes. Just as suddenly his arm and hand pulled free, leaving the trumpet behind.

In the second before Atwood began scrambling out of the would-be grave, an overwhelming sense of loss hit him. His magnificent house was gone. He had seen it disintegrate; now he could see no part of it. All his possessions were gone, all his clothes, all his paintings and guns and mementos and pictures.

But until a second ago, he had still possessed his trumpet.

Now he no longer had even that. Releasing that prized instrument had been the equivalent of parting with his last worldly possession in a world gone berserk.

Chapter 6

Seward, Alaska, 5:36 P.M.

Dan Seavey was staring intently at a mason jar of silver half-dollars collected by his friend and fellow teacher, who had just made him an offer he couldn't refuse.

"Seavey, guess how much is in that jar and I'll give it to you!"

"You mean, exactly?"

"Yeah, exactly."

Seavey rubbed his bearded chin and thought for a second. The visage of Seward's waterfront to the east, right outside the picture window, registered in his peripheral vision, as did the sound of a northbound freight train just starting to move down by the shoreline.

Seavey sat back suddenly and looked his friend in the eye with a grin.

"Well," he began, "I'd say fifty dollars even."

The other man looked shocked, then incredulous.

"That's exactly right!"

As the words were spoken, the table began to move.

In fact, the entire house was in motion, slightly at first, a soft, gentle rocking, as if some giant hand were gently shoving the foundation back and forth. There was no rattling, just the wavelike motion.

Dan Seavey cocked his head, a perplexed smile on his face.

"What . . . is that?"

The question was matter-of-fact, slightly amused, and very collected. Seward's climate had presented the Seavey family with all manner and variety of weather in the past year, but the ground hadn't moved. This feeling was not familiar. Somewhere in the back of his mind, an explanation involving seismic waves was triggered and placed in reserve, but his conscious mind suddenly was open

79

enough to accept any explanation: the heavy freight train moving down by the waterfront; traffic vibrations; some large machine in his friend's basement. Ideas which later seem silly sometimes rush to the forefront in the split second before logic takes over.

Before Seavey could pull up a plausible answer himself, his friend filled the void.

"I don't know, Dan . . . but I think it's an earthquake."

The motion was becoming more insistent now, and the fifty dollars' worth of coins, title to which had only seconds before come into question, began to bounce gently on the tabletop.

The two men sat and looked at each other in confusion for a moment, the seismic waves continuing to increase in amplitude, now rattling the dishes and glasses in the cupboard.

Several blocks to the south one of the last customers in the Brown and Hawkins store had completed a small commercial transaction—or so he thought. The man handed Virginia Darling a dollar and three pennies for the can of Red Wing shoe oil she was holding in her left hand. The slightly worn dollar bill, a silver certificate, was placed in her right palm, the three pennies following in succession. As she began to pull her right hand back and extend her left hand with the product, the first P waves flashed beneath the store from the northeast, vibrating the counters and the ceiling boards and the cash register.

Instinctively Virginia looked around. Her husband was at the back of the store, coming forward, a reassuring smile on his face. Obviously this was another of their periodic shakers, and just as obviously it would be over in a matter of seconds.

"Earthquake, I guess," she told the man, who turned to look toward the street through the plate glass windows of the store.

With the arrival of the first S waves seconds behind the compression wave front, the direction and urgency of the shaking changed, and increased—and increased some more. Fifteen seconds had gone by, and the customer was gripping the counter, trying to stabilize himself against the vibrating floor.

With each second that crawled by, the shaking seemed to increase. There was a rumble, a roar in the distance that now seemed to come up through the floorboards as the building itself joined in with the sounds of creaking wooden joints and vibrating products on glass-top counters.

Virginia's husband was moving faster, headed for her.

"I think we'd better get out . . . now!" She moved in response, as did the customer, not remembering their exact footsteps but somehow traversing the distance between counter and front door in a few seconds, spilling onto the dirt street, which was beginning to buck wildly.

Trees in her peripheral vision were swaying back and forth slightly, and power lines had been set in motion. People from the bank of stores across Fourth Avenue were also rushing into the street, looking puzzled—and scared.

Still holding on to the dollar and three pennies and the shoe oil, Virginia Darling turned to look at her building, which was suddenly beginning to move.

"I'd better hightail it home!"

Dan Seavey jumped to his feet and half wobbled, half ran out the door, down the steps, and into the cool air, now filled with an amazing rumbling noise he had never heard before. His house was a half block away toward the south and the railroad docks—his wife and three young children inside, none of them any more familiar with this phenomenon than he. Somewhere in the back of his mind he knew the word "frightening" should apply; but right now it was more exhilarating than scary, and he wanted to share it.

Seavey tried to get his rubbery legs to run on the bouncing surface of the street, but it was becoming increasingly difficult.

Dean Smith, the longshoreman at the controls of the gantry crane on the Alaska Railroad dock, had not recognized the vibrations at first. Now he had no doubt. The cold chill of reality pressed in on him: alone, exposed, sitting above a dock built over a deep ocean berth, suspended fifty feet above the concrete—and the damn crane was beginning to move of its own volition. By all rights and previous experience, this should be ending, he told himself.

Hang on, boy, this will stop!

But it wasn't stopping; it was getting worse. The front of the crane, beyond his control, had started whipping back and forth laterally, and suddenly the whole thing was coming off the tracks, one side lifting up off the metal rails, then slamming back down while the other side lifted into the air, higher and higher with each cycle, throwing him around in the control cab, "walking" like some sort of giant metallic spider in a grade B horror movie—walking right down the dock, toward the water!

That was enough. If he was going to die, he was going to do it fighting.

Dean Smith ripped open the cab door, gripped the metal rungs of the ladder with all his strength, and launched himself out of the protective cage.

The drunken motion of the gantry crane had captured Dan Seavey's attention as he wobbled the last few feet to his front door steps. The crane was getting ready to do something unplanned and potentially catastrophic. Seavey paused, holding on to his hand railing, waiting to see what was going to happen, not spotting the tiny figure of a man suddenly emerge from the control cab, clinging perilously for a moment to a small ladder, as he swung wildly with the huge crane's gyrations.

It had taken a few seconds before the Alaska Railroad engineer realized what was happening. His engine had begun swaying on what appeared to be straight and steady tracks, and a cold fear of impending derailment hit him, even though he was moving at only two to three miles per hour. The swaying then became urgent, hysterical vibrations, bouncing and lurching, throwing him around in the seat and threatening to throw the whole train off the tracks.

He let go of the deadman's throttle, hearing the diesel decelerate, the electric power decrease, and the electric motors wind down. The brake lever was in his hand now, and he pulled it, gently at first, bleeding off the air pressure, trying to bring the train to a halt.

The tracks looked as if they were wavering, and the motion was getting stronger. He had been through many earthquakes before, and they always let up after twenty or thirty seconds. He hadn't been worried at first, but now he was.

As he watched in horror, his train still moving, cracks began to appear in the roadbed in front of him.

L. C. Lamberson had joined the crew of the *Alaska Standard* for dinner on board before climbing back down the gangplank and returning to his office at the head of the dock. Lamberson was the only supervisor on duty, in fact, the only Standard employee on duty; everyone else had gone home. Twenty minutes of calm had passed as he sat at his desk.

Like most of Seward's residents, Lamberson was only mildly impressed when the first waves flashed beneath the Standard Oil dock and office and made their presence known with a slight rocking motion. Obviously it would stop soon. They always did.

Even the arrival of the surface waves didn't particularly upset him, though the rumbling and clanking of metal that had begun within twenty seconds shot a supply of adrenaline into his bloodstream. He was, after all, sitting in the middle of thousands of gallons of petroleum distillate fluids such as gasoline and propane and other things that could explode with ridiculous ease.

When the building and dock began joining in the noisemaking, rattling and squealing, shaking and booming, with things crashing down inside, Lamberson quickly decided this was not going to fit the normal scenario. He came out of his chair and ran onto the dock, glancing first at the *Alaska Standard* and then to his left at the set of storage tanks on the side of the dock.

What he saw froze him in his tracks: The maze of pipes was beginning to come apart, the first streams of fuel already shooting urgently, threateningly toward the ship, others straining at their attach points.

Lamberson turned on instinct and ran back into the office, picking up speed as he entered the warehouse, running through the building toward the town, weaving over the bucking floor and emerging on the western side, picking up speed again as he hit the railroad tracks and prepared to dart around the south end of a moving freight train. As he calculated his trajectory—pacing his footfalls so as to get over the rails and ties without tripping or breaking stride—a fissure opened, snaking its way from left to right dead ahead of him, opening up the ground exactly where he had planned to step, throwing him off-balance, into confusion, and into the widening crack—with a line of heavily loaded tank cars on the other side.

Seward Police Officer Eddie Endresen and his brother Andy had been in deep discussion about the family fishing boat when the first compression waves arrived. The boat was out of the water and inside a large shed at the head of the small-boat harbor, just north of the Texaco tank farm on the northeastern shoulder of the town.

83

Both brothers decided to wait it out at first, but when the building began shaking violently and threatening to collapse, the two streaked out of the door—just as the walls and roof came down, crushing the boats inside.

Some forty seconds had passed since the first waves reached them on the north side, microseconds before they coursed under the Standard Oil dock, the Seavey residence, Brown and Hawkins, and the railroad dock on the south end, less than four thousand feet away.

Both men were alarmed; Andy's son, Frank, was on another of the family boats, this one tied up at the foot of the ramp below the shop. As Andy Endresen ran in that direction, his son clambered onto the ramp, which was starting to gyrate violently, forcing him to crawl, inching his way up toward his worried father.

Ed Endresen had turned to go run to his car when the chimney of the boat shop joined the rest of the structure in collapse, flattening his car in the process.

The son, Frank Endresen, had almost reached the head of the ramp, which was swinging crazily. He reached out, inching along, grabbed his father's hand, and pulled over the top to safety just as the ramp gave way and crumpled into the turbulent sea water.

Frank Endresen dashed ahead of his father toward higher ground, but the surface was rupturing in lateral cracks everywhere as the surface continued to buck and bounce in wild motion. Frank and Andy Endresen had almost reached the pickup when a fissure opened beneath its rear wheels, and the truck began sliding slowly, inexorably, into the maw of the trench, now filling with water.

The two men watched in horror and fascination as the fissure ate the pickup. They would have to escape on foot—if at all.

Ed Endresen had already tried escaping, and was failing. After the chimney flattened his car, the policeman dashed for the railroad crossing, which had been blocked by the freight train, which was now slowing. Cracks were opening up everywhere, brown, muddy water filling them, spurting and spilling over on the adjacent gyrating ground, making everything extremely slippery.

Sixty seconds had passed since the shaking started, and Ed realized all his escape routes were gone, cut off, or blocked. With a sickening feeling and a knot in his stomach he saw his last path to safety blocked by the line of boxcars moving and shaking ahead of

84

him on the vibrating tracks. The train was still in motion. He couldn't get past it unless he went under the cars, but if he fell beneath those wheels . . .

The sounds of cracking wood and screeching metal, roaring water, and the incessant rumble of the quake itself filled his ears and seemed to come from directly behind him, gaining on him, leaving him no other choice but to get past the train. He could barely stand up on the lurching ground, which seemed to be in motion in all directions at once. His brother and nephew had disappeared, he had no idea where.

Precisely what made the decision for him was unclear, but suddenly Ed Endresen was in motion again. The policeman began running toward the moving train, diving in one incredible, frantic motion behind the heavy wheels of a boxcar, hoping to roll out on the other side in time to stay out of the path of the heavy wheels, reaching, grabbing for the stretch of ground on the other side of the tracks.

"Oh my God, I've got to go back in and get Mother!"

Why she hadn't thought about her before, she didn't understand, but Virginia Darling *had* to get back in the Brown and Hawkins building. Her frail mother was on the second floor of this building, which was now beginning to lurch and bounce as much as the street.

Her husband, however, was restraining her—holding her arms.

"We'll both go," he told her.

But he wasn't moving.

Her frame of reference rattled, her eyes glued to the family store, the booming and bouncing and thunderous roar of the quake still increasing, she wondered for a fleeting instant if he'd lost his mind. *He said we'd both go,* she thought, *but he's holding my arms. I've got to get back in there!*

Memories of the 1933 quake in Long Beach fluttered across her mind. Memories of all the small shakers they had lived through replayed in her consciousness. Why hadn't this subsided?

There was another sound now, another noise, the sound of glass. That was it, glass breaking, exploding, somewhere behind her. The waterfront was behind her, and she was facing west, facing her storefront, listening to the sound of windows exploding sequentially behind her, getting closer and closer. It would be, she thought, merely a matter of seconds before hers went. *She had to get in that building!*

Dan Seavey saw it at the same time the spectacle filled the eyes of other shell-shocked citizens: a tremendous explosion to the east, flame and smoke shooting vertically hundreds of feet, seemingly at a forty-five-degree angle canted north along the eastern shoreline, balls of flame and heat and light roiling into the air. To Dan Seavey it was amazing—fascinating. As he looked back at the railroad dock, Seavey realized the gantry crane he had been watching was gone, and he felt cheated. *Damn,* he said to himself, *I missed the show!*

To Seward veterans the explosion held its own set of imperatives. The one most feared occurrence in the city was the specter of the Standard oil tank farm exploding—and now it had happened.

And as everyone knew, that meant Seward would burn.

The flames from the exploding fuel tank behind reflected off the glass of the Brown and Hawkins front window seconds before the glass collapsed in a million shards. With the ground still bucking and shaking amidst horrendous noise, there was no time for explanations or entreaties. Virginia Darling yanked herself free of her husband's grip and ran toward the frantically shaking frame building, disappearing into the hallway leading to the upstairs section as her husband raced to catch her—to keep her out of what he knew any second now might be a collapsing pile of rubble.

And in the middle of town, heard by only a few, the old bell in the tower of one of Seward's older churches had begun to ring thirty seconds into the quake. It was now a frantic, maniacal, maddened series of clangs and rings, the striker hitting all sides of the bell, the bell itself flailing around. To one who heard it and would later remember, the sound could only be described as hysterical. Seward was starting to come apart at the seams.

The first surface waves from the point of the great underground fracture 130 miles away beneath Prince William Sound had undulated into Seward from the northeast, shaking the town and the mountains from north to south, back and forth, finally imparting a different and deadly kind of motion to the water-saturated mound of sand and gravel and small clay particles on which Seward was built—the alluvial fan (or delta) leading from the western wall of

Resurrection Bay to the waterline, sloping some 500 feet beneath the water down to the floor of the bay.

The entire waterfront was built on the outer edge of that gravel mound where it met the water, but forty-five seconds after the seismic waves had begun yanking it back and forth, the weight of the gravel and sandy material into which a hundred pilings had been sunk, on which a thousand railroad ties had been laid, and around which the entire economy of the Seward community had been based began to sink.

The cracks were the first horrifying indication that something catastrophic was about to happen. The cracks and fissures formed north to south, alongside the railroad tracks and between them and the waterline, opening and closing, spewing muddy water and liquefied sand, marking the beginning of a migration toward the bay. As the entire surface of Seward's waterfront above and below the waterline began to flow like a viscous liquid down the underwater slope, it pulled with it the Standard Oil dock, the new San Juan cannery dock, the railroad marshaling yards, the Army dock, the breakwater and moorings of the small-boat harbor, and the economic base of the town. All of it began to move toward the bay, stretching and dropping slowly at first, the massive, moving underwater landslide displacing thousands of tons of water instantaneously, and causing a mound of seawater many feet high to begin forming a mile out in the bay—a mound of water which would not treat the battered remains of the Seward waterfront kindly.

Third mate Ted Pedersen had been all alone on the end of the Standard Oil dock by his tanker, the *Alaska Standard,* when the shaking began to reach alarming proportions. He never saw L. C. Lamberson momentarily emerge from the Standard Oil offices before heading back for higher ground. What Pedersen did see was the explosion of one of the storage tanks. As fellow townspeople turned to see the rolling fireball ascending into the clear, blue sky, they were looking from the relative safety of land. Pedersen's vantage point was different. With a fire storm beginning at the head of the docks and fuel gushing everywhere along the shore, the realization came fast: He was cut off.

At that point the feeling of wooden pilings and dock planking sinking beneath his unsteady position joined the bouncing and shaking of the seismic waves. The image of the town moving upward registered in his mind a split second before the explanation of what was really happening: The office, the storage warehouses, the tanks on the waterline, and the dock on which he was trying to stand were slipping down, sliding—to where and for what reason he had no idea, and no time to consider.

Pedersen was already in motion, turning abruptly and beginning a dash toward the ship and the boarding ramp, which hung tantalizingly close to the bucking surface of the wooden dock. His feet seemed to move in slow motion, the heat and light from the petroleum conflagration behind him burning hot on the back of his neck. The ship was close, yet still yards away. He tried to keep moving in a straight line on the bouncing surface, but it was more a frantic wobble toward the gangway than a run. Unseen by the crewmen on board, who themselves had been startled to feel the tanker dropping, Pedersen ran with every ounce of strength he could muster.

But suddenly his target—his haven of safety—was in motion, too. The boarding ramp was off the dock, swinging up and away from him. The ship itself had begun to roll slightly, throwing the ramp out of reach. Now, however, the edge of the boarding ramp had disappeared as the ship dropped in front of him faster than the dock.

Pedersen realized he wasn't going to make it. He saw it was futile. Perhaps there was another way.

The veteran crewman turned around and started back toward the inferno of the dock, trying to make himself believe that he could find a safe path to the shore. But the planking of the dock in front of his wobbly steps was beginning to come apart. The earthquake was still gripping everything. It seemed as if it would never stop. Exactly how much longer he could continue to find a place for his frantic footsteps and his pathetic attempt at running was uncertain. He was frantic yet calm, full of adrenaline yet running harder than he had ever run in his life—right into the chasm that suddenly opened in the dock before him, a rush of water and wood and steel passing his confused field of vision in such a blur that it was unclear what was happening, where he was falling. One thing seemed certain, however: He wasn't going to make it. That thought coursed through his brain as he lost consciousness.

Although gantry crane operator Dean Smith didn't see the Standard Oil facilities sinking into the bay, he was very aware of the explosion of the storage tanks. But Smith already had a tiger by the tail, trying to get down the fifty-foot ladder from his control cab with the huge machine swaying and walking along its tracks. Hand over hand, holding on to cold metal with what could be called a true death grip, Smith somehow managed to hit bottom and race over the lurching and bucking surface out of the way before the crane reached the deepwater edge of the wildly gyrating railroad dock.

The dock was breaking apart. Smith had seen the cracks in the paving deck a foot wide and getting wider. The coffee shop and offices were settling toward the water, and smoke—or steam—was shooting from broken windows.

Finding a fellow dockworker, Smith stumbled out the front gate onto higher ground before thinking about the possibility of fire from loose power lines. Someone had to cut off the main power supply to the dock, and he would have to do it. It was a futile and dangerous mission since the dock and all the buildings on it were already disintegrating, but Dean Smith turned anyway and started running back through the gate toward the collapsing dock.

Somehow Virginia Darling managed to get up the first of the wildly shaking and vibrating steps leading to the second floor of the Brown and Hawkins building, desperate to get to her frail mother. Behind her, Oscar Darling had followed her across the street, unable to catch up with his wife until now. For some reason, this time he didn't try to stop her. With Oscar behind her on the steps, Virginia pulled herself hand over hand up the stairwell, fearing what she might find at the top. The sound was still horrendous, and the report of things falling on floors above had met her ears the second she entered. There was fire somewhere in the building, she was sure. If their building stayed up long enough for them to get out, it was probably doomed to burn along with the rest of the town. Those were simply passing thoughts. The welfare of one of Seward's most senior pioneers—her mother—was her only focus.

The railroad engineer realized it was hopeless. The cracks in the roadbed in front of his locomotive had been just the beginning. What he now knew was a massive earthquake had finally derailed him, he was sure. He dumped the air pressure to lock the brakes and decided to abandon his engine.

The engineer half jumped, half climbed down the left side of

89

the big diesel, which seemed to be in sideways motion along with the disintegrating tracks. He hit the dirt running toward the west, toward the streets of the town, instantly realizing that he would have to get past an obstacle course of shaking rails and ties, fissures opening and closing, and several lines of boxcars. As he scrambled in and out of the first water-filled fissure, the engineer didn't have time to see the growing mound of water in the bay and what it was doing. He didn't have time to consider how fast that mound might form a wave, and how fast that wave might move back toward the waterfront, seeking equilibrium. He was focused on only one thing: reaching higher ground and getting out of this hellish railyard. The growing shadow over his shoulder remained unseen.

The mound of water began to dissipate by the third minute of the quake, forming huge waves. One growing wall of water began moving toward the Seward waterfront, where the eastern shore was now disintegrating, the San Juan and Army docks no longer visible, the Standard Oil area in flames, the dock in pieces, and the small-boat harbor partially collapsed and by all appearances devoid of water.

Dean Smith realized almost the instant he had started back through the gate of the railroad dock that the effort was fruitless. He also realized his gantry crane had disappeared, the whole thing was nowhere to be seen. That made no sense, even though he knew instinctively that it had walked all the way to the edge and tumbled in where now a wall of water was now breaking over the eastern edge of the concrete ramp. With a fascination born of disbelief he watched the east point cannery actually riding the wave, surfing fifteen feet above the remains of the dock on the crest before sinking from view. It was moving toward him, the wave lifting several cars like corks as Smith whirled around and resumed running as hard as he could back out the gate toward the Brown and Hawkins building on Fourth Avenue, escaping just ahead of the wave before it played itself out over Railroad Avenue, the backwash pulling ruined buildings, cars, and debris back into the bay along with thousands of gallons of flaming gasoline.

L. C. Lamberson stopped by the bowling alley, two blocks up from where his Standard Oil office had been. He could see only the

90

wall of smoke and flame and exploding rail cars now. There was no visible sign beyond that of the dock or the *Alaska Standard*. The terrific heat from the explosion and fire had followed him up the street, and his heart had nearly stopped when the sound and vibrations of the explosion hit him as he had stumbled out of a water-filled crack in the switchyard and over the rails to safety. The wave crashing in over the remains of the dock and the waterfront was adding insult to injury. Carrying a swell of flaming gasoline and floating railcars along with it, the wave was just a footnote to a holocaust. A great sadness pressed in on him. He was sure the tanker had gone down with all hands. He couldn't see a trace of her.

Frank Endresen was frantic when he reached the relative safety of Fourth Avenue above the railyards and the small-boat harbor and realized that his father, Andy Endresen, wasn't with him.

Like his brother, Ed Endresen, Andy had been blocked by the fissures and the rail cars. He had fallen into and paddled across several cracks and rolled under the boxcars only to be faced with another horror: more than a foot of spilled, menacing green aviation gasoline now covered the stretch of ground in front of him like a lethal lake, spillage from the Texaco tanks which had split open, cascading thousands of gallons of the stuff into the railyards. As he ran through the gas, the flames from the Standard Oil tanks just to the south were all too apparent. One spark would be all it would take to incinerate him—and the sounds of explosions were getting closer.

While Andy Endresen had been fighting his frantic battle to escape, his brother, Ed, unseen some fifty yards to one side, also had fallen victim to an opening fissure. The crack had become an instant chasm opening on the other side of the boxcar Ed Endresen had rolled beneath. Barely getting out of the way of the rear wheels of the boxcar, Ed had reached out instinctively as he tumbled into the trench and caught the far edge, his feet dangling over what seemed a thirty-foot abyss below. Just as rapidly as it had opened, the fissure began closing, belching up a cascade of muddy water, which helped the police officer get his elbows over the slippery edge of the crack. He pulled himself up, one knee first, then rolled most of his body over the top before trying to pull his right leg out of the closing crevasse.

Too late! The ground closed around his boot and his leg, pressing hard, the shaking and undulating of the terrain still in full cry. Endresen looked at the boxcar and the swirling water on the other side and realized he had to act. With a violent lurch he yanked his foot free, wrenching his back terribly in the process, and got to his feet just as the boxcar beside him toppled over and began sinking toward the bay. Endresen stumbled, ran, hobbled, fell, and raced the remaining five hundred feet to Fourth Avenue through the same lake of spilled fuel his brother Andy had forded, worried, like his brother, that any second it could ignite.

As the three Endresen men reached safety, the first wave reached their escape route, finishing the demolition of the small-boat harbor, washing scores of boats over the disintegrating seawall, drowning several people on board two separate vessels, washing over the spot where most of the fuel-covered railyard had stood moments before, and carrying a wave of flaming gasoline and debris toward the lagoon, which stood on the other side of the only road out of Seward.

The engineer had cleared the last line of freight cars in his footrace to safety as the wave broke behind him. His abandoned eighty-car train was already ruined, most of it having rolled seaward off the tracks as the land beneath the loaded cars slumped toward the bay. He had heard the Standard Oil tanks explode as he struggled over the pitching, cracking railyard, and then realized with horror that the additional explosions that kept going off sequentially to his left were the tank cars at the rear of his train, exploding one by one from the rear toward his position as he wobbled toward the safety of higher ground.

And then the line of upset boxcars was in motion again, lifted by the harbor wave as it crashed in on the remains of the switch-yard, lifting the tons of metal in the air and surging them forward toward the last line of rails, where he had stopped for a second to look back.

Adrenaline taking over, the engineer was in motion once again, moving as fast as he could toward Fourth Avenue, the sound of crashing metal and roaring water in his ears, finally reaching the relative safety of a street with no cracks.

Standing on the still-gyrating ground, he could hear his heart pounding. Emil Elbe, a heavy-set fellow railroad worker who had run across the same obstacle course, appeared on the right side of the engineer now, trying to keep his balance, his face contorted in pain.

Elbe grabbed his chest, panting for breath, terrible pain shooting through his body, the pounding of his heart now erratic. With ashen features the veteran railroad man slumped to the ground at the feet of the engineer, losing consciousness as the last vestige of the first wave began its backwash to the bay, carrying most of the train with it.

He had escaped the quake and the fire and wave, but it had been too much for his heart. Emil Elbe died where he had fallen.

The entire crew was in shock, but somehow the *Alaska Standard* had survived. Battered and thrown around, with one crewman missing, she was nevertheless not taking on water. The tanker kept her engines on standby and kept to the center of the bay, aware that further waves might be inbound. Back to the west there was only destruction to be seen. A wall of flame and smoke covered the city from the southeast edge to the location of the small-boat harbor, which could no longer be seen. The company's dock was gone, as were all the other dock facilities as far as the captain could see. Just flames and smoke were visible.

Looking at the same scene of utter destruction from several decks below the wheelhouse, the shocked radio operator of the *Alaska Standard* returned to his radio room and made contact with an operator somewhere in the lower forty-eight, tapping out in rapid Morse code a simple and sad chronicle.

"Seward," he transmitted, "is burning!"

Chapter 7

For nearly four minutes the Alaskan landmass had shaken, rolled, raised, dropped, and undulated with the wildly complex series of seismic energy waves emanating from beneath as the rock layers broke, readjusted, cracked, shattered, and moved again, finally reaching a point in this sequence of elastic rebound in which the stored energy was decreasing, breaking fewer and fewer snags, letting the plates finish their major readjustments. Smaller and smaller lurches of the rock occurred with each passing second. The wave fronts diminished slowly, the gyrations winding down until at last the plates had stopped moving again.

There would be weeks and months of additional readjustments—aftershocks—as the layers shrugged and shuddered and pushed and wriggled like a large animal slowly sinking into a deep sleep, searching for the most comfortable position.

In the meantime, as the battered residents of south-central Alaska began to despair of the seismic waves ever lessening, the last part of the sequence was just beginning.

Valdez, 5:39 P.M.

"Captain! Captain, over here. Fast. Please!"

The voice from the right side—the starboard side—of the bridge finally broke through Merrill Stewart's high-speed mental calculation of what was happening to his ship and what could be done.

He jerked his head to the right and remembered the image of his third mate lying on the floor. The man had just asked to be relieved seconds after the *Chena* had thundered down on the re-

95

mains of the dock. Now the helmsman was beside him, asking for help, listening to the captain's reply.

"Get some sailors up here, and let's get him to his room."

Stewart still had a dying ship to worry about, but Thompson might be a dying crew member. He looked very ill—conscious, but obviously in shock and very weak. The man was only thirty-eight, but the possibility of a heart attack crossed the captain's mind.

Several crewmen materialized and helped Thompson up, half carrying him toward the interior stairway to the deck below, trying to stay upright against the continuous shuddering and bouncing of the seismic waves being transmitted through the thin layer of water beneath the ship.

She was rising again, rolling suddenly once more to port, another incredible gyration threatening to capsize the vessel, pushing them toward the shore and forward, throwing the crew members off their feet again.

Stewart had the handle of the engine telegraph in his hand. It had been on "one quarter ahead." Now he slammed it forward to "full speed ahead" and noticed the pointer respond as one of the engineers answered the command from down in the battered engine room some two hundred feet away.

To his left Stewart could still see the tortured town gyrating and bouncing, the tanks of the Standard Oil and Union Oil tank farms in violent motion. He expected to see an explosion from what had to be spilled fuel, but so far it hadn't happened.

The ship was over thirty degrees to port again, but this time the rate of roll seemed to be slowing—stopping—as the big vessel paused, rising on the new wave, shuddering at the top, beginning to roll back the other way to the starboard side as the water again passed beneath the ship, the wave unable to push that much weight ahead of its crest. As Stewart watched, the wave smashed into the interior of the harbor, playing out before hitting the edge of town.

The ship was coming down approximately where the small-boat harbor had been. It had not been raised as high on the second wave, so the impact when the flat bottom smashed onto the mud the second time was nowhere near as violent and bone-crushing as the first. She shuddered, no water beneath her for a second, and then seemed to refloat almost as quickly on a combination of the backwash and a new wave growing beside them to starboard.

Stewart noticed the rpm needle move. The screw was begin-

96

ning to turn, barely and dead slow, but at least he was getting some steam. Maybe, maybe he could get some headway before the waves put them on the beach.

As the ship came up for the second time, Stewart could see they were just inside the shallow ledge of the interior harbor, the huge vessel seemingly inches above the bottom, barely refloated on the incoming water. He dashed out the door onto the port wing again and looked aft, trying to assess whether they had maneuvering room, trying to decide if he could order a turn, wondering if he still had a rudder.

The scene that met the captain's gaze was as near hopeless as anything he had seen in three decades at sea. The *Chena*'s stern was sitting in the middle of a floating junkyard of broken pilings, rocks, mud, and the remains of the dock. The blades of the ship's propeller would be smashing into that debris even now—if it could even continue to turn.

He whirled to look forward. No solace there, either. In front of the bow lay another impossible barrier: the floating ruins of a cannery that had been on the collapsed end of the parallel dock which bordered the southeastern end of the small-boat harbor. The cannery's foundation was gone, but the cannery itself lay right across the only path to deeper water.

And they were too close to the mudbank to turn. If he ordered the wheel in either direction, they would run aground.

The *Chena*, he realized, was trapped.

Fifteen hundred feet from the *Chena* thirteen-year-old Tom Gilson was frantically trying to make headway toward the First Bank of Valdez, getting nearly half a block from the waterfront intersection behind him before he really noticed that he was running up the middle of what had become a growing stream. With a shock he realized the water wasn't coming from behind him (which was what he expected somewhere deep in his parcel of fears) it was coming toward him. Muddy brown torrents of water forced up from the saturated soil mixed with the effluent from the destroyed sewer system and destroyed water mains in the town and coursed down the street at least a foot deep, maybe more, channeled by the high snowbanks on each side of the avenue. Tom was half running, half wading up Broadway while the surface of the street continued to undulate beneath the current, hundreds of cracks ripping through the surface as the loosely consolidated soil beneath the city settled and stretched toward the bay in the continuous grip of the seismic waves.

The shaking had not let up, but Tom was finally learning how to time his movements in order to stay on his feet. He had given up waiting for the quake to end. It was not going to end, apparently. He didn't understand why, but it was obviously a fact he would have to accept for the moment.

Fissures were opening everywhere in the street in front of him, and with the water getting deeper he was having trouble staying upright—avoiding the cracks. Ahead of him was the Alaska Hotel, the principal lodge in town, built of concrete blocks and stucco. As he looked up at the building, one wall peeled away and the front disintegrated, debris falling onto the inundated pavement before him. Other walls farther up the street were waving and threatening to shatter as well. He kept telling himself the bank building would not be one one them.

Marion Ferrier had refused to leave without her purse and galoshes, and her daughter was furious with her. Giant waves were headed up the bay, and the house sat by the waterfront. They had to leave!

Marion pulled on her boots and grabbed her purse, following her daughter outside, the sound of her overturned clock's incessant chiming filling her ears as she rushed through the door. The gyrating of the building seemed to be slowing now, but it wasn't over. She could see a car coming up the street, still bouncing on the quivering roadway.

Larry had already fled into the street, flagging the driver, trying to get them a ride out. The station wagon filled with a neighbor family slowed enough for the Ferriers to pull open the doors and jump into the moving vehicle, which immediately sped away up Wickersham Street toward higher ground. The unspoken thought in everyone's mind revolved around the horrific sight they had seen in the harbor two minutes before; surely there would be another giant wave, and that one would get their houses.

The propeller speed was up to five revolutions now. Merrill Stewart checked the gauge as the *Chena* rose off the bottom for the third time. She was plowing through mud and debris, scraping along the bottom, barely floating, headed right for the remains of the cannery and doomed unless she could be turned. Ahead of her was the muddy stub of the causeway to the cannery, and she wouldn't clear it.

Stewart was aware of the backwash from the previous waves, but he hadn't noticed the cascade of water from the Valdez streets. Now, without warning, a gush of water pushed in from the port bow, mixing with the backwash from the third wave, putting an incredible field of floating debris into motion, the sound of roaring water rising above the noises of cracking timbers and screeching wooden beams scraping along the hull of the ship.

The shaking of the quake could no longer be felt. But at that moment his finely tuned nautical senses detected something else. The rudder was positioned straight ahead, yet the *Chena*'s bow was beginning to swing to starboard. It moved slowly at first, just a hint of a movement, something most people would never feel. It hadn't even registered on the compass yet, but it was there.

The backwash wave was pressing on the port bow, putting the twenty thousand tons of metal into a right-hand rotation, acting like an aquatic tugboat pushing the bow to sea. If there was enough of it—if the current lasted long enough—maybe they could avoid the mud ahead.

Stewart, still on the port wing of the bridge, watched as his ship rolled slightly to starboard and the bow began to move a few degrees at a time to the right, the propeller turning even faster now, the sounds of the ship's bottom scraping and screaming past untold debris still ringing in his ears.

In the number three hold it was too late for two of the longshoremen, one of them crushed to death and the other dead of a heart attack in the excitement. But with the wild rolling of the ship now apparently over, several men had come to Jack King's rescue, and King was alive, though in great pain with two crushed feet. His rescuers knew instinctively that King would need quick medical attention and a hospital, and with what the ship was going through, they also realized that neither might be possible. There were no doctors aboard the *Chena.*

The noise of the impact with the remains of the cannery was considerable, but Captain Stewart counted it as a victory. The bow was more than ten degrees right of where it had been, and speed was picking up, the distance between the ship and the mudbank on the left giving him the ability to order a slight turn of the wheel to increase the turning rate to starboard, toward the relative safety of the bay. Merrill Stewart couldn't believe it, but it looked as if they were going to avoid becoming a permanent feature of the Valdez waterfront.

Of course, they would undoubtedly become a permanent underwater fixture. With what the *Chena* had been through, Stewart felt instinctively that she was sinking. He would take her into the channel, drop anchor, and prepare for the worst.

Red and Delbert Ferrier had never experienced anything like the shaking and bucking that had kept throwing them on the beach for the previous five minutes. Within seconds, it seemed, an avalanche started down the slope right above them, breaking into the stand of trees right above the shoreline and stopping before reaching them. Red realized that if another slide occurred, they wouldn't be so lucky—the trees wouldn't hold. Father and son had bolted to their skiff and frantically paddled to the *Falcon* on the crest of a wave. The skiff suddenly washed up to deck level, and the two men jumped out and into the Falcon, abandoning the skiff.

Within moments they had the engine going and pulled in the anchor, heading to the southeast across the narrows toward Jack Bay.

It was then that the wall of water caught their eye. The first backwash from the huge wave created by the collapse of the Valdez waterfront had begun racing westward down the ten-mile fjord less than two minutes into the quake. Now it could be seen bearing down on the narrows, cresting, gigantic in height.

The *Falcon* could manage only seven knots of speed, but they were coaxing every ounce out of her, trying to get to the shelter of the other side, trying to outrun a wave that was obviously going to outrun them.

The lighthouse at the north entrance of the narrows was nearly a mile behind them now as Delbert looked back, watching the crest as it bore down on the concrete installation, which sat twenty-five feet above the waterline. The wave was on it in an instant, snapping the entire structure off its foundation as if it were a matchstick, rising above the top of where the lighthouse had been seconds before.

100

"We'll take it on the stern. Hang on!"

Red had no idea what their chances were, but with a fantailed stern and a lot of luck, they might survive.

The wave lost its crest after it had moved into the narrows and taken the lighthouse. Now it was bearing down on the Ferriers' boat, mere yards behind them, a wall of water in the form of a huge swell, which suddenly picked the thirty-four-foot boat up, surfing it along before it, inundating it, consuming it, upending it, and disorienting its two occupants, the deck angle unbelievable, the boat's prow seemingly pointing straight down.

And just as quickly it was over. Profoundly shaken, Red and Delbert Ferrier watched the wave recede to the south and tried to let the fact sink in: They were still alive.

It was followed by the cold fear inherent in the next thought: If that wave had come from their town, what had happened to Valdez and their family?

John Kelsey's building had tipped partially off its foundation. It was now leaning over at a shallow angle; but amazingly, it was intact, and his family had made it through the incredible shaking unscathed. Even his mother-in-law had won her battle to catch the gyrating coffeepot without injury. He emerged from the building into the torrent of water and looked toward the waterfront—to one of the most profound shocks of his life.

He just couldn't see them at first, he thought. They must be there. Seven million dollars' worth of buildings and causeway and docks don't just disappear.

But with a cold knot in the pit of his stomach and the effort to fight the growing confusion with denial failing, his training in facing reality far too well developed, John Kelsey realized that was precisely what had occurred. The docks were gone! The buildings were gone. Most of the causeway was gone. And the people . . .

Oh, Lord, what about his people out there—where were they?

It was unbelievable. Beyond belief. Impossible to accept. But there it was. Nothing but debris beyond the stub of the causeway, nothing but wreckage—and the *Chena,* which registered in his peripheral vision off to the left, still afloat.

Oh, my God! he said to himself. *Anyone not on the ship couldn't have survived. Did they make it? Did anyone make it?*

The *Chena* held that answer. The ship, he realized, was doing something quite odd: It was steaming through the middle of the cannery, smoke coming from her stack, obviously running for safety.

Through the middle of the cannery? Was nothing left?

The vivid mental image of all those men, their wives, and the children, good people in a festive mood as he had seen them fewer than twenty minutes ago, played in his mind's eye.

John Kelsey, his world in ruins, stood in the middle of Alaska Avenue for a brief moment, neither seeing nor feeling the rush of water coursing around his ankles and legs as he stared into the void.

Seward, 5:40 P.M.

Like the rolling thunder of a high-speed freight train a second after the caboose passes, the deep-throated, soul-shaking rumble and roar created by the seemingly endless chain of seismic waves punishing Seward began to subside. Slowly at first, the jerking and twisting motions diminished just enough to raise a faint glimmer of hope in a thousand minds that maybe, just maybe, it was not the end of the world after all. After nearly five minutes of progressive disintegration of their city and whatever trust they had held in the security of the ground beneath their feet, it was hard to believe that Armageddon had not arrived. Five minutes had become an eternity of disorientation and disbelief.

Wave by wave, undulation by undulation, Seward came slowly to a halt, its wild north-south, up-down, booming and tilting motions subsiding as if someone were turning down a giant control knob.

Virginia and Oscar Darling finally reached the top of the stairs and raced down the hallway toward the far end, where the form of a tiny woman stood, braced, in a doorway.

Emma Hawkins was as white as a sheet. As her daughter and son-in-law rushed up to her breathlessly, the final surface waves were passing underneath the Brown and Hawkins building, the sound of screeching nails and groaning wood, rattling dishes and jars and crashing canned goods now subsiding, the noise down to an occasional quiver.

102

The kitchen floor behind her looked like a casualty of war, but the owner was simply angry.

"I couldn't get off the bed!" she began.

"Mother, come on, we've got to leave!"

Emma Hawkins had tried for a full five minutes to get up as her building bucked over the seismic waves like an out-of-control raft on a white-water river. Every time she tried, however, another lurch would throw her back on the bed, and that had left her furious. The Seward pioneer had weathered just about everything else this land could throw at her, and she was in no mood to be thrown around by a mere earthquake. With the contents of shelves, pictures, and almost everything else breakable or movable in the small apartment hurling themselves to the floor, she kept trying to get to her feet and at last succeeded, moving quickly then to the presumed safety of the door. She had handled it and survived, thank you. Why on earth should she leave now?

Emma Hawkins looked at her daughter with a puzzled expression.

"It was only an earthquake, Virginia, and it's over now."

That brought the two rescuers to a mental halt.

"But," Virginia began, "they say there's going to be a tidal wave."

The retort was instantaneous.

"Oh, they always say that, but it never happens."

The elderly lady had her jaw set and her arms extended, holding on to either side of the door, oblivious of the battle zone of canned goods and kitchen contents strewn in crazy profusion behind her.

"Mother!"

She looked up at her daughter.

"Mother, there's a fire someplace awfully close, and that *is* real—I saw it myself. We've got to get out!"

Emma Hawkins thought over that new bit of information, thought about her building, the town's other wooden buildings, and the fuel tanks down by the shoreline.

"Well," she said finally, "that's different. Let's go."

Within minutes after the shaking had stopped, the rumbling of the massive quake was replaced by the sound of car engines starting up all over the central area of town as people decided a burning city was no place in which to stay. Cars began collecting residents and heading north, out of Seward, across the lagoon road, which moments before had been washed by a debris-ridden wave full of spilled fuel and the remains of small boats. The twenty-foot-wide strip of concrete was still open as Scotty McRae, accompanied by his son Doug, drove the family car past the lagoon. With Mrs. McRae, children Robert and Linda, Doug's wife, Joanne, and their baby son, plus one neighbor aboard, the presumed safety of Joanne's family home south of the airport at the head of the bay was their destination. They would wait there at her parents' house while Scotty, a volunteer fireman, went back with Doug to help fight the blaze which would surely consume Seward—and their homes with it.

As Scotty and Doug helped unload the family and prepared to return to town, a dark shadow of water entered the southern end of Resurrection Bay at high speed, gaining height as it moved, spanning the bay—the logical result of the sudden uplift of hundreds of square miles of seawater which had occurred minutes before during the progressive breakage in the rocks of the Alaskan subduction zone.

As it moved, cars on the northbound road to Anchorage that had reached the northern limit of the town, just north of the mile-long airport runway, came screeching to a halt. The road ahead was, in a word, destroyed. Impassable. Impossible. The remains of a series of small bridges were twisted and broken off to the side, visible to the lead cars as a jumble of concrete and twisted beams. Such an occurrence on the only surface route in and out of Seward meant only one thing, of course: The entire town was trapped.

The fire was not spreading. Dan Seavey had noticed that fact within the first five minutes after the shaking stopped. Virginia and Oscar Darling with Emma Hawkins in tow noticed it, too.

The plume of smoke and flame was going straight up. Without wind, the flames were staying confined to the waterfront—or what was left of it.

But the silent, black wall of water that would enter the harbor some fifteen minutes later would catch the populace unprepared. The first wave had been a harbor wave, created by the underwater landslide.

The next one would be a true tsunami.

Volunteer firemen had gathered helplessly near the flaming eastern shore. All the water mains were severed, and one lone pumper truck was racing north to find fresh water, its driver hoping no buildings would catch fire until he could get back. Soldiers from the Army barracks above the destroyed Army dock had fanned out into town along with dockworkers who had left the docks minutes before the shaking started. Many were now back near the destroyed railyards, looking at the damaged and missing tracks and the capsized lines of rail cars, as well as the boxcars half submerged on the other side of the Texaco tanks.

With a sudden vengeance which betrayed its force and fury only at the last second, the dark wall of water which had flashed unseen from the south end of Resurrection Bay now found itself limited by the bottom. It rose to crest twenty to thirty feet above the muddy surface of the upper bay and the area which had been the small-boat harbor, now seemingly drained of water as the huge wave built itself up to a crescendo, crashed ashore all at once along the ruined eastern waterfront, carrying a secondary tidal wave of burning petroleum on a fiery crest toward the buildings of Sixth Avenue, threatening anything and anyone in its path.

Dockworkers and townspeople who had ventured in a dazed state close to the wreckage of the first wave saw the deserted diesel engine shudder for a second, then rise like a wounded beast, pushed and propelled toward the town, 250,000 pounds of machinery shoved like a surfboard ahead of the flaming wave crest, bracketed by boxcars and tank cars and disconnected flying wheel trucks from the disintegrating railroad cars in its path, all of it hurtling into small buildings and over the shattered ties and roadbeds to form an amazing, flaming windrow of wreckage from the southeastern corner of Seward's ravaged waterfront to the northeast corner, where the remnants of the small-boat harbor had been seconds before.

The image of that gigantic railroad locomotive in mid-flight would become a metaphor in the minds of those who saw it for the immense forces of nature unleashed on Seward and other Alaskan communities—as would pictures of the smashed diesel's final resting place: on its side nearly two hundred feet to the west of its original position.

105

Bob Clark and his wife, Blanche, were headed for higher ground when they saw the wave, a dark line moving fast toward the town and toward their tiny neighborhood at the head of the bay, just south of the Seward Airport.

"Oh, my God . . . we'll never make it!"

Clark jammed the car in reverse and wheeled around, racing back a half block to their house, leaving the car and pushing Blanche along before him toward a backhoe parked by a tree in the adjacent yard. The Clarks clambered up on to the bucket of the backhoe, and were halfway into the branches of an adjacent tree when Bob noticed the McRae family's car coming slowly past them. They hadn't known of Scotty and Doug McRae's plan to leave the family in the house across the street. All they could see now was that father and son were headed back toward town across the flat, sea-level stretch of ground separating the small housing area from the lagoon road. Bob Clark could tell the two McRaes didn't know what was coming. And he knew that if they drove into that flat area head, they wouldn't make it.

"Go back! Scotty, Doug, get back!"

Clark's voice seemed inaudible against the wind.

"Back! Go back!" he yelled at the top of his lungs and was relieved that the McRaes hit their brake, looked around, and understood him at last.

Scotty and Doug heard the words "tidal wave" and reversed course, racing back to the house, yelling for the rest of the family to get out. Doug found a barrel at the rear of the house and began pushing his family one by one up on the garage roof. Joanne McRae's parents' home was deep in a grove of trees. The Clarks' house was just across the road to the south, blocking the view of the bay. However, the sound of the oncoming wave had already reached them, a roar as menacing as the earthquake.

Doug's mother was up, the neighbor had made it, his brother, Robert, and his sister, Linda, carrying his newborn son, and finally his wife were all on the garage. Scotty McRae jumped up to the eave and helped his son up, both looking toward the bay simultaneously—and both realizing the water was too high.

A mountainous wave maybe twenty feet high could be seen now between the trees in the distance, a growing roar filling the air, headed toward the low-roofed garage.

106

"Up, we've got to get higher. Get up on the roof!"

The McRaes began scrambling again, jumping from the garage roof one at a time to the higher roof of the one-story residence. The wave was over the north edge of the bay, headed right for them.

Doug was up, having lost his footing for a second, then turning around in time to see his dad leap to the higher roof just as the first wave crashed into the house and the garage, ripping the structure from its foundations and carrying it off to the woods behind them.

The house held with the first wave, teetered, shook, and moved, but held—probably on the strength of the plumbing. The wave, however, inundated the family, cascading over them and drenching everything.

The Clarks could not be seen, but they, too, had held on in the branches of their tree a half block away, bracing for the second wave, which hit with even more force, tearing loose from its foundation the house the McRaes were riding, rafting them back in the same direction as the garage in the fading twilight.

Doug McRae held on to his family and tried to hold on to the roof. It was a terrible battle to stay in one place. He assumed there would be a third wave. His sister still held his baby son, his wife was to one side, and they all were hanging on. He had seen the Clarks' house destroyed by the first wave. The house they were riding had lost the garage in the first wave and been swept off the foundation with the second. He understood the horrendous power of that water, and he knew instinctively there would be more waves.

And he doubted they could hang on through a third.

The passage of the first tsunami wave from outside the bay, the second devastating wave to hit Seward, had barely disturbed the *Alaska Standard* as she stood out from the town slightly down the bay, the shell-shocked crew recovering rapidly from their ship's close call. As the crewmen once again ventured outside, knees still shaking, eyes filled with the awful sight of Seward apparently in flames, they heard a weak voice from somewhere above a forward hold.

On a catwalk some ten feet above the main deck of the tanker, third mate Ted Pedersen had regained consciousness in total confusion. He had thought himself doomed. Now here he was aboard the ship he thought he had been unsuccessful in reaching. Was he really alive? Was this some sort of delusion?

Pedersen had no idea how he had been washed up on the catwalk, but the pain in his badly broken leg began to reinforce the point that he was, in fact, alive—and in need of help. With no docks left to receive the ship in Seward, and those ashore rather occupied with their own problems, that help would be hours away. For Ted Pedersen, as with the McRae family and many other Seward residents, there would be a tomorrow and survival, but only after a long, cold, agonizing night.

Anchorage, 5:41 P.M.

The shaking in Anchorage had almost stopped. Bit by bit the buildings had regained the ability to keep up with the direction their foundations were moving as second by second the bucking and lurching and side-to-side motions lessened, then quit altogether.

A gigantic series of fissures and grabens (collapsed or depressed areas left when blocks of land move apart) had formed in the shape of a boomerang, with its midpoint touching the middle of Fourth Avenue, the right "wing" coming very close to the Westward Hotel, the other "wing" describing a path of slumped land and ruined buildings to the east across Third Avenue. The clay beneath had turned to viscous liquid, and blocks of ground above, with their frozen, snow-covered surfaces bearing the weight of rows of shops and buildings, had begun to break away and slump down in relation to the south side of the fissures. Buildings like the Denali Theater and scores of shops both dropped and slid to the north a few feet.

At the west end of the city, a similar "block glide" over the viscous liquefied Bootlegger Cove Clay had occurred on L Street—one of the fissures opening beneath the Four Seasons apartments and bringing it down in a heap. More than thirty city blocks of buildings shook, rattled, and slid over the layers of clay below, one six-story apartment building relocating itself eleven feet west of where it had been built, but without fatal damage.

The Westward Hotel, however, had stayed in place. As its designers had planned, the huge foundation and careful construction paid off. There was damage where the hotel and an adjacent building flailed away at each other, but as the last waves diminished, the new hostelry stood relatively intact.

108

In the Petroleum Club a shaken Bob Reeve felt the waves slow and stop at last. He picked himself up from the base of the bar railing and looked out with amazement on the devastation around him. The General Motors dealership by Merrill Field had collapsed, the concrete roof now lying in pieces. The J. C. Penney store was in ruins, the Four Seasons apartment building had collapsed, and damage was visible in every direction—though overall Anchorage was still standing.

Three miles to the east of town, Baxter and Robert Rustigan realized they had survived, but their knees were still shaking. With bloodstreams full of adrenaline, the two brothers held on to the now-wobbly fence in their front yard until they were sure the quake was really over, then headed back inside the house.

Like the majority of the wooden frame homes in large earthquakes, the Rustigan house was a terrible mess inside with most of the shelves and cabinets unceremoniously emptied, furniture overturned, and glass broken. The bathroom was a noxious mixture of perfumes, after-shave lotion, mouthwash, and other assorted fragrances now in a slush of broken glass on the tile floor, the kitchen covered with broken plates and glasses amidst dented pots and pans. Characteristic of wooden frame homes when the foundation doesn't fail, though, the basic structure of the house was intact.

Baxter and Robert Rustigan plugged the fuel oil tank at the back of the house and decided to drive into town to sightsee. It was logical to assume that everyone had survived as well as they. Not in their wildest nightmare would the two boys have imagined what had just happened to their mother in downtown Anchorage: Mary Louise Rustigan had seen the growing shadow of the falling slab from the J. C. Penney store, recognized what was happening, and given her daughter a final shove a split second before the force and fury of the falling concrete ended her life in the middle of the rubble-filled street. Bonnie Rustigan had been propelled to safety. Her mother had not.

Anchorage was getting dark. There was no electric power. Telephones were out in many areas, water mains had been broken all over town, and the maze of natural gas lines had been shut down automatically and immediately by a model system of automatic emergency shutoffs that probably prevented the city from burning.

Roads were broken in various areas, emergency radio communications were sketchy, the city's radio stations were off the air, and in the moments following the last undulations, people all over the Anchorage area tended to think that they had been sitting on the epicenter of the quake. The idea that other areas might have been hit harder simply didn't occur to such people as Bill Tobin, the *Times* managing editor who had watched people being killed and figured the world was ending in front of Penney's.

Tobin was in a state of shock. The Penney's building in front of him was destroyed, and he assumed there would be a score of dead customers inside. He raced to the nearby Holy Family Cathedral to find a priest for the dead at Penney's, then went straight to the newspaper, bursting into the city room to find a photographer.

The lights were off in the Anchorage Times Building. The composing room looked like a war zone, with people standing around stunned. Bill Tobin was equally stunned to hear that his photographer was next door taking pictures of a liquor store.

"He's got to go down to Penney's. A lot of people have been killed there!" Tobin was a bit frantic, the galvanizing images from Penney's still playing in his mind's eye.

"Bill, there's a real mess next door. All the bottles are broken, and Joe's gone to get some shots."

Bill Tobin just stared at him, not comprehending.

The staffer tried again.

"Bill, didn't you hear about the earthquake?"

There was silence. A deep, all-pervading silence like nothing he had ever heard. Not a sound, no birds, no water running, no waves crashing, cars honking, planes flying—nothing.

Warren Hines, still holding on to his frightened little sister, who was now absolutely silent herself, stood on the promontory chunk of Turnagain Heights' real estate some thirty feet above the devastation all around and looked back toward the south, more startled by the total lack of sound than the destruction.

He had given up hope that it would stop, but finally it had—slowing bit by bit until there was no movement.

Warren had no idea why the neighborhood was in pieces. He could see the landscape was broken in crazy chunks of tilted ground, groves of trees at weird angles, ten or twenty spruce trees all heeled over at forty-five-degree angles from their chunk of ground brushing another grove lying at an equally steep angle in the other direction. There were cracks and gullies and crevasses and roofs of houses strewn around in all directions. Some walls and garages were still visible, cocked over on their sides. Some had disappeared altogether, like Bob Atwood's house.

Everywhere Warren looked there was desolation, and the entire world might look that way for all he could tell.

A figure suddenly appeared and then disappeared behind a chunk of ground in front of him. Warren watched, hopeful, searching the spot where the figure had disappeared.

There he was again. A man in a blue sports jacket came around the side of the mound in front of him, and Warren Hines realized with a start who it was.

Bob Atwood was known as one of the most immaculately dressed gentlemen in Anchorage. Now his clothes were dusty and his hair somewhat rumpled, but to Warren Hines he was a very welcome sight.

"Bob!"

"Yeah. Wait a second."

Atwood clambered up the sloping side of the Hineses' promontory chunk, joining them on top.

Warren Hines, many years his junior, looked at the city's publisher, whom he knew as a family friend, and smiled.

"Well, Bob, you've got yourself a story."

That stopped Atwood for a split second.

"You two all right?" he asked.

"Yes. You?"

"Well . . ." Atwood paused, looked back over his shoulder. "The house is gone, and . . ." His voice trailed off. The destruction they all were looking at was beyond grasp.

The three of them walked carefully down the slope of the thirty-foot rise that had protected Warren and Mitzi and began threading their way between the huge chunks of upended ground, trying to find the new edge of the bluff visible occasionally in the distance. People were starting to gather along that ridge—hopefully to help.

The concern over Mrs. Hines was growing. Bob Atwood's wife, Evangeline, was in town on a shopping trip, and he assumed she was okay. But in the middle of the nightmare, Warren had seen his mother—he thought.

111

Now he heard her voice from somewhere above them.

Atwood and Hines looked up to see an amazing sight. Perched on top of another singular chunk of ground forming a tiny mesa were Margaret Hines and her car. They had been carried away from the edge of the bluff as she had opened the door of the vehicle in what had been her driveway. Now the surface she was standing on had enough room for the wheels of her car and her feet—no more. They helped her down, walking on gingerly to the edge of the bluff, where a gathering crowd of neighbors helped them up the thirty-foot embankment with ropes. Ten minutes before that embankment had been in the heart of Turnagain. Now it was view property.

In the minutes following the last of the seismic waves, husbands and wives turned the corner into Turnagain and other neighborhood roads, standing on their brakes with horror at the sight of what lay ahead: half the neighborhood broken away and strewn in pieces toward Knik Arm. Family, friends, and neighbors were milling around, trying to figure out where houses had gone, where their loved ones were, and what had happened. Some houses had slid so far it took a bit of detective work to track them. Others were left hanging off the new cliff, or were undercut by fissures a few feet back from the new cliff. Bob Atwood's house held the record. It had traveled 1,280 feet before coming to rest in pieces.

Wanda Mead had been away on an errand when the seismic waves slammed into Anchorage. Now, as she turned into her neighborhood, she braked to a stop, seeing that the road ended much too soon. She left her car with heart pounding at the realization that her home was no longer where she had left it—her children no longer safe within.

She was helped down the slope by a neighbor who told her he had brought Penny and Paul out of the ruined area to safety minutes before. The two children had seen their mother as she passed, tears streaming down her face, determined to go in after Merrill and Perry, relieved that at least two of her children were safe.

There was nothing left of the house. It was down there—somewhere. She assumed that Merrill and Perry would be nearby, maybe standing, confused, beside one of those blocks of ground.

The words from the young man helping her at first made no sense. Now they were beginning to sink in along with a cold fear. He had talked to Penny, talked to others who had seen Perry and

Merrill scramble from the house, talked with the one other person who had seen Perry and Merrill fall from view into the crevasse.

"I'm very sorry, Mrs. Mead, but I'm afraid they're gone."

"What?" Uncomprehending, she looked at him.

"We can't find them. I'm afraid they're buried."

Wanda Mead looked toward the north where the home had been, where her sons still were. The landscape was insane. Her sons were down there somewhere, but where? Was there any time left? Where could they dig? The horror of it all—the uncertainty and the fear that time was running out—pressed in on her.

Chapter 8

Seattle was swarming with scientists. The annual meeting of the Seismological Society of America had inundated the campus of the University of Washington and several downtown hotels with seismologists, geologists, marine geologists, and others from both the U.S. Geological Survey and universities throughout the nation. Now, at 7:44 P.M. Pacific standard time on Friday, March 27, 1964, most of them were too busy with early-evening seminars or dinner meetings to notice the city shiver.

The local newspapers had given lukewarm coverage to the meeting so far, with a combination of tepid interest and routine interviews producing routine answers. But one question kept coming up nationwide, and several members of the Seattle press had used it as well: Will we be able to predict earthquakes someday?

The question was always a long shot. Research scientists—especially the type of scientists who studied earthquakes, the seismologist—were hard to pin down on such major questions.

Geologists always seemed eager to talk about their work, but too often no one outside the scientific community seemed to want to listen. The press chased after seismologists, however, asking for simple explanations of complicated processes on short notice whenever earthquakes rumbled onto the news wires. In being professionally careful, the seismological community had developed a reputation for being circumspect and hard to interview.

"Seismologists"—one research geologist sniffed—"tend to be quiet, brilliant little fellows with thick glasses who spend their lives in basement labs reading squiggly lines transmitted in from halfway around the world." A scandalously inaccurate stereotype, of course. But in the early sixties seismologists were found in numbers too limited to defend themselves, and the science they pursued still

115

seemed quite a mystery even to the informed layman—its practitioners somewhat akin to modern-day alchemists armed with seismographs instead of beakers.

Earlier in the day of March 27 the question about future earthquake prediction had landed in the laps of several seismologists as they talked to newsmen between professional sessions. The response of one California Ph.D. was typical.

"Who knows?" he said. "We're looking for clues, but we don't even agree among ourselves about the overall mechanisms which cause quakes—especially major ones. Until we solve that riddle, it's hard to imagine how we could predict them."

Dr. Otto Nuttli, sitting high above Seattle in the Space Needle restaurant, knew something had rumbled beneath his chair, but since it was sitting on a rotating platform traveling at one revolution per hour inside the panoramic windows of the restaurant, the realization that the vibrations might be seismic waves was a bit slow in coming. Five hundred and ninety feet beneath the distinguished seismology professor from St. Louis University the site of the 1962 Seattle world's fair was bathed in a soft sea of artificial illumination, the glittering, twinkling lights of Seattle's Queen Anne Hill, the harbor, and the downtown area in the background.

Nuttli's dinner companions were puzzled, too. Fellow seismologists, professors, and scientists from across the United States looked up one by one, realizing something had happened, expressions of curiosity raising eyebrows. They were here to talk about earthquakes. Could that have been one?

Or was it the wind?

The turntable in the Space Needle restaurant had stopped, it's automatic systems sensing an out-of-balance condition, tripping a relay, and shutting itself down as the ground so far below imparted a tiny back-and-forth motion to the well-engineered structure, a motion amplified to a gentle rocking at the top. The sounds of a first-class restaurant—muffled conversations and the tinkling of cutlery on plates punctuated by the occasional pop of a wine cork—died rapidly as the complement of guests began searching one anothers' faces for an explanation.

The rest of nighttime Seattle looked normal and calm and unaware of the fact that the first S waves from the second greatest known earthquake of the twentieth century had just passed beneath them, headed southeast at twelve thousand miles per hour.

116

In the campus district two miles to the east where the day's meetings had been held, U.S. Geological Survey geologist George Plafker settled into a booth in a small, ground-level restaurant. Plafker, an energetic thirty-five-year-old scientist from New York, who now lived in Menlo Park, California, had become an expert on south-central Alaska's geology. As a member of the Alaska branch of the survey, he had mapped much of the area that held the epicenter of the colossal eruption of seismic energy which had just lashed Alaska for nearly five minutes—energy the equivalent of 250 million tons of TNT. As George Plafker studied his menu, unaware of anything out of the ordinary, the entire wave train began passing beneath the Seattle-Tacoma area. The waves shot by unheralded, marked at ground level only by a slight shiver or shudder beyond the notice of most people, leaving Washingtonians unaware of what had just occurred fourteen-hundred miles to the northwest.

The shaking had stopped in the forty-ninth state, the breakage which had begun beneath Prince William Sound was now complete, but outside Alaska no one knew for sure it had even started. No one knew that the Seattle-based *Chena* was at that moment fighting for its life, churning through the remains of the Valdez cannery. News of the wall of fire that shrouded Seward had not yet reached the outside world in the form of a radio transmission; and the deathly quiet of the alien landscape that was now Turnagain Heights was unknown to those a half mile away—let alone in the lower forty-eight.

As Warren Hines watched Bob Atwood appear around a mound of broken earth in Anchorage, the great seismic waves shot beneath Portland, Oregon, fifteen hundred miles to the southeast, and simultaneously beneath Petropavlovsk, Siberia, on the Soviet Kamchatka Peninsula to the west, headed relentlessly out from the epicenter, identical wave fronts expanding all over—and through—the globe. Seismograph needles in locations all over the United States jumped into motion, traveling almost instantly to the stops, bouncing back and forth between those mechanical limits, describing waves so large that their full magnitude could only be estimated.[1]

By 7:48 P.M. Pacific standard time the seismic waves had shivered unnoticed beneath the western shoreline of Canada's Hudson Bay, beneath the ice pack over the earth's North Pole, and beneath the Menlo Park, California, USGS headquarters. In another two minutes they were racing through the concrete of Main Street USA in Disneyland as George Gryc, the chief of the Alaska branch for the survey, strolled with his family on holiday from his duties at Menlo Park.

At approximately fifteen minutes after the break, the S waves rippled through Dallas, Texas, which lifted along with most of the central United States as much as three and a half inches with the surface waves which followed—the soufflé type of rise much too gentle to be noticed by anything but future interpretation of distant, sensitive instruments. Dallasites considered themselves virtually immune to the effects of earthquakes, even though largely unknown, major faults lurked in the rock strata a hundred miles to the northwest. Like so many Americans living east of the Rockies, seismic problems seemed a West Coast worry. The idea that their city could be moved around, even without damage, by an event three thousand miles away was unthinkable. But it was happening.

And moments later the same wave front, expanding like a gigantic doughnut thousands of miles in diameter, passed simultaneously beneath Memphis, Tennessee (a city built on a seismic time bomb ticking away beneath the Mississippi River basin); Detroit, Michigan; the Canadian capital city of Ottawa; Goose Bay, Labrador; Reykjavik, Iceland; the northern coast of Norway; the Barents Sea north of Murmansk, Russia; Vladivostok, on Russia's east coast; Sapporo, Japan, on the island of Hokkaido; and the state of Hawaii (all of which live with earthquake hazards of their own). Within the following forty-five minutes the waves touched most of the planet, the surface waves beginning a circumnavigation of the earth that was to last for nearly thirty days—the planet responding like a struck gong and vibrating, slowly, silently in space as a result of the enormous power that had been unleashed.

By 11:00 P.M. in Seattle (9:00 P.M. in Anchorage) the first detailed reports on the seismic cataclysm had reached the outside world, and men such as Dr. Plafker and Dr. Nuttli and scores of other earth scientists began hearing sketchy details of what had obviously been a large earthquake that seemed to be centered somewhere in Alaska. As excitement and interest grew and telephone lines came alive with calls among their hotel rooms, unbeknownst to them a dark mass of water, a true tsunami created by the sudden uplift of twelve thousand square miles of Alaskan seafloor, began rising near Port Alberni, British Columbia, on Vancouver Island, funneled in from the Pacific thirty-four miles up an inlet. One by one, four waves in all, the water pummeled the community, tossing several cars around and pushing buildings from their foundations.

                              *   *   *

The staff of the Seismic Sea Wave Warning Center in Hawaii had been in a dilemma for nearly an hour after the first seismic waves coursed beneath the sands of Waikiki, running the needles of their seismographs to the mechanical stops. Realizing a great earthquake had occurred somewhere to the north in Alaska, the men who staffed the center and worked to guard against giant waves crashing in on Hawaiian (or other Pacific Rim) communities without warning tried in vain to get through to Alaska to find out how bad it was, and whether this obviously mammoth event could have generated a sea wave. As the very wave they feared radiated out across the Pacific at greater than four hundred miles per hour, the warning center writhed in frustration. Calls to almost every branch of the U.S. military, urgent teletype messages to Sitka, Alaska (unanswered), seismic laboratories and observatories at Caltech in Pasadena, Berkeley near San Francisco, Tokyo, Guam, and others discovered nothing more than what they already knew. Within a half hour, with seismograph needles leaping to the edges of their drums at more and more observatories around the globe, urgent calls began coming into the center, requesting tsunami information from them—calls from Manila, Hong Kong, the Federal Aviation Administration (FAA), the military, and others. Communications with Alaska were nearly impossible. No one knew what had happened, until an amateur radio operator talking on a car radio managed to get through with a chilling message: Cordova (to the southeast of Valdez) had been "wiped out by a great tsunami!"[2]

With that, the decision was made to issue an evacuation order for the Hawaiian Islands—a decision stopped at the last minute by a phone call from the Navy installation on the island of Midway to the northwest. The tsunami, they reported, had passed Midway like a cat in the dark, the waves rising a mere two feet higher than normal.

More uncertainty and confusion resulted. Should an isolated Pacific island like Midway expect anything more significant from a killer wave? Did that prove anything? No one really knew; the business of monitoring tsunamis was too new. Minute by minute the staff discussed, worried, phoned, thought, and, worst of all, waited.

Until midnight on the West Coast, that is, when word arrived that a great wave had roared ashore at Depoe, Oregon, the backwash carrying four children away from their family campsite and into the sea, drowning them. Within an hour the wave had come ashore as a series of four breakers in Crescent City, California, just south of the Oregon border, demolishing much of the town, throwing redwood logs everywhere, wrecking a sawmill, and drowning ten people.[3]

The evacuation order was issued with the wave less than an hour away, and Hawaii braced for the worst.

In Anchorage's Providence Hospital the sight of Dr. Perry Mead in constant motion professionally attending to patients was in contrast with the tears streaming down the man's face. He had arrived home twenty minutes after the quake to find it gone, his wife standing on the roof of their destroyed house, his daughter, Penny, hugging him in tears with the word of her brothers' disappearance.

"Daddy, we're never going to see Merrill or Perry again."

He had known in an instant it was useless to dig, useless to search anymore. His boys could not have survived a half hour below ground, without air. He had stood and stared at the wreckage for what seemed like an eternity. Now he was trying to keep busy—to help those who could still be helped. The hospital staff was nearly in tears watching him, knowing the magnitude of his loss.

If Doug McRae had been able to read his watch in the darkness, he would have placed the last major wave to hit Seward at a little after 10:00 P.M. Alaska time. Bob and Blanche Clark had left the protection of their tree hours earlier to join the bedraggled McRae family on the roof of the battered house just after the first wave had hit. As darkness enveloped the area, the men had cut a hole in the roof, wrapping the women and Doug's tiny infant son in fiberglass insulation for warmth—a necessary move, but one that would have them scratching tiny glass fragments from their skin for weeks. After each wave, Scotty and his son rekindled the fire behind the house, which now rested in the woods many yards from its foundation, and brought the family down to huddle around it for warmth. It had been around 10:00 P.M. that the all too familiar sound of roaring water caused them to scurry back to the roof again, riding out the last major onslaught of black water in the dark—a darkness still punctuated by the sight of the Seward waterfront on fire.

The sight of creosote-soaked wooden pilings floating vertically all over the bay, their top ends on fire like some sort of aquatic candle, was a sad and eerie contrast with the flames from the ruined fuel storage tanks. Now, at 1:00 A.M., however, with their tiny camp-

120

fire going again, they felt a surge of hope. The waves had been getting progressively smaller, and it seemed certain that the worst was over. The rest of the night would be a numbing procession of relighting the fire, watching for additional wave crests, and trying to keep the family warm, but they knew they were going to make it. Battered, dispossessed of their property, probably burned out back in town—but alive and uninjured. Even Doug's infant son was holding up well and sleeping most of the ordeal away.

Daylight, they knew, would be only hours away, and when it came, Doug McRae planned to walk to the nearby highway for help.

The heart of Seward was in far better condition than the McRaes and the Clarks had feared. There had been 86 houses totally destroyed and 269 heavily damaged; but their homes were standing, and the center of town had not burned. Though the ruined tank farms and fuel-soaked debris would burn for days, the heart of Seward was safe.

The continuous plume of black smoke from the town, however, was the funeral pyre for Seward's economy. There was no longer an Alaska Railroad dock, or a Standard Oil dock, or a San Juan fishing dock, or a small-boat harbor, railyard, trackage, or fuel storage facility in Seward. There was no longer any way to send and receive cargo whether to and from Anchorage or the outside world by water. In the blink of an eye—in the space of five minutes—the massive federal, state, and private investment in Seward as the aquatic front door to Anchorage had been virtually destroyed. And the slide of the entire waterfront into the muddy bottom of the bay had taken with it any chance for rebuilding in the same area. Thirteen people had lost their lives, five were injured seriously, but the vast majority of the nineteen hundred residents would survive physically, only to be faced with near economic strangulation. Dan Seavey would stay in Seward and teach, Brown and Hawkins would stay in business, the Endresen family would claw their way back into the boat and fishing business, and the core of the town would remain. But with the docks gone, the longshoremen would have nowhere to work for months, if not years, and the railroad payroll would never return to the same levels. Even though the federal recovery programs and cleanup jobs would sustain many through 1964, the long-term prospects were grim. Worst of all, Anchorage

121

would finally have the excuse to open its own deepwater channel to the outside world.

To the northeast of battered Seward, anchored several hundred yards off Valdez, the captain of the *Chena* was amazed to find that the reliable old ship was not sinking after all. Stewart and the chief engineer had searched all through her interior, expecting to find a rising tide of seawater. But she was dry. Somehow the *Chena* had absorbed the abuse and would stay afloat, arriving in Seattle battered but operative a week later.

Some of the human beings aboard and around her in Valdez, however, had not been as fortunate. Third Mate Ralph Thompson, two of the longshoremen, and all those who disappeared in the swirling waters which had closed over the dock in Valdez had not survived. And Jack King, the longshoreman whose feet were crushed in the *Chena*'s forward hold, had spent the night in agony aboard the ship (though he would survive after an emergency airlift to Anchorage the next day). For the next fifteen hours Stewart and the *Chena* stood off the stub of the ruined piers, the anchor holding the ship at the end of several hundred feet of chain.

Within minutes of finding the docks gone, John Kelsey and his brother had begun damage control operations, trying to keep the fuel tanks by the waterfront from burning, and trying to help their mortally wounded community. Within an hour many of the wives and children in town had gone up the road to higher ground while others tried to bring some organization to the chaotic nightmare. As in Seward, the spirit of cooperation and altruism would carry the Valdezans for several weeks before a more organized level of outside help would come.

Valdez had more problems than just the loss of people and pier. The town had sunk. The surface of the community had dropped an average of ten feet and stretched some twenty-five to thirty feet toward the bay as the unconsolidated alluvial rocks and gravel settled and crept westward during the shaking. Now Valdez's water table was at the surface, the underground utilities were broken in hundreds of places, and the main streets of the town were underwater at high tide.

The one realization, however, that did not dawn on them for some time was apocalyptic: Valdez could not remain where it was. Alone among the major Alaskan coastal communities, the entire

122

town of Valdez would have to be abandoned and physically relocated farther to the west along the north shore of the bay. It would take years of hard work and dedicated effort on the part of scores of residents, leaders, and government officials, but Valdez would eventually be uprooted and relocated in an amazing story of human determination which would position the town for a massive recovery when the Trans-Alaska Pipeline project began a decade later.

But in the darkness of Friday evening in the midst of wreckage and pain and ruin, those thoughts and prospects for recovery were hard to grasp—mere threads of hope in a tapestry of disaster.

In the early hours of the morning the tsunami waves reached the north shores of the Hawaiian chain, causing extensive coastal flooding and some moderate damage on Maui, but killing no one. Without the evacuation, people would have been caught in some of the low-lying areas when the wave, which was more of a sudden high tide than a breaker, came in. As the wave continued south toward the equator, the weary employees of the tsunami alert center continued sending out reports on wave height, speed, time of passage, and direction to other parts of the Pacific basin—just in case.

Reuben Katchadoorian, another USGS geologist in the Alaska branch at Menlo Park, California, had reached his bed a little after midnight in the San Francisco suburb after a quick trip to the homes of fellow geologists George Plafker and Arthur Grantz to pick up extra clothes and winter coats. Grantz had accompanied Plafker to the Seattle meeting. Now the two of them were tasked to join Katchadoorian in a hurried trip north to Alaska. The three had been on the phone by late Friday evening, planning what to do, making last-minute arrangements, and exchanging the latest word on what had occurred.

It was very clear that the survey needed to be there in force —fast. The types of surface effects that such a quake could cause— phenomena such as sandblows and cracking in lake ice—could disappear rapidly, yet the information such clues might provide could be invaluable in searching for answers to the question that was already circulating like a brush fire in the geologic and seismologic community: What on earth—or more specifically below the surface of the earth—could have caused such a massive disaster? Although no one really knew many hard facts by midnight Friday, it was becoming apparent that this could be an extraordinary opportunity to study a great quake in the survey's own backyard, and maybe, just maybe, advance the science more rapidly than they had dared think possible.

George Plafker, Art Grantz, and Reuben Katchadoorian were part of an army of scientists who had begun advancing on Alaska as soon as the word of what had happened echoed across the scientific community. Nearly six hours after leaving Seattle on Saturday morning, their propeller-driven Super Constellation had landed at Elmendorf Air Force Base in Anchorage (since the main Anchorage airport was still unusable), carrying a planeload of scientists, worried returning residents, and newsmen. After securing parkas, boots, rooms in the visiting officers' quarters, and a rental car with the help of the military, the three USGS men headed into Anchorage for an initial look at an incredible sight.

This was virgin territory for the trio. Not one of them had ever participated in researching the aftermath of an earthquake—especially not a great earthquake. All they had known before leaving Seattle was that Anchorage had been hit hard and that there was some ocean wave damage to a few outlying villages. Within minutes of arrival they were hearing rumors and worries about Seward, Kodiak, Valdez, and many other significant communities to the south.

And Anchorage was indeed a mess. The Fourth Avenue collapse, the destroyed buildings, the L Street slide, Turnagain Heights, Government Hill (where a school and several homes had slid halfway to oblivion) were astounding features. Katchadoorian was oriented to engineering concerns, and decided to work in the Anchorage area. Plafker and Grantz would move to the outlying areas.

Meetings with local and military officials followed, triggering questions about where to look for the greatest hazards and how to pinpoint potential landslides. People wanted quick opinions on the scope and the breadth and the causes of the damage.

Sunday morning, while Katchadoorian worked in the Anchorage area, Grantz and Plafker got on board a Twin Otter twin-engine propjet aircraft for a reconnaissance flight, winging over the Kenai Peninsula, Whittier, Chenega, Seward, and down Resurrection Bay toward Soldotna and back up past the Kenai lowlands. On Mon-

124

day, all three of the USGS men flew in an Army Huey (HU-1 helicopter) over the Anchorage region, looking at the quake's effects on the ground. And Tuesday, Grantz and Plafker once again boarded the Otter, flying a second time over devastated Seward, along the coast eastward to Montague Island and Cordova and (after a fuel stop) to Valdez.

What they were seeing was unbelievable. Geology is a science of interpreting both very slow change and cataclysmic alterations. Of the two, cataclysmic changes are the most frustrating; geologists seldom have the chance to see one in progress or examine one in the immediate aftermath.

Here beneath them, however, was a landscape in twisted agony, a land which had undergone a cataclysm of change in a matter of minutes. Landslides and avalanches, twisted tracks on a destroyed Alaska Railroad bed throughout its length south of Anchorage, Seward's waterfront collapsed and destroyed, the city's industry in ruins, Kodiak awash in debris with wrecked fishing boats strewn everywhere, the coastal community of Chenega completely washed away with twenty-three lives lost, an entire village gone—it was incredible.

They flew over glaciers which had been covered by landslides miles in length, coastal towns with their waterfronts strangely inundated, and others with boat harbors now completely above waterline, all for reasons they couldn't fathom at first.

It was, above all else, a mammoth laboratory, Plafker realized. Dispite his empathetic feelings for the people and the communities, his excitement was growing by the minute. The things they could learn from this!

But why and how could such force be unleashed without anyone's having a clue that it was coming, or that it could occur? Alaska had quakes all the time—he had experienced them himself—but nothing like this had ever hit the Alaskan landmass. At least there were no historical records or stories of such major seismic events.

It was also significant, he thought, that the loss of life was so low, despite the bombardment of the seismic convulsion the area had undergone for what people kept telling him was an impossible five long minutes.

Five minutes? He was no seismologist, but how could a quake last that long? They would have to get an initial report out within

125

weeks, but he was going to have to do some very rapid reading up on earthquakes and tsunamis.

What, for instance, had wrecked the Seward waterfront? From the air it was obvious the docks were not just awash, they were gone. He and Grantz had obtained maps from the local USGS man in Anchorage and diagrams of the facilities. They knew what the Seward waterfront should be like, but it wasn't that way any longer. An underwater landslide seemed possible, but they would have to study it in person.

Could some enormous fault running many miles through the area south of Prince William Sound have caused this cataclysm? With his nose pressed to the Plexiglas of the Otter's windows, George Plafker stayed alert for anything which looked like a fresh fault trace of mammoth proportions. So far there was nothing. Perhaps, he thought, it was underwater.

And then there was Valdez. Below them now, the first few blocks of the town awash since it had apparently dropped in relation to sea level. The scars of a great wave could be seen from the air on a nearby shoreline west of Valdez, but the docks at Valdez were truncated, and the same sort of underwater disaster that had struck Seward looked possible here. More pictures were snapped and more notes taken as they continued, flying low over glaciers on the way back, landing at Elmendorf Air Force Base a short while later.

Plafker was now more excited than he'd ever been as an earth scientist. He, Reuben Katchadoorian, and Art Grantz would have to work their tails off to find out all they needed to discover to write just a preliminary evaluation, but the potential value to science was staggering. It was going to be an agony, but it was going to be fun to be the first to study it.

He felt a twang of guilt for enjoying this, for being excited. People had lost their lives and their homes and their economic futures in this earthquake. True, the initial death toll was just over a hundred, compared with thousands in other major quakes, but that didn't lessen the human impact.

But what excited him was not just the pure science of it, the pure thrill of discovery, of being on the cutting edge of understanding a side of nature that few had possessed an opportunity to study. What was also exciting was the possibility that this quake, if forced to yield its seismic secrets, could be one of the last killer earthquakes to catch an American—or any community—completely un-aware. Perhaps there were keys to where and when such things occurred, how they occurred, and how to prepare for them. Maybe there were valuable lessons on how to build to survive such high-amplitude earth shaking. Possibly there were clues that could lead to predicting such quakes, and recognizing the precursors, if any, which could herald their occurrence. Such knowledge would be of enor-mous benefit to mankind. That was exciting, and that would keep what one newsman would later describe as the "foot soldiers of science" roaming the tortured Alaskan terrain for years, putting to-gether the pieces of the puzzle. Various thoughts of that sort crossed George Plafker's mind in the first few days as the task began.

The base commander at Fort Richardson next to Elmendorf in Anchorage seemed to have everything under control, Plafker noted. He had offered them unlimited support. Airplanes, cars, offices, any-thing they needed they had only to request.

But he wanted—needed—one thing in return from the USGS men. With aftershocks constantly rattling the area ever since the main quake on Friday, threatening the nerves and the safety of those beginning the task of piecing the state back together, he needed information.

"I need to know," he had explained, "can it happen again? Will it happen again? And if the answer is yes, then how soon can we expect it? When will the shaking hit us again?"

George Plafker, Reuben Katchadoorian, and Arthur Grantz were as diplomatic as they could be, but the answer for the general was frustratingly obvious.

They didn't know. No one knew. It could be years or decades before questions like that could be answered.

But with the thousands of square miles of outdoor laboratory the great quake had created, they could dare to hope that the an-swers might be within reach.

Chapter 9

En Route to St. Louis, Missouri—March 28, 1964

As Otto Nuttli knew so well, the great quake which had just hit Alaska with such devastating force would further imperil the safety of the middle and eastern United States. That seemed a strange result, but he knew it would be inevitable. The national focus on Alaska's agony would reinforce the mistaken idea that damaging earthquakes occurred only west of the Rockies.

The seismology professor from St. Louis University had spent much of his career studying what lay beneath the surface of the eastern part of the nation, from Colorado to the Atlantic coast. He knew, as did most geologists, that the thousands of feet of sedimentary rock layers deposited over millions of years at the bottom of ancient oceans which once covered what had become North America were now the heartland of the country, from eastern Colorado to the Appalachians. He also knew that below those layers—forever hidden from easy observation—was the bedrock of the North American continent (also called the North American craton). All that was standard knowledge, but few people understood that those hundreds of thousands of square miles of bedrock forming the foundation of the United States undoubtedly held many significant faults, invisible beneath the wheat fields of Kansas and rolling hills of Kentucky and the urban sprawl of the industrial East. Yet these were faults which could easily be capable of producing unexpected, major earthquakes.

No one knew—no one could know—where the faults were beneath the eastern or midwestern United States until future technological breakthroughs provided ways to "look" beneath the surface. Any particular city in the nation might be sitting on an ancient fault under incredible pressure and close to the limits of endurance.

129

Nuttli had been warning for years that if such a breaking point were reached in an unknown buried fault, the resulting snap could send an unexpected cataclysm of seismic waves slamming into cities that were totally unprepared to deal with major earthquakes.

And of course, as Otto Nuttli had come to realize, the ground beneath the eastern two-thirds of the nation had one very special, very dangerous characteristic which the West Coast didn't share: It could transmit seismic waves for hundreds and even thousands of miles with terribly damaging efficiency.

There were many ways to illustrate the point. A catastrophic 8.5 magnitude quake in the Los Angeles area which could do sixty billion dollars of damage to L.A., for instance, might scarcely bobble San Francisco nearly four hundred miles to the north because the convoluted folds and differences in the geologic structure of the landscape in California (and everywhere west of the Rockies) absorb too much of the seismic energy, attenuating—or lessening— the seismic waves with increasing distance.

But the eastern two-thirds of the nation has no such built-in protection. Place the epicenter of the same quake near St. Louis, and the surrounding landscape of the Midwest and the eastern seaboard will transmit the seismic energy with a hundred times greater efficiency, causing monstrous levels of damage and the potential for thousands of deaths in such cities as Chicago, Detroit, Indianapolis, Memphis, Nashville, Pittsburgh, Cincinnati, Philadelphia, and even Washington, New York, and Boston in addition to the horrific destruction it would cause in St. Louis. Therefore, a smaller earthquake of, for instance, only 7.0 magnitude could cause distant widespread damage the equal of which would require an 8.0 magnitude great quake in California.

Otto Nuttli knew that even fellow seismologists were hard to convince of the heightened dangers east of the Rockies, but the entire Midwest and East act like a solid, continuous slab of material when shaken. Strike it hard or shake it back and forth, and the waves will travel faithfully from one end to the other. Masonry buildings anywhere in the path of such waves could collapse, dams could break or liquefy, and high-rise buildings in distant cities could fall.

Dr. Nuttli knew he was developing into a bit of a Cassandra (as one local newsman would label him), but, damn it, these things were real and threatening.

"Okay, but what do we do about it? Abandon the East Coast

and the Midwest on mere speculation that there might be a fault which might cause an earthquake someday?"

It was a typical question, almost always asked by someone who did not realize that the danger to the eastern two-thirds of the country came from almost total lack of preparation, as well as of understanding. Few, if any, of the communities east of the Rockies had building codes which gave the slightest consideration to the possibility of earthquakes. In fact, few, if any, of those municipalities and states had ever seriously considered looking into the potential seismic hazards in their areas—hazards which begged questions of intelligent land use planning and zoning. There was little or no official concern over buildings placed on saturated, unconsolidated soils that could liquefy if shaken, because they never expected them to be shaken. Almost none of the city fathers or county commissioners east of Denver realized the extreme vulnerability of unreinforced masonry buildings common throughout the Midwest and East, or the potential vulnerability of skyscrapers built with little or no thought to seismic resistance engineering. And, of course, the idea that local governments might need coherent rescue and recovery plans to guide them in case a damaging earthquake did occur was laughable. Dangerous earthquakes, you see, just don't happen east of the Rockies. Tornadoes, floods, hurricanes, and fires, yes. But not earthquakes.

Modern-day New York City, for instance, has never been devastated by a major earthquake.[1] Neither has Philadelphia, Washington, D.C., or Chicago. Therefore, none of them ever will be. That, as Professor Nuttli knew, had always been the popular perception—and the problem.

However, if the land beneath any of those cities had undulated with catastrophic seismic waves in the recent geologic past—five hundred or a thousand years ago—we would not know about it. And wherever such quakes have occurred once, they may occur again, violently shaking landscapes that once held only forests and grassy plains, but that now hold tens of thousands of buildings and residences, bridges, roads, sewers, pipelines, water mains, and a bewildering maze of the physical works of man—almost none of it engineered to survive severe earth shaking. There was a basic truth that Nuttli was determined to keep hammering into his students and anyone else who would listen: For any particular spot in the nation, the fact that we don't know of a history of past earthquakes

131

must *not* be interpreted as evidence that no earthquake threat exists.

And, in fact, for the eastern United States, there *is* a recorded history of earthquakes.

In 1727 the New World colonists in New England were shaken by a significant quake. Then again, shortly before dawn on the frigid morning of November 18, 1755 (seventeen days after Lisbon, Portugal, was leveled by a catastrophic earthquake), Boston and the entire eastern seaboard from South Carolina to Nova Scotia were rattled by a series of sharp tremors. Fifteen hundred chimneys were toppled, gables fell from brick houses, mantels and heavy wooden furniture crashed into floors, the famous gilded cricket atop Faneuil Hall's weather vane in Boston snapped off, and the inhabitants of the eastern seaboard were shaken to the depths of their being. A one-thousand-foot-long fissure opened in Newington, New Hampshire; cracks opened elsewhere near Massachusetts Bay, spewing dust and sand; and people spoke of seeing the landscape covered with waves as if it were the surface of the sea. Within the dour and dark philosophies of Calvinist New England, the earthquakes gave preachers the fuel for their fiery verbal indictments of the human misdeeds and wickedness which surely had called down the displeasure of the Almighty in the form of shaking ground. Prayer and fasting, frenetic church attendance, and pulpit pounding marked the following months, but did nothing to explain the geophysical causes of the quakes.[2]

Then, more than a hundred years later, in August 1886, Charleston, South Carolina, was badly mauled by a massive quake which probably approached a magnitude of 7.5 on the Richter magnitude scale.[3] But no one yet knew what had caused either seismic event—or whether such things would occur again anytime soon. Certainly no catastrophic East Coast earthquakes had diverted anyone's attention from California after 1886, with the 1906 San Francisco quake seemingly a confirmation that the problem was entirely a western phenomenon. Nuttli knew the reaction to expect from the Alaska quake. It would provide misguided confirmation to the smug and the unconcerned that only the earth beneath Californians and Alaskans was not to be trusted.

Watching his fellow scientists in a grand state of excitement in Seattle brought such ironies to mind. Of course, he shared that excitement, too: The Alaska disaster was a major scientific opportunity, and he could hardly wait to get back to the university's seismological observatory to look at the first seismogram tracings to get a feel for the magnitude of the event. The quake would undoubtedly teach them much, and they certainly had a lot to learn.

Otto Nuttli sat in a window seat of the Boeing 707 lifting off from the Seattle-Tacoma Airport and bound for his home in St. Louis and watched the magnificent image of Mount Rainier swim into view, one of the crown jewels of the world's stratovolcanoes, and merely sleeping at that. Rainier was listed as dormant and considered highly subject to future eruption, as was its sister volcano, the beautiful Mount St. Helens, visible now just to the south.

The beauty of this region was almost jarring. Through the windows on the left side of the cabin he could see Mount Baker, another snowcapped, dormant volcano just inside the Washington line to the south of British Columbia. Back to the right side—the south view—beyond Rainier and east of St. Helens sat Mount Adams, and to the south of those two the sharp, snowcapped pinnacle of Mount Hood jabbed the sky east of Portland, Oregon. Several other major stratovolcanos of this group, including Crater Lake in southern Oregon and Mounts Shasta and Lassen in Northern California, formed a coherent line of volcanic peaks marching down the northwestern coast. All of them were set back a hundred miles or so from the seashore, providing mute testimony to the forces and the processes that push molten rock up from depths fifty miles below to form such magnificent—and geologically temporary—sentinels.

But what, exactly, was that process? Fellow earth scientists within a developing, separate subdiscipline known as volcanology were scratching their collective heads over that question. This straight, north-south rampart of volcanoes was stark evidence of some specific planetary process at work. As with the other volcanoes around the Pacific basin which joined the American volcanoes in forming the so-called Pacific Rim of Fire, the process was not unique to the Pacific Northwest—just unexplained. When it was finally discovered, knowledge of that geologic mechanism would probably spur great advances in seismology as well. There were some intriguing new theories, Nuttli knew, and some people out there who wanted to resurrect a now-discredited idea more than forty years old called continental drift. But there were sure to

133

be years of hard work and (they hoped) exciting discoveries ahead before they really knew.

As the jetliner cruised east, gaining altitude steadily, leaving the Cascade Mountains and the Cascade volcanoes behind, the convoluted geology of the western United States began to unfold steadily below. At speeds and altitudes like this, the Boeing was as much a flying geology lab as a means of conveyance. The erosional deltas of mountain streams, the sudden upthrust of a range of mountains, or the grand sculpturing of the Columbia River flowing steadily through the canyons it had carved were spread out in living color. The geologic processes which were so hard to interpret at times at ground level were clear and obvious from thirty-five thousand feet.

It would be nice if seismologic facts could be seen as clearly. It was incredible what could be learned from a seismograph tracing—carefully comparing the vertical, north-south, or the east-west tracings of the seismograph stylus and determining which were P waves, which were S waves, when they arrived, and from which distance they had come. It was similar to reading a specialized language, but the process was one of interpretation, mathematically and logically.

Again that brought Nuttli's thoughts to the eastern seaboard. California could see its faults. Missouri seismologists could only look at the ink lines on the seismograph drums and guess what was down there.

Nuttli was more of an observational seismologist and academician. He left the fieldwork to others, such as the cadres from various universities and the USGS who were gathering portable seismographs and field notebooks and getting ready to race north to Alaska even as he flew east. There was much to be learned from reading the various seismograms they would record of the aftershocks which were still occurring almost hourly beneath Alaska, but Otto Nuttli had classes to teach back in St. Louis.

Nuttli's academic home, St. Louis University, had come rather naturally to a position of prominence in geophysics and seismology. As a Jesuit school, it joined several others around the nation as principal academic centers for earthquake research. There were many Jesuit fathers who had been deeply involved in the field over the decades, leading to the joke that in fact, seismology was a Jesuit science because only Jesuit priests had the patience and the time to

134

tend basement seismographs and interpret miles of seismogram data.

But Otto Nuttli was not a priest. He was a professor and researcher who had been spending more and more time in recent years on the questions of seismic risk to the central United States. It was an area of increasing worry, especially when Nuttli thought back to the granddaddy of all American earthquakes—the most awesome, powerful, and frightening seismic energy release ever recorded on the North American continent. It was an earthquake most Americans knew absolutely nothing about, yet it was possibly the most important earthquake in American history.

A series of massive tremors had rocked the western fringes of a young nation, releasing seismic energy which had reached every city, killing some, frightening many. It was a monstrous release of tectonic forces of unknown origin, which had exploded beneath the bed of the Mississippi River halfway between the young settlements of St. Louis and Memphis, near a tiny, dying town that one promoter had planned to make the capital city of Spanish America: New Madrid, in the Louisiana Territory. Somewhere beneath the alluvial muds of the great river in an area geologically known as the Mississippi Embayment, for some reason, and at great depth, something snapped on a frigid morning in December in the year 1811.

Chapter 10

Louisiana Territory—1811

With St. Louis getting colder and winter definitely on its way, John Bradbury had been anxious to start his journey to New Orleans. The previous two years of exploring the Missouri River's upper limits all the way to its headwaters in the frontier fringes of an unknown land had left the Scottish naturalist exhilarated but exhausted. It had also left him frustrated with a nagging fever and confinement to bed for several months in the small frontier town. St. Louis wasn't much in 1811, but it was at least a pocket of civilization, tucked conveniently near the confluence of the Missouri and the mammoth river named Mississippi. It had served well as his jumping-off point—his outpost in the New World. Now, however, it was time to go.

The expedition of Lewis and Clark had opened the way into the fascinating interior of the North American continent just five years before, and although Bradbury had not traveled nearly as far to the west as that expedition, he had walked on land and crossed streams no white man had ever seen before. Many brave souls were setting out each year from St. Louis, some with visions of empire in their heads, such as Zebulon M. Pike with his recent discovery of a wall of mountains several months journey to the west; others were spurred only by the desire for adventure or profit, or both. The Missouri River (also known as the Big Muddy) ran heavy each spring with flatboats and canoes carrying French trappers, American explorers, and many others westward into the unknown.

For Bradbury, riches were measured in discovery. New plants abounded in this land; he had samples of thousands of specimens, which had preceded him down the Mississippi to New Orleans, bound eventually for Liverpool and home. It would take years to study all he had collected—provided the samples made the journey intact.[1]

The shipment had left in early November, shortly after Bradbury began feeling well again, and now he, too, was on his way south, signing on as temporary master of a commercial flatboat laden with thirty thousand pounds of lead consigned for delivery in New Orleans. With more than a week on the river behind them, John Bradbury and his crew already had passed Island Number Ten, more than a hundred miles south of St. Louis.[2]

Bradbury's tiny entourage formed an interesting cross section of humanity: four Creole oarsmen, a patron (crew boss or bosun) by the name of Joseph Morin, and a fellow of slightly greater refinement named John Bridge, who also hailed from England but was apparently on a rather aimless pursuit of his fortune.

If the crew was strange to Bradbury, he was stranger still to the crew. Two years of plunging into his work in thickets, swamps, forests, or mud flats to get the specimens he sought had given a routine and a rhythm to his single-minded pursuit of nature. His zeal constantly seemed to startle the others. He thought nothing of cajoling the patron into landing the boat at strange, tangled places along the river, jumping into the water and disappearing for protracted periods in the most inhospitable mess of vegetation, returning hours later with nothing more than a handful of "seedpods and leaves." The energetic botanist would climb aboard, filthy and mud-caked, smiling through a sweat-stained face which always seemed ruddy and sunburned, and then discourse for hours more on technical matters beyond the grasp (or, it can be surmised, the interests) of the crew.

Even after a day of such antics, Bradbury would spend half the night carefully entering observations in his journal or plotting the course of a comet the men had been watching with apprehension in the northern sky. While he scribbled notes about the comet, they "crossed themselves and offered a pinch of tobacco to the river."[3]

John Bradbury's flatboat and crew had reached the Kentucky Bend section of the Mississippi by the afternoon of December 14, 1811, stopping for the night at the small riverfront town of New Madrid (pronounced Mad'-rid, unlike the Spanish capital), a confused and tenuous little community that had suddenly found itself a part of the United States just eight years before.

The young nation to the east was in an official state of confusion in the last days of 1811. Dolley Madison and her quiet and somewhat indecisive husband, the fourth president of the United

138

States (and the hero of the Constitutional Convention), were at home in the new Washington, D.C., mansion built for the chief executive, as James Madison grappled with a full range of problems. The country's foreign policy—if, in fact, there was one—was in deep trouble. The nation had yet to command much respect in the world community of established kingdoms and empires, and the British in particular had been treating their former colonies with utter contempt. British ships had for the past six years helped maintain their oaken wall of naval strength against Napoleonic France by impressing British subjects as sailors wherever they could find them, and that included grabbing American sailors on American ships. The humiliation of having U.S. shipping subjected to constant harassment by the British and the French had led Thomas Jefferson's administration to declare a total embargo on foreign trade several years earlier, a disastrous policy which nearly drove the New England states to rebellion. Now Madison's administration had begun permitting American trade with only France, falling into a trap set by the wily Napoleon (who would meet the limits of *his* power the following year on the fields of Waterloo). To make matters worse for Madison, a noisy group (known as the War Hawks) led by thirty-four-year-old Henry Clay of Kentucky, was clamoring for war with England, looking for an opportunity to seize Canada and England's western possessions. It was a time of unrest, and with slow communications, a time of rampant rumors on the frontier.

Several hundred miles of twisting river to the south of New Madrid, the city of New Orleans was still adjusting to American control. The "capital city" of French America had been sold suddenly by Napoleon to a startled Thomas Jefferson eight years earlier for a mere fifteen million dollars. What shook Jefferson was the additional land that came with New Orleans: the entire Louisiana Territory, an expanse stretching from the western shores of the Mississippi all the way to what would later become Utah and Wyoming. Overnight the real estate holdings of the fledgling United States had doubled.

For New Madrid, however, the Louisiana Purchase was a disaster. The town had been laid out originally with a grandiose plan by promoter Colonel George Morgan, a Revolutionary War officer, to become the capital of Spanish America. It had served as a mandatory tax collection stop for river traffic through what had been

139

first Spanish, and later French territory, but with the land on both sides of the river now part of the United States, there were no more taxes to be collected. Suddenly, New Madrid's chief reason for existence had evaporated.

When John Bradbury and crew stopped at New Madrid on December 14, 1811, all that was left of the community was a collection of two small stores carrying a desultory arrangement of merchandise, perhaps a hundred cabins scattered in the immediate vicinity, one Catholic church without a priest, and (by some reports) one schoolhouse. It was hardly a garden spot of the Mississippi, and Bradbury was not sad to leave it.

Having traveled one hundred miles farther south on the river, by two o'clock on the frigid morning of December 16, Bradbury's flatboat was tied to a grove of willows a few hundred yards above a dangerous area of the river called the Devil's Race Ground, where the Mississippi flowed past a half-submerged island. Running such shallow narrows in darkness would have been suicidal, so the crew had decided to bed down for the night in the roughhewn cabins on the flatboat beneath a starry sky.

The sounds of the mighty Mississippi formed an audible backdrop of soothing white noise as the tired boatmen dropped off to sleep. The distant roar of the rapids just to the south balanced by a constant burbling and splashing of waves against the bank blended with the gentle rocking of the wooden craft. The heavy scent of wet vegetation intermingled with the musty smell of Mississippi mud and the aroma of kerosene in the drafty shipboard cabin. Wrapped in equally odorous buffalo robes against the freezing temperatures, Bradbury and the others were fast asleep in different cabins at the moment that massive tectonic pressures that had been building unseen and unknown beneath the region finally reached the breaking point.

Suddenly, with no warning, cubic miles of rock shifted, causing other blocks and faults to activate, the moving, reverberating mass lashing out with massive waves of seismic energy.

The P waves and the S waves from miles directly beneath the small settlement of Little Prairie, sixty-five miles north of Bradbury's boat, arrived twenty-four seconds later, crashing into the riverbed beneath the boat. With an initial, monstrous heave accompanied by a deep-throated rumbling of soul-shaking proportions, the banks of the Mississippi began moving, the water churning in violent waves.

Bradbury was awake in an instant, the incredible noise all around him blending with the sudden motion of the heavy boat—a motion which made no sense. With the sound of trees beginning to crash nearby, he threw off the heavy buffalo robe and tensed his body to leap through the entrance to the tiny cabin, when it was filled instead with several of his crew, eyes wide, a look of uncomprehending terror on their faces.

"*O, mon Dieu, Monsieur Bradbury, qu'est-c'qu'[il] y a?!* [What is *that*?]"

Bradbury had to push past the men to get to the door, running over the bucking deck of the cabin, his senses rebelling at the magnitude of the shaking and the noise—the horrendous noise—all around them.

The river looked as if it were in the midst of a storm, agitated, confused waves chopping in different directions, but not wild enough to explain the lurching and shuddering of the boat. Something else had hold of it and seemed to be shaking it with a vengeful violence.

The sound of wildfowl screaming in various directions in the dark willows all around the bank pierced the low rumbling. The image of white foam on the river blended in a confused rush with the sight of the trees to which the boat was tied, whipping in incredible arcs toward the water and back up.

All he could think of was their mooring lines. They must hold, or the current would take them!

The men were behind him now, all of them out of the other cabin, where they had also been jolted awake. Joseph Morin, the patron, met Bradbury's gaze with a wild look as the botanist turned back to the terrified faces and half screamed the answer:

"*C'est un tremblement de terre!* [It's an earthquake!]"

As his words reached them, a large mass of riverbank crashed into the water somewhere nearby in the dark. Bradbury had been satisfied that their mooring was safe; now he wasn't sure. If they snapped loose and got shoved into the Devil's Race Ground at night in this upheaval, they would surely drown. John Bradbury didn't need years of experience on the river to arrive at that conclusion. It was self-evident.

But at the moment he had a panicked crew and a seismic nightmare with which to contend. With the second crash of riverbank into the churning waters, the patron's voice rose like a shriek over

141

the awful rumbling: *"O, mon Dieu, nous perons!* [Oh, my God! We're perishing!]"

The seismic waves reached the town of New Madrid approximately seven seconds after they began assaulting Little Prairie, slamming into the roughhewn houses simultaneously, jolting awake the residents, many of whom were thrown unceremoniously onto cold floorboards in pitch-dark rooms still heavy with the woodsmoke of last evening's fire and early morning's embers, the thunderous noises from below blending with the squealing of tortured wooden joints and crashing metal pans, shattering glass windows, and disintegrating stone chimneys and hearths.

A young woman named Elizabeth Bryan was one of those who awoke to a nightmare in total darkness when her bed rammed the wall of her small bedroom at flank speed. Fumbling, terrified, and unsure of where she was for a few seconds, she could hear the panicked screams of geese someplace outside along with the frightened yells of fellow humans.

Scrambling over the pitching floor to the doorway, fighting the sickening motions, Bryan lunged at the bolt and nearly fell outside when she yanked it back, the door pitching open into the darkness of an alien landscape.

The world she entered seemed to be ending. Most of the residents of New Madrid must have had similar thoughts as they fought to get outside, then fought to stay upright. Trees were still whipping back and forth in the little town with awful splintering noises and the bellowing of cattle melding with the "most awful roar" as people staggered seemingly in all directions at once.

There were a few smoky torchlights now as the townspeople gathered, confused, scared, and not even noticing the freezing temperatures as they stood in nightshirts and nightgowns, bare feet on frozen soil, listening to the winding down of the noises that Elizabeth Bryan would later describe as "very awful ... resembling loud but distant thunder, but more hoarse and vibrating."

The sky had been crystal clear as the people spilled into the freezing night. Within five minutes, however, a cloud of dust and "vapour" with a sulfurous smell filled the air and blocked out the stars.

Through the night there were eight more minor shocks, followed by a major jolt just after 6:30 A.M. and culminating with a

142

monstrous shaking worse than all the others which hit a little after 7:00 A.M., this one strong enough to shock the famous bird watcher John Audubon as he rode his horse in the barrens of Kentucky several hundred miles to the east.

This time, in the subdued morning light, weird geysers of sand and what appeared to be a black substance mixed with water broke out in several locations nearby, some spouting up to fifteen feet in the air, the heavy sulfurous odor again overtaking everyone, getting in their eyes and obscuring their vision. The seismic waves yanked the ground beneath New Madrid from side to side, further collapsing houses and chimneys in the midst of a hoarse, frightening roaring mixed with the screams and yells. The bewildered people were in mass confusion as their community and their houses crashed around them.

One hundred miles to the south John Bradbury and his boat had managed to stay tied to what was left of the bank, but as the shaking died down, he plunged into the water with a candle, following two of the crewmen, trying to see whether the lines were still secure.

What he found was a profound shock. Shielding a candle, he saw "a long chasm bridged with fallen trees [separating the bank they were moored to from the new bank of the river]; at its end the sheer bank had caved into the river. Their boat would have been buried had it been moored fifty feet above."

Bradbury finally gave the order to abandon the craft, and all of them spent the remaining long hours of darkness on the shaking bank, huddled around a small campfire and counting the impacts of succeeding shocks. The earth seemed to never stop moving.

Six hundred miles to the east the waves passed beneath Thomas Jefferson's home shortly after two in the morning. The grand mansion of Monticello had begun shaking, the sight of kerosene lamps swaying back and forth greeting the startled ex-president of the United States as he sat bolt upright in bed and wondered what had happened.

The seismic waves set bells ringing in New York and Boston moments later, "throwing down" houses as far east as Cincinnati (where residents ran outdoors), spreading over all of the fledgling nation, waking residents in farms and villages, towns and tents from the foothills of the Rockies to the Atlantic shores. In a thousand dark rooms puzzled humans looked around and wondered what had shaken them, unaware that what they were feeling was a catastrophic earthquake. It would be weeks before word spread throughout the country, explaining that what had startled them had begun on what were at the time the western fringes of their nation, an unfathomable distance away.

As daylight crept into the shattered remains of New Madrid, a muddy, turbulent Mississippi River could be seen laden with debris (including the cargo of several destroyed river barges, barrels of flour and pork, and personal possessions), and the aftershocks continued. In fact, the earth seemed to stay in a constant state of agitation throughout the day of December 16 and into the next, as hundreds of stunned settlers simply lost track of the number of jolts.

As a sad Christmas season came and departed, the band of traumatized survivors at New Madrid continued to live in temporary tents and shelters, without money, without much hope, and without help. Much of their townsite had slumped into the river, and numerous houses had been destroyed or damaged. Word began to filter in that a small lake had been tremendously enlarged by a massive slumping of the land to the east in Tennessee (it was named Reelfoot Lake), and stunned rivermen spread reports of islands which had disappeared while new ones had risen in strange places, the channels with which they had become so familiar now completely altered.

On January 7, 1812, it happened again. Another mammoth quake erupted amidst the constant smaller quakes, this one coming in the early darkness as well, causing widespread sandblows, strange lights in the sky, more slumping of the riverbank, and horrendous noises and traumatizing people almost as severely as the first major jolt of December 16.

More chimneys were destroyed on January 7, and from that day until February 1, the tremors continued on a daily basis.

Then, suddenly, about February 1, all was quiet again. The smaller quakes stopped, the periodic shocks ceased, and people began to dare hope that maybe the worst was over.

It wasn't. At 4:00 A.M. on February 7 another series of breaks directly beneath New Madrid radiated massive waves of energy that smacked into the pitiful community with a force and vengeance

144

greater than all that had come before. Elizabeth Bryan, still clinging to hope and living on an adjacent hillside, watched sand geysers erupt in all directions, saw the remaining buildings in New Madrid utterly destroyed, and listened to the raging water of the Mississippi as its bottom was thrust up in several places, creating a series of tremendous (but temporary) waterfalls on the great river.

The awful darkness of the atmosphere, which, as formerly, was saturated with sulfurous vapor, and the violence of the tempestuous thundering noise that accompanied it, together with all the phenomena mentioned as attending the former [earthquakes], formed a scene, the description of which would require the most sublimely fanciful imagination. At first the Mississippi seemed to recede from its banks, and its water gathered up like a mountain, leaving, for a moment, many boats which were here on their way to New Orleans, on the bare sand, in which time the poor sailors made their escape from them. It then [rose] fifteen or twenty feet perpendicularly, and expanding, as it were, at the moment, the bank overflowed with a retrograde current rapid as a torrent. The boats, which before had been left on the sand, were now torn from their moorings, and suddenly driven up a little creek. . . . The river falling immediately as rapidly as it had risen, receded within its banks again with such violence that it took with it whole groves of young cottonwood trees which lodged its borders. . . . A great many fish were left on the bank, being unable to keep up with the water. The river was partially covered with the wrecks of boats, and it is said that one was wrecked in which there was a lady and six children, all of whom were lost.

In all the hard shocks mentioned the earth was horribly torn to pieces; the surface of hundreds of acres was . . . covered over to various depths by the sand which issued from the fissures which were made in great numbers all over the county, some of which closed up immediately after they had vomited forth their sand and water.[4]

The townspeople had had enough. Almost to a person they fled what was left of ravaged New Madrid for a nearby encampment on a small hillside, one family in such panic that their injured seventeen-year-old daughter was left behind on her bed where a falling timber had broken her leg.[5]

The town of New Madrid was gone, totally destroyed. What had not been shaken to the ground had fallen into the river with the calving riverbank.

The Mississippi waterfalls which were reported by Bryan and others gave rise to reports that the great river had actually run backward, but whether it was a temporary "retrograde current" or a genuine flow reversal (highly unlikely, considering the volume of water), the river had been forever changed.

On the adjacent land the remains of sandblows dotted the destroyed countryside, forests lay cocked at strange angles, trees lay broken by the millions, an area of land four miles long had dropped twelve feet, a huge lake had been created, and many boats were missing. There were no officials in what was left of New Madrid to decide how many had died, but because of the small population, the number of people who did not live through the quakes was minimal. Not so, however, on the river. Although John Bradbury and his crew had made it safely to New Orleans by February 7, others simply disappeared with their cargoes. There was no way to know how many.

The February 7 "hard shock" was felt and noticed throughout the nation. Major topographic changes had ripped through an area of fifty thousand square miles, and an area of one million square miles had been badly shaken. St. Louis suffered substantially, with many houses damaged, some collapsed, chimneys down by the dozens, and the population thoroughly frightened. New Orleans, Boston, New York, Chicago, Colorado, Montana's wilderness, and even southern Canada weighed in with excited newspaper accounts in the next few months. Repeated strong shocks rocked Louisville, Kentucky, two hundred miles away and St. Louis to the north. Cracks developed in buildings in Savannah, Georgia; a chimney was lost in Richmond, Virginia; pavement cracked in Washington, D.C.; and bells rang by themselves all over the country.

The New Madrid region was sparsely populated before, but the few people who had been there during December and January scattered to the four winds (except for a few hearty souls). Many decades would pass before anyone would make a systematic assessment of the surface damage, but even a hundred years later it would be staggering. Each of the three quakes would have registered near magnitude M_w 8.5—sufficient to classify them as "great quakes" in the West and well over that threshold in the east.[6]

As Professor Otto Nuttli would come to find out 150 years later, the New Madrid sequence was the largest seismic energy release ever known or suspected on the North American continent, and it had managed to do major damage to sturdy one-story frontier buildings in a sparsely populated wilderness. By 1964 that "wilderness" had become the center of a great nation, with major cities radiating in all directions on land that in 1811 and 1812 quaked and gyrated with a force great enough to destroy a nonseismically engineered structure at distances of many hundreds of miles.

What if it occurred again? Is there any reason to believe that it can't? Is there any assurance that it won't?

Such questions had begun to haunt men like Nuttli, who had begun to research the immense intensity of the great New Madrid quakes and who realized the extreme vulnerability of cities like St. Louis and Chicago, Louisville, Cincinnati, Detroit, Dallas, Little Rock, Kansas City, and many others.

And then, of course, there is the matter of the high mudbanks on the eastern side of the Mississippi some 110 miles south of New Madrid. Several thousand acres of grassy plains covered the area in 1811 on a bluff overlooking the river, the grass roots growing in humus above a type of alluvial Jell-O of sedimentary outwash piled up over sixty feet of windblown loess seated over thousands of feet of other sedimentary rocks into the depths of the Mississippi Embayment—a water-saturated, unconsolidated aggregate of sand and clay and pebbles which vibrated, heaved, shook, split, lurched, jerked, and twisted with sickening motion during all three of the New Madrid main shocks, throwing down trees, rippling the ground with fissures, the sympathetic vibrations of the poorly consolidated muds increasing the effect of the seismic waves, rendering it unsuitable for anything not built to withstand a tremendous lateral beating of ground motion.

Even as a park it would be dangerous in an earthquake the size of any one of the New Madrid events. Yet on that very spot 150 years later would sit the brick and masonry buildings and homes, the nonseismically engineered roads and bridges, of one of America's major cities: Memphis, Tennessee, its inhabitants largely ignorant of the degree to which their city sits squarely in the cross hairs of a seismic gunsight.

147

Chapter 11

Isla Guamblin, Chile—1968

The differently shaded bands along the sea cliff told the story. George Plafker sat back for a second, contemplating the obvious lines of demarcation—the layers visible beneath the lip of the cliff on the other side of the small bay—and thinking about their significance.

Hatless under a bright Chilean sun, he had to squint a bit to look at the whitish upper band running along the top half of the fifty-foot bluff. That one was merely a marker. It was the band beneath that was important, the one that held a vital record etched graphically in the rocky face of the Tertiary sandstone.

It was a gray layer 18.7 feet thick which had been underwater part of each day for hundreds of years. The layer ran completely around the bay, wherever the cliff was showing, clearly marking the area that during each tidal cycle had been washed by the waters of the southeastern Pacific, depositing small marine animals (such as barnacles) and supporting the algae and other plant life that had lived there.

Until the evening of May 22, 1960, that is, when it suddenly became dry land.

A day and a half before on May 21 something had snapped beneath the South American continental shelf a thousand kilometers to the north, triggering a large earthquake that reached a magnitude of M_L 7.5, a serious upheaval that left destroyed houses and shaken Chileans in its wake.

The nightmare for southern Chile, however, had just started. Some thirty-three hours later, at 7:11 P.M. on the night of the twenty-second, a second quake began with another subterranean failure in an ancient snag between rock faces, and this time a ruinous torrent of seismic waves erupted in all directions, surpassing a magnitude of M_L 8.5, releasing energy in greater amounts than the planetary convulsion which would rip through Alaska four years later in 1964.[1]

Suddenly the entire Chilean coast was in sickening motion, the seismic cataclysm tearing through the seashore and countryside, killing thousands, pulverizing masonry buildings, creating a devastating tsunami that headed out across the Pacific to kill more people in Hawaii and Japan, and rearranging the altitude of the seashore for more than a thousand kilometers north and south.

In a matter of seconds the island Plafker was sitting on had been thrust upward a total of 18.7 feet. At the same time, hundreds of square miles of land to the east up and down the coast had dropped as much as 6.5 feet, plunging some farmlands underwater and rearranging seashores and port facilities, docks and fishing beds throughout the country. The gray band George Plafker was contemplating—the intertidal zone of wet vegetation and marine organisms—had suddenly become high and dry even at high tide, and within days the organisms and vegetation were dying, left to bake in the sun during the following eight years until Plafker and his team members arrived by boat to find their remains and write their epitaph. It was a startling document, showing with precision exactly how much uplift the quake had caused at this exact location—and the technique of reading that visual record was the same one George Plafker had developed to a science in Alaska during the summer of 1964.

Now, in January 1968 during the Chilean summer, the thing that kept getting to Plafker was the similarity of the surface changes in Chile to those in the Alaska quake. Amazingly, the Chilean quake of 1960 and the Alaska quake of 1964 were dead ringers in many respects.

Of course, it was also amazing that the scientists who originally visited Chile right after the 1960 quake had missed so much. They never fully documented the vast areas of raised land and seafloor (emergence) or the incredible expanse of dropped real estate (subsidence). They had arrived with a preconceived idea, convinced that they understood the Pacific basin and the "accepted" model, which dictated that only steep vertical faults ring the coastal continental boundaries. They expected that an examination of the seismic wave records trapped from around the planet by the new World-Wide Standard Seismograph Network would show evidence

150

of a buried steep vertical fault running roughly north-south along the Chilean coast.[2] For some reason (which they made little effort to explain) their postulated fault had stored energy and released it in the form of a great quake. It was a neatly conceived theory, and it was also dead wrong.

Another team of eminent seismologists had reached the same conclusion about the Good Friday quake four years later in Alaska, bypassing the implications of Plafker's 1964 work and his exhaustive documentation of raised and lowered Alaskan real estate. They concluded that just as in Chile, the cause of the great quake was a steep vertical fault (this one presumably situated along the southern Alaskan coast).

Both they and Plafker had read the very same seismograms, but had arrived at two entirely different conclusions.

"You see," Plafker had explained to more than one friend outside geology, "you can interpret the seismographic data to mean either a steep vertical fault, or a shallow, subhorizontal dip-slip fault. That's a radical difference, but the math will support either conclusion. If it's steep and vertical, then there's no indication of the seafloor moving or thrusting beneath the continental landmass of Alaska. It's just a fault, a crack in the crust, that for some reason moved. But, if you read the same data the other way, you get a ninety-degree change in the indicated 'plane' of the fault that caused the quake. In that case it could only be a shallow dip-slip fault plane, which would mean that one layer has to be pushing under the other layer, alternately sticking and slipping—each slippage resulting in large earthquakes."[3]

Plafker had not been aware of the impending conflict as he sloshed through the tidal areas of south-central Alaska during the entire summer of 1964. But as a geologist, he had been aware that there was no substitute for field observation. Foot by foot, beach by beach, Plafker and his associates in the USGS had documented the effects on the Alaskan seashore, gaining a reputation for near eccentricity by carrying around pocketfuls of barnacles to see how long they could live out of water (and thus figure out how reliable an indicator dead barnacles could be on seaside cliffs, and whether they could indicate when and how far the seashore had been raised). The exhaustive studies documented a staggering expanse of raised and lowered landscape, which helped answer questions ranging from the cause of tsunamis to the amount of energy released by the 1964 quake.

The record was fascinating, but while George Plafker was working hard on observational field geology, he was also unwittingly establishing the inestimable value of a rather radical new form of seismic research that would shortly take seismology out of basement laboratories, bringing seismologists into the sunlight of geological fieldwork, and geologists like Plafker into the field of seismological research. It was a terribly simple concept of looking for records of seismic occurrences in geologic features, but it would take a decade to gain legitimacy, and twenty years formally to take on its proper title: Paleoseismology.

When George Plafker returned to Menlo Park from Alaska in the fall of 1964 and put it all together with the seismological evidence, the conclusion on the cause of the 1964 upheaval had seemed compelling: It had to be dip-slip. It had to be one massive section or layer of rock sliding beneath another. In this case that meant the Pacific floor was sliding beneath the Alaskan landmass, which was part of the North American plate. There was no way the quake could have been caused by a vertical fault running hundreds of miles along the Alaskan coast and cutting more than a hundred miles into the crust and the mantle of the planet.

And, as George Plafker realized, the exciting part was that if the causative fault was in fact dip-slip, there had to be some massive force pushing at least one of the two layers. The discovery of what that force was and how it operated might provide an element of proof of a new, evolving, and very controversial theory which would later be called plate tectonics.

There was another aspect to the mystery hidden beneath the surface of the Pacific. In Alaska's case, a long trench in the seafloor (called the Aleutian Trench) ran to the south of the Aleutian island chain, paralleling the chain almost exactly from fifty miles offshore as it angled to the northeast toward the south-central Alaskan landscape. When Plafker had plotted out the raised area in Alaska and those parts which had been lowered, they formed a band of affected territory (and seafloor) which ran from southwest to northeast, paralleling the Aleutian Trench. Was that coincidence?

Plafker knew well the theory espoused by such masters of seismology as Hugo Benioff—a developing theory that such trenches are boundaries between sections of the earth's crust, and that they most likely mark the spot where ocean floor is being shoved beneath an adjacent landmass. Benioff had published in 1954 a landmark paper which tracked earthquake hypocenters (a hypocenter is the exact spot and depth where an earthquake starts) from the ocean trenches landward at several different such spots on the globe. To everyone's amazement, he found that when earthquake hypocenters were plotted in three dimensions, the greater the distance from the trench toward the continent, the deeper the hypocenters became. In fact, when drawn on graph paper from the side, his findings indicated a zone of earthquake activity from such trenches sloping downward beneath the landmass, which was labeled the "Benioff zone." Could it be, he had asked, that the ocean floors were being consumed beneath the continents, and that the dipping layer of earthquake hypocenters he had identified revealed places where the layers above and the sliding layer below had snagged, then broken? If so, the prevailing model of the earth was all wrong.

George Plafker sat in the Chilean sun and watched one of his assistants working with a level, determining the exact height of a point on the distant cliff. The boat they had used to get here bobbed in the foreground in the bright sunlight, lending an almost Mediterranean feeling to the scene, even though the latitude was nearly forty-five degrees south.

These were very exciting times geologically. Plafker was glad in some respects that so much time had elapsed since the terrible death toll of the 1960 disaster here. It was hard to enjoy "good science" when so many had died or suffered. Yet enjoyment was exactly what he was deriving from finding further confirmation that on-site investigation—surficial evidence—could take a statistical ambiguity and resolve the conflict. What he was documenting here, like Alaska, had to be a dip-slip earthquake, caused by something shoving the floor of the Pacific under South America and Chile. Perhaps those who stayed in the lab and examined the numbers and the seismograms couldn't tell what was happening, but here on the affected shoreline in person it was crystal clear.

He thought back to an incident of a few years before when he, an obscure geologist from Menlo Park, suddenly found himself unintentionally challenging the two-thousand-pound gorillas of the seismological world. He could laugh about it now, but at the time it

153

had been unnerving. His definitive report on Alaska (a 1965 paper printed in *Science* magazine more than a year after the Good Friday quake) had taken careful issue with those scientists who thought a steep vertical fault had caused the great quake, and who, by inference, did not believe that the Pacific Ocean floor was pushing beneath the North American continent along south-central Alaska.

The problem was that the scientists with the opposing viewpoint included none other than Dr. Frank Press, one of the most respected seismologists and geophysicists on earth (based at Caltech), and Dr. Ari Ben-Menahem, a brilliant Israeli mathematician and seismologist (also at Caltech). Shortly after publication of the paper, *New York Times* science writer Walter Sullivan had interviewed Plafker at an East Coast symposium about his postulated model for the Alaska quake and how it implied that the radical new idea of plates slipping beneath other plates might be the cause, and how that differed from the other experts. Plafker talked freely, never dreaming that in bold headlines a few weeks later there would be a major story about the competition between two dynamically opposed theories, one espoused by Dr. George Plafker, the other by Dr. Frank Press.[4]

George Plafker was stunned. Here he was, a geologist who knew next to nothing about earthquakes and seismology, one who had never even studied an earthquake before the Alaska quake of 1964, and he had ended up constructing a model for the cause of the earthquakes that diametrically opposed the most brilliant and respected men in seismology.

Half hiding in his office at Menlo Park, George Plafker wasn't entirely sure whether to be professionally proud or professionally frightened.[5]

But he was sure of his conclusions. While the others had relied on the ambiguous mathematical analysis of seismograms, he had pulled on his boots and walked the whole damned Alaskan countryside, documenting raised and lowered landscape that simply could not have been moved in such directions by a vertical fault.

And there was a larger issue than just the correctness of his Good Friday quake fault model. George Plafker's conclusions about Alaska, and the curiosity which led him to the southern coast of Chile in 1968, were about to take on a pivotal role in changing the way earth scientists viewed the earth. His 1965 paper on the Good Friday quake was about to provide one of the last missing pieces to a global puzzle—the tectonic puzzle—which had been falling into place with accelerating rapidity since the early fifties. The science of seismology was soon to be catapulted into a brave new world of understanding in a blinding series of advances that would touch the lives of almost everyone on the planet.

Slowly, inexorably, like a recurring bad dream which begins to take on the trappings of reality, a new model of the earth had begun to creep into the periphery of earth science. It was a very troublesome model for many dedicated scientists because with each successive discovery, the traditional scientific model of the earth's crust was beginning to crumble. The worst part was that the picture that was beginning to emerge from an increasing snowstorm of papers and articles bore a frightening resemblance to a heretical and thoroughly discredited idea first espoused in 1912, a postulation which had been received by the serious scientific community with universal derision and scorn, and one which had been sneeringly dismissed as Wegener's theory of continental drift.

It was a ludicrous idea. It was, said the leading scientists of the early twentieth century, a ridiculous manifestation of unprincipled and unfettered imagination. "It" was a theory dreamed up by an obscure German scientist, theorist, and meteorologist named Alfred Wegener, who had brazenly announced that the earth's surface features were in constant horizontal motion.

The earth, in fact, was like a drying apple. That was the accepted view of the planet: a hot molten-rock interior covered by a thin, cooling crust, which over the eons had contracted as the crust had cooled, wrinkling and shearing into mountain ranges and valleys while collapsing and settling in spots during violent earthquakes.

But all that was primarily vertical motion. No right-thinking scientist would even laughingly propose that the major continents did anything but remain where they had first formed. Therefore, Alfred Wegener could not be a right-thinking scientist.

Wegener, a curious and energetic man trained in a variety of scientific fields, had found a naked emperor. The "accepted theory" of the cooling, drying apple could not explain why mountain ranges and vast plains were not evenly distributed worldwide. It failed to provide even a hint of explanation as to why the west coast of Africa seemed to fit the east coast of North and South America like pieces of a planetary jigsaw puzzle. And after some transoceanic investigation of the plant life and microbiology of both seashores (which turned out to be very similar on shores thousands of miles apart), Wegener began to look for reasons to believe that the continents, in fact, did move around.

From his early discomfort with the prevailing theories, Wegener, by 1912, had proceeded to what he called the theory of continental drift, a radical idea which he published in 1915 in a book entitled *The Origin of Continents and Oceans,* a book which emerged to the universal howls and abusive laughter of a scandalized world of scientists who knew that they already had the final answer, and a globeful of roaming continents was not a part of it.[6]

Established science would have nothing to do with Wegener's fanciful ideas about drifting continents (despite two additional books on the subject by other scientists published a decade later), and for the next three decades the matter received little serious attention. Worse, any scientist who attempted to explore the theory ran the risk of professional ostracism.

But there were problems with the dried apple theory as well, and they kept cropping up every now and then to bother earth scientists who were beginning to discover new facts about earthquakes that wouldn't fit the classic model of the earth's crust.

A Japanese seismologist by the name of Kiyoo Wadati was one of the first to realize that his data formed a square peg in the round hole of the accepted view of the planet's surface features. By the late 1920's he had spent enough time poring over seismograms of Japanese earthquakes to discover a curious trend: There was a dipping plane of earthquake epicenters diving from a shallow depth under the east coast of Japan to a great depth under the Asian continent. They seemed to start at the Japanese Trench, a great underwater valley or canyon off the Japanese coast, but they became progressively deeper as they moved to the west. Wadati recomputed and refigured and rechecked his data endlessly to be certain, but the conclusion remained the same: The epicenters recorded on Japanese seismographs reached startling depths of four hundred miles down beneath Manchuria.

The dried apple theory held that below fifty or sixty miles the earth's interior was hot liquid rock, and molten rock can't shear in such a way as to cause earthquakes. What, then, was happening? Wadati kept probing, but reached no overt conclusions before the investigation was taken up by a man who had helped refine the design of the modern seismograph, Caltech's Dr. Hugo Benioff. Benioff began documenting the same phenomenon in other ocean trenches around the Pacific, finding the same dipping trend, which he reported in his breakthrough paper of 1954.

But the same rejection of the idea of a mobile planetary crust that led the scientific community to such abuse of poor Alfred Wegener began eroding Benioff's findings almost immediately, although in a more metered way. Benioff had obviously done his "homework," supporting his findings with excellent and voluminous research which showed that the entire Pacific basin was ringed with such zones of dipping earthquake hypocenters always radiating out and down beneath an adjacent continental landmass. At the end of the paper Benioff concluded that these were actually mammoth sections of the ocean floor—slabs—which were plunging downward into the earth's interior, and since they did not melt until at great depths, their continuous downward movement created the constant earthquakes which he had mapped.

Collectively, the seismological and geological community acknowledged that *something* was happening, but it was too soon, they said, to conclude that whatever it was had anything at all to do with moving slabs of ocean floor, plunging or otherwise. After all, if gigantic slices of the earth's crust were plunging back into the planet's interior, what was replacing them? The dipping planes of earthquake hypocenters dubbed Benioff zones might be evidence of some other process, said the established seismologist. Perhaps, some suggested, the plates were emerging from the earth's interior at those ocean trenches rather than submerging. Benioff "obviously" had jumped too rapidly to a conclusion.

Dr. Hugo Benioff was a quiet and studious scholar of great capability who held the respect of the scientific community (no less a giant of seismology as Dr. Charles F. Richter of Caltech was a Benioff protégé). He took the criticism in stride, but increasingly it sent him back to reexamine his research, concerned that perhaps he had overlooked something or indeed had published too soon.

He hadn't. More geological and seismological discoveries were starting to come in with relative rapidity by the late fifties, the more startling among them the results of several initial years of marine geological research in the Atlantic ocean.

No one had really known what lay on the bottom of the Atlantic Ocean. Certainly it was assumed that miles of sediment overlay bedrock, but no one had mapped the ocean floor and its substructure. In the mid-fifties, however, Columbia University's newly established Lamont Geological Observatory (later renamed Lamont-Doherty) began to do just that, using a specially outfitted three-masted schooner, the *Vema*, in a multiyear effort to find out what the bottom of the Atlantic looked like, and what it was made of. The scientists began using seismic refractive devices, which "listened" to the echoes from underwater explosions bouncing off the rock strata below the ocean floor, giving clues to what types of rock structures were down there. It was a crude beginning filled with shadowy returns that required much interpretation. To almost the same extent as seismology's efforts to deduce the structure of the center of the earth by reading the seismic waves that passed through and around it, the *Vema*'s task was as complex as an attempt to reproduce the entire structural blueprint of a fifty-story building by tapping the outer wall and interpreting the echoes returning from within.

Nevertheless, from the very first the results were startling.

To begin with, the depth of the sediments was not the same in different parts of the Atlantic. They were thickest along the shores of North America and Europe, but progressively thinner toward the middle of the ocean. That made no sense—or did it?

Then the picture of a zone of mid-ocean underwater mountains began to emerge as a unified system of incredible proportions. The Atlantic Ocean was bisected from north to south for thousands of miles by the strangest mountain range on earth. Instead of sharp peaks in the middle, there was a valley running the entire length of the north-south underwater mountain system, sometimes many miles wide. What's more, at certain points the range simply came to an end, its southward march beginning again miles to the east or west, as if it had been torn apart by a right-angle fault. Additional data showed the temperature of the ocean floor near the mid-Atlantic rise (as the mountain range was quickly named) was hotter than the crust near the edge of the continents, and by 1960 data had begun to show that the age of the rocks at any point on the eastern side of the mid-Atlantic rise was the same as the rocks an identical distance to the west of the rise.[7]

Marine geologists, as they were being called, were becoming active all over the world as the new World-Wide Standard Seismograph Network came on-line in the early sixties, and the data they were gathering showed similar mid-ocean ridges in parts of the Pacific (the East Pacific rise off Central and South America) and other oceanic areas. In addition, when small underwater earthquakes occurred, they seemed to center exclusively in mid-ocean ridge areas.

It was becoming increasingly difficult to avoid putting the evidence all in a row and coming to the preliminary conclusion that new crust was being generated in the mid-ocean rises, and was moving away in both directions, accumulating more sediment with time like some sort of planetary conveyor belt system.

But where did it go?

At the same time that the evidence was mounting for a moving ocean floor, several prominent marine geologists, such as Lamont's Dr. Maurice Ewing, were concluding that mid-ocean trenches (of which there were none in the Atlantic but many in the Pacific) were actually zones of extension, or at least stable areas.[8] That not only failed to dovetail with the tentative theories arising from research in the Atlantic, it contradicted Dr. Benioff head-on.

Despite an eloquent presentation in 1963 by Dr. Harry Hess of Princeton, which provided one of the earliest models of what was probably happening (crust coming up in the middle of the rises, moving the continents along like a conveyor belt, and the ocean floor on the other side being consumed beneath the advancing continent), the emerging picture was still considered radical. In fact, Professor Hess himself, tongue firmly planted in doctoral cheek, described his theoretical model as "geopoetry" in a rather brilliant turn of phrase which at once defused the expected criticism of nervous colleagues while it raised the structure of the emerging idea into the light of further worldwide examination. No one yet dared breathe the name of Alfred Wegener, but all those in earth sciences who were following the exciting march of discovery were holding their collective breath, waiting for a breakthrough, or a definitive statement.

And, in March 1964 Dr. Hugo Benioff, having been professionally pushed and shoved, niggled and attacked (however gently) for his supposedly premature conclusions, disregarded the broader implications of the newest research and succumbed to the pressure. Benioff issued a new paper in which he reinterpreted his own data—the data he had so brilliantly presented in 1954—concluding that the first time around he had been wrong to deduce that his Benioff zones had anything to do with dip-slip faults, or plates thrusting one beneath another. Using the purely mathematical approach as his basic guide, and disregarding even Professor Wadati's findings published before him, Benioff fell into line with Dr. Frank Press and others in concluding that the engine of the great quake in Chile and similar quakes in Benioff zones was actually counterclockwise *horizontal* movement of the Pacific Ocean floor, or steep faults deliniated by the Benioff zones.[9]

"Poor old Benioff," George Plafker recalled as he sat on the shoreline of southern Chile in January 1968 and prepared to return to the boat. What Plafker had seen in Alaska and Chile left no doubt that Dr. Benioff's original conclusions had been prophetic and dead right, yet the eminent senior seismologist had lost the confidence of his original conviction and thrown in the towel with that paper.

But the irony—the extreme irony—was in the timing. Benioff's retreat was published on March 27, 1964—the very day of the Good Friday quake, the examination of which would eventually prove him right.

Chapter 12

Menlo Park, California—Fall 1970

Fuzzy facts.

It was a phrase he loved to use—a phrase scientists weren't expected to use.

"We geologists tend to gather fuzzy facts, and after evaluating them, we seem to want to go out and gather even more fuzzy facts."

Dr. Robert Wallace's wry, almost impish sense of humor was evident around the corners of his phraseology as he described the differences separating seismologists, geophysicists, geologists, and engineers. Emphasizing such contrasts, however, was part of the melding process—part of his constant, gentle preaching on the subject of how the various scientific disciplines needed one another to solve common scientific problems facing them all.

"Geophysicists think differently than geologists. It's the mental process. Like seismologists (who consider themselves geophysicists), they tend to be more mathematically oriented, and so they tend to take a problem and simplify it so they can describe it mathematically. That produces some very important constraints. The problem, in other words, can't lie outside this boundary over here or that boundary over there. That's marvelous."

Wallace seemed perpetually amused at the differing methods of problem solving used by colleagues in diverse areas of the scientific community.

"Geologists end up coming to a synthesis of multiple suggestion. I'm perfectly comfortable as a geologist with a lot of loose ends, a lot of things that don't fit, lots of things that are not hard facts, [that are] fuzzy observations. Geophysicists and seismologists [on the other hand] want to go out and get a hard fact, a number, and if it shows on an instrument, then it's real to the geophysicist, and you can analyze [it], and that's good. Good science!

"The point is, they're both reproducible, and that's the essence of science, the fuzzy facts and the hard facts."

Bob Wallace sat back in his chair in his neatly packed and organized office in the U.S. Geological Survey's western headquarters in Menlo Park and looked at the autumn leaves blowing around the adjacent tree-shaded parking lot in the gentle embrace of a late-afternoon zephyr. He was alone now at the end of the day, and cascading through his mind were thoughts and ideas, projects and observations, a germinating overflow spilling from a cornucopia of excitement in the scientific community—an excitement which always seemed to exhilarate him.

It had been six years since a phone call from his wife had found him similarly deep in thought at the office on the night of March 27, 1964. She had heard the news of the great quake in Alaska, and though the Menlo Park complex all around him was the epicenter of West Coast seismic research projects, the after-hours quiet of his office (a block from the nearest seismograph) had isolated him from the news. Thinking of that quake now was quite significant because it had altered so much so very rapidly. The changes in professional life within the U.S. Geological Survey from 1964 to 1970 were, well, seismic. Suddenly earthquakes were important items.

But Wallace was a senior geologist, not a seismologist, which made his present, increasing interest in things seismological all the more intriguing. Yet that had been one of the most important changes, the technical transfer of information, research, and expertise among the various scientific disciplines.

For one thing, people were talking to each other across professional lines, at long last. Wallace had become a passionate advocate of the concept that there was great synergistic value in the cross-pollination of ideas and observations between seismology and geology, though that had traditionally seldom occurred in any structured way. It was obvious to him, however, that both fields needed each other to understand the problems they faced.

And now, thank heaven, that kind of communication was occurring with increasing regularity.

Before the 1964 cataclysm in Alaska, geologists and seismologists exchanged pleasantries in the hallways of Menlo Park and occasionally at parties, and that was about it. The two disciplines were miles apart. Suddenly, however, geologists such as George

Plafker had come along to hand the seismological world some seminal observations from geology. Plafker, in addition to his other research, had found benches (flat areas above a beach eroded in past centuries when the bench was, at that time, the beach itself) in Alaska, clear evidence that previous great quakes had dropped and raised beachfront property many times before 1964. That was a geological revelation contributing directly to the quest for an answer to a seismological question.

George Plafker had impacted geophysics as well. His paper on the Alaskan quake of 1964 had provided one of the last important keys to the emerging theory of plate tectonics. In fact, it was during a landmark meeting of the American Geophysical Union that Plafker's paper, along with some seventy others, was read, helping push the theory over the top with his clear evidence that oceanic plates were being shoved under the continental plates. The result was the final, utter destruction of the last, battered elements of opposition to the general concept that Alfred Wegener had postulated fifty-three years before. It became obvious from that meeting that the earth's crust indeed *is* composed of segmented plates of mammoth proportions that are in dynamic and continuous motion.

Overnight the entire geophysical world changed. Suddenly in that model of moving continental plates were answers for which no one had yet formulated questions.

And—a rarity in the lives of earth scientists—suddenly there was research money available. Not an unending cascade of cash, but a newly uncorked pipeline of funding for studies and projects which were beginning to change the face of science on what seemed like an ever-accelerating basis.

The great Alaska quake of 1964 was responsible. It had shaken up not only the forty-ninth state, but the governmental establishment as well. The fact that an American community could be hit so hard (and that its misfortune could cost its fellow taxpayers so dearly), instantly focused many political minds on the reality that such disasters could occur as well in the continental United States. From the White House to Capitol Hill there was sudden recognition that the country's knowledge of the true level of risk from major earthquakes, and of what could be done about that risk, contained questions that must be answered, and soon. Thus the national spotlight began to shine on the campuslike atmosphere of Menlo Park (and the USGS headquarters at Reston, Virginia).

As Wallace and his colleagues watched with growing optimism, research projects that had been fiscally impossible to finance just a year before were being discussed with real hope of future funding.

One of them was his, a stillborn project in 1963, when he and Dr. Parke Snaveley had tried to sell it. The two of them had lobbied long and hard to convince the USGS to fund the two million dollars necessary for an ambitious program of research into the mechanisms of the San Andreas Fault. The famous rift, which cut through California from south to north and was the culprit in a great quake at Fort Tejon (north of Los Angeles) in 1857, as well as the great quake that devastated San Francisco in 1906, was still largely a mystery. It was an incredible fact, but very little really was known about the potential for more great quakes on the San Andreas. It was assumed that ruinous quakes were both possible and probable, but Wallace knew that the body of geologic knowledge about just what made the San Andreas Fault move (and what happened seismically when it did) was in its infancy.

Before the plates had snapped beneath Prince William Sound, there were no funds to go any further into the question. The USGS wouldn't buy the idea—which was to say that it did not consider the study of long-range earthquake potential sufficiently urgent and promising to warrant taking someone else's funding—as would have been the result.

By 1965, however, neither the public nor the USGS leadership could get enough information on the subject of damaging earthquake potential in California. Suddenly Bob Wallace's project on the San Andreas was viable, and with funding and approval in hand, he had happily dusted off his field equipment and, in a professional sense, gone home.

Wallace's roots as a geologist were in the San Andreas. As a young graduate student at Caltech in 1938 he had been required to do two complete theses. His first concerned vertebrate paleontology, but the second—which would grow to be a passion—was focused on the nature of the San Andreas Fault, the worrisome geographic and geologic oddity which split California nearly end to end.

As the world drifted toward global war from 1938 through 1941, no one really knew the true nature of the fault. It was possible, some postulated, that it was a very old surface feature that for some reason had started to slip laterally just in the last two million years. Of course, everyone in the field knew that it had last slipped catastrophically in 1906, displacing the countryside (as well as fences and roads) in Marin County to the north of San Francisco by more than 5 meters (16.4 feet) at some points, and causing the great San Francisco earthquake in the process.

But how far had it slipped in historic times? And how deep did the rift in the earth go?

The fault trace (the visual surface evidence of it) ran from above Point Reyes north of San Francisco south through Daly City, down the peninsula, through the small farming community of San Juan Bautista, south through the tiny community of Parkfield (and twenty miles to the west of Coalinga), south-southeast through the barren Carrizo Plain, through the middle of the Tejon Pass north of San Fernando and Los Angeles, south of Palmdale, and on to the south-southeast, breaking into several subsidiary faults as it entered Mexico.

It was there, but what it could do, and when it might be expected to do it, were unknowns. Those were the questions which confronted Bob Wallace during the sultry summer of 1938, when he arrived, hot and sweaty, piloting an aging car along the margin of the Mojave Desert (where the fault trace of the San Andreas stands out with amazing clarity as a series of straight ridges running northwest to southeast), intent on finding answers to what seemed to be a purely geologic question.

Levi Noble, a geologist with the survey whose house literally sat on the fault, had produced some papers in the twenties that Wallace had read—papers which concluded that there could have been as much as twenty-four to twenty-six miles of total slippage along the San Andreas since the tear in California's landscape first formed. The scientists at Berkeley's School of Earth Sciences, however, steadfastly disagreed. Their position was that the fault had slipped no more than one mile at best.

Standing on the fault itself in nose-to-nose confrontation, Bob Wallace could see the evidence quite clearly: The offset stream and riverbeds and the lateral features and hills on the eastern side were now scores of miles to the southeast of where their counterparts resided. It seemed obvious, geologically, that the fault had slipped far more than even Noble had suggested, at least a hundred miles over millions of years.

It never occurred to Wallace to phone Berkeley and talk to the

165

people who held the opposing view. Long-distance calls cost money he didn't have (research money was nonexistent, and even the National Science Foundation was yet to be created), and that sort of thing just wasn't done anyway. He didn't know the people at Berkeley. To write or call might be unacceptably forward, and he certainly couldn't afford to travel to Berkeley to discuss the matter. The geologists there could have just as easily been located in Mongolia. Communication about conflicting ideas and theories simply didn't exist from 1938 to 1942—especially not at the behest of a shy, studious doctoral candidate who had no desire to breach protocol.

With the nation at war by 1942, Bob Wallace ended his four years of research before feeling he had truly finished the project. Four years of studying the San Andreas had not provided the hard evidence he needed to solve all the problems (and he had filled in some of the questions with answers of his own construct); but he *had* produced an important paper, and in the process he had managed to boldly suggest with elegant understatement that the total slippage on the San Andreas Fault might be as much as seventy-five miles (many years before others discovered not only that it had slipped seventy-five miles, but that the total distance is measured in the hundreds of miles).[1]

It had been twenty-three years before time, circumstance, and money had permitted Bob Wallace to get back to the San Andreas, but thanks to the effect of the Good Friday quake on the USGS's research budget, 1965 found him once again on the trail (and in the Carrizo "desert").

Experienced where he had been green in 1938, tempered now by decades of research, and carrying a fresh mandate to help answer the multitude of questions about earthquake risk in California, Wallace focused on documenting streambed offsets and trying to find ways of pinpointing slip rates at various sites along the fault.

It was geology contributing directly to seismology, providing basic information which might help seismologists construct a basic framework from which to answer the increasing drumbeat of questions coming from government leaders, insurance companies, businessmen, and citizens.

The problem, of course, was the simple fact that no one knew what had happened (if anything) along the San Andreas before the middle of the nineteenth century.

166

There had been only one great Fort Tejon quake (1857) and only one great San Francisco quake (1906) in the recorded human history of California, but that "history" was only a few hundred years old—a mere heartbeat in geologic time. Without a longer base line of historical knowledge with which to "bracket" major quakes at different locations along the fault, some other method was desperately needed to know when—and if—they had occurred. And though it still seemed rather bizarre in 1965 to the ordered analytical methods of seismological analysis, Bob Wallace, George Plafker, and numerous other geologists were beginning to understand that there might well be ways to look at the sedimentary deposits of the recent geologic past—the past thousand years or so—and find evidence of when and how badly the earth had shaken from fault movement. Perhaps, thought Wallace, the process could be developed into a science in itself, providing seismology with the much needed seismic history undreamed of by previous seismologists.

Of course, there was the bedrock recognition that while geologists were not trained to read seismograms with the sophistication of a Charles Richter, seismologists were not experienced in reading the surficial record—yesterday's dirt in geologic time scales—and deriving vital information on where significant quakes had happened before, how they had affected the surrounding terrain, and how often they might recur.

The question Bob Wallace had worked on during 1965 and 1966 was very direct and not a little troubling: How dangerous is the San Andreas Fault?

And there was another question, always in the background, flowing inexorably from the realization that anyone who could emerge from a study of the fault with the answers to "when, where, and how much" would be offering the world (and California in particular) a genuine, unabashed earthquake prediction.

Was such a thing possible? The question of whether science would someday be able to predict with accuracy where and when damaging earthquakes would occur had been around for centuries. But finding a method of prediction would be akin to the discovery of dynamite—a breakthrough which would carry with it an entirely new and serious set of problems.

What would major population centers do in response to a prediction? What should they do? What should government leaders do or recommend? How do you prevent either apathy or panic among the general population? And, of course, what happens if you're wrong, and a predicted earthquake does not occur? Such questions leaped from the neat confines of geophysics and seismology, the observational confines of geology, and the strictures of structural engineering (an art of the possible) and raced with mad abandon through the hitherto unexplored recesses of sociology, psychology, law, public policy, and economics. Such disciplines were not part of the required curriculum for a Ph.D. in seismology, yet the trail from one question to its logical conclusion would require the involvement of all such fields. If the presence of geologists at the doorstep of seismological research was startling, then the image of what stood in the shadows behind the smiling, helpful cadre of geologists (offering their emerging techniques of finding seismic history in the dirt) would be somewhere between upsetting and terrifying to the more insular members of the science. The confines of that neat scientific discipline were about to crumble, and though the best and the brightest of the field (such as Professor Charles Richter) had never tried to confine the science to the basement lab or insulate its implications and teachings from the real world, research seismology was about to be hauled, blinking and looking somewhat off-balance, into the messy area of real-time human existence to a far greater extent than even Richter had thought possible.[2]

Prediction was not science fiction. The question of whether it could be done was regarded as a reasonable possibility by the scientific community, given enough research time and sufficient research budgets within both the USGS and the academic communities. Perhaps only long-range warnings of earthquakes would be possible, or maybe a deep understanding of the quake mechanism itself would develop in the years and decades ahead, handing seismologists the key to effective prediction methods on a widespread basis. Possibly (as with so many other scientific breakthroughs in human history) a serendipitous fluke of a discovery would occur somewhere along the line of meticulous research. There was hope that in a few decades (or even years) seismologists would be able to predict earthquakes as regularly and effectively as meteorologists predict the weather. If that were to occur, people in general and Americans in particular could know when their buildings would be shaken to the limit, their freeways imperiled, their schoolchildren threatened by falling ceilings and bricks, and their employers put out of business.

168

Perhaps they could be told with precision exactly how a given piece of real estate would behave in a future quake, as well as how large that quake would be, preventing municipal auditoriums and nuclear power plants from straddling active faults, and multistory apartment buildings from rising on alluvial Jell-O, poised to sink, collapse, or capsize in a moderate tremor.

Since earthquakes can cause such damage, there just must be a way to determine when, where, and to what extent they will occur. That holy grail might be years down the road, they knew, but it was an unspoken, common goal of the broad collection of seismologists and interested earth scientists such as Plafker and Wallace, who were increasingly convinced that perhaps, just perhaps, the answer lay in the recent geologic record, right beneath their feet.

And to an amazing extent, one of Wallace's heroes had started that very process ninety-five years before in Utah.

Grove Karl Gilbert, one of the most admired geologists in the history of the American West, was best known for producing a classic study in 1907 of the great 1906 San Francisco quake with an attention to detail that had become legendary.[3] But Gilbert's inquisitive mind had married geologic evidence and questions of where earthquakes might occur as far back as 1872. He had participated in the Wheeler surveys of Utah, and recognized that certain scarps (long, relatively straight scars running horizontally, which he named piedmont scarps) along the base of the Wasatch Mountains near Salt Lake City indicated slippage related to earthquakes. For Gilbert's brilliant mind, it was a short logical distance from that realization to the conclusion that the populace of the Salt Lake area needed to be informed of the risk. In 1883 he published a warning to the citizenry, pointing out that in places where no such scarps exist (such as Salt Lake City), yet where they *should* exist according to the reading of the geologic evidence in the mountains on either side, there was reason to believe that a damaging earthquake could be expected in the future. His warning—the first serious U.S. earthquake prediction and the very first paper on earthquakes by the fledgling U.S. Geological Survey—was a century before its time (although the predicted quake has not yet occurred). Equally important was the fact that his observations were based entirely on surficial evidence—what he could see in the terrain, evaluated by his "natural talent for deductive reasoning."[4]

169

Gilbert had gone far beyond that propitious start in the decades which followed, but his most important contribution to seismology ended up effectively lost, buried in dusty stacks of his work, never cited in any significant paper until Bob Wallace discovered his amazing blueprint for earthquake prediction and hazard mitigation more than two-thirds of a century later.

In 1909, with San Francisco still rebuilding from the great quake of 1906, Gilbert had given an otherwise unremarkable keynote address to a January 1 meeting of the American Association of Geographers. Though already well known as a geologist and geographer, Gilbert wanted to pour forth a flood of ideas and insights into the problems of coping with, predicting, and preparing populations for damaging earthquakes. With the destruction of 1906 very fresh in his mind, and the power of the San Andreas Fault's sudden slippage the subject of his insightful study for the previous three years, Gilbert had much to say. His speech, however, fell on deaf ears.

These were geographers. While they were respectful and interested, the words Gilbert lofted into the room held no greater meaning for them than the immediate effect of any intelligent speech from a distinguished scientist. Those words (and the paper on which they were based, "Earthquake Forecasting," issued the same year), would remain effectively lost for the following seventy-one years. They spoke of the hope that someday the proper seismological tools and understanding would enable the seismologist to serve society the same way the meteorologist can, and they outlined the basic considerations for a major program to minimize—mitigate—the hazards of earthquakes to various populated areas. The areas Gilbert covered included a primer of earthquake prediction, earthquake engineering, land use, risk evaluation, and earthquake insurance. In the distant future, Bob Wallace would refer to the speech as the "most perceptive, encompassing, and balanced analysis" to come out until the 1960's. But the tragedy was, of course, that those ideas and concepts and the blueprint to action were needed then and there—and they were ignored.

The years that followed would provide ample evidence of what could have been done, how many lives and dollars could have been saved, as quake after quake struck communities, not only in California but throughout the world, that were totally and abysmally unprepared to deal with the threat—or the aftermath. Earthquakes remained natural occurrences to which mankind could only react. The concept of advance preparation or planning was largely nonexistent—though the blueprint had been offered in 1909.

Bob Wallace watched the streaks of late-afternoon sunlight playing like an infinite row of dancing spotlights through the gently moving limbs of the eucalyptus trees that surround Menlo Park, wafting their pleasant and distinctive fragrance through the air and through his window to permeate his office with the scents of nature at her best. It had the feel of a university campus, but without the presence of frenzied students dashing back and forth to classes.

Not that students weren't a part of the Menlo Park culture. Wallace's office was just a short distance to the north of Stanford University—a mere bicycle ride away. It had become somewhat axiomatic that Stanford geology and seismology students naturally gravitated to the USGS "campus" for summer research jobs, or just to hang around the working cadre of the survey's ranks of experts. It was like studying political science in the basement of the White House with full access to the President—an amazing continuous opportunity for intellectual exchange and ferment, the young students learning from the veteran scientists, and (as always) vice versa.

Campus was the right word for it, as well. Unlike any other agency of the United States government, the survey was run like a university, with senior scientists rotating in and out of administrative positions in large measure in accordance with their desires, and with information and planning exchanged in a freewheeling way which led some of the more organizationally oriented (some would call them bureaucratically calcified) members of the U.S. civil service to refer to their organizational structure at USGS-Menlo as "benign anarchy."

But, it worked. While the loose organizational structure might create coronary instability in the heart of a senior civil service administrator from, say, the Treasury or Commerce Departments, the survey's way of doing things produced results, creating an ongoing climate of dynamic support for intellectual curiosity that, when gently guided (and occasionally shoved), provided the nation with cutting-edge earth science technology and vital ongoing scientific leadership of university programs throughout the nation.

Money, of course, was a constant battle, even after the 1964

Good Friday quake. The mere mention of money—funding priorities—in a major project proposal could raise blood pressure, trigger tempers, and create infighting over scientific research turf by men and women who knew well that at any given time there was only so much of it available from either the taxpayers or various foundations. The monetary pie was very finite, and their task was to divide properly (and to protect their share of) that pie each year. The pie might get larger, as it had in 1964, but everyone's share was still a matter of percentages.

This reality had already had an impact on the efforts to translate the growing excitement over earthquake potential and possible earthquake hazard mitigation into some sort of coherent program. Just after the catastrophe in Alaska, for instance, Dr. Frank Press had chaired a panel for the President's Office of Science and Technology which produced a major report and recommendation for an ambitious ten-year program on earthquake prediction, a program which naturally would cost money.[5] The report emphasized that no one was adequately studying the threat of earthquakes or what to do to minimize damage and deaths from earthquakes in the United States, a significant national mistake.

The engineering community, however, had been working on ways to plan structures to withstand earthquakes for many decades. It had amassed years of research and stacks of documents and suggested building codes to enable its practitioners to freeze the existing structural technology at any point and build the most resistant structure possible, given what they might know about the earthquake potential of the piece of land they were using.

Suddenly here came the report from Dr. Press and his panel stating an urgent need for federal funding of new programs and seeming to bypass all the efforts of the engineering community. Press had spotlighted seismology, not engineering, as the savior science. The members of the National Academy of Engineers, for one, were not amused. The idea of earthquake "prediction" as a national goal was, to them, a completely incorrect focus, and they countered by preparing their own major report (eventually issued in 1969), a quality document which predictably relied on potential engineering solutions as the cure for 90 percent of whatever threats earthquakes might pose to civilization.[6]

That, said many, is great for future buildings and those you can force into reconstruction, but it ignores the basic questions of what

172

causes earthquakes, when and where they will occur, and what happens to the ground when they do. In addition, ran the reaction, how do we deal with older buildings which were constructed at a time when earthquake-resistant technology was in its infancy (or ignored completely)? What do we do with thousands of unreinforced masonry buildings in San Francisco, for instance, which will turn to lethal falling rubble with the next major quake? The most stringent engineering codes and standards for future construction will never touch that problem.

In 1968 the survey's director waded in bravely with an attempted compromise proposal that tried to put the problems into perspective, balancing the engineering goals against the predictive goals and research needs. But the director made a small, significant political and strategic mistake: He put a price tag on the project.[7] As a result, the USGS report had nothing more than a temporary impact as interest in his compromise declined in direct inverse proportion to the dollars required to fund it.

And there the matter sat—until 1969.

Sometimes, as Bob Wallace had pointed out to many colleagues and visiting students, a galaxy of diverse individuals and interests ends up heading in the same direction, but unable to communicate and combine their efforts for one principal reason: the lack of a catalyst. In chemical terms, the explanation went, a catalyst is "a substance that [starts] a chemical reaction and enables it to proceed under milder conditions than otherwise possible," but at the end, the catalyst itself is unchanged. In life, it is often a single dedicated and concerned individual who, through force of personality, intellect, and social skills, manages to weld a diverse group together and prod it on to achieving something as a group that never would have been realized as a gaggle.

In 1969 such a person had emerged from extensive governmental work in the insurance industry to accomplish exactly that. Dr. Karl V. Steinbrugge had accepted appointment as chairman of a task force (within President Nixon's Office of Science and Technology) that included such leading scientists as seismologist Dr. Clarence R. Allen of Caltech, and Bob Wallace's close friend and classmate from the same institution, Dr. Richard Jahns, by then dean of the School of Earth Sciences at Stanford.

There were six other professional people from different disciplinary areas in the group as well, and under Steinbrugge's leadership, they began to cross the lines of normal interdisciplinary defense systems to state both their mutual objectives and their individual professional concerns, moving toward the formulation of a list of things that needed to be accomplished by the nation regarding the subject of damaging earthquakes.[8]

"The mission of this Task Force," wrote Steinbrugge in his introduction, ". . . is to develop an appropriate national action program for the reduction of the human suffering and property damage attendant upon an earthquake. . . ."[9]

But the rather brilliant move which pulled the final report (issued in 1970) out of the mire of internecine squabbles in the scientific and technical community and enabled it to become a catalyst for the beginnings of the nation's first coherent move toward earthquake hazard mitigation, came in the organization of the report. In effect, the task force members avoided placing any one group's interests in a higher priority than another. Instead, they developed a list of "High Priority Recommendations," each of which was ranked according to whether the benefits to the public could be expected within five years (short term), between five to ten years (intermediate term), or in more than ten years (long term). By use of that technique, no one's ox ended up gored, and interests as diverse as basic seismological research and engineering research found themselves admirably represented and recommended on the same page with such short-term "after-the-fact" elements of the equation as disaster response planning on the federal level.

And, wisely, they did *not* mention money. Of course, the report dropped enough funding hints to create small earthquakes of its own, but there was no price tag attached, and thus no direct threat to the various interests around the country that guarded their percentages of the research pie like a hungry mother hawk.

In the end, the effectiveness of the report was not only an accolade to (and an affirmation of) Karl Steinbrugge's tour de force performance in the deft social management of the diverse people and interests involved, it was also an affirmation of worth for the principles that Bob Wallace had been advocating so quietly yet so effectively from his office at Menlo Park—always seeking to be a mediator, and always seeking to increase the degree of communication across scientific lines.

In many ways, Wallace's role as a pivotal catalyst in the process of intellectual ferment would be of inestimable value, not only during the formative period following the Good Friday quake, but in his widespread influence on the young seismologists and geologists whose maturation as major forces in earth science in so many cases included exposure to the teachings and melding influences of Dr. Wallace.

As the veteran geologist checked the following week's appointments on the few pages remaining in his 1970 calendar, getting ready to head home from his Menlo Park office, the larger national stage outside had been set for massive—seismic, if you will—change in the landscape of America's (and the world's) ability to perceive and cope with dangerous earthquakes. But even with the distance traveled—even with the release of the Steinbrugge task force's report, renewed interest in Washington, and growing excitement in the earth sciences community—the body politic and its representatives would need much more convincing.

And, as always, the forces of nature were preparing to give the process another formidable push. The pressures building in the rocks four hundred miles south of Menlo Park would not wait for human initiative.

Chapter 13

Long Valley Caldera,
California—February 1971

The snows of winter, once melted on the eastern slopes of the majestic high Sierra Nevada mountains in central California, cascade and tumble as the freshest form of water down into myriad streams and rivulets, in constant motion through such beautiful areas as Mono Lake, Long Valley (near the resort town of Mammoth Lakes), and south through Crowley Lake into Bishop, dropping from seven thousand feet to four thousand feet in altitude southbound into the breathtaking Owens Valley. Funneled between the Sierras on one side and the White and Inyo mountains on the other, the crystal-clear waters pass over some of the most seriously disturbed, volcanically active, fault-ridden and earthquake-prone territory in the United States as they head for the water faucets of Los Angeles.

Flowing out of the Owens Valley through the southern portion of a 338-mile-long pipeline-aqueduct system that starts at Mono Lake, the water flows inexorably across the main trace of the east-west Garlock Fault in the western margin of the Mojave Desert, across the San Andreas Fault within twenty-five miles of Fort Tejon (site of the great Fort Tejon quake in 1857), and approaches the northern foot of the San Gabriel Mountains, using simply the force of gravity to push the continuous flow up and over a low pass lying along the highway as it crosses the mountain ridge within the confines of gargantuan water pipes. On the other side, at the head of the San Fernando Valley, the water spills into the two reservoirs forming an important part of the water supply for the Los Angeles metropolitan area of 3.6 million people.

In the surprisingly warm predawn hours of Tuesday, February 9, 1971, 6.7 billion gallons of water diverted from the high Sierras lapped at the dam of the Lower Van Norman Reservoir, an earthen dam built in 1915—some 27.9 million tons of liquid ready for delivery to the maze of water mains in Los Angeles.

And below the Lower Van Norman Dam—literally across the street from the foot of the huge dirt structure—lay a trusting segment of American suburbia. Twenty square miles of attractive middle American homes stretched toward L.A., homes which just before sunrise held some eighty thousand residents (many of them still asleep) living in a natural aquatic channel more than two miles wide and stretching some eight miles to the south.

Charlie Richter had warned them.[1] Many times during previous years he and other seismologists had pointed out that the exact mechanism driving the San Andreas Fault did not have to be understood for the seismological community to know that it was hazardous to the health of Los Angeles. Obviously there was slippage along the hundreds of miles spanned by the fault. Obviously the portions of the fault that had not slipped in many, many years were building up strain. And just as obviously, when that strain ultimately was released, the elastic rebound of the rocks on both sides (and for many miles below the surface of California) would send seismic waves of energy coursing through the earth, shaking the state in various directions and with various intensities.[2]

Los Angeles was not ready for a major quake, and certainly not a great quake. There were innumerable things which needed to be done to prepare and which would save lives and property—but such efforts cost time and money. And, more than anything else, such efforts and expenditures require leaders who are convinced of the danger. What evidence do we have, the questions commonly went, that a major quake will hit in our lifetimes? What certainty do we have that we need to prepare?

The answers, of course, were in the history of the cataclysmic quake that jolted sparsely populated Fort Tejon in 1857. In the clear record of what those seismic waves did to the land south of Fort Tejon—the land on which Greater Los Angeles sits today—lay all the facts that politicians and businessmen alike really needed to justify massive expenditures of time, effort, and money to get ready for the next one. As Richter knew well, if present-day Los Angeles were hit by a quake the magnitude and intensity of the 1857 event, tens of thousands of Angelenos would die beneath the rubble of buildings and freeways and homes and offices from the damage that

178

the earth shaking would cause—damage that could run as high as sixty billion dollars.

The point was very simple—and very hard to get across. The San Andreas had not slipped north of Los Angeles since 1857. Therefore, another large or great earthquake at or near Fort Tejon just north of the San Gabriel Mountains (twenty-five miles north of L.A.) could occur again at any time. It could be in ten minutes or a hundred years; but the risk was real and deadly—and the buildings of L.A. (not to mention the residents) were unprepared.

As Professor Charles Francis Richter slept in the early hours of February 9, the needle of a small seismometer he kept in another room of his Altadena home (just above Caltech's Pasadena campus) continued to run, jerking occasionally from small waves arriving at random through the metamorphic bedrock of the San Gabriel Mountains, which sat just to the north of his property.[3]

Suddenly, at forty-seven seconds past 6:00 A.M., the needle began cycling wildly in both directions as a primary wave front of intense magnitude rippled beneath Dr. Richter's den, shaking the foundations of his house, and shaking perhaps the world's best-known living seismologist bolt upright and instantly awake in bed.

Charles Richter yelped something incoherent as his wife, Lillian, awoke and watched him disappear at amazing speed through the bedroom door, which was shaking and gyrating. While the family cat hung on to the bedroom rug (as much in terror from his owner's sudden passage as from the shaking), Richter made his way over a shifting, shaking floor, now obviously in the grip of S waves from somewhere close.

Was this it? Was this Fort Tejon? The thought had been crystal clear in his mind the second he awoke, but the shaking was not yet catastrophic enough to be a Fort Tejon magnitude quake. Richter continued in motion, heading for his seismometer.

Twenty miles to the west and a bit over five miles beneath the surface, something had snapped less than ten seconds earlier at a point where the San Gabriel Mountains had been pushing for millions of years over the alluvium (sediments) that formed the San Fernando Valley. The sudden movement of the rocks had created massive seismic energy waves which lashed out from the hypocenter to reach the surface somewhat to the southwest, combining with newly created surface waves to kick the ground up and sideways below the Pacoima Dam in the foothills, beneath the Veterans Administration hospital (the VA's "garden spot" facility) in Sylmar, and underneath the earthen Lower Van Norman Dam, as well as the ground structure of the entire San Fernando basin.

Within six seconds of the first P wave arrival, the north-south and up-down needles on the strong motion seismographs at the Pacoima location recorded a pulse of energy which would make seismic history. Acceleration—the rate at which the ground is yanked in any direction—had never been recorded at greater than the force of one gravity. Now, however, the needles registered 1.25 times the force of gravity in two of the three axes—at the very same moment that the walls and the structure of hundreds of masonry buildings all over the immediate area of San Fernando and northern Los Angeles began to fail.[4]

Robert Dutton had been sitting in his wheelchair, unhappily waiting for yet another medical test (this one much too early in the morning), when the first waves shuddered in from just a few miles distant. Deep inside the third story of the four-hundred-patient VA hospital where he was being treated for a back injury, the military veteran felt the shaking begin, felt the building respond with a massive rumble, and instantly knew he was in danger. Time became elastic, giving him more room to think as he catapulted himself from the wheelchair, oblivious to the consequences to his back, somehow moving through the doorway to the hall just beyond in a matter of seconds. The smell of hospital disinfectant from the freshly swabbed linoleum floor caught the periphery of his attention as he passed through the doorframe, intent on escape from the shuddering enclosure of the third floor, which was shaking now, vibrating, lurching (seemingly in all directions) with a horrendous noise of groaning and screeching and rumbling. He knew there were patients throughout the building, but only the thought of escape filled his head. With the doorway behind him, Dutton turned to look at the waiting room from which he'd come.

There was nothing there. The room was gone, falling away even as his eyes focused on the void where it had been.

Two of the wings of the hospital were in free fall, concrete floors pancaking down on the ones below, instantly crushing many of the human beings between them, throwing others into alcoves and corners, traumatized, uncomprehending, but alive. With an unbelievable noise of protesting metal, shattering glass, and rumbling concrete, two wings of the forty-five-year-old building, which had just passed a major engineering inspection following a face-lift, collapsed into rubble, instantly taking the lives of at least thirty-five people, and pinning dozens of emphysema and tuberculosis patients (along with some staff members) in the twisted wreckage.

Among those who would not emerge were several veterans who had just returned from America's stalemated jungle war—men recovering from wounds received in Vietnam.

The sight from the breakfast table was beyond belief, but as the young high school student watched from the den of his uncle's house just to the west of the Golden State Freeway in Newhall, the water in the swimming pool next door lifted up as a unit—all of it—holding together in exactly the same kidney shape as the pool which had contained it, rising like a semitransparent blue bubble ten feet into the air as the ground, which had suddenly lurched upward with a neck-snapping jolt, now slammed back down, out from under the water, leaving the pool's contents suspended in midair. In a slow-motion sequence like nothing he had ever experienced before, the young man watched the pool and the entire backyard of his neighbor's house descend out from under the giant lens of water *and lurch sideways*!

The water began to descend, but the pool was no longer exactly beneath it. In fact, the pool was now off to the south, it seemed, maybe only a few inches, maybe a few feet. In what seemed an eternity, a substantial portion of what had to be thousands of gallons of chlorinated swimming pool water crashed like a mini-tsunami onto the back porch and through the sliding glass doors of the neighbor's house to inundate the interior.

At the same moment, responding to the initial lurch upward and the following 1.25 gravity descent of the terrain, hundreds of other swimming pools in the Valley had danced the same dance, and within minutes hundreds of homeowners would emerge from the terror of the earthquake to find their living rooms and dens filled with their swimming pools.

Less than two miles to the west of the VA hospital, the enclosed five-story stairwells attached to each end of the brand-new twenty-three-million-dollar Olive View Medical Center (an 850-bed facility run by the county) peeled away in opposite directions with

181

the force of the major shocks, only six seconds into the quake. The remaining structure slumped and tilted at the same time, preserving the lives of most of those inside the main section, but completely destroying the building. The facility had been described as "earthquake-proof," but in the grips of a real earthquake it had lasted exactly seven seconds.

To the immediate east of the Lower Van Norman Dam concrete dust was rising in a billowing cloud, as freeway overpasses from Interstate 5 and Interstate 405 twisted and crashed onto, and through, the concrete decking of the roadway, crushing two men in a small delivery truck that happened to be in the wrong place at exactly the worst possible moment on the otherwise deserted freeway, and creating a scene which would be described from the air as resembling the scattered toys of an angry child.

But the ultimate horror had been reserved for a man who lived above the level of the reservoir on the western side, and whose house overlooked the earthen structure holding back the water. Reservoir keeper Clyde Carney had been thrown off his bed onto the floor by the first heavy jolts of the quake. Waking up in an instant, aware that his house was still vibrating violently, the image of the dam a few hundred yards away filled his mind's eye as he got to his feet and ran to the front door.

What he saw nearly stopped his heart. The concrete roadway atop the dam had split in two and slumped into the reservoir, and the dirt face of the dam—the dam itself—was beginning to crumble. As he watched, helpless, his mind reeling at the specter, layer after layer of the water-side portion of his dam shook loose and slid backward into the water, the saturated soil seeming to be part liquid as it slumped and slid. There were only a few feet left between the water level and the top now. The far side of the dam, the part to the east, was going fast. There was no concrete left on top, and the level of the remaining dirt seemed mere inches away from disaster. And there was nothing in the world he could do but watch with his heart in his throat.

Carney knew without forming the words what would happen if a single shaft of water shot over that disintegrating mound of dirt. It would carve a vertical slice into what remained, the rush of water (propelled by the force of 27 million tons of liquid weight) pushing ever faster and in greater volumes through the channel, taking more and more of the dam with each second, growing within a minute or less to a torrent, and then to a massive, horrifying cascade as the dam gave way completely, 6.7 billion gallons of water forming a wall of instant death for the tens of thousands of sleepy people in homes which stretched as far as he could see to the south.

But the shaking had stopped. Carney saw a last slice of dirt slough into the water, then nothing. Nothing else was sliding. There couldn't be more than two or three feet of remaining dam surface above the waterline, but thank God, at least there was some. Would it hold? Was there time? Carney knew he had to move fast. Pumps would have to be started immediately to begin drawing down the lake, pumping the water into the Los Angeles River and to the sea. There might be pluggable breaches in the face of the dam. Those would have to be filled, fast. With every pump and every man they had working nonstop, the process would take hours—days—to be really safe. In the meantime, the dam could go at any second.

As Carney turned and headed back into his house to summon crews to the scene and tell the police they'd better evacuate the area, the realization that the lake had not been full weighed heavily on his mind. It had been at only about 60 percent of capacity as the result of routine drawdown. Now the top of the dam was far below where the waterline normally stood. If the lake had been filled . . .

In only ten seconds it was over. There would be thirteen mild aftershock sequences in the following six minutes, but the main quake was over. The San Andreas had not slipped. The great quake that Charles Richter and so many other earth scientists feared had not yet occurred.[5]

But the seismic waves that had been generated by the essentially moderate "event" (which would be rated at M_L 6.6 on Professor Richter's scale) had killed forty-one people at the VA hospital, two at the Olive View facility, two on the freeway, and seventeen others across the city—including several people killed in their beds by falling beams and ceilings and nine who died of heart attacks before they could get medical help. In all, 944 buildings suffered major damage or were destroyed, and 139 others would be unsafe for occupancy without repairs. In addition, eighty thousand people had to be evacuated for nearly three days from the area below the Van Norman Dam until the water could be drawn down far enough for safety, and the lifelines—electrical power, sewers, water, telephone and other communications, as well as the normal chain of food supplies—were seriously disrupted for the same length of time.

All in ten seconds. All from a M_L 6.6 earthquake, which had even managed to destroy a supposedly earthquake-proof public building.[6]

Los Angeles hadn't had as bad a scare since March 10, 1933, when a major tremor flattened Long Beach (on the southern edge of Los Angeles), killing 120 people and destroying scores of school buildings which were empty of schoolchildren only because it was late afternoon (5:54 P.M.).

In other words, the Los Angeles area had been extraordinarily lucky in 1933. And in the confusion and the destruction of February 9, 1971, with sirens filling the air all over the San Fernando Valley, it was chillingly obvious to those who remembered the history of the 1933 disaster that Angelenos had been saved by luck and timing once again. Had the quake hit during rush hour when the freeways and many of the heavily damaged commercial and office buildings were occupied, had it struck when the Van Norman Reservoir was full, had it lasted another five or ten or twenty seconds (as it would in a major or great quake), the carnage could have been in the thousands, or worse.

Disasters, of course, breed changes and safety precautions that no amount of worried rhetoric could otherwise force. Thirty-eight years before the San Fernando quake the citizens of the Long Beach area had gathered in shock before crushed and broken school buildings in their city, holding their unscathed children tightly, and realized the magnitude of what would have occurred had school been in session. Within days experts were estimating that thousands of students would have been crushed to death beneath collapsing unreinforced masonry walls and ceilings, pancaking concrete floors, and poorly braced doorframes. Perhaps tens of thousands more would have been injured, and some of those maimed for life.

The jolting realization that the schools themselves had threatened their children's lives grew into a tide of public and parental outrage which rapidly spilled over into the political arena and carried new legislation through the California statehouse in record time on a flood of concern—a landmark bill which required public schools in California to be built to survive earthquake damage. The new law was a significant step, one of the first, in fact, in what

184

would become known as the process of hazard mitigation. Suddenly all California public schools, regardless of which school district owned the facility, were charged with doing something about the risk of building collapse in a major quake. The Field Act, as it was known, was the beginning—but it was only a beginning.[7]

Recriminations and angry statements of who was to blame for what element of damage and lack of preparedness began within hours of the San Fernando quake as well. Questions of why the Olive View and veterans hospitals had been destroyed, why a dangerous dam had been allowed to continue holding water, and why the existing building codes had not been enough to protect the citizenry of San Fernando and Los Angeles echoed back and forth for months.[8]

But memories are very short when it comes to expediency. Considerations of how much it costs to tear down dangerous buildings, how much it costs to build to higher standards, and how much it costs not to build on unstable ground once again become paramount after the rubble has been removed and the dead have been buried. Just as Charleston, South Carolina, had rebuilt many of its badly damaged buildings of unreinforced masonry on the very same ground after the 1886 earthquake—just as San Francisco had permitted the reconstruction of questionable structures on shaky ground throughout the city following the 1906 catastrophe—so, too, would Los Angeles try to brush aside the message inherent in the San Fernando earthquake as it had in the years following the Long Beach quake. Dangerous construction techniques and designs not prohibited by codes or other new laws would continue. Dangerous unreinforced masonry buildings sure to crumble when the San Andreas slipped again were left standing—and occupied. Land with commercial value would be used regardless of seismic risk or hazardous location. And police, fire, and rescue agencies would continue to talk on different radio frequencies in more than 140 different area jurisdictions like an electronic Tower of Babel sure to contribute to confusion when the inevitable finally happened.

Of course, there was severe disagreement over just what should be done in the face of such a threat. There was very little knowledge or understanding among political leaders and municipal officials about how to respond to such worries. Disaster response—how to pick up the pieces efficiently and quickly, guard damaged areas, care for the injured and restore vital lifeline services—was what city officials always seemed to think of when earthquakes were mentioned. The massive strengthening of building codes and seismic zoning, the forced destruction or rebuilding of hazardous buildings, and education programs to warn people of the many quick and inexpensive things they could do to protect themselves were ideas yet to be born. Certainly the 1970 Steinbrugge report had touched on many such subjects, but few officials had a real, visceral grasp of what was required.

Then, too, the San Fernando quake produced some genuine seismic surprises which seemed to indicate that even the best of existing seismic building codes might be inadequate. One of Charles Richter's protégés (and a senior Caltech seismologist in his own right), Dr. Clarence Allen, was appointed to head a quickly convened National Research Council panel just after the quake. Within days the members became sufficiently concerned about the possible inadequacy of the building codes to rush their report into print while the memories—and the public support for change— were still fresh.[9]

The accelerations recorded at the Pacoima Dam (more than one gravity) and the severe ground motion at the foot of the San Gabriel Mountains (where the collapsed hospitals had been located) were startlingly violent for a moderate earthquake. In an April article (printed in *Science* magazine[10]) one of the panel members was quoted as saying, "I don't want to overstate this, but if we can't tie [the severe building damage near the foot of the mountains] to some [unrelated, nonseismic] geologic hazard, then problems of land-use planning and seismic zoning are going to become pretty damn rough."

"Such uncertainties," the magazine continued, "underscore a long-standing belief held by many seismologists and structural engineers that a concerted federal program is urgently needed to expand basic and applied seismic research and to assist . . . 'high-risk' cities . . . to reduce existing earthquake hazards." But that had been recommended before, the scientific community responded. What about the Press report in 1965 that called for a federal program after the Alaska quake—and got nowhere? What about the 1968 interagency committee report which also called for a ten-year program—and was ignored? What about the engineering report of 1969? And, of course, what of the latest and best—the comprehensive earthquake hazard mitigation recommendations from the Office of Science and Technology team welded together by Karl Steinbrugge?

"The upshot of all these reports," *Science* quoted an unnamed "prominent seismologist" as saying, "is that we've had enough reports." What we need, he continued, is action. Perhaps, the scientist told the magazine, the San Fernando quake had "shaken the dust off these many proposals" and would spur action at the federal level. After all, the damage in the Los Angeles area had by then been tabulated, and the bill, which exceeded that of Alaska in 1964, was more than a billion dollars.

"You know, we've been lucky before, and we were even more lucky this time."

The seismologist stood on the eastern flank of the now-empty Van Norman Reservoir complex and looked toward the destroyed dam that had slumped to within three feet of killing tens of thousands of people. Disasters waiting to happen such as this, he had said, must be found—and defused.

"The problem—always the damn problem—is that unless we can tell [city officials and government leaders] when the big one is coming, they think they have forever to handle the problem. And, of course, forever means sometime after they're no longer in office. Somehow we have to get them the answers they need."

The scientist pointed to the north, toward the ridge line of the San Gabriels and toward Fort Tejon.

"As Clarence Allen has said, some day, the San Andreas . . . will break in a major quake. In the meantime, we're going to have to figure out how that thing works, and approximately how much time is left before whatever is locking up in this area breaks." He paused, shaking his head.

"Because when that finally happens, luck won't be enough."

Chapter 14

**Stanford University, Palo Alto,
California—March 1974**

The waiting was intolerable. His entire future—at least his future as a geologist—hinged on the message that would come through the door with Dean Richard Jahns in a few minutes.

Twenty-three-year-old Kerry Sieh fiddled with a pencil and sighed. He knew he was a bit of a rebel in the Stanford graduate program. There were two ways to travel to a Ph.D. in geology, and the path most often taken—the one the faculty had wanted him to follow—was to become an apprentice to one of the resident masters, letting that professor assign him a Ph.D. thesis project to work on and to specialize in afterward.

And there were two professors under whom he could have apprenticed: one a stratigrapher with strong ties to the oil industry; the other an expert in the mechanics of folded rock layers and how the earth's crust develops such features. But neither subject had captured Sieh's imagination. He had his own ideas, and he did not want to adopt somebody else's program of research.

Sieh had known from the first that going it alone was the tougher method. And he knew it seldom worked. He would have to find a professor who would be his adviser on an independent project that Sieh himself would shape and control. That would take research money, and established professors already had enough trouble getting grants and contracts for their own projects. It was a long shot to think that he could get a piece of that same pie for his own use. Then, too, he would have to overcome the natural bias of the faculty. The professors already had more technical problems to work on than they had graduate students to assign. It was going to be an uphill battle to find one who would support a maverick student with yet another subject of research.

189

Nevertheless, when he had written his three-page Ph.D. thesis proposal (part of the all-important second-year exam), he had outlined just that: an independent probe aimed at understanding how often the San Andreas Fault generated great earthquakes.

And, in a few minutes, Professor Jahns (dean of the School of Earth Sciences, one of the most respected geologists in academic captivity), would walk through the door and pronounce sentence.

Sieh found himself listening for footsteps in the linoleum hallway outside the office, stiffening every time the sound of shoes on the stairway echoed through the door, relaxing only slightly when they passed and died down. It was probably too late now to second-guess, but had he done the right thing? Would he find any allies on the three-man review panel?

And, basically, had he passed or failed? The seconds ticked by like some diabolical form of ancient academic torture, butterflies performing aerobatic maneuvers in the pit of his stomach.

Kerry Sieh had never been interested in rocks. He was fascinated by a wide variety of subjects, such as political science, economics, music, and many others—but earth sciences had not been originally on his list of favorites. In fact, the Southern California high school senior who had entered the University of California at Riverside in the fall of 1968 had been very confused about what to pursue as a profession. There were some anxious times that first collegiate semester within his dorm room at UC, Riverside, as the eighteen-year-old stared at the math and chemistry tomes in front of him, feeling lost, unnecessary, and adrift.

He had never had a very good image of himself. Since his family had moved to Newport Beach, California, from Iowa in 1962, he had just more or less drifted as a loner—a teenager who liked being outdoors and at the beach, but by himself. Nevertheless, he had enrolled at UC, Riverside with the vague idea that he would focus on economics, or music, or perhaps political science, or maybe even prelaw. None of those particularly excited him, but they provided some potential answers to the ubiquitous campus question: And what's your major?

As the fall semester approached an end, Kerry became more and more apprehensive about what his future as a college graduate would hold: a life in an office, which he had always assumed to be the inevitable consequence of higher education.

But as January 1969 approached (and campus riots, hippies, activism, and social consciousness competed with folk music for the attention of college students), it dawned on him that there were students approaching their degree who didn't fit the stereotypical image of corporate clones. One senior in particular had caught his attention whenever he returned from field trips. The senior would be physically and mentally exhausted, yet exhilarated from the experience, the intellectual challenge, and the balance of working both indoors and out. What the fellow was doing, in fact, was studying geology.

Maybe, thought Sieh, *there might be a future for me in that area.* And with that idea in mind, Kerry Sieh signed up for an introductory class in the spring semester and immediately fell in love with the earth, and the immensity of geologic time and geologic processes.

It was the challenge of finding answers to intriguing questions that came through loud and clear even amidst the rote rhetoric of first-year basics. And there was a visceral excitement to the methodology of charting one's own course with a backpack and a geologic map (held in the teeth of a battered clipboard), and of striking out for paths untrod and cliffs unclimbed to get the answers to what the surrounding landscape was made of and how it happened to arrive at that particular condition.

Suddenly there was a purpose and a direction to his life that began to grow with each passing course. It was a field in which he had a definite talent, and for which he had rapidly developed an affinity. It was amazing how many other scientific and professional disciplines were involved—how many other areas might be needed to solve a geological problem. Chemistry, physics, engineering, seismology, and many others touched geology, and vice versa. He liked problems that were messy, that required being outside and getting his fingernails dirty—literally. There was something deeply satisfying and therapeutic about geology, and thoughts of a career began to coalesce.

But there was something missing. By the time the San Fernando quake rumbled through his apartment in Riverside on February 9, 1971 (jolting him awake and sending him wobbling sleepily for the protection of the doorframe), he was becoming concerned that whatever he could do in geology might not be socially relevant. Just searching for oil or working out esoteric research problems would not be enough. The social activism of the late sixties had not been lost on Kerry, who by 1970 had become overtly religious and convinced that everyone had a responsibility to contribute in some way to the betterment of his fellow man. But precisely how a geologist could contribute was unclear to him. It wasn't a constant worry, just an unfilled hole in the emerging jigsaw puzzle of his professional future.

Until the following month, that is, when the Geological Society of America held its annual convention on the Riverside campus.

The San Fernando Valley and Los Angeles were still picking up the pieces following the earthquake as the first of March rolled around, but Kerry Sieh still had not traveled the sixty miles to the west to view the damage. A fellow geology student had tried to get him to go, but earthquakes seemed a seismological problem of the present, while geology was a science of studying and interpreting the past. It hadn't occurred to him that the two disciplines fit together. Nor had it occurred to him that an upcoming professional meeting of geologists and geophysicists on the university campus might plant in his head the seed of an idea that would help change his future radically.

It was purely by chance that Kerry Sieh was in the audience when two engineering geologists began presenting a new method they had developed to determine exactly where active faults were located so that their clients' buildings could be constructed a safe distance away. Traditionally the process of locating precisely where faults were often depended on broad guesswork and interpretation of surface scars that had long since been disturbed or erased by other building activity. Their solution was first to dig a hundred-foot-long, three-foot-wide, ten-foot-deep trench at right angles across the general area of a suspected fault zone. Then, by examining the sedimentary layers exposed in the walls of the trench, they could find the exact trace of the fault itself by locating places where the layers had been broken or vertically torn by past slippage of the fault during earthquakes. That, quite simply, eliminated the guesswork.

A light of sorts went on in Kerry Sieh's head. All semester he had been struggling through a class on stratigraphy and sedimentation, learning the nature of sediments, and how they're laid down. Geologists who master such techniques can examine a cross section of strata and discover a wide range of facts about the history of the

192

place where the sediments were deposited, what the environment was like, when floods occurred, and perhaps even the date and severity of any event which disturbed the layers. In addition, Kerry's junior year as a geology student had thrust him into the heart of structural geology, the understanding of faults, and how the upper crust of the earth ends up arranged the way it is.

Sediments and layers, in other words, were arrayed in living color before his mind's eye as the two engineers talked, and the thought that kept imposing itself seemed terribly simple: *They aren't getting all the information out of those trenches that they could. They're only looking for the location of the faults.*

I'll bet, Kerry thought, *you could stand in one of those trenches, examine the sediments in great detail, and find small scarps that collapsed from small earthquakes, triangular wedges, and perhaps sandblows which could provide a lot of clues as to the nature of those earthquakes.*[1] And, he realized, if enough plant material could be found in such a place to permit carbon dating, a geologist might be able to discover when the various quakes that had left such telltale evidence had occurred.

But the two engineers weren't addressing such questions. They wanted to know only where faults had slipped, not when and how.

Kerry Sieh left the meeting with those ideas beginning a process of fermentation in the back of his mind. It would be a long trail from March 1971 and the meeting room at UC, Riverside to an office at Stanford with two years of graduate work almost complete and an idea firmly in mind of how to proceed in researching faults, but at least he had a direction, and a reasonable hope.

Kerry Sieh looked at his watch again. What was keeping the dean? It had been just a few minutes since he last glanced at the hands of his watch, but those minutes were dragging by at a glacial pace. Various thoughts occupied his distracted mind, thoughts and worries such as what on earth he would do if he didn't pass the exam. In addition to the doctoral thesis proposal, there had been the classroom examination, and although he was pretty sure he had done well, he wouldn't truly believe it until he heard it from Dr. Jahns in person—whenever that was going to be.

Jahns had been quite helpful to Sieh, but then that was his way. He was extraordinarily approachable and personable for such a senior scientist, and he genuinely cared about his students—which was one reason he was so well regarded by them. That, and his rather famous sense of humor. His friend at the USGS, Bob Wallace, claimed that half the risqué jokes floating around the country had been crafted and circulated by Jahns, whom Wallace labeled a "world-class raconteur."

His practical jokes had become legend as well. Of course, Caltech tended to instill such propensity for energetic nonsense in its students, and Jahns had taken to the practice with an extraordinary dedication.[2] There always seemed to be some joke in progress perpetrated either by, or on, Professor Jahns—so much so that at one point as a Caltech professor (before making the jump to Stanford), the school's administration felt they had to reprimand him for "unprofessorial conduct."[3]

But first and foremost, Dick Jahns was a highly respected geologist who had a visceral love of getting into the field and getting his hands dirty trying to solve messy problems that refused to yield to easy solutions. In that, he was as much a role model for young geologists as he was a professor. He was that rare sort of academician who can look far beyond the normal strictures of academic qualifications and recognize genuine talent and occasional genius, the sort who could see something more than the average in the young doctoral candidate named Kerry Sieh who had ended up on his Stanford doorstep almost by chance.

A pamphlet had started it—a small flyer sent in 1971 by the National Science Foundation to undergraduate-level geology professors telling about the Student Originated Studies Program. It was a three-million-dollar plan designed to entice science students into socially useful research by inviting research proposals directly from undergraduate students. A certain number of the proposals would be selected and funded with a small NSF grant.

The pamphlet landed in the hands of one of Kerry Sieh's geology professors at UC, Riverside, who handed it to another student, who discussed it with still another student, who collared Sieh one afternoon in his senior year.

"You're the only one with a sufficiently high grade point average to qualify as director of something like this, Kerry. How about joining us?"

He had hesitated at first, worried that the time spent applying could lower his grade point average. But however remote it was, the opportunity to try out the idea that had been stewing in his

194

head since the lecture six months before was worth a chance—so he accepted, and began preparing a proposal.

They would study the nearby San Jacinto Fault, sixty-nine miles from the campus, by using the same trenching technique discussed by the two engineering geologists, but with a different goal: to find a recurrence interval for the earthquakes that occurred there.

If they succeeded, they would be the first to find earthquake history in the geologic record—in the ground itself—rather than just in human memory.

But Kerry Sieh did not realize how audacious his plan really was. The possibility that they might fail to find such evidence never crossed his mind. The fact that he might be opening the door to a major new method with planetary implications for advancing seismology was never considered. The pure logic of the proposal and his ideas for finding a new way of answering some very old questions seemed quite straightforward. The only real problem was whether they had a chance for the grant.

The application was, in essence, a long shot. Even with the polished proposal, which took two full weeks to put together, there were no assurances it would have a chance. There was a lot of competition nationwide. The odds were probably too great. It probably wouldn't work.

But it did. Some five months later the group was shocked to receive word from the NSF that their proposal had been accepted. Sieh and friends, it seemed, would get their grant.

Of course, there were strings attached, including a requirement that the project director must agree to go on to graduate school. Kerry had made up his mind to become a high school physical sciences teacher or a consulting geologist. He didn't need a doctorate for either position, but if graduate school was the price of the grant, he'd change plans. By the time his team arrived at the San Jacinto Fault in the summer of 1972, Kerry Sieh had been admitted to Stanford's School of Earth Sciences as a graduate student.

The NSF research project was at once a success and a failure. The team failed to establish how often earthquakes originated on the fault, but they gained a wealth of experience working with the evidence—experimenting with the methods appropriate to carry out such a project. For Kerry Sieh, it was an exciting, enticing dress rehearsal. And when classes began at Stanford in the fall, Sieh's ideas about finding earthquakes in the geologic record had matured significantly.

The hallway was still empty. Another half hour had passed. Sieh chuckled to himself, thinking of the NSF grant two years before. If he got his doctorate and contributed anything, that would be government money very well spent! It was the government, after all, that had seduced him into geology to begin with.

Dick Jahns was filling the doorway suddenly. Kerry hadn't even heard his footsteps, but now he looked up at the dean with hope and inquiry showing on an anxious face.

"Well, Kerry, we've decided on one thing." Professor Jahns sat down on the edge of the desk and smiled at his student.

"What's that?"

"You're damn bullheaded!" Jahns was chuckling gently, easily. "The others feel like they offered you something you could do for your thesis project and you didn't want to do it, and they don't think you're going to succeed in what you're proposing to do."

Kerry was stunned. There it was. God, there it was. He had flunked! He fought the growing knot in his throat.

"Now, there's nothing wrong with your candidacy exam, you did fine on that, and you're plenty smart, and I think you might be able to make something of this."

The words almost didn't register at first. Jahns had delivered the academic death sentence, then commuted it, holding out some hope. Fighting hard for control of his emotions, Kerry listened as the dean told him to rethink his research proposal, take the other professors' criticisms into account, and then he, Jahns, would send Kerry out in the field to see if trying to find records of earthquakes in the dirt of the past few thousands years had any possibility of success.

"What should I work on? Should I work on the San Jacinto?" Kerry asked.

"That's just a little thing. Let's go for the big one. Let's go for the San Andreas. A lot of people are crawling around on it, but no one is doing what you're proposing."

The days that followed were brutal. Despite the lifeline from Dick Jahns, and the fact that he'd passed one part of the exam, technically his research proposal had been rejected. He had failed. His carefully nurtured idea had been rejected, and only the kindness of the dean was keeping any hope alive that on reconsideration the professors would reverse themselves and accept his proposal. It was also clear that it was entirely up to him to justify the dean's faith. If he were to keep his doctoral program on track, he would have to prove to these doubting experts that what they believed couldn't be done, in fact, could.

His project, Kerry realized, had become far more than just a doctoral research program. He believed in it. He believed he could do something no one had yet done with the simple concept of looking for evidence of past earthquakes in yesterday's dirt. In fact, he was more worried about losing the chance to prove his idea, than about getting his Ph.D.

The NSF project had not only whetted his appetite and provided good practice, it had focused him on a geologic problem that had immense social significance, which is exactly what the NSF had intended to encourage. They wanted to divert young scientists from esoteric research into areas of immediate benefit to mankind, and in this case that meant probing the possibility that earthquakes could be predicted by finding out when they had occurred in the past. By 1974 there was a lot of discussion in the scientific community about the possibility of earthquake prediction, especially with the advent of plate tectonics and the resulting models of how the different plates were moving, and how fast they were going. What he could find out by examining the San Andreas could make a difference—but now it was an uphill battle. He had to convince them that he could find the evidence in order to earn the opportunity to do so.

Kerry Sieh was extraordinarily depressed. People jump off bridges because of such failures, he told a friend. People quit school forever because of such catastrophes. He felt devastated, yet thankful that Jahns had encouraged him to pick up the pieces. After all, he had another year of classes ahead, and during that time he would work like a demon to prove the project's efficacy. Bob Wallace of the USGS knew the area in middle California around the Carrizo Plain that Kerry wanted to target, and he knew Dr. Wallace had done his Ph.D. thesis and additional research work on the same subject. Dr. Wallace might even be on his doctoral board, if he could stay in the ball game. Such thoughts and ideas whirled through his mind as he fought to recover from the blow. Pulling himself together, he started planning. He would get Wallace's help. He would make it work. He simply had to.

Chapter 15

Carrizo Plain, California—June 1975

Another dead fox lay before him, grotesque and pitiful, baked by the unmerciful desert heat, and looking very tiny in contrast with the stark floor of the broad valley.

Kerry Sieh had found dozens of dead animals so far—a grisly greeting during the first day of fieldwork—many of them lying in the dry, golden brown grass on dusty, hot ridges and in the depressions along the fault trace as it cut through the Carrizo Plain. Dead rabbits, squirrels, and even songbirds littered the ground at intervals.

What on earth? The question kept diverting Kerry's attention from his primary mission. It was bizarre and depressing—and frightening. For nearly nine miles of parched grasslands there had been nothing alive—except him.

The inanimacy of the scene was almost total. The arid landscape undulating ahead of him in the 105-degree heat declared itself unfit for human habitation and mocked his presence. It was an alien environment in which the brutal rays of the sun washed out the color of the place and bleached the souls of its trespassers.

Fifteen difficult months had passed since that awful day at Stanford when Dean Jahns had told him that this project, and his degree program, were hanging by a thread.

There were times he was certain of his ideas, and there were times—lonely times like these—when the isolation and the enormity of the task seemed to mock his confidence, making him examine in great depth whether his accomplishments were a mirage and his hopes for success merely the stage props of a dreamworld. It was a type of self-doubt which every ambitious and self-confident person faces at one time or another, the agonizing fear that someday you'll pull yourself over the top of the highest ledge of the mountain, exhausted and excited, only to find that the mountain was merely a foothill that the real masters conquered years before. It's the fear that someday you'll find you've been dealing in self-delusion, and that you're not the expert you thought you were. It was, he realized, an industrial-strength version of the same hollow panic that an overconfident high school valedictorian would feel in his first semester of college if he realized he couldn't pass freshman English, or the sickening impact to a straight A Phi Beta Kappa of receiving a failing grade on his first paper in graduate school.

That type of fear can metastasize into an intellectual paralysis, halting the audacity and originality of new ideas carried on the shoulders of enthusiasm and intellectual curiosity—cooling the fires of passion with the wet blanket of caution and self-doubt. Kerry Sieh had faced such fears before, and had conquered them with a self-confidence born as much of his passion for geology and determination to contribute to society, as from his growing intellectual maturity. He could do it—it was just damned hard.

The weight of his backpack was beginning to tug at Kerry's consciousness as he pushed his two-pound hiking boots forward, committed to covering the last few miles before sunset to reach the place where he had pre-parked his bicycle early in the morning. He had left his car nearly nine miles back before beginning the day's trek.

Normally he would be watching his path for snakes, but it was far too hot for rattlers, if indeed any of them had survived whatever had made this desolate country a killing field. The dead animals he had seen all day were a nagging problem. What had killed them? Was this area poisoned? Such thoughts distracted him as the shimmering waves of heat beat down on the twenty-four-year-old graduate student like the growing worry that maybe the place he was searching for did not exist.[1]

Kerry had become fascinated with the Carrizo Plain, and Bob Wallace had helped to build that interest. The fault trace was so visible and visceral as it ran through the area that Wallace long ago had decided that much could be learned from studying its geologic features. If he knew where to look (and what questions to ask), then there were answers to be found.[2]

Kerry Sieh was still astounded by how little was really known of the San Andreas, especially about the southern sections of the great fault. The San Francisco quake of 1906 had focused the geophysical community on the northern segment for seventy years while the potentially dangerous six-hundred-mile stretch to the south remained an obscure curiosity. Of course, to anyone who really looked to the south, the fault appeared to be relatively harmless. In San Juan Bautista, for instance (about a hundred miles south of the Bay Area), the two sides of the fault merely crept past each other at a very slow and steady pace, creating nothing more than minor temblors from time to time. True, a few buildings, curbs, and sidewalks were being wrenched apart slowly, where they sat literally on top of the fault, but the threat was predictable and tame.

Even in Parkfield (a tiny farming community located right on the fault about halfway between San Francisco and Los Angeles) the periodic earthquakes that seemed to occur every twenty-two years reached only a Richter magnitude of 6.0 (M_L), and did little, if any, damage. And to the south of Parkfield was the nearly deserted Carrizo Plain, which didn't really contain enough civilization to worry about.

But then there was Fort Tejon, south of the Carrizo Plain. It was common knowledge that a huge earthquake had struck that portion of the fault in 1857, but no one knew how far the fault had slipped during that quake, or how badly it had affected the area that was now the densely populated Los Angeles basin.[3] For that matter, no one even knew if there had ever been great quakes in that area before 1857, even though that question would obviously have a bearing on what Los Angeles could expect in the future.

Considering all those elements, Kerry had decided to structure his thesis project to answer three key questions. First, he needed to know how much the fault had slipped during the 1857 Fort Tejon quake. Secondly, he wanted to find how fast the fault was slipping year by year—the average slip rate over the past few millennia (the last few thousand years). And finally, he wanted to pinpoint when past earthquakes had occurred during the previous few thousand years in order to determine if there were a regular rhythm to their recurrence. Such information could lead to earthquake prediction, at least in the long term.[4]

The answers to at least the first two questions lay in the offset streambeds of the Carrizo Plain. The aerial photographs he had studied showed numerous small creeks and streams that had been dislocated—wrenched apart—where they crossed the fault. Finding the right ones of those to study would be a starting point.

In the beginning, each of those streams had started as a relatively straight channel flowing from the hills to the east directly across the fault toward the west. But in the early years of each new stream, the day inevitably came when the fault suddenly moved, the western side slipping northwestward, carrying the western part of the streambed with it.

One key to the puzzle lay in discovering when those streams had been created as a straight channel across the fault. Kerry theorized that most of them dated from the tremendous outflow of water from the last ice age, about ten thousand years ago, but he had to be sure. If there was enough carbon in the upper levels of those beds to determine when the channel was first cut, he would have the date—and a starting point. Then, by measuring how far the western channel had been carried off to the northwest on the Pacific plate side over the ensuing centuries, and by dividing the distance with the number of years since the stream was created, he would have the average yearly slip rate.

That still left a problem, however. How many feet did the fault slip with each earthquake? The key to that question, he figured, lay in the offsets of the newest streams, which had been displaced only once—in 1857.

If, for instance, the 1857 quake had caused ten meters of slippage, it just might be that each time the fault moved, it moved in ten-meter increments. Kerry knew that if *that* were the case, he would find all the offset streams displaced from their original location in ten-meter multiples—ten-meter jumps—as well. And that was exactly what he thought he saw in the aerial photos and in Bob Wallace's original work.

"The point," Kerry had explained so many times, "is that if I know the fault is moving at, say, 5.5 centimeters per year on the average, and I know that each time the fault slips in an earthquake it slips a total of ten meters, then I can divide ten meters by 5.5 centimeters, which gives me 181 years. That could mean that it takes 181 years on the average for the fault to store up enough strain (at the rate of 5.5 centimeters per year) to break whatever is snagging it, which would mean that on the average the area has a great earthquake every 181 years."

Apparently the San Andreas had been snagged in the Carrizo Plain since 1857, and it seemed inevitable that someday that snag would break, allowing the fault to slip back to equilibrum suddenly in a major earthquake which would relieve the strain and start the process all over again.[5]

Kerry Sieh sat down on dusty rock to rest, looking around at the hills in front of him, the reddish sun now throwing long shadows over the valley. He would need all the bullheadedness and determination he could muster if he were going to succeed here. He felt deep down that this was the right thing to do and the right time to do it, and that this parched terrain would yield its secrets if probed long enough. But he had no more guarantees than a gold miner—and gold miners can grow old waiting for that one, big find.

So far all he had was one particular stream which was typically offset as it crossed the fault in such a way that he might be able to date its origin. That one held promise, although the layers of sediment were not the sort he needed to answer the other question: when the previous quakes occurred.

The same stream also had been featured by Bob Wallace in one of his papers. It would be appropriate, Kerry thought, to name it after the senior USGS geologist. Even in the middle of a semiarid wasteland, a place called Wallace Creek would confer a certain importance. Now all he had to do was dig up the answers—make Wallace Creek yield the right information.

Kerry got to his feet, balancing his bicycle and climbing on for the ten-mile trek back to his car. He would return in the morning. There were many more miles of the San Andreas to cover, and somewhere along that line were gullies he had to find.

Pallett Creek, California—July 1, 1976

"Beautiful! Look at that!"

Kerry Sieh moved closer to the vertical face of dirt his brother's shovel had exposed, a layer cake of sediments with interbedded peat layers deposited over the last two thousand years. As with every other cut they had made for the past month, this one was replete with clearly defined breaks in the horizontal layers, and areas in which material that looked like sand had pushed up from its natural level through some of the layers above, forming what looked like an upside-down bowling pin.

"It's a sandblow, right there!"

Rodger Sieh moved closer, puzzled over Kerry's excitement. "What?"

Kerry began tracing the history they had exposed.

"There, Rodger. Right there!"

The summer sun had been merciless, but the thrill of discovery was making the hardships endurable. The results from nearly two months of work were already proving to Kerry that his initial excitement was justified—excitement at finding this shady bend in an otherwise obscure creek on the edge of the Mojave Desert. It was *the* spot he had been searching for in the previous year, up and down the San Andreas Fault, through the Carrizo Plain, and throughout this country of arid landscape and desert vegetation. And the answers it could provide were going to be exciting.

Kerry sat nose to nose with the exposed dirt wall of Pallett Creek's northern bank. As he looked at the near-vertical break in the strata which could be traced from just below the upper surface of the present-day meadow downward through other breaks in the alternating dark and light layers, it was rather amazing to realize that his left foot was on the Pacific plate, and his right one on the North American plate. He was in effect staring the San Andreas Fault down the throat.

On the surface, as he looked back to the west-northwest, the now-familiar outline of two small sloping ridges terminating in a tiny draw running from the west exactly toward his position betrayed the line where the two plates had been sliding past each other for thousands of years. It was typical rift topography. The markings weren't as clear and stark as they were in the Carrizo Plain 125 miles to the northwest, but there was no mistaking that sort of miniature "valley."

His practiced eye and careful precision in really looking at what lay before him had spotted a rich, recent geologic history from the very first days of digging. For a few thousand years, it seemed, up to about 1910, the spot where the brothers were standing had been a swamp. With the water table at the surface, the area was washed by the waters of several adjacent springs, and covered periodically by flash floods coming from the nearby north shoulder of the San Gabriel Mountains, waters rich with sediments that buried the grasses and plants over and over again, providing a marvelous stack of layer upon layer of carbon-rich strata which could be carbon-dated.

A free-lance surveyor named Henry Hancock had slogged through the swamp in 1855 as he slowly worked on mapping the southern boundaries of the Mojave Desert.[6] At that time, as with another survey in 1904, Pallett Creek was little more than a surface stream flowing through a soggy marsh—the same as it had been for centuries.

Sometime after 1904, however, floodwaters carved a channel through the swamp, eroding the layers drastically, slicing out a gorge thirty feet deep in an ever-widening streambed, which at some point had acquired the name Pallett Creek from a pioneer named George Pallett who had settled the area in the 1860's. When the elevation of the streambed dropped, the water table dropped as well, draining the swamp, and the layers of saturated soil dried out in the space of a few years as the desert grasses reclaimed the land. Cottonwood trees, which needed constant moisture, followed the waterline down, growing in the stream channel but forsaking the upper surface, where the marsh had been. By the time a small biplane with an aerial photographer flew over in 1930, the stream gorge had filled with fast-growing cottonwoods and willows while the upper surface had become a desertlike meadow standing, hot and dusty, where the willows and marsh grasses of the soggy swamp had been just three decades before.

Now, with a handful of unimpressed horses grazing the slim supply of grasses in that meadow, the two Sieh brothers chopped away at the remains of that dried marsh while below in the stream channel the summer sounds of locusts and unseen buzzing insects accompanied the visual richness of the cottonwoods that typically responded to hot desert breezes by spreading their cottonlike seeds in the air, creating an ocasional incongruous desert "snowstorm."

The climate simply was not fit for human habitation, the brutal temperatures hardly noticed by Kerry, but increasingly onerous to his new wife, Laurie, whose brief honeymoon (following their May 29, 1976, marriage) had ended in the Mojave Desert at Pallett Creek. By late June their lives were revolving around the arid former swamp—with Kerry and his brother Rodger (a divinity student) attacking the streambank by hand with shovels during the day while Laurie, by her own description, served as chief cook and bottle washer. Because they were working with very limited funds, the motel rooms they were renting in nearby Palmdale were a luxury, but also a necessity. By July, Laurie was spending the blast furnace days hugging the air conditioner in one of the tiny rooms while her husband and brother-in-law worked on at Pallett Creek, Kerry getting more excited with each sunrise.

He had hoped for a place with multiple layers going back a few hundred years. Pallett Creek's dried banks had that and more. He had needed carbon-rich plant material in each important layer. The strata were filled with peat layers, rich in carbon 14. He had needed a place in which previous earthquakes had ripped open whatever surface existed at that time, and which rapidly building sediments had covered and preserved. Pallett Creek, again, was more than he'd dreamed of finding. And of course, all those requirements had to be fulfilled by a spot whose sediments and telltale strata were on the San Andreas Fault. At Pallett Creek, the main fault trace of the San Andreas ran right through the dried-up swamp, less than five yards from the lip of the creek gorge, where it paralleled the stream for a distance before cutting diagonally across the channel.

It was, in a word, ideal—or at least as close to it as he could have imagined.

Kerry was also beginning to feel more confident about the answers he had found in the Carrizo Plain, with which he might be able to answer at least two of his three key thesis questions. At the end of the previous summer he had found evidence that the western side of the fault had slipped 10 meters (approximately 30 feet) in the 1857 Fort Tejon earthquake. To the south, however, closer to Palmdale, the offsets in the San Andreas were in multiples of only 4.5 meters. That would indicate that the Palmdale section could store only about 5 meters of accumulated strain before it would jump forward, producing a major earthquake in the process, while the Carrizo Plain section could store 10 meters of strain before breaking.[7]

Did that also mean that the San Andreas Fault, which appeared to be a single rip between the two great plates, was moving at different speeds in different locations? No one knew as yet. Deep in the earth beneath the fault the two plates continued to move at a steady rate past each other according to the accepted theory. The brittle surface, however, was a different story. At each point along the fault the western side would slip forward in a jerky motion of sudden release and slippage, followed by periods of no movement, followed by still another buildup of strain, ending in sudden release and slippage, each cycle causing approximately the same magnitude of earthquake. (What governed how much strain could be contained before a snagged area broke was basically the strength of the snag.) In addition, when all the distances through which the fault had slipped were added up and divided by the number of years, the result yielded the average movement per year—the same rate, of course, as the movement of the plate at great depths.

If the average slip rate per year was the same everywhere along the fault, then a five-meter-jump-per-earthquake rate for the Fort Tejon section would mean that great quakes occurred there, on the average, twice as often as in the Carrizo Plain.

At first Kerry had become very excited when offsets on the Carrizo Plain suggested an average slippage of only 1.5 centimeters per year. "That would mean . . ." he had figured, rather excitedly, "that the San Andreas only has great quakes about once every seven hundred years, and since the last one was only one hundred and eighteen years ago, that means Southern California has already had its big earthquake and would be out of danger." Even at half that cycle—350 years—the Fort Tejon area, too, would be still for centuries to come.

It wasn't, however, that simple, or that fortuitous upon further examination. The evidence he was still evaluating in the Carrizo Plain and at Wallace Creek pointed to a slip rate anywhere from 1.5 to 3.5 centimeters per year, and while that would be slower than the rate indicated by the marine geological studies (5.5 cm/year), the interval of recurrence of great quakes in the area could be on the order of only a couple of hundred years or less. The story would have to come from detailed studies of the offsets in the Carrizo, as well as the actual record of past quakes at Pallett Creek. And to get the latter information, he had to find "the" spot.

Kerry entered the fall semester of 1975 poring over aerial photographs, looking for offsets to the south that were as clean and definite as Wallace Creek, but were located south of Palmdale just north of the San Gabriel Mountains, which bordered the northern Los Angeles area. There were quite a few, he noticed, that had offsets of 130 to 150 meters. If the slip rate of 1.5 centimeters per year (which he still thought might be accurate for the Carrizo Plain) held up as the slip rate all along the San Andreas, and if the streams on the north slope of the San Gabriel Mountains had come into being about ten thousand years ago at the end of the last ice age, offsets of 130 to 150 meters would be about right. (Kerry had made plans to return to Wallace Creek in the fall to begin the work of carbon dating and measuring offsets, but his initial figures on average slip all were speculation.)

Sometime in the fall, before returning to the Carrizo Plain, he had driven down the back roads south of the small desert town of Pearblossom toward the fault, finding one promising site several miles away from Pallett Creek. Just as in the Carrizo, he needed enough carbonaceous material in the upper surface of the landscape bordering a stream to carbon-date, with the hope that the resulting date would give him the starting point at which the new creek channel had been cut straight across the fault. From there he could measure the distance to the offset streambed on the other side of the fault and figure out the average yearly slip rate.

Levi Noble, the geologist who in the 1920's had originally raised the radical idea that the San Andreas might have slipped a total of thirty-five miles since its creation, had mapped much of the fault in the same area. When Kerry looked at one of those maps, he was startled to find Noble's comment that the Pallett Creek drainage contained "interbedded sands, gravels, and peats" at the fault crossing. That was exactly what he needed, and in November 1975 he had driven back to the area to climb the barbed-wire fence by Pallett Creek and take some peat from the top of the streambank (and an old embedded log from the bottom) for carbon dating. This, he thought, might be the ideal place to measure the offset streambed. If the carbon dating could tell him when the stream had first cut a channel in the swamp, he could get an average slip rate.

The creek appeared to have a very typical, characteristic jog where it met the fault, with an offset of 130 meters. Kerry returned to Stanford convinced that the top layer would be dated at ten thousand, and the bottom log at perhaps twenty thousand years.

And he was thunderstruck when the results came in.

The top layer was only two hundred years old; the bottom only two thousand.

Kerry was devastated! The best-looking streambed in the area, and the dates were useless. Obviously Pallett Creek had not been wrenched 130 meters apart in only two hundred years; that would be an incredible rate of 65 centimeters per year, 5.41 centimeters per month, or 1.8 millimeters per day! You could set up bleachers, sell tickets, and bring in crowds to watch the daily slippage if such a rate were realistic. Obviously it was not. Obviously the Pallett Creek samples were a bust, and he had found the wrong layers, missing the ones which could tell him how many thousands of years it had been since the creek first crossed the fault. Obviously . . .

Within minutes Kerry Sieh realized that what he had was far from a disappointment—it was a triumph. If the layers he had sampled ran thirty feet vertically through two thousand years of geologic history clearly interbedded with enough peat to carbon-date the entire array, it would be infinitely more valuable than just a place to measure the offset and get a slip rate.

As he stood there and looked at the lab report on the carbon dates, he began to understand what he had found. Pallett Creek was the very place he had searched so hard to find—the key to the third and most difficult phase of his thesis project—the key to dating historic earthquakes along the San Andreas.

"Kerry, I want you to know something." Dr. Richard Jahns was looking at the final copy of the finished doctoral thesis that Kerry Sieh had placed in front of him. Jahns knew what it contained, of course, having served as Kerry's adviser throughout, but as with any ceremonious milestone, the quiet impact of those several hundred pages on the desktop was in stark contrast with the weight of the effort, research, and determination behind it—and a mere whisper of the immense impact that the research contained in those pages would have on the seismological community.

"When you first walked in here with this idea, Kerry, I thought you were crazy. I didn't think there was any way you could work this out. All of us thought you'd hang yourself."

Kerry Sieh—soon to be Dr. Kerry Sieh—was surprised. He knew the other professors had had no faith in his idea, but Dr. Jahns had always been supportive.

Jahns patted the thesis, obviously proud of the fact that despite his misgivings, he had seen something in Kerry Sieh that he thought deserved a chance. The idea that one motivated, bright student who believed fervently in his project could overcome the odds with hard work and ingenuity had proved right.

It was July 1977, the month Kerry was to begin as a new geology instructor at Caltech in Pasadena, some four hundred miles down the San Andreas Fault to the south. Most of the previous eight months had been spent refining data, finalizing conclusions, and drawing the last sketches of the strata which had yielded so much (not to mention the late hours typing and revising the manuscript). While the thesis marked the end of the project, it really marked the beginning. Kerry knew he would have to continue digging at Pallett Creek. There were many more secrets to be found—not that he hadn't unearthed a staggering number already.

There had been a cornucopia of datable material and clearly visible breaks in the various layers representing specific earthquakes, interlaced with sandblows and gopher holes and complex "horizons" of peat and sand and sediment. Kerry had mapped with meticulous precision more than eleven different views of the strata across the fault (which he had exposed through digging long trenches), and had documented Fort Tejon magnitude quakes (within plus or minus forty years) in 1745 (during the American colonial period), 1470 (before Christopher Columbus's voyage), 1245 (when only Indians occupied North America), 1190 (a century after the Battle of Hastings), and the years 965, 860, 665, and 545. Through his work at Wallace Creek, he had postulated an annual slip rate of 3.4 centimeters along the length of the fault and had constructed a profile of the average offsets—sudden slippage—of the fault from Parkfield to San Bernardino during the 1857 quake. In short, he had asked and answered all three of the major questions.

The significance of what he had found, and what he had validated with such careful precision, was profound. The list of prehistoric earthquakes alone meant that no longer could residents or government officials of Southern California treat the prospect of great earthquakes on the southern San Andreas as the mere armchair postulations of theorizing scientists. This was hard-and-fast proof. Great quakes hit the Fort Tejon area of the fault on the average every century and a half, Kerry had discovered, and had done so at least nine times in the prior fifteen hundred years.

But the fault had not stopped slipping, and therefore, the research meant that with virtual certainty, the fault would break again at some point in the future.

Many people had accepted that fact before, but seismologists always were in such disagreement about *when* it would happen that

210

Valdez before March 27, 1964. John Kelsey's city dock is on the lower left. Dashes indicate the line of destruction. *(Courtesy U.S. Geological Survey)*

Seward prior to March 27, 1964. *(Photo by U.S. Army Corps of Engineers; Courtesy U.S. Geological Survey)*

Seward on March 28, 1964. *(Photo by U.S. Army Corps of Engineers; Courtesy U.S. Geological Survey)*

Inside image: Old Valdez with truncated docks

New townsite under construction

Valdez area, looking east. *(Photo by U.S. Army; Courtesy U.S. Geological Survey)*

Seward's Texaco tank farm and rail yard the morning after. *(Photo by U.S. Army; Courtesy U.S. Geological Survey)*

J. C. Penney's new Anchorage store, April 1, 1964 (5th Avenue and D Street). *(Photo by Dr. George Plafker; Courtesy U.S. Geological Survey)*

The effect of shaken Bootlegger Cove clay: 4th Avenue near C Street in downtown Anchorage, March 28, 1964. *(Photo by U.S. Army; Courtesy U.S. Geological Survey)*

The Hines family home where it came to rest in reorganized Turnagain. *(Photo by Lloyd Hines)*

Dr. Robert Wallace of the USGS—the driving force behind the new science of paleoseismology. *(Photo by John J. Nance)*

Dr. Brian Atwater of the USGS in the field near Willapa Bay, Washington—digging for evidence of ancient earthquakes. *(Photo by John J. Nance)*

Charleston, South Carolina, September 1, 1886. *(J. K. Hillers/Courtesy U.S. Geological Survey)*

Train thrown from tracks north of Charleston, South Carolina, by quake of August 31, 1886 (note funnel-shaped smokestack). *(J. K. Hillers/Courtesy U.S. Geological Survey)*

Sadly typical scene of downtown Coalinga, California, May 1983. These shops were occupied when the waves arrived. *(Courtesy U.S. Geological Survey)*

Duane Hamann in the laser house on Car Hill, Parkfield, California. *(Photo by John J. Nance)*

Like a ticking bomb poised over the heads of nearly ten thousand residents, the remaining water of the lower Van Norman Reservoir laps at the remains of its shattered earthen dam as engineers frantically work to drain the lake. *(Courtesy U.S. Geological Survey)*

San Francisco freeway interchange, 1971. The result of seismic waves 1/100th as large in magnitude as those produced by the 1857 Fort Tejon quake just to the north of Los Angeles. *(Courtesy U.S. Geological Survey)*

Dr. Kerry Sieh of Caltech explains his breakthrough at Pallett Creek. *(Photo by Henry Spall; Courtesy U.S. Geological Survey)*

Carbon-dated layers at Pallett Creek, and graphic evidence of past great quakes on the San Andreas Fault just north of L.A. (numbers on tags are approximate years of each earthquake's occurrence). *(Photo by Henry Spall; Courtesy U.S. Geological Survey)*

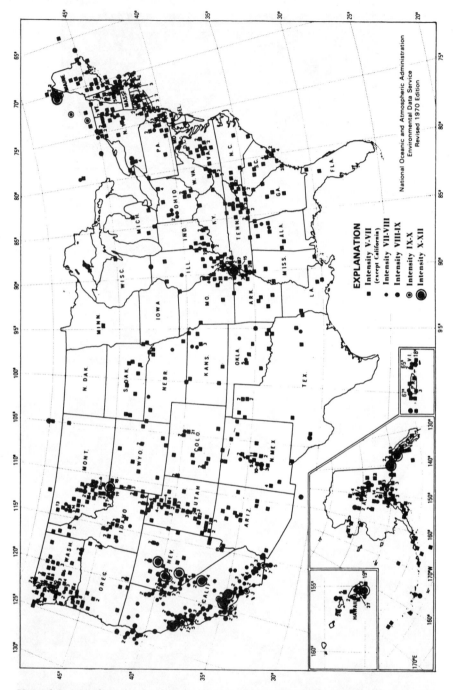

National Oceanic and Atmospheric Administration
Environmental Data Service
Revised 1970 Edition

EXPLANATION

■ Intensity V-VII
  (except California)
■ Intensity VII-VIII
● Intensity VIII-IX
◉ Intensity IX-X
◉ Intensity X-XII

United States, showing locations of earthquakes of modified Mercalli intensity V or greater from colonial times through 1970. (*From* Earthquake History of the United States *{U.S. Department of Commerce, National Oceanic and Atmospheric Administration and U.S. Geological Survey Publication 41–1 revised edition (through 1970), reprinted 1982 with supplement (1971–80)}*) there was no sense of urgency. However, simple math—subtracting 1857 from 1977—yielded the figure 120. It had been 120 years since the last quake, and since the record at Pallett Creek indicated clearly that some quakes had been separated by less time than that, the possibility of a repeat performance of Fort Tejon at any time had to be faced.

Now there would be powerful ammunition for scientists and government leaders who wanted to adopt some of the hazard mitigation proposals that Dr. Steinbrugge's task force (among others) had recommended in 1970. Suddenly the ethereal nature of the concern was about to evaporate under the hot lights of reality which had been turned on by what one solitary young scientist had believed he could find—and did find—in yesterday's dirt.

But there was more. From his office at Menlo Park Dr. Robert Wallace had followed Kerry's progress with great interest and enthusiasm. While he knew that the inevitable flurry of interest in the hard facts and implications of Kerry's thesis would have quite an impact, the project's success carried a higher magnitude of benefit for geology, and, in fact, for geophysics and seismology as well. The idea that seismologists and geologists needed each other—the concept that such cooperation across interdisciplinary lines could develop a synergistic momentum—had been validated in an exceptional way. This was another quantum leap in the usefulness of the sort of research that Gilbert had pioneered, Plafker had practiced, and Wallace had advocated for decades. This was a field in search of a new title, and Wallace was prepared to name it. The term "paleoseismology" would be exactly right, though it would take some time to gain acceptance.[8]

But the greatest benefit of all would be in the jolt of enthusiasm that Kerry Sieh's triumph would give to a growing hope—a yearning—that had fueled papers and studies and endless discussions of what seismology could do for society in the future: the hope of earthquake prediction. In effect, Kerry Sieh's thesis was an inherent long-term prediction, thoroughly supported and neatly encapsulated. What happened before on the San Andreas at Pallett Creek would obviously happen again. The challenge would be in determining *when,* for Pallett Creek, Los Angeles, and for all other areas seismologically in harm's way.

And while the dirt had been flying at Pallett Creek, on opposite sides of the planet new hope had broken out that perhaps there were ways to do it.

Chapter 16

Beijing (Peking), People's Republic of China—July 28, 1976

The offices of the State Seismological Bureau were quiet and nearly empty in the predawn darkness of summertime Beijing, where only a few personnel remained on duty to monitor the twenty-four-hour-a-day seismographic network and receive incoming calls and teletypes. With more than ten thousand Chinese citizens engaged in watching for early indications of earthquakes throughout the far-flung nation, messages arrived at all hours.

With the vast majority of the one billion men, women, and children in China still living in mud-brick, tile-roofed, unreinforced masonry houses, the fact that much of the nation was riddled with major faults and tectonically active seismic zones was very well understood. Millions of Chinese had died in previous centuries when large or great earthquakes collapsed their brittle homes, and the building materials had changed little over the years in the confines of the ancient civilization that was China.[1]

In 1966, for instance, a couple of massive shocks fragmented houses and buildings in a region two hundred miles south of Beijing, killing thousands. As Mao Zedong and Premier Zhou Enlai were beginning the disastrous (and murderous) Cultural Revolution (which was to rage for ten years and set Chinese modernization back twenty), Zhou also began a "People's War on Earthquakes." He had been shocked by the destruction and the suffering in the Hsing'tai region.

Within the framework of massive social upheaval, and despite the rout of the nation's scientists and intellectuals (sent into the countryside by the thousands to be retrained by the *Red Book*–waving peasants), the Chinese somehow managed significant advances in seismic research and seismic knowledge. By 1974 they

225

had set up a nationwide army of 10,000 full-time seismic observers, thousands of local monitoring stations and seismographs, 250 regional seismic stations, and 17 major observatories. The amazing network of people and instruments set about monitoring tremors, well water levels, animal behavior, radon gas emissions in wells, strain gauges, and numerous other possible precursors (many such monitoring efforts helped quietly by the displaced expertise of banished scientific minds).[2]

And by 1975 it had paid off.

Nearly 300 miles to the northeast of Beijing in southern Liaoning Province, Manchuria (about 320 miles north-northwest of Seoul, South Korea), something was happening. The seismologists and the observers alike knew that the continuous reports of everything from weird animal behavior to small swarms of earth tremors marked more than just an active seismic zone; they were the chatterings of a tectonic warning. Since the Hsing'tai disaster, the epicenters of a number of intermediate-magnitude quakes seemed to be "walking" toward the southern Manchurian region, and Liaoning Province in particular. The port of Luda (Dairen) had been rocked by a massive quake in 1856 (a year before the Fort Tejon quake in California), but there had been little industrialization and fewer people at the time. Now, as the menacing northwest march of epicenters continued, the fact that no quakes had occurred in the province for fully 119 years was worrisome in itself. In addition, after much surveying and monitoring, the seismologists had discovered that something was lifting the area around Haicheng and Yingkou, and tilting it slightly to the northwest.

From January through May 1974 the nearby tremors increased to a rate fully five times that of normal years, and the Beijing seismologists decided to put their reputations on the line: They issued a tentative forecast for a major quake within two years.

On December 22, 1974, another swarm of quakes began, the largest measuring just under 5.0 (M_L Richter magnitude). In response, the Seismological Bureau tightened its forecast: Expect the quake, they said, in the first six months of 1976. By the first of February the Beijing office was knee-deep in reports from the area. Wells were bubbling, animals were doing exceedingly odd things at unpredictable times, and most of the measured and observed parameters were registering in one direction or another.

Then, on the morning of February 4, a swarm of more than five hundred minor tremors shuddered and rattled through the region, reaching a crescendo with an ominous M_L 4.8 jolt, followed by abrupt, absolute seismic quiet.

Suddenly it all had stopped. There were no tremors, no microquakes, and no jolts. No seismic waves of any sort wiggled the seismograph needles. The ominous threat contained in those now-straight lines on the seismograph drums was not lost on the scientists in Beijing. The minutes of seismic quiescence built like the image of a swollen reservoir filling to the breaking point behind a temporary dam.

The seismologists of the State Seismological Bureau, being Chinese, were all very well trained both as scientists and as political realists. They were acutely aware that most difficulties in Chinese life must be considered a political problem, and by that measure, this one was a granddaddy.

They knew they had the power to order the population of several million people out of their homes, and that in their society the people (for the most part) would obey. They also knew that the temperatures in Haicheng and Ying kou were below freezing. And, they remembered only too well how embarrassed they had been over the issuance of a false alarm a few months before—a well-meaning evacuation order that had sent thousands of people fleeing their homes into the Manchurian winter at Panshan (several hundred miles to the northeast), only to be followed by continuous seismic calm.

But the sudden quiet in this case—and after years of activity —was unnerving. While the remaining minutes of the morning of February 4 ticked by with flat seismogram tracings, a worried consensus began to develop as the seismologists slowly resolved their political and sociological worries. Obviously, the consequences if they were right and did nothing would be far worse than the consequences of issuing another false alarm. The total absence of seismic waves could mean only one thing: A great quake was imminent. By 2:00 P.M. they could stand it no longer, and the order went out to evacuate.

Tens of thousand of Chinese began extinguishing cooking fires, shutting down machinery in scores of factories throughout the heavily industrialized area, collecting food and blankets, and setting up camp on lawns and in parks. Three million people were affected, all of them told to expect a cataclysmic earthquake sometime in the next few hours. As the seismologists knew only too well, the audacity of their prediction in naming place, time, and magnitude was unprecedented.

It was also dead right.

At 7:36 P.M. the last snag holding back the dam of seismic strain below the region fragmented, and the rock faces below jerked past each other along one of the major fault planes, pulsing a torrent of P and S waves from the focus of the break. First the compression or primary waves (push-pull waves; P waves), roared beneath them, followed within seconds by the side-to-side ruinous undulations of the secondary waves (S waves). The monstrous waves of pulsed S wave energy had roared a short distance to the surface of the Chinese mainland, and were now yanking the foundations of the cities to one side while throwing them upward in violent and sickening waves of movement, and doing what all great Chinese earthquakes traditionally have done in a nation that has limited lumber resources and great need of masonry for building their homes: destroying 90 percent of the structures within seconds.

As the roofs fell and the walls crumbled, great sheets of strange lights flashed across the sky in all directions, clearly witnessed by millions of frightened people.[3] Rail lines twisted like spaghetti, bridges and highways collapsed, sandblows spouted all throughout the area, sending jets of sandy water fifteen feet in the air, and factories fragmented as if hit by a nuclear burst. In 120 seconds southern Liaoning Province lay mortally wounded, and the towns of Haicheng and Yingkou lay utterly destroyed.

However, of the three million Chinese citizens who had fled their deathtrap homes and businesses, only three hundred had died.

As the shell-shocked but living residents began to pick up the pieces, and the Seismological Bureau in Beijing realized that it had averted an unspeakable human catastrophe, the word of the Chinese scientific triumph began to spread to the rest of the planet almost as rapidly as the powerful P and S waves that announced the great quake to a thousand seismographs worldwide.

The successful prediction was a stunning orchestration of manpower, scientific prowess, insight, information, government support, popular cooperation, and bureaucratic intestinal fortitude in the face of dangerous odds. Few outside the People's Republic of China really appreciated how dangerous (politically, professionally, and personally) had been the actions of the seismologists in Beijing. The fact that mattered to the world—especially the world of seismology—was the profound and undeniable realization that the growing expertise of the science of seismology had directly contributed to the saving of perhaps millions of fellow human beings.

It did not mean that suddenly all earthquakes, there or elsewhere, had become predictable as to place, time, and magnitude, but, to any rational scientist who had ever considered the question—to every governmental official or municipal leader who had ever faced the dilemma of what to do—the Haicheng forecast meant that the possibility of successful earthquake prediction as a tool of the overall process of earthquake hazard mitigation held greater credibility than the day before.

That realization alone would be of great force and influence in the following seventeen months, especially in the United States.

Even within the quiet halls of the crowded Seismological Bureau offices, the relative quiet of the early-morning hours of July 28, 1976, was in marked contrast with the din of daytime Beijing. The sound of passing vehicles could be heard periodically outside the windows—the muffled sounds of engine and tires rising above the chatter and buzz of nighttime insects, then diminishing again, as the capital slept. In a few hours the cadre of scientists and assistants would arrive once more in a wave of bicycle-borne humanity as the constant roar of the great city rose to full cry in the background.

And today, one of the areas waiting for more study would be the intensely conflicting data coming from an area just a hundred miles east of Beijing, a city of one million known as Tangshan.

There had been a number of medium-size tremors in the area of the industrial city the year before (just after the successfully predicted Yingkou-Haicheng quake), but there was a growing concern that perhaps those tremors were something other than aftershocks of the Haicheng quake. Maybe, in fact, they were precursors of a larger quake coming in the Tangshan area. The scientists knew that a major fault ran exactly beneath Tangshan; but there was no record of its having caused an earthquake in recorded history, and in China recorded history encompasses several thousand years.

Nevertheless, the bureau had decided to lace the area with a web of sensors and surveillance, which documented a few puzzling magnetic changes and gravitational anomalies, but which in the end justified no more than a carefully vague forecast that there might be a large earthquake in the area sometime in the future.

By late July there were scattered reports of strange animal behavior and fluctuating well water levels, but no clear pattern had emerged. During the dog days of July in the mainland heat of Beijing, the seismologists had pored over the conflicting reports and agreed merely to keep watching. The Haicheng prediction had been a resounding success, but in that case the indications that something was going to happen had become overwhelming to the practiced scientific mind. The situation in Tangshan, on the other hand, was indeterminate.

Just prior to 4:00 A.M., while twenty-three members of a visiting French delgation slept in their Tangshan hotel rooms a hundred miles east of Beijing, the lights suddenly went on. In milliseconds some of the visitors along with hundreds of Tangshan residents awoke to an amazing display of red and white lights in the sky outside, lights flashing like an aurora borealis gone berserk, reflecting through their windows, booming away silently like sheet lighting from a violent storm—yet without a storm. One second it had been dark; now it was bright as daylight. Those who watched searched their respective minds and memories for an explanation—as did other startled people up to two hundred miles away in all directions.

What on earth?

As the question formed in a thousand minds, the long-dormant fault beneath Tangshan was disintegrating a last snag that had held back unmeasurable seismic strain accumulated over centuries, and hundreds of square miles of unseen rock faces rumbled past each other just a few miles below Tangshan, sending an incredibly powerful pulse of P and S waves that arrived at the surface almost simultaneously, striking the foundation of the city like a mammoth sledgehammer, propelling everything upward with accelerations exceeding one gravity, hurling thousands of people into the ceilings of the mud-brick, masonry, and tile homes, which instantly shattered, the roofs dislodging and descending on top of them, crashing back down with the other side of the very first wave. With the city simultaneously in the agonizing grip of unbelievably massive transverse wave fronts shaking the terrain like some sort of monstrous, angry dog, Tangshan simply collapsed.

230

Surface faults rippled through the middle of the city like snakes as buildings disintegrated, roads and canals that crossed the faults were ripped apart laterally (some places with displacements of four feet or more), and almost all of Tangshan's industrial facilities were reduced to rubble. The wave fronts ripped into Beijing as well, splitting a major hotel, destroying some older structures, shattering glass throughout the capital, throwing the contents of desks (including those at the Seismological Bureau) on the floors, and sending millions of residents into the streets—some of whom remained there, living outdoors for days to wait out the inevitable aftershocks.

In what was left of Tangshan, the hotel housing the French delegation had come apart with the first shock, somehow killing only one of the group. The stunned survivors, adrift in a sea of wreckage, picked their way barefoot through the rubble, bruised and shaken—and amazed to be alive.

The same, however, could not be said for the endless ocean of ruined masonry and embedded humanity in all directions. When the shaking had stopped, well over half a million men, women, and children—a population greater than the number of Americans who reside in Washington, D.C.—lay crushed to death or dying beneath the rubble of their buildings.

The deeply shocked and embarrassed seismologists who scrambled to get to the bureau in Beijing within hours of the Tangshan disaster knew only that a catclysmic earthquake had occurred without the benefit of a useful prediction. They were horrified to find it was Tangshan. Amidst the despair that permeated the Seismological Bureau with each upward revision of the death toll, there was a chilling sense of failure and hopelessness in the face of nature. China had thrown societal effort and resources into preventing this sort of thing from ever happening again—and the year before all their hard work had saved millions. But this time no wells had bubbled, no earthquake swarms had provided prior warning, and no clear and certain danger had given the scientists any reason to call for an evacuation. They had not failed, but their method had—at least insofar as the seismologist in Beijing or elsewhere might have considered it consistent and reliable. Clearly, routine short-term prediction of killer earthquakes was not yet an operable reality.

Chinese government officials, feeling acute disgrace at being unable to control their own destiny, internationally embarrassed by the utter reversal of their 1975 Haicheng prediction, which had been a triumph of Chinese scientific ability and public resolve, acted with characteristic totalitarian insularity and refused to acknowledge the details or the scope of Tangshan's death. Officially they would admit that a great earthquake had occurred (they could hardly deny it; worldwide seismographs, the French delegation, and Western visitors to Beijing brought the news within days to the rest of the world), but there were to be no discussions of death tolls or damage, no foreign visitors, no foreign seismologists, and no admission of failure. To the rest of the world, China would simply pretend the great Tangshan disaster had never happened (in terms of social and human impact).

Nevertheless, one of the Frenchmen who had returned home told a waiting world press that in the whole of Tangshan he had seen one solitary smokestack still standing, and that in the midst of hundreds of thousands of people, he had seen only handfuls of survivors—nothing more.

But when so many members of the human family perish in modern times, the reality cannot be suppressed forever. Within months Western experts had arrived at a death toll of between 660,000 and 750,000. In other words, Tangshan had been the greatest killer earthquake on the planet in four hundred years.

There was no doubt that the growing excitement over the possibility of earthquake predictive methods (which had grown substantially in the wake of the Haicheng success) had suffered a heavy blow with the Tangshan cataclysm. But by no means was it dead or dying. After all, Haicheng had proved that under certain circumstances at least some great quakes could be predicted in the short term, and outside China there had been many new and promising advances that had in no way fallen victim to Tangshan's sudden, unheralded onset. Perhaps the most exciting of those new methods had originated with a Russian discovery which itself grew out of a major human tragedy.

In October 1948 nearly twenty thousand people had been obliterated by a catastrophic earthquake that roared in without warning along the northern rift zone of the Kopet Dagh Mountains in the extreme south-central Soviet Union city of Ashkhabad, 20 miles north of the Iranian border, and 280 miles east of the Caspian Sea. Nine months later another monstrous quake rumbled through the Garm region of rugged mountains in Soviet Tadzhikistan (700 miles east of Ashkhabad), crushing the village of Khait along with twelve thousand residents beneath a tremendous rockslide.

Even in Joseph Stalin's Russia that was too much. The murderous Russian dictator had never hesitated to slaughter his own citizens by the tens of thousands for the flimsiest of political reasons, but natural disasters which killed his subjects without his authorization were irritants—and economically disruptive. Accordingly, the Soviet Academy of Sciences was mobilized to find ways of preventing such disasters from striking without warning, and a large-scale study of the seismically dangerous Garm region began in earnest. The ensuing years of geologic and seismologic measurements and observations produced warehouses of information, but fifteen years passed before the Soviets had sifted a significant finding from their incredible data base. In an international geophysical symposium in Moscow during 1971—four years after the international death of the traditionalist view of the earth and the acceptance of plate tectonics—the Russians reported that before earthquakes, the seismic waves were slowing down as they traveled through the rocks.

The ratio of the speed of P waves and S waves is always the same, or so it had been thought. That constant ratio was the very factor that enabled seismologists to read a seismic wave at any distant location on Planet Earth, and to calculate rapidly the distance of the originating earthquake by finding the difference in the arrival time of the first P wave from the later arrival of the first S wave, then applying the fixed ratio of 1.75 (P waves, in other words, travel 1.75 times faster than S waves).

But the Russians had noticed that prior to earthquakes in the Garm region, the ratio seemed to change, and dropped as low as 1.6. The drop could go on for days or months or even years, and there seemed to be a correlation between the length of time the drop continued and the size of the earthquake that eventually followed.

The revelation created an invigorating sensation of a possible breakthrough. Was this the key? Was this the long-sought mechanism that would always work exactly the same anywhere on earth, and would permit accurate earthquake predictions?

American seismologists, including Dr. Lynn Sykes of the Lamont-Doherty Geological Observatory in New York (who had pio-

233

neered many of the marine geological discoveries of seafloor spreading that in turn helped prove the theory of plate tectonics), returned to the United States interested but skeptical.

Seven years before, Dr. William Brace of MIT had noticed that when rocks are squeezed under tremendous pressure in a laboratory environment, a rather strange thing happened just before they shattered: The rock would swell. Because of thousands of hairline fractures that appeared just before failure of the rock, its volume would increase slightly, and along with such swelling came a fascinating change in its ability to transmit high-frequency waves.[4]

Lynn Sykes assigned one of his graduate students to a doctoral program centered on the Soviet finding, and with the results of those efforts and those of a growing number of excited seismologists in the United States, a picture began to emerge of this process, which was called dilatancy.

The seismograms for many small earthquakes and for the 1971 San Fernando earthquake, when reexamined, all seemed to show the very same phenomenon noticed by the Soviets: For a period of time—years in the case of large quakes—the P waves slowed down, then returned to normal, followed by the quake. There was, in addition, a predictable correlation between the length of time the slowdown continued, and both the size and the timing of the eventual quake. Given Dr. Brace's experiments, it appeared that rocks in a fault zone under increasing pressure, just before breaking and permitting the fault to move, would develop the same network of hairline fractures. Since the fractures would be voids, filled with air if with anything, compressional P waves would not be able to travel through the rock as quickly, and would slow down. That slowdown could be spotted in an instant by any seismologist reading any seismogram, and such a discovery would be a warning that the rocks were under increasing compressional strain.

When groundwater eventually filled those cracks, the speed of the P waves would return to normal. But the presence of water would lubricate and hasten the failure of the rocks and the slippage of whatever fault was involved. Within a certain period of time, the earthquake which had been building would finally occur. That, too, could be spotted in advance by a seismologist, especially one who had noted the initial slowdown and had been watching for the P waves to return to normal in an area already suspected to be building toward a quake.

234

"If all this holds up," one eminent seismologist postulated very much off the record in 1976, "we may have found the key that will give us the ability to accurately predict earthquakes based on the slowdown of the P waves, and we may even be able to issue short-term warnings when the P wave speeds return to normal. It seems too simple, I know, but that's where we are."

By the time the State Seismographical Bureau of China had issued its first warning about Haicheng, it, too, was watching the speed of P waves. (Haicheng, however, showed no evidence of the slowdown. Nor, for that matter, did Tangshan.)

As the seismological community emerged from the crushing news of Tangshan's death, one bright hope stayed intact, from the halls of Menlo Park to the halls of the U.S. Congress. With dilatancy possibly handing the scientists a key to short-term prediction, and with plate tectonics providing the explanation of the basic planetary engine which propelled earthquakes, there was every reason to believe that someday in the future the prediction of earthquakes could become a significant part of mitigating the hazard of earthquakes.

And that recognition in itself combined with political happenstance and a disturbing phenomenon called the Palmdale Bulge to create a critical mass on Capitol Hill.

Palmdale, in the Mojave Desert north of Los Angeles, sits astride the San Andreas Fault not far to the southeast of Fort Tejon—an area of the fault which had been locked tightly since 1857. Suddenly, in 1975, however, USGS scientists discovered that Palmdale was rising. When elevation survey data from 1959 were compared with those of 1975, it appeared that the entire Palmdale area—at least thirty-two thousand square miles of desert—had risen as much as eighteen inches. In view of its location on a locked portion of the largest exposed active fault in the country, even a first-year geology student could find reason to believe that the Palmdale Bulge (as it was quickly dubbed) and the "big one" (the great earthquake that lay in Southern California's future) were related. The bulge just had to be a precursor of the impending earthquake, but how could it be used to determine a specific date or a reasonably precise time period in which the inevitable tectonic snap would occur? From F.E.M.A. in Washington to the California Seismic

Safety Commission (which had just been established in 1975), concern began to grow over what to do, and when to do it.

By the first months of 1977 with a new president, Jimmy Carter, in the White House, a bill to establish a national earthquake hazards reduction program, which had been batted down for five years in a row in Congress, finally attained administration support. In the previous session of 1976 the Senate had passed the bill only to have it defeated by the House, largely because the Ford administration believed there were already enough federal agencies with authority to handle disaster preparedness.

But the problem was not disaster preparedness, or preparing to react *after* a disaster had occurred. The problem was learning how to prepare *before* a disaster, and government on all levels was unfamiliar and uncomfortable with such an approach.

The problem was finding ways to fund basic research, and to foster basic education of the citizenry that earthquake hazards could be minimized if older, highly vulnerable buildings were torn down or reinforced, new building codes were encouraged in all seismic areas, and people were taught what to do ahead of time to prepare their homes and themselves for surviving the aftermath of a major quake—whether in New York City or Los Angeles. In addition, there was a crying need for better coordination of disaster response agencies, especially in areas that didn't realize they could be sitting on a seismic bomb.

The bill had grown out of the ideas and efforts of the 1970 Steinbrugge task force and the upset over the pitifully inadequate state of preparation exposed by the 1971 San Fernando quake. But its greatest contribution would be to focus the nation's attention on the fact that by no stretch of the imagination were earthquakes simply a "West Coast problem" or an "Alaska problem." Fully thirty-nine states were high-risk zones, and most of the rest would bear the economic brunt for a disaster anywhere else.[5]

The Palmdale Bulge provided the final shove over the top. Answers were needed to questions of what the bulge meant, and such answers would cost money in the form of research and coordination of projects to figure out ways of predicting earthquakes. With the success of Haicheng (and despite the disaster of Tangshan), the excitement over the dilatancy theory, and the growing confidence of the seismological community that it was in full cry on the trail of ways to predict the place, size, and time of damaging earthquakes, prediction became the goal. That coupled with worry over the Palmdale Bulge and the last-minute support of the outgoing Ford administration (along with the support of the incoming Carter administration) to get it past both houses of Congress and onto the President's desk—at the same time Kerry Sieh was finalizing his doctoral thesis, which would provide a significant leap forward in both prediction and the new infant science of paleoseismology.

The Earthquake Hazards Reduction Act of 1977 would not be the final solution, but it would be the start of a consensus that might one day lead to a full national resolve. At long, long last the United States was going to pull its head at least partway out of the sand and face the fact that Americans did not have to wait helplessly to be victims of seismic disasters.

Chapter 17

Pasadena, California—November 29, 1978

Karen McNally was practically yelling at her car radio as she pressed the accelerator toward the floor, the vehicle's speedometer already reporting illicit velocities to an inattentive driver.

"Where is it? *Where?*"

Some announcer in some station somewhere in the Los Angeles area had read the item—obviously a fast-breaking five-bell story off the news wires—but he hadn't said enough.

As she wove between several cars, trying to make headway through the usual L.A. freeway traffic toward Caltech in Pasadena where she could get answers, the possibility that this was the very thing she had been waiting for and working for during the past nine months filled her with a sense of frustration.

"There has been," the announcer had said, "a major earthquake in Mexico."

"Oh, damn!" had been Karen's first response. The squashed accelerator had come a few seconds later.

I'll bet this is our quake! The words echoed in her head as she changed lanes once again, downtown Pasadena sliding by her now, the off ramp leading to Caltech just two miles ahead.

The image of her colleagues from both the United States and Mexico tending the array of seismographs placed around the southern coastline of Mexico in the state of Oaxaca, 290 miles south of Mexico City—the thought that the very earthquake they were trying to capture might have occurred on the very day she had returned to the United States to finish a technical paper (which had gone begging for weeks)—was very upsetting. But it was an upset filled with excitement that the earthquake prediction might have come true on schedule, and perhaps—just perhaps—right in the middle of their seismograph network.

"Where, dammit, *where?*"

News from everywhere else poured from the radio, but there was no further mention of the quake. Karen was still fumbling with the tuning knobs as she pulled up in front of the Caltech lab and abandoned the car to race inside to the seismograph drums.

All the needles had jumped toward the mechanical stops with the wave arrivals of a genuine great quake, and initial calculations (which were already under way when she burst through the door) seemed to indicate that the tremendous pulse of seismic energy was coming from south of Mexico City, from the southern coast of Mexico.

Karen's first suspicion was exactly right. It was indeed her earthquake!

A team of Texas seismologists had first indentified the area as ripe for a seismic "event" a year before in 1977, predicting a 7.25 to a 7.75 great quake within one and a half years. But she had been the first to build a net of seismographs in an attempt to "trap" the quake they thought was coming. Now here it was, roaring in on schedule (nine months into an eighteen-month forecast) and at an M_s magnitude of 7.8, which was on the upper end of their magnitude prediction.

Karen McNally, Ph.D., senior research fellow at Caltech and one of the brightest young seismologists on the trail of earthquake prediction, was ecstatic—and eager to get right back to Los Angeles International Airport and aboard any flight that could carry her south once again. Her paper could wait.

Something had been missing from the seismic puzzle of Mexico's southern coast. The fact that a certain area near Oaxaca had not suffered a major earthquake since 1928 had been noticed by seismologists at the Geophysics Laboratory at University of Texas (UT) at Galveston as they pored over some global seismicity data in 1977.[1]

The Texas team realized that a 185-mile stretch of seacoast was involved—an area which had stayed still while areas of coastline to the northwest or to the east (into Central America) had suffered great quakes much more recently. Yet the Oaxaca area of Mexico's coast sits atop a classic seismic bomb—a highly active subduction zone in which the floor of the Pacific Ocean (the Cocos plate at that point) is being shoved beneath the North American plate near its

240

southern border with the Caribbean plate. Since great quakes had occurred many times in Oaxaca's past, and since great quakes had occurred on either side of that 185-mile-wide sector in recent years, and further, since the rate of subduction for the plates could be assumed to be the same for the Oaxaca sector as well as the adjacent sectors, logic would dictate, they pointed out, that at some point in the not so distant future another great quake would take place under or near Oaxaca.

In other words, the Oaxaca sector was a "seismic gap," an area along a fault or subduction zone which could be identified as due or overdue for an earthquake because of the rate of plate movement and the history of earthquakes on either side of the gap.

It was the validation of the theory, not the theory itself, that was new. Japanese seismologist A. Inamura had identified Tokyo as sitting on a seismic gap before 1923. Since continents were thought to be stationary at that time, his method involved a study of past earthquakes in the Tokyo area. He had concluded that if the adjacent coastal areas were periodically hit by major quakes, and if they had suffered such quakes more recently than the last one in Tokyo (as was the case), then Tokyo was overdue. Tokyo, he said, must be sitting on a seismic gap—a gap which would be considered filled only when an earthquake of substantial size occurred.

Sure enough, Tokyo was hit in 1923 by a devastating quake which touched off a ruinous fire storm and killed 140,000 Japanese. Five years later, in 1928, Inamura identified another seismic gap: the Tokaido-Nankaido region in southwestern Japan, which was subsequently "filled" by two more great quakes in 1944 and 1946—events which further verified that he was on to a new method that might just mark the threshold of earthquake forecasting.[2]

But in Oaxaca's case, there was another factor. Not only had the region been devoid of major earthquakes, it had been devoid of *all* earthquakes large and small since 1973. Since subduction zone pressures never stop, sudden cessation of seismic activity in the vicinity of a subduction zone means something has really welded the plates together far below. Naturally that "weld," or asperity, cannot last beyond a certain level of strain, so the day inevitably will come when the snag breaks, the plates lurch forward, massive amounts of previously stored tectonic energy are released as the strain dissipates, and the region is again lashed by seismic waves.

A developing theory of subduction zone quakes held that such seismic gaps went through two phases before the inevitable major earthquake. During a so-called alpha phase (which might start many decades after the last major earthquake), all activity large and small would cease. Seismographs in the area would register little more than large ocean swells hitting the beach, passing trucks, and occasional hard landings by airliners at nearby airports. The area, in other words, would be locked tight tectonically, and would be under great, increasing stress.

The end of the alpha phase and the beginning of what was called the beta phase would be heralded by small earthquakes resuming in the area. If those small quakes and swarms of quakes (many of them too tiny to be felt by the population) resulted from the progressive fracturing of rock preparing to break under increasing strain, then there would be only a certain preparation period before the thunderous impact of a large or great quake completed the cycle.

Oaxaca, said the Texans, seemed to be in a classic alpha phase. Therefore, they reasoned, at some point in the next decade the beta phase should begin, announced by a sudden onset of small or moderate earthquakes. According to the theory, once the beta phase had begun, a great quake could not be far behind.

Discovering what a beta phase pattern looked like in living black-and-white on a seismogram, and getting a finite feel for the length of time between the beta phase onset and the main event (a M_s 7.5 earthquake or greater), were problems the Texans were eager to address. Such answers take research money, so with renewed optimism that the 1977 earthquake hazard reduction act (which was moving toward passage in the Congress) might open the floodgates for increased research funding of any program that might advance the science toward the goal of earthquake prediction, the University of Texas researchers submitted a proposal to the USGS for a two-year study costing a quarter of a million dollars. The plan was to place a sophisticated network of seismographs around the Oaxaca area in hopes of "capturing" the inevitable beta phase (as well as the eventual main earthquake). The data they could record from such a network might go a long way toward identifying the telltale signs of a subduction zone earthquake about to occur. A quarter of a million seemed a small price to pay for possible clues to prediction of great quakes that could kill thousands of people and ruin billions of dollars of property (in the absence of extensive earthquake hazard reduction programs).

242

The USGS funding officer in Menlo Park, California, however, turned it down. The 1977 bill might send a wave of new funding into the USGS the following year; but this was fiscal 1977, and the funds just weren't available yet.[3]

In the meantime, storm clouds of a sociological nature were gathering over the Mexican coast—and over Galveston. The UT, Galveston team's conclusions had been interpreted inadvertently in Mexico as a "prediction," altered from a long-range statement of probability into a forecast by a local psychic (quoted in the press), and twisted into a specific prediction by the members of a scientifically uninformed population (who had filled in the blanks on their own and arrived at a precise date the earthquake was "supposed" to occur). The entire affair had escalated within months to a near panic in Oaxaca, which culminated with a nonevent: The earthquake did not occur as "scheduled."[4]

The Mexican authorities were, to say the least, less than impressed with the state of advancement in earthquake prediction—especially that aspect which permitted carefully hedged technical forecasts to balloon into unscientific predictions of date, time, place, and magnitude.[5]

Karen McNally and several other junior and senior scientists at Caltech had followed the ideas, reports, papers, proposals, and local overreactions with great interest, looking at the same data the Texas team had digested and agreeing that the Texans' conclusions were probably right. It did appear that Oaxaca was in an alpha phase, and it was quite possible it would emerge at any time into the beta phase. It would be a tragedy if the complex seismic waves large and small that would course through the Oaxaca region when that happened were not carefully recorded for years of future study.

It was with such knowledge, and against such a background, that Dr. McNally flew to Mexico City in August 1978 at the invitation of the Institute of Geophysics (a division of the Universidad Autónoma de Mexico) to deliver a lecture to the Mexican seismologists and geophysicists looking at the same question: Is something about to happen in Oaxaca that bears close watching?

It was somewhat stuffy in the small auditorium in Mexico City—a combination of the Mexican capital's high altitude and the heat of a near-equatorial summer. Though she was enjoying the topic, it was with some relief that Karen McNally began wrapping up the talk, heading toward the question-and-answer period that would probably be the most productive part of the day. Those arrayed before her all were graduate students or practicing scientists, listening intently as she described what research American seismologists were pursuing in California, how it pertained to Mexico, and her view of the Oaxaca situation.

Speaking English (her Spanish was good but somewhat limited), Karen's voice rose and fell over a surprising range of volume, a voice of cultured smoothness on a wave of expressive tones. The daughter of highly educated Danish parents who had settled in Central California's San Joaquin Valley, her accent bore the hints of European pronunciation, rounding out a captivating verbal style that was holding the rapt attention of her English-speaking Mexican hosts and colleagues as she told them of her recent efforts to find identifiable patterns in the seismograms of recent earthquake swarms which had preceded great quakes in other parts of the world. To what extent were they precursors? Was there a characteristic "signature" of such seismic noise before a great quake? Was there, at least, a characteristic pattern in each particular locality before a great quake? Could they find, in other words, a specific pattern of small and moderate earthquakes which could be read like a fingerprint—the fingerprint of a killer subduction zone quake lurking just around the corner? Perhaps someday they could point to such a pattern and say, in effect, "This is the signature of an upcoming Alaskan quake," or, "This is the unmistakable pattern of an impending M_s 8.0 Chilean quake."

Dr. Karen McNally had been walking them verbally through a logical matrix of possible solutions when the fact that a small bell had rung somewhere in the auditorium gave way to the realization that someone had stuck his head in the side door, interrupting her.

"There's been an earthquake," he said simply, and in English, to a group of scientists who had felt nothing.

It was a rather startling sight to passing students, the gaggle of seismologists, geophysicists, and geologists following their guest lecturer and spilling out of the auditorium en masse (after having instantly decided to abandon the question-and-answer period for some more specific answers regarding the announced quake), headed at flank speed for the old, imposing Tacubayn Observatory adjacent to the university. The huge, ancient metal gates of the place creaked open slowly as the elderly record keeper let them in, conducting them at a slower, more respectful pace—like a monk leading the rabble into the inner sanctum of an ancient monastery. There were three small seismic networks in Mexico, two of them digital and modern, the third—and oldest—consisting of very basic seismographs whose inked needles on the revolving drums recorded the "bare bones" wave arrivals from a few sensors around Mexico City and a couple of outlying areas. It was to these elderly machines that the group went, fingers pointing to ink scratches on white paper, pencils flying and calculators clicking as they pinpointed the P and S wave arrivals, calculated the time difference in between, applied the mathematical ratio representing the different speeds of the two types of waves, and derived the distance. They were in Mexico City, which had been unaffected. The quake had to be on the coast. Looking at the north-south drum, the east-west drum, and the up-down drum (seismic waves are three-dimensional and, in classic seismic stations, are measured by three different seismographs, each representing one axis), Karen and company quickly calculated the direction from which the seismic undulations had come.

All the while Karen McNally knew that the Texas team had not been monitoring the Oaxaca coast in recent months and might not have seen any patterns of tiny quakes preceding this moderate one. The Texans had anticipated that Oaxaca might break its quiescence by showing how it had happened, historically, two times before. But could this be it? On one level it was far too perfect a solution—not to mention the timing. Here she was, vitally interested in just this subject and just this area. Was it possible that she could be standing here, giving a lecture on the very subject at the precise moment the region came alive? That seemed too fantastic. Too exciting. It was like finding you have five digits on a six-digit lotto ticket for several million dollars, and waiting with bated breath for the last digit. And, scientifically, this was indeed a type of lotto. Could that last number be hers?

Suddenly the calculations seemed to reach a consensus. It was a clear case of suspicions confirmed. The waves had come over three hundred kilometers, and from the south-southeast. They had come from a moderate earthquake in Oaxaca, and that could mean only one thing: The seismic quiescence had broken. The Oaxaca seismic gap had entered the beta phase, and a great quake couldn't be too far behind.

245

Dr. Karen McNally was excited! They would have to move fast. But first, they would have to find some money. Karen knew that however limited were American funds, the funds her Mexican colleagues had to work with were dismal by comparison. The Mexican scientists did, however, have a cadre of volunteer scientists and students as well as vehicles and equipment, along with some limited research funds. Karen, on the other hand, had Jack Everendon, her project manager at the USGS, to whom she normally turned for research money, and she would have to convince him to help.

Quickly returning to Pasadena, Karen McNally assembled a team of seven Caltech scientists and graduate students, and talked Everendon into approving a transfer of $3,700 from an existing USGS-funded project to finance an expedition to the Oaxaca coast. It was very obvious that time was of the essence. Since the beta phase had begun, it could be anywhere from weeks up to eighteen months before the expected great quake occurred. If they were going to be able to find distinctive characteristics in the signature of seismic waves from the small earthquakes that would probably continue up to the main break, then they had to get an array of sensitive seismometers (as well as strong-motion versions which would not go off scale in large tremors) into the field rapidly. Mexico's sparse, existing seismograph network was far too inadequate.

But $3,700? Everendon gave McNally approval for the transfer, not for new funds. But the project he was approving on an emergency basis essentially proposed to do for $3,700 what the seismologists and geophysicists at UT, Galveston had wanted to do for $250,000. Everendon seemed just as convinced Karen's quest would fall short of finding a method of prediction, but for that price, it was worth a try.

By the first week in November 1978, the network of portable seismographs was in place around the state of Oaxaca—only seven stations scattered through the wild Mexican countryside, but a network of instruments sensitive enough to find the signature, if there was one. For approximately eight days the needles traced flat lines. Then a series of small tremors rattled the area, reaching only magnitude 3.2 M_s. After mid-November it quieted down again, and for nearly two weeks, the only thing happening seismologically at the surface was the arduous daily work schedule kept by the team in constantly visiting each machine, checking and resetting the time signals (using satellite clocks for precision), changing paper, performing maintenance, and driving—constantly driving—between sites.

On November 28, a second swarm of tremors shuddered the needles, these rising to M_s 3.7, sweeping from one end of the gap landward and toward the center.

And eighteen hours later, as Karen McNally was landing at Los Angeles International Airport, the final snap occurred. With a magnitude of M_s 7.8, the great waves of seismic energy lashed out for nearly a minute, rocking and undulating the Mexican countryside (sparsely populated in that area), damaging rural towns, throwing down some stone walls, cracking adobe houses, and damaging some buildings as far away as Mexico City, 290 miles to the northwest. Had such a quake occurred underneath Los Angeles, the results would have been catastrophic. Because of its location, however, no one died.

When McNally's team members looked at the data, it was incredible. They had trapped the earthquake exactly in the middle of their portable seismographic net. With strong-motion seismograph tracings coupled with the weeks of buildup seismic activity, they had amassed an unprecedented record of a great subduction zone earthquake, including the train of microquakes that would never have registered meaningfully on the main Mexican seismic networks.

As the team members prepared to wait out the aftershock sequence (and Dr. McNally returned at high speed from L.A.), they all were very aware of what success could mean. If standard signatures could be found—if typical foreshock patterns could yield reliable formulas for calculating how long a beta phase would last before a major or great quake—seismology could take existing long-term predictions based on the identification of seismic gaps, and turn them into viable intermediate-term predictions. In fact, with enough work and enough data and a good measure of cooperation on the part of nature, it just might be that foreshock patterns could also provide reliable short-term prediction.

By February of 1979 Karen McNally was back in her Pasadena office, seismograms happily draped over a desk which in turn held various strata of books, papers, notes, information, lesson plans, and copies of professional journals. There would be years of study of the

247

reams of information from Mexico, and many more field trips to the Mexican coast to work on other seismic gap areas. But things did seem, in a somewhat disjointed way, to be falling together.

There was an excitement in the air among the seismologists, geologists, geophysicists, and even volcanologists—an excitement which went beyond the natural exhilaration of advancing the science. In part it was a continuation of the rush of enthusiasm that followed the acceptance of the plate tectonic model, and in part it was a result of additional funding and support through the 1977 Earthquake Hazard Reduction Act. For those like McNally, whose insatiable curiosity was channeled by the happy and heretical faith that each individual researcher could make a difference, the renewed chance to keep looking for the answers and clues—the hope of finding ways of predicting earthquakes—meant a limitless horizon.

But another aspect of that excitement was the general impression that having been handed the prodigious task of finding methods and constructing the systems within ten years for effective earthquake forecasting (one of the stated goals of the hazard reduction act), the geophysical community was actually meeting the challenge.

For one thing, the definition of what really constituted an earthquake prediction had already begun to change. The Chinese were responsible for starting that alteration, recognizing on reexamination that while predicting a great quake within hours could obviously save hundreds of thousands of lives, there was equal value in knowing where a great quake (or even a lesser quake) would strike sometime in the future, or in knowing that (as with seismic gaps) a quake was due within months to a few years. There were different things that a society could do when faced with different levels of predictions. Obviously a short-term warning that a major seismic calamity was due within a few hours to a few weeks would not provide sufficient time for reconstructing buildings or dams, enacting new standards of land use planning, or encouraging resettlement away from high-risk areas. A long-term prediction, however, would permit just such activity, and if the recommendations were carried out faithfully as the years passed, the value of such a prediction and the hazard-reducing actions it sparked could save thousands of lives and untold billions of dollars of property.

By the same token, an intermediate-term prediction within a few weeks to a few years would provide valuable time for rechecking existing structures and preparing emergency response agencies and functions for the inevitable.

When a particular area is identified as subject to a damaging earthquake, that fact alone is a prediction, and each stage of refinement in terms of probable time of occurrence can be of immense value to a nation. Therefore, a failure to predict precisely time, magnitude, and location within days or hours, may not be a failure at all. But that attitude had not yet been accepted in America.

The startling element, as Karen McNally would write in a professional paper a few years later, was the fact that "The locations of most large earthquakes likely to occur in the future are rather well known based on the seismic gap method, which integrates the history of previous large earthquakes, the rates of plate motion, and geologic slip rates. Similarly, the size of a future large earthquake can be estimated from the dimensions of a seismic gap."[6]

In other words, within a few years of the passage of the hazard reduction act, long-term prediction was already within the realm of possibility, and in some cases, effectively operational (for major quakes).[7]

As a result of the work of scientists like Karen McNally and Kerry Sieh, and so many others, intermediate-term forecasts were also showing great promise.[8] In the same paper ("Variations in Seismicity as a Fundamental Tool in Earthquake Prediction," published a few years later), Karen McNally characterized the progress by pointing out that: "The current stage of research is comparable to that existing prior to the understanding of plate tectonic theory. A number of systematic patterns are observed which are suggestive of underlying processes, other patterns appear random, and no unifying model has yet been found with which earthquakes can be predicted."

But as she and her colleagues knew, there would need to be a substantial revision in the understanding of just what it was that seismology was supposed to accomplish within the ten-year period foreseen by the 1977 hazard reduction act. There was growing pessimism that the problem was far more difficult than originally thought, and that pessimism was beginning to retard progress—and recognition of what had already been accomplished.

"Being perfect scientists," she explained, "we want the perfect solution. When we can't find it as readily as we want, we get frustrated, and get to thinking that perhaps we can't find a perfect solution, so the entire thrust of the research project is a failure."

The Russian-discovered, American-refined dilatancy theory was a prime example. The 1977 bill washed in on a wave of optimism created in part by dilatancy—but by 1979 the bright hope that P wave slowdown and speedup could provide a unified key had been dashed by the reality that some earthquakes exhibited no changes in wave speed, and in others the behavior patterns were not predictable. Instead of scientists' using what aspects of dilatancy might be helpful in looking for a multifaceted array of indicators that a quake was coming and when it would occur, dilatancy as a theory had been largely discredited and in too many cases discarded. There was still some value to it, though. P waves did, in fact, slow down and speed up in certain cases, and some successful predictions had been made solely on the basis of the phenomenon.

Nevertheless, by early 1979 there had been at least one stunningly successful intermediate-term prediction that had nothing to do with dilatancy—the Oaxaca quake. What's more, by January 1979 another intermediate-term forecast had been made with a degree of courage which gave real hope to the scientific community that perhaps—despite the highly restrictive definition of what a prediction was supposed to be—real progress was being made.

Specifically a pattern of small tremors (anomalous seismicity, they were called) had occurred six months prior to a pair of large earthquakes (magnitude M_s 7.1 and 6.9) in the High Sierras of California in 1954. The seismic murmurings had begun after a lengthy period of seismic quiescence, and the record of the ensuing flurry of activity had been preserved on older seismograph tracings.

Suddenly, in late 1978, after another period of quiet, the same pattern began again. Several seismologists who had paid close attention to Karen McNally's success in Oaxaca concluded that what they had was a pattern preceding an earthquake, and taking a deep breath, they forecast what they thought was coming: a large quake in the vicinity of the beautiful resort community of Mammoth Lakes, California, nestled in the High Sierras to the east of Yosemite, at the north end of the Owens Valley, and in a fascinating formation ringed by ridgelike volcanic cliffs known as Long Valley.

The prediction, it seemed, was only the beginning.

Chapter 18

Vancouver, Washington—
Thursday, May 22, 1980

As Rob Wesson looked up, the President of the United States came through the door.

Sweeping in suddenly past two typically dour Secret Service men and accompanied by Dr. Frank Press, his science advisor, Jimmy Carter looked around the crowded second-story office as a half dozen USGS scientists looked back in stunned silence.

They knew the President was due to visit the ground-floor level of the U.S. Forest Service headquarters in Vancouver, but they had intended to stay out of the way. Now, without warning, he was in their midst.

The smoking hulk that had been the beautiful snowcapped Mount St. Helens had drawn the constant attention of the survey's volcanologists for the previous two months, as a growing cadre of scientists edged ever closer to an open prediction of the cataclysmic explosion that, in fact, occurred on Sunday morning, May 18, at 8:27 A.M. Now, four days later, deeply shocked by the volcanic eruption which had killed sixty-one people (including USGS volcanologist Dr. David Johnston), spread ash over a quarter of the nation, halted the economy of Washington State for several days, and grabbed the attention of the world, the President had come to see for himself. U.S. Forest Service headquarters in Vancouver—the building being used as a temporary headquarters by the USGS "mission"—was the first stop. Carter would fly around the mountain by helicopter later in the day.

"Hello, Frank." Dr. Robert Wesson, still stunned, extended his hand to the familiar form of Frank Press, who was standing slightly in front of President Carter. It seemed the appropriate thing to do. No one else had moved.

The President was searching for something to say, and someone to say it to, amidst a rather awkward situation. The roomful of scientists were still frozen in awed silence, all staring at the commander in chief and waiting for someone to break the ice.

"Rob! How are you?" Dr. Press responded.

Carter turned toward Wesson and Press.

"You two know each other?" The familiar Georgian accent broke the silence as Dr. Press began introductions, starting with Wesson, who had been sent out hours after the explosion as the personal representative of the USGS director, Bill Menard.

"Certainly. Mr. President, meet Dr. Robert Wesson of the USGS."

Rob Wesson had not wanted to come to Vancouver, but the relationship between the USGS director and the field detachment monitoring the explosive situation at St. Helens had been choked by poor communication through the intermediate bureaucratic layers, and Menard wanted a personal representative on the scene. Wesson tried, unsuccessfully, to talk him out of it, then caught a red-eye flight on Sunday to Portland, Oregon, arriving at the USGS outpost in Vancouver in time to watch the awful expression on the face of the USGS team leader as he got the news of Dr. David Johnston's last radioed words:

"Vancouver . . . Vancouver, this is it!"

"This mountain is a powder keg, and the fuse is lit," Johnston had told the press a month earlier, ". . . but we don't know how long the fuse is." The thirty-year-old Ph.D. in geology from the University of Washington had made several helicopter-borne dashes into the new crater of the reawakening volcano after it cleared its throat with ash plume eruptions in late March. On Sunday morning, May 18, 1980, Johnston awoke from his first night on the ridge south of Coldwater Creek, dubbed Coldwater II, and began checking the array of monitoring instruments trained on the deadly mountain, which stood a mere six miles away. At dawn he had radioed that all was quiet and beautiful, the sun just breaking over the verdant forest to the east, a wisp of steam and ash curling from the conical top of the peak.

Suddenly, at 8:27 A.M., an earthquake of 5.0 magnitude shook the mountain, the epicenter from somewhere beneath, the seismic waves radiating upward to shake the north face of the volcano,

252

which had been bulging—swelling—at the rate of five feet per day during the last few weeks, a bulge now some three hundred feet displaced from normal. With the episodic earthquakes that had rocked the area before the first ash plume of March (announcing the movement of magma beneath and the reactivation of the volatile mountain) and the more recent harmonic tremors, indicating larger amounts of liquid rock flowing somewhere below, the precursors of a possible major eruption were obvious. Johnston and many others fully expected the mountain to erupt in a major, vertical explosion so typical of subduction zone volcanoes with magma rich in silica.[1]

It was these worries that had prompted Washington Governor Dixy Lee Ray—herself an accomplished scientist and former head of the Nuclear Regulatory Commission—to establish a "red zone" around the mountain, giving state officials and county officials monstrous headaches in controlling the entries and exits of citizens and residents who couldn't believe the threat was real.

At 8:27 A.M. David Johnston felt the tremors. He watched the mountain for the next few minutes, the possibility of further quakes or some activity triggered by the quake now very high. No volcanologist at that point would have been surprised to see a monstrous plume of ash and steam and pyroclastic material (molten and partially cooled rock in a mixture of searing, glowing gases) shoot straight up from the peak, perhaps taking much of the top cone with it.

Instead, at 8:32:37, five minutes after the seismic waves had unhinged the critical structure of the north face—the lid of the pressure cooker—a landslide began on the north flank, a debris flow descending down in a mammoth movement of material at the very spot that Johnston and others had documented the worrisome bulge, and at the very point where an ancient magma flow had formed a massive plug, bottling up the incredible forces of the volcanic bomb which had pressurized behind the wall of rock on St. Helens' flank.

In mere seconds the falling curtain of rock was replaced by the plume of ash and steam which came shooting out laterally, to the north, toward Johnston's position, followed by a vertical plume and then a lateral blast. In the seconds after the blast had started, Johnston grabbed the microphone of his VHF radio with excitement

253

tinging his voice, beginning the unfinished message to Vancouver: ". . . this is it!"

Fourteen seconds after the start of the landslide, a cataclysmic surge of pyroclastic material carried on a deadly two-hundred-mile-per-hour wave of superheated gases shot out to the north, taking approximately one minute and forty-nine seconds to reach Coldwater II, blowing the young geologist off the ridge as it seared him and his equipment with unsurvivable temperatures cloaked in a fog of unbreathable ash.

President Carter was shocked by the destruction he saw below as the presidential party flew back and forth around the smoking remnants of what had been the crown jewel in the stunning array of the Cascadia volcanoes. It looked like a moonscape, he remarked, as several officials, including Governor Ray, pointed out various areas and discussed the differing problems and needs. Without question this segment of Washington was a disaster area, and without question federal assistance would be needed in significant amounts. Most of the budget of the state for emergency services had already been exhausted.

The governor had been faced with an agonizing two months of controversy. Would St. Helens blow up or not? That was the central question. How much responsibility should the state take to prevent people from putting themselves in harm's way? Where was the dividing line between our hallowed freedoms to determine our own individual levels of acceptable risk, and the state's responsibility for preserving life and property? As property owners in the region griped and worried, resisting evacuation efforts while listening attentively to the opinions of the uneasy scientists and government leaders, the agony of predicting a major and deadly geologic event became all too clear.

The USGS team members kept monitoring Mount St. Helens with the increasing belief that an explosion was coming, but with a corresponding reluctance to make that a blanket prediction. Though they were besieged for conclusions and opinions, it was all too obvious that the social and economic consequences of making the wrong call could be severe, and no one really knew what the mountain was going to do. Volcanology was shrouded in more mystery and uncertainty than was seismology.

As the first week of May passed, it was puzzling to realize that

254

even with a smoking hole in the top of the mountain spouting ash, and a cadre of scientists monitoring earth tremors and saying worried, cautious things, there were still scores of people in the area refusing to believe that the mountain was dangerous. The Mount St. Helens they knew—the Spirit Lake they loved—had never been blown away before in their lifetimes. Why should they expect such a result now? Even with eruptions as recent as mid-April 1857 to validate its status as an active and dangerous volcano, Washington state and county officials faced a constant battle enforcing the evacuation of the red zone around the mountain.

One of those battles had been lost from the first, as Spirit Lake resident Harry Truman (no relation to the former president) refused to leave the mountain and his commercial lodge no matter how serious the threat. Truman's constant interviews on radio and TV in the weeks before the explosion (at the behest of a fascinated media) made him an overnight celebrity, but on May 18 he paid the ultimate price: He and his lodge were swept away and buried by the first wave of firey, pyroclastic materials down the north slope.

And with the explosion of May 18th came the typical finger pointing and recriminations over those who were in the zone, and who did not come out. People such as Dr. David Johnston were there for a valid purpose—many more were not. Despite the hundreds (if not thousands) of lives saved by the forthright actions of the state, the dark worry of what would have become of the evacuation effort if it had been Mount Rainier and the populated regions of Pierce County (which contains the city of Tacoma, among others) that had been threatened weighed heavily on the minds of the officials involved. There were serious lessons there. In fact, St. Helens, as bad as it was, was merely a warning. Someday, undoubtedly, Mount Rainier could reawaken as well.

Air Force One had reached cruising altitude as President Carter and Dr. Frank Press talked about the amazing things they had seen.

"I just can't believe the destruction down there," the President remarked at one point.

Dr. Press, long an advocate of hazard mitigation for geologic threats, especially those of earthquakes, and knowledgeable of the latest research, including Dr. Kerry Sieh's breakthrough findings on the southern San Andreas, looked Jimmy Carter in the eye.

"That, Mr. President, is nothing compared to the scope of the disaster we're going to have in Los Angeles when the great quake that's coming finally occurs."

The President was astounded. As Press filled him in on the scope of the human loss which would inevitably occur, the deaths and injuries, the loss of property in the tens of billions, and the danger to American defense installations up and down the southern coastline, Carter made the decision to form an immediate ad hoc committee within the National Security Council to look into the matter and what the country needed to do to prepare.

As much as the original paper Dr. Press had written in 1965 on earthquake hazard reduction, as much as the decade-long efforts to enact the 1977 earthquake hazards reduction bill, that one exchange between the President's science advisor and the occupant of the Oval Office pushed the national understanding of earthquake threats past another milestone. By the time Air Force One reached the ramp at Andrews Air Force Base near Washington, D.C., the framework for a rejuvenated look at the problem was in place— even as the puzzle of what was to become of Mount St. Helens deepened back in America's other Washington.

More than the ash plumes which continued to spout from the crater, more than the destruction of vast square miles of forests and industrial installations, the partial damming of the Columbia River, and the threat to the state's resources in dealing with the cleanup, there was a growing concern in Washington: Was life in the Pacific Northwest going to be the same? What had always been a beautiful, picturesque area of wooded landscapes and mountains, rivers, and inland waterways was becoming a periodic ashtray for the now squat and ugly mountain which had changed its personality overnight.

The problem was the uncertainty, and the inability of anyone in the physical sciences to answer the question: What now?

The last major eruption along the Cascade volcanic chain had rocked Northern California in 1914 with the beginning of a three-year eruption of Mount Lassen which included some spectacular displays of capricious behavior on the part of the mountain (at one point it chased a forest fire lookout down the mountainside by hurling boulders the size of houses at his lookout tower). Would St. Helens rain ash clouds on the area for three years, or more? The prospect was very depressing. Residents of Yakima and Spokane

256

(both covered by the ash plume's initial fallout), along with their fellow Washingtonians on the western side of the mountains from Vancouver, Washington, north to the Seattle-Tacoma area, were tiring fast of waking up to gritty coverings of gray ash. As the days immediately following the eruption had shown, St. Helens' ash could grind an engine down to a major repair bill in no time, as well as ground aircraft and imperil health.[2]

But it did appear that there would be no more cataclysmic explosions. The seismic activity beneath the mountain seemed to confirm that the May 18th explosion had relieved the lion's share of the pressure, and other than sporadic throat-clearing eruptions and dome-building lava flows, the mountain and the population of the Pacific Northwest might even learn how to coexist—though periodic tremors felt as far north as Seattle would continue to raise questions of what, exactly, was occurring below, and the worrisome question of whether seismic or volcanic activity touched off by St. Helens could reactivate Mount Rainier.

It was a chicken and egg argument, the relationship of volcanoes and earthquakes. Sometimes, as with St. Helens, an earthquake could trigger the final phases of a volcanic reawakening, setting the stage for (or actually causing) a major eruption. Were the earthquakes themselves, though, caused by volcanic activity below? Obviously the movement of subterranean rivers of glowing magma was what created the episodic (or, at a more developed state, harmonic) tremors so familiar to volcanologists and seismologists monitoring volcanoes. But where did the other earthquakes surrounding such events as St. Helens fit into the puzzle? Which, in fact, came first? The volcanic or the seismic event?

Since the acceptance of the plate tectonic model, one thing seemed certain: The movement of the plates provided the principal engine for most volcanic activity worldwide.

The Cascade chain of volcanoes, for instance, is very similar to numerous other volcanic mountain chains throughout the world in that it is the direct result of plate subduction. Chains such as the Andes Mountains in South America, or the string of volcanic peaks on the Aleutian Islands in Alaska, are formed when the oceanic plates which are being consumed beneath the continental plates melt into magma. That magma—usually rich in silica—is lighter than the surrounding rock structures (which are as much as fifty kilometers [thirty miles] beneath the surface of the earth), so the

257

colossal blobs of newly liquefied rock, thousands of degrees hot, begin rising to the surface, melting overlying rock layers as they ascend, taking thousands of years for the inverted teardrop-shaped masses called plutons (sometimes measuring miles across) to reach areas beneath established volcanic chains, where they fill faults and tubes and other venting systems which can energize anew an existing volcano. (Old, cooled plutons now lay exposed as the Half Dome and El Capitan mountains in Yosemite National Park in California.) It is such plutons which fuel the eruptions of volcanoes such as Washington's Mount St. Helens.

But no one yet knows what role earthquakes—especially great subduction zone earthquakes—may play in the process of accelerating the plutonic masses of molten rock in their journey to the surface.

All up and down the coast of the Pacific Northwest the evidence of this process can be seen from the ground, from the air, or on a map. The majestic beauty of Mount Shasta in Northern California; the collapsed remains of a mountain we now call Mount Mazama (Crater Lake) in southern Oregon; the Three Sisters in middle Oregon; Mount Hood east of Portland, Oregon; Mount Adams, St. Helens, Rainier, and Baker in Washington; and Mount Garibaldi in British Columbia—all are stark evidence of the presence of a subduction process many kilometers below—and evidence of the approximate point inland from the seashore where the Pacific plate is melting thirty to fifty miles beneath. In fact, the reason that Mount Lassen (to the southeast of Shasta in North California) is the southernmost member of the northwestern volcanic mountain chain can be seen on any tectonic map: Lassen marks the approximate southern limit of the Cascadia subduction zone along the Pacific Northwest coast. (From that point south, the two great plates are sliding past each other along the planetary crustal seam of the San Andreas Fault.)[3]

Like the mythical phoenix, small amounts of the consumed oceanic plates rise again, their remelted material forming the very rock of such mountains as Fuji in Japan (near Tokyo) or Mount Rainier near Seattle and Tacoma (originally called Mount Tacoma).

But there are other types of volcanoes. Hot spots such as that which formed the Hawaiian island chain channel basic basaltic magma from the earth's mantle to the surface without the mixtures of silicas and other minerals found in the remelted crustal rock of subduction zones.[4] There is, in fact, a hot spot beneath the continental United States. A massive pluton—magma chamber—which sits beneath Yellowstone National Park energizes the geysers and the other geothermal activity which, in our geologically brief time on this continent, has attracted so much attention and justified our first national park.[5]

And, there is the sort of volcanic region which results from the tectonic stretching of the crust of the earth, a process which thins the crust and permits magma from the mantle of the earth to intrude into the cracks, rising to the surface to form the type of volcanic region still visible in northeastern New Mexico and southern Colorado—and in recent times just to the east of the High Sierras in California.

In the area due east of Yosemite between the rising Sierras and the White Mountains, north of the present-day town of Bishop at the head of the Owens Valley, a huge mountain rising perhaps fifteen thousand feet stood with a volcanic bomb in its heart less than a million years ago. Fueled by basaltic magmas rising through a thinning crust (a hundred miles from the nearest subduction zone), the mountain disintegrated in a thunderous planetary cataclysm some seven hundred thousand years ago—an explosion of ash and clouds of glowing pyroclastic plasma which makes the explosion of Mount St. Helens seem totally insignificant by comparison. St. Helens blew one-quarter of a cubic mile of rock and ash into the air on May 18, 1980. Before that it had thrown out 1 cubic mile around 1900 B.C. Mount Mazama's explosion which resulted in the collapsed caldera that formed Oregon's spectacular Crater Lake ejected 10 cubic miles of rock in 4600 B.C., and in more recent times, in 1815, Indonesia's Mount Tambora blew 19 cubic miles into the atmosphere (compared with Krakatoa's 4.3 cubic miles in 1883) as it killed twelve thousand people and caused the "year without summer" of 1816.

But when the mountain which sat to the south of present-day Mono Lake blew up, it injected a staggering *250* cubic miles of rock and pulverized mountain into the atmosphere, spreading a layer of ash as far east as Nebraska, undoubtedly darkening the atmosphere of the earth for several years, and leaving behind a collapsed caldera to cap the throat of the spent volcano. The rubble from the collapse formed a roof over the spent magma chamber (which had been reduced to one-quarter of its previous volume) and formed a beau-

259

tiful high-altitude desert floor ringed by the remnants of the former volcano's flanks—an awe-inspiring area which seven hundred thousand years later was named Long Valley by the humans who had so recently arrived in the last few seconds of geologic time. Into this eight-thousand-foot-high setting of ponderosa pine and active hot springs came a trickle of prospectors and miners, following Indian trails and building boom towns and mining camps in the High Sierras, followed by ranchers and cattlemen and farmers, who eventually gave way to the interests of a distant, growing California metropolis (Los Angeles) which began to drain the area of water in the early twentieth century, reducing the agriculture and leaving the high terrain of Long Valley with only one significant economic activity: the status of being a resort community dependent on tourism.

It was this valley that had been tagged as a seismic gap in 1978, a prediction hardly noticed by the residents of the resort community of Mammoth Lakes within the southwest rim of Long Valley— residents who were quite used to small tremors.

And it was the community of Mammoth Lakes that found itself catapulted into a seismological-volcanological mystery which began with a series of four moderate earthquakes of magnitude M_L 6.0, 5.8, 5.8, and 5.9 all on the same day of May 25, 1980, just before the economically important Memorial Day weekend, and precisely one week after the explosion of Mount St. Helens.

Chapter 19

Mammoth Lakes,
California—August 25, 1982

Denial.

The reality was, quite simply, that these people did not want to believe the facts. Their town was literally sitting on a volcano that might be ready to erupt, but the residents were refusing to accept the truth.

The panel of scientists from the USGS, the California Office of Emergency Services, and the California Division of Mines and Geology had come together for a long-delayed meeting with the outraged community of Mammoth Lakes—and it was turning into an agonizing encounter, to say the least.

For scientists such as Dr. Roy Bailey, the USGS volcanologist who had helped trigger the alert to begin with, the anger made no sense. Scientific facts were scientific facts. He and his colleagues were only reporting them—telling Mammoth Lakes a truth they obviously did not want to hear. In that, the USGS was merely the messenger, bringing the unwanted news that Mammoth Lakes might be facing a major and deadly volcanic eruption. But from the emotional and angry attitudes in the room, it was obvious that the survey had become the enemy—a messenger the townspeople wanted to strangle.

"You people have destroyed this community! You've . . . you've gone off half-cocked and scared everyone to death with this stupid warning, and now you tell us that you really don't know if anything is going to happen or not. Why the hell did you go shooting off your mouths to the press and destroying our season before you had any idea whether there's a threat or not?" The angry businessman, face flushed with anger, regained his seat as his neighbors applauded, many other frowning faces nodding in agreement throughout the room. It had gone that way since the meeting began. After three months of bureaucratic fumbling among the various government agencies over the date and location for a public meeting to explain the USGS warning, tempers had grown very short. Many local merchants were facing a lean winter after a curtailed summer season, and the opportunity to broadside the "egghead scientists" who had "caused the problems in the first place" was not going to be lost. It was, it seemed, open season on USGS volcanologists. In fact, to some of the men on the panel (sitting on the raised stage at the northeast corner of the auditorium and feeling just a bit cornered), the level of upset sparked old movie images of indignant villagers carrying lighted torches and dark resolves.

To hear these people tell it, Bailey knew, the USGS had maliciously devastated the community's economy by issuing a Notice of Potential Volcanic Hazard. (Some even openly accused the survey of timing the notice to help somehow with new USGS budget requests on Capitol Hill!)

But as Dr. Bailey knew, a major cause for the anger had been the outrageous way the people of Mammoth Lakes had been told that their beautiful little community might be facing a volcanic nightmare. More accurately, it was the way they had *not* been told—at least not by the USGS. The information had come in the form of a newspaper story from Los Angeles.

Somehow the information on the upcoming USGS warning had leaked to Los Angeles *Times* science writer George Alexander, who broke the story under the May 25th headline MAMMOTH AREA TREMORS HINT VOLCANISM. The USGS had dated and sent the formal release the same day, sending copies to a long list of government and community leaders by regular U.S. mail. Predictably, however, the Los Angeles *Times* arrived first.

No one in the Mono County government, no one in the community of Mammoth Lakes, nor anyone in the Chamber of Commerce had been told of the warning before copies of the paper reached the public on the twenty-fifth. Mammoth Lakes community leaders, such as Gary Flynn and Gail Frampton (both in the real estate business and already fighting tough times), had been shocked, horrified, and infuriated, in that order.

The perceived discourtesy was bad enough, but it was just the beginning. The USGS notice unleashed instant national publicity, echoing across the nation on TV, radio, and wire services, telling the world various versions of what Alexander had accurately reported. In some publications Mammoth Lakes was simply in danger; in a few it seemed on the verge of annihilation (as would be anyone foolish enough to travel there, it was implied). In perhaps the most bizarre version, lava was reported running through the streets of the town. Whatever the outside world was told, there was one thing made quite clear: Mammoth Lakes was a potentially dangerous place to spend a vacation.

And all this descended on the resort a mere six days before the biggest weekend of the year, the Memorial Day influx of tourists and tourist dollars which inevitably led to new condominium sales, booked-up hotels, packed restaurants, and as much as 15 percent of the gross revenues of the year for some businessmen. The timing of the USGS notice and the perceived "holocaust" of negative publicity could not have been worse. Mammoth Lakes had already been reeling from a national recession and an overbuilt real estate market. Now, suddenly, people began calling Long Valley with cancellations, erasing many hotel reservations, collapsing real estate deals like a house of cards (most recreational real estate sales in escrow were dumped within hours), and inundating the Chamber of Commerce in the unincorporated community with worried inquiries about friends, relatives, and summer homes thought to be in harm's way. One caller phoned specifically to ask if "the lava has cooled enough for us to take pictures [of it]."[1]

The shared opinion of many local merchants and real estate brokers in the first week following the botched release was that their federal government could hardly have hurt them more had the Air Force simply lobbed a bomb into the center of town. For a community so completely dependent on summer tourism, the economic damage attributed to the USGS warning seemed the final straw—and far worse than any coup de grace which might be administered by any volcanic explosion. The conclusions were ridiculously apocalyptic, and the rhetoric hyperbolic; but to the business community, those conclusions reflected the financial damage they were sure had occurred.

There was little interest, then, in the scientific justifications of the USGS volcanologists who had "attacked" their town and their livelihood, and there was little enthusiasm for listening to the carefully structured two days of presentations planned for this meeting—presentations designed to show why Dr. Roy Bailey and Dr. Alan Ryall and many others felt Mammoth was possibly sitting on a reawakening volcano in a preeruptive phase. (It was startling enough for the townspeople to hear that for all the years they had been there, they had been living inside a volcanic caldera!)

But the evidence was there—had been there—and would continue to be there. And it had started with the scientists' puzzlement over the four moderate quakes which had struck Mammoth two years before on May 25, 1980, seven days after the explosion of Mount St. Helens eight hundred miles to the northwest—quakes which heavily damaged only three buildings (including the high school) in a community largely consisting of wood-frame buildings which tolerate seismic waves quite well.

Dr. Roy Bailey had been studying the Long Valley caldera for years, and had published a paper on the volcanic activity and history of the area in 1975. It had been only a decade since scientists had first recognized the fact that Long Valley was an ancient caldera from a seven-hundred-thousand-year-old cataclysm, and even later that they discovered the widespread evidence of a still-active magma chamber beneath the valley floor.

But Bailey was also aware that Long Valley lies on a very active fault zone which runs the length of the eastern front of the Sierra Nevada range. Just to the south of the caldera, in Owens Valley, one of the three largest earthquakes in California's recorded human history occurred in 1872—a great quake which probably registered M_s 8.2 in magnitude. Even longtime residents of Mammoth were used to constant tremors and seismic rumblings from barely felt quakes to "pretty good shakers." It was assumed by many geologists that the continuing uplift of the Sierras (which were rising continuously in altitude by tiny increments each year) caused the periodic tremors, and the occasional large quakes. Therefore, the reasoning went, the quakes of May 1980 were probably more of the same: tectonic in origin.

Because of the 1978 forecast of a moderate quake in the area (based on seismic gap theories) and the large number of smaller-magnitude quakes following the four main jolts, the USGS issued an earthquake hazard watch on May 26, 1980 (the mid-level warning of a three-level notification system adopted by the USGS in 1977).[2]

But other evidence that there was something more to the mystery than tectonic forces began to stack up rapidly. A "level line" run through the valley adjacent to the major highway U.S. 395 in the summer of 1980 showed something quite odd, and quite dis-

264

turbing: The area was bulging, rising slowly like a mound of dough in an oven. The rise was very small—a matter of some ten inches since 1979—but it was very significant, because it was centered over the preexisting magma chamber, which (according to theory) had been slowly cooling and contracting down to a depth of six miles below the surface over the intervening fifty thousand years (since the last significant eruption). The logical explanation for the bulge, then, would be magma pressure—*new* magma pressure—coming from within the magma chamber below. Perhaps the bulge, the magma chamber, and the earthquake were connected. Perhaps "the chicken or the egg" problem was surfacing in yet another volcanic setting. Did something volcanic cause the earthquakes? Or did a tectonic earthquake series trigger something volcanic?

Then there was the ominous discovery that the seismograph tracings of the Mammoth aftershocks bore a chilling resemblance to the seismographs of continuing volcanic activity beneath Mount St. Helens. What that suggested was the movement of magma somewhere beneath the street level of Mammoth Lakes, California.

The town had been picked as the site of a small conference on continental scientific deep drilling in May of 1982, an unrelated U.S. Department of Energy probe to discuss a deep-drilling geothermal project in the Mono Craters area at the north end of Long Valley. It was also a convenient midpoint location for researchers from the University of Nevada's seismological lab and USGS scientists from Menlo Park to meet (though Roy Bailey had come from USGS headquarters in Reston, Virginia). In the cool, crisp, rarefied air tinged with the sweet aroma of pine and spruce and woodsmoke, with the vista of snowcapped peaks and the clean, if overbuilt, resort community's collection of stores and restaurants and hotels, it was a very pleasant place to be. All the natural attributes which made the area so alluring were in evidence in the bright, sunlit afternoons and the sparkling starscape of the evenings. The setting was soothing; some of the information, however, was not.

The seismologists from Nevada had come with seismographic information on Long Valley meant to be of use to the Department of Energy's project, but as Dr. Bailey sat up and took notice with increasing alarm, it impacted directly on his knowledge of the volcanic situation. The previous two years of earth tremors, it appeared, had not been scattered all over the caldera, as Bailey had expected. Instead, according to the Nevada seismologists, the epicenters were bunching up and becoming more frequent. And the area of those "bunched" epicenters was almost directly beneath the conferees in Mammoth Lakes, along the south margin of the caldera.

More precisely, he learned, the seismographs indicated that one area a mere two miles east of town—and almost directly beneath the only road into and out of the community—seemed more active than any others. And, it appeared that the depth of the shallowest earthquakes had been creeping closer and closer to the surface, from about five miles below in 1980 to about three miles beneath them in 1981.

Finally, the Nevada group reported that they had also confirmed the presence of "spasmodic tremors," the phenomenon associated with active volcanoes and considered to be the result of rocks breaking under the pressure of flowing liquid rock—magma—or from the gases released by the magma.

As if to underscore the warning, a series of tremors rumbled through the town the day after the conference, shaking up an already worried Roy Bailey, the coordinator of the USGS volcanic hazards program.

Here, right at Roy Bailey's feet, seemed to be a growing volcanic hazard. The realization that they had been mistaken to treat the earthquake patterns as merely a seismic problem weighed heavily. If there was magma moving around at depth, and if it ever reached the surface, the result would be an eruption. Knowing that the type of magma likely to surface in Long Valley was rich in silica and explosive potential—remembering the deadly pyroclastic plasma flows which had killed and destroyed everything in their paths so rapidly in the St. Helens explosion—Bailey knew with crystal clarity that this was nothing to be coy about.

A final phone call from Dr. Alan Ryall, one of the seismologists from the University of Nevada who had attended the conference and returned home the following day, was perhaps the last straw. Ryall had read the seismograms of the postconference tremors. They were now within 3.5 kilometers of the surface, he reported, squarely beneath State Highway 203, the front driveway to Mammoth Lakes and the only escape route.

That got everybody in the USGS camp excited, and immediate conferences began in Menlo Park and at USGS headquarters in Reston, Virginia, culminating in the notice that was typed up, readied for release, and delivered to the hands of the U.S. Postal Service on May 25, 1982:

266

United States Department of the Interior
Geological Survey, Western Region Menlo Park, California
94025

Public Affairs Office
For Release: Upon Receipt (Mailed May 25, 1982)

*NOTICE OF POTENTIAL VOLCANIC HAZARD ISSUED FOR
EASTERN CALIFORNIA*

Because of recent changes in earthquake and thermal activity, a notice of potential volcanic hazard—the lowest
of three levels of formal concern—was added today (May
25, 1982) to an existing earthquake watch for the Mammoth Lakes area in east-central California, by the U.S.
Geological Survey, Department of the Interior.

In a statement prepared for state and federal emergency
officials, USGS Director Dr. Dallas Peck said, "The discovery in recent months of ground deformation and new
steam vent (fumarolic) activity, apparently associated
with the earthquake activity, indicates that the outbreak
of volcanic activity is a possibility but by no means a certainty. The concentration of these phenomena near Mammoth Lakes in the southwestern part of the Long Valley
volcanic caldera suggests this as a possible eruption site,
but neither the probability nor the nature, scale or timing
of a possible eruption can be determined as yet."

The notice went on to outline the "recent events" that had led
to the issuance, adding, "The ultimate consequences of this activity
are uncertain. It is quite possible that no eruption will occur, that
the magma will cool and solidify to form an intrusion at depth."
The immediate consequences had been economic. Now, three
months later on August 25, as the meeting at Mammoth Lakes High
School lumbered on, the exchange of information and forthright
answers of the scientists slowly diffused some of the anger—if not
the monetary loss.[3]
As the meeting broke up, it was obvious to the USGS men that
the locals were still dissatisfied and deeply upset. They didn't want

267

to believe any of it. They wanted to believe the USGS had over-reacted, and the lack of certainty was the key to that conclusion.

"Will our town be destroyed?"

None of the USGS men could answer that for sure.

"If an eruption does occur, how bad will it be?"

Again they had received only a broad range of possible scenarios as the answer.

"How long will it be before you guys do know anything for sure?"

Not even that question could be answered.

There would probably be adequate warning and time to get out if the worst occurred. More than that was shrouded in uncertainty. Bailey and Hill and the others could only repeat the fact that the hazard was real, but no one yet knew what would come of it. The science simply wasn't there yet. Someday, perhaps, with enough research, and enough bright minds focused on the geologic, tectonic, volcanic, and geophysical problems—but not yet.

"Why, then," was the recurring question, "did you issue the notice?"

"Because, sir, the hazard is real."

"There are no winners," Dr. Dave Hill would say much later. "We're in a bind because anything we say may impact negatively [on] the economic structure. But, if something happens and we *haven't* said anything, then we'll really be between a rock and a hard place."

The two groups were talking past each other; that much was painfully obvious. The fact that the magma, which was apparently moving around beneath their community, might explode in the near future, destroying anyone or anything in its path, seemed unreal, especially since there were no obvious changes to the landscape. All the local residents had were the words of the scientists, and the economic setback those words had brought to the community. Predictably, but unfortunately, all the things that needed to be done to prepare the community for a mass evacuation were being blocked by concern over the economic impact. If the town built an alternate escape road, for instance, it might be interpreted as a confirmation that the threat was real, and further damage the economy. Twisted thinking such as that dominated during the remaining months—until, that is, January of 1983.

268

Suddenly the seismographs were alive again with earth tremors from beneath the Mammoth Lakes area. Swarms of hundreds of small quakes, many large enough to feel, rumbled and rattled through the landscape, migrating ever closer to the surface, still centered near the only road into town, beneath a picturesque campground and a mountain stream.

Now the townspeople began to worry. Further deformation of the ground was documented by the scientists, and for the first time spasmodic tremors, potential evidence of moving magma, were identified on the seismograms. By mid-January the magma was less than ten thousand feet beneath them.

Suddenly the attention of Mammoth Lakes citizens was drawn to the cause, not the effect. The growing volcanic threat, and the growing worries of the volcanologists that perhaps the rise of magma would not stop until it hit the level of groundwater and built up enough pressure for a major explosion, took precedence over the economy. USGS informational meetings began to be crowded, the daily update meetings drawing little of the sound and fury of previous months. Lines appeared at grocery stores and gas stations. Property owners began purchasing earthquake insurance with volcanic hazard riders, and the Mono County supervisors began coming under fire for not having provided an alternate escape road for the town—an omission promptly corrected as a dirt road was immediately plowed from the town over the hills to the north, rejoining U.S. 395 six miles away from the epicenter of the rising magma.

Emergency evacuation warning and coordination plans were drawn up, and the county sheriff's department began coordinating with the National Forest Service personnel, Bureau of Land Management employees, and the local fire department, figuring out what to do and how to do it if the volcanologists finally decided an eruption was imminent. For the remainder of January, each new quake and each new announcement sent shivers of fear through the residents who had innocently chosen to live in the maw of a great volcano, triggering quiet prayers and deep anxieties, and raising the inevitable question of whether this was the wrong moment in geologic time to be occupying the ancient caldera.

Then, as suddenly as they had begun, the tremors began to recede. Work on the road proceeded at flank speed, but the earth scientists watching the seismographic evidence hour by hour began to have some renewed hope that maybe—just maybe—an eruption was not on the way after all. Perhaps, they thought, the rising magma had been a dike intrusion in which molten rock had filled one of the vertically trending cracks which bordered all margins of the caldera, and had risen as far as it could go. Perhaps, in other words, it would stop short of reaching groundwater or a vent system, and thus stop short of an explosive eruption.

Slowly, caution merged into relief for the residents of Mammoth Lakes, and as March passed and the seismic activity continued to decrease, so did their interest in the reality of the volcanic processes at their feet. By May, where hundreds would have been present, only a dozen citizens attended a two-and-a-half-day USGS meeting of open presentations, even though it was held in the heart of the town.

And, just as suddenly, the unspoken moratorium on criticism of the Survey ended. Letters to the editor began appearing once again in local papers, some repeating the essentially ridiculous (and completely false) accusation that the USGS volcanologists had issued the original notice only to squeeze more funding from Congress. (One even suggested that the whole affair was a USGS maneuver to obtain government-paid vacations in Mammoth Lakes for the scientists!)

The speed with which the very real danger of January was relegated first to a false alarm, then to a grossly misinterpreted nonevent, was frightening. The fact that a disaster had not occurred was cited as proof that there was never any danger in the first place, and the focus of the community once again turned from public safety to potential economic setbacks.

"It was all a bunch of public relations hooey by the government scientists to get national attention," the Mammoth Lakes merchant said.

"But what happens if an eruption does occur?"

"We'll just sidestep the lava and carry on, son, that's what."

State and congressional representatives were peppered with demands to force the USGS to rescind its notice. At the same time, developmental plans to open a second major ski area and expand the recreational base of the community beyond the summer season and ski season began again, even though such expansion would significantly raise the number of visitors (and probably the number of residents) exposed to any renewed volcanic activity (the peak daily summer crowd was over thirty thousand, and the winter daily aver-

270

age above fifty thousand, and those figures were expected to double by the year 2000). While the new emergency escape road had been plowed, the developers knew well the difficulty of getting thirty thousand people out of the caldera within any reasonable period of time, even in the middle of the summer. In the winter, however, Mammoth was sometimes cut off for many hours by snowstorms. The prospect of a sudden volcanic eruption alert coming in the middle of the ski season with more than fifty thousand people trapped by snows in a community about to be annihilated by pyroclastic flows should have been a chilling prospect to anyone interested in expansion. However, the normal human tendency is to let economic growth push aside such "ethereal" concerns.

Nevertheless, the facts needed to be faced: What would Mammoth Lakes leaders and Mono County officials do in such a situation? Would there be enough time? And, of course, would it be irresponsible to permit expansion of the ski facilities, and the daily numbers of recreational visitors, in light of such a threat?

Clearly, the easiest and most cost-effective way to answer such questions was to deny the basic reason for asking them in the first place. If there was no credible volcanic threat, there was no problem. End of debate.

To their credit, the supervisors of Mono County and California authorities continued to face the problem, however weakly. (Within six months, two of the county supervisors who had been most supportive of facing reality would be thrown out of office in a recall election in the fall.)[4] By June, an Incident Command System had been set up, coordinating the various emergency response agencies and their communications systems, and federal funding had been obtained to pave the emergency escape road (a project completed in nine months rather than the usual three to four years).[5]

There was still a missing element, however, and it was the ability of a city or county to control its citizens' exposure to seismic risk. The same dilemma haunted Anchorage, Seward, and Valdez, Alaska, after the 1964 quake, and confronted Los Angeles and its surrounding communities with every new confirmation of what awaits in the San Andreas Fault to the north. The very same specter haunts those who know that such American cities as New York and Washington, D.C., Charleston, South Carolina, Memphis, Tennessee, St. Louis, Missouri (and many other locales), face major seismic hazards, but who also know that such cities have inadequate (or non-existent) controls over seismic engineering or rational land use.

The question—and the lesson—which was beginning to emerge from such controversies as that surrounding Mammoth Lakes had confronted enlightened urban planners for decades: Where, in fact, do we draw the line between public and private interests in a free society? How far can we allow ourselves as individuals or individual companies to go in accepting a major risk of natural disaster? Certainly there is a point at which our collective interests as a people to have a reasonable level of public safety must intervene (through the operation of government) to override conflicting private interests and to say, "No, you can't build a collapse-prone convention center on that liquefaction-prone tide flat," or, "We will not allow you to build a major hotel on a block of land that someday in the future will slide into Knik Arm," or, "No, we will not allow the number of winter visitors potentially at risk in Mammoth Lakes to be doubled simply because you want greater profits for yourself and the community."

We know what will happen when private economic interests win out (or governmental ignorance of a hazard prevails) and hundreds, or thousands, end up killed or injured—physically, financially, or both. We will point fingers and level accusations. We will throw out politicians and nominate committees and wring our hands. We will make loud noises about how we will never again allow something so negligent and heinous to occur.

But until something happens, it is excruciatingly difficult to bite the bullet economically and politically, recognize a hazard, and ask the ultimate question: What should we do now that we will wish we had done after a disaster?

Of course, failing to acknowledge that a threat even exists neatly blocks this process. For the people—and especially the real estate interests—of Mammoth Lakes, that denial was the solution.

But as one real estate salesman in Mammoth pointed out six months after the January scare, "We live here. We accept our own risk on our own buildings, and if we want insurance against a volcano, we buy insurance. And the USGS tells us there will be enough warning. Why shouldn't we expand?"

There was no question that the notice issuance and the publicity had hurt. Property values dropped at least 35 percent (from an already-inflated level), and would stay depressed (even though the number of visitors both summer and winter would continue to increase over the following years).

In the meantime, the USGS scientists hurried to install an impressive array of monitoring instruments in Long Valley, but refused to rescind the notice for want of any evidence that the hazard had abated. As far as the volcanologists could tell, the cessation of the magma flow could last for decades, or only for weeks. The underlying threat was still there (and the bulge in the caldera continued, although at a somewhat slower rate). Therefore, they concluded, the notice would remain.

But the USGS men and women had been slammed into the wall of societal reality. Their concentration on the "pure science" of the problem had led them in all innocence to trigger a series of human events which, in the absence of a volcanic event, added up to possibly unnecessary damage. If in no other way, the survey's insensitivity to the delicate nature of the public response to a warning or a notice had led to instant polarization of the populace. After that, mutual understanding was difficult at best. The lesson, however costly to Mammoth Lakes, had national overtones. The ability of the USGS to bring a community properly and carefully up to the point of understanding the true scope and depth of a seismic or volcanic hazard will be critical. As the science progresses, the knowledge of who is at risk will expand. Delivering such news will never be easy, but obtaining community (and political) cooperation will be essential to reducing the exposure of the public to danger.

But what of the uninformed who blunder in? What of the retiree who, on arriving at this new place called Mammoth Lakes with his life savings and a desire to settle in the mountains, sees only pure air and blue skies, pine trees and sweet-smelling woodsmoke wafting from beautifully attractive condominiums? What can protect such a person who knows virtually nothing of the volcanic threat?

The USGS eventually replaced its three-tiered warning system with a simple warning or no-warning system (a move prompted in part by the outcry from Mammoth Lakes). By 1984, though the threat had not changed, it would no longer rise to the threshold criteria of the new warning system—thus the hated notice was allowed to expire. But without the notice, there would be no formal truth-in-advertising legislation or other structured means of assuring that the incoming uninformed became informed.

The real estate salesman sat in a corner of his Mammoth Lakes office, pondering the question. "What of that innocent, uninformed potential buyer?" he was asked. "There's no formal warning out there. Are *you* going to tell him?"

The agent shook his head in the negative. "No."

"No?"

"No! There are no warnings . . . there are no alerts . . . there's no reason for us to have to say anything."

He paused again, pondering his own words.

"I've never told anyone about it. . . . I don't think that's anything that any of us [in real estate] would discuss . . . Christ, we wouldn't make a sale if we did. Period."

Chapter 20

Coalinga, California—May 2, 1983

It looked, she thought, like Germany during the war. Like Dresden after the air raid—a bombed-out shell of a city.

Standing in the middle of Elm Street, Marlene Dakessian perceived only rubble and destruction: The old Coalinga Inn was on fire, its brick facade collapsed along with its upper floor; the Flower Pot restaurant's back wall was gone; and the wreckage of the Service pharmacy was visible a block farther to the northeast, bricks and pieces of jagged concrete littering the street as if an angry child had taken a grand swipe at a carefully constructed stack of blocks—and walked away.

Her mother had painted such scenes for her as a little girl, weaving dark memories of terror-filled nights in wartime Germany into word pictures for her young daughter to understand—images of a shattered world of rubble and destruction and screaming, exploding air raids in which life carried no guarantee but those of the present moment. She had wanted Marlene, in the security of her American youth, to understand what could happen in war. Mrs. Dakessian had wanted her daughter to see and feel and understand the reasons why immigration to America had been so important, and had brought such security.

Until now. Before living through the horrid scene in front of her—a scene of dust and rubble and flames consuming the formerly sedate image of her town of Coalinga—the thirty-three-year-old divorcée had never understood such images, or such destruction.

Nor had she appreciated how fast it could occur. It was frightening to see other dazed people running back and forth like ants, firemen appearing from behind her to flail away at the fire, others clawing at rubble, some with otherworldly expressions, obviously even more stunned than she.

It had been only minutes before that the first jolt had thumped Marlene out of a late-afternoon nap, the frantic scampering of her cats toward the back door of the daintily decorated owner's apartment at the Kruger Motel motivating her dash to the doorway—the ingrained response all native Californians are taught to trigger when the ground begins to move.

Her cats had streaked off into the alley when she threw open the door to stand there, being shoved back and forth with increasing violence as the doorjamb itself gyrated into a parallelogram and back through the vertical, back and forth, nails squealing in wooden members as she turned to see her precious possessions—little glass figurines and books and records, a crystal piano, a treasured lamp— all catapulted from their shelves and tabletops to crash on the floor. With the roar of the quake in her ears and the sounds of the internal destruction of brittle materials and tinkling glass providing the upper range of accompaniment to the cacophonous symphony of domestic disaster, she had briefly thought her own end might be near—then rejected the idea. After all, Coalinga did not have disastrous earthquakes.

Whoever is at the center of this is really getting hurt! That thought was clear. It might be Bakersfield, or the San Andreas Fault some twenty miles to the west (which would mean Parkfield was getting a far worse hammering than expected). It never occurred to Marlene that the seismic waves shaking her town apart had originated moments before beneath the oilfield to the northwest in Coalinga's backyard. Coalinga had earthquakes, but never anything like this!

Thirty feet to the east in an adjacent house the terrified wife of the man who had built Marlene's home and business, the Kruger Motel, fought a combination of panic and grief as the cherished bric-a-brac she had collected during a lifetime (and during her early years in Germany) disintegrated all around her. The Krugers, like Marlene's parents, had been refugees from wartime Germany, and there were disturbing memories and overtones to the violence of the earthquake—overtones which ran very deep.

And in the downtown area, two blocks away, heavy bricks had begun raining from disintegrating facades, as walls undulated away from floor beams, and roofs and ceilings dropped onto stores and offices and shops below. One man rode a disintegrating second story down to the first, a woman at the Coalinga Inn crawled

276

through a minefield of bouncing tables to safety, and the owner of an auto parts store ran headlong into an avalanche of bricks as he tried to escape.

In his small stationery and gift shop, John Bunker, now in his senior years, had felt the quake start, and watched the work of a lifetime rapidly disintegrate into shards of glass and overturned shelves amidst fallen ceiling tiles and overturned fixtures as he dove beneath a counter to survive. A half mile away his wife, Florence Bunker, a former Coalinga City councilwoman, watched their china and furniture smashing onto the floor and worried about her husband. Anyone caught in the midst of Coalinga's downtown section of unreinforced masonry buildings dating back to 1912 would be in danger during an earthquake; she knew that instinctively.

And in forty seconds it was over. Marlene Dakessian glanced at the disastrous remains of her possessions on the apartment floor, realized that being alive made the mess a small matter, and turned her attention to comforting Mrs. Kruger, who had emerged into the alley in tears, her home's interior equally in ruins.

Outside the downtown district the damage was less apparent, but in some cases just as catastrophic. Hundreds of homes had been jerked partially or completely from their foundations, chimneys were down, brick walls cracked or crumbled, some roofs completely collapsed, and the interiors covered with the debris of whatever had not rested on the floor when the shaking started.

Several blocks from the heart of Elm Street, Paul Lopez looked at his destroyed home and wondered. His family was safe, but their thirty-three-year-old house was obviously a total loss: cracked, shattered, thrown off the foundation, and ruined.

Four days before, however, on Thursday, Paul Lopez had stopped in town to renew his homeowner's insurance policy. Remembering a small quake the previous year and feeling nervous about their brittle masonry home, Lopez had paid the additional amount for earthquake insurance.

That had been on Thursday. This was Monday. Was he covered? Would they pay? And, of course, the central question that thousands of Coalingans were asking themselves in silent panic: Can we recover?

The thirty-two-year-old mayor of Coalinga thought a bomb had gone off at first. It was a curious idea—he had never heard a bomb—but through endless television portrayals, Americans vicariously experience many things with a contradictory, distant realism that at times of stress can make unfamiliar situations very familiar, and very frightening.

The rapid arrival of the side-to-side S waves had solved the puzzle, of course, and Mayor Keith Scrivner had hung on as the forty seconds of battering seismic undulations tossed his office around. At first he raced around the shattered town, locating his wife and four kids, gathering all four daughters one by one from various locations—all of them shaken, but all of them safe. Now he stood at City Hall with other wide-eyed, shell-shocked, city officials, each person trying to muster reserves of personal strength, and each of them struggling to think with crystal clarity and maturity. They had been hit, and they had been hurt badly as a community, and so far the outside world did not know. The city had plans for disasters, but when something massive and totally unexpected occurs, only one question really ricochets around the cranium of a young city official: What on earth do we do now?

Most of the phones were out, electricity was out, and crews were already running as fast as possible to turn off the gas lines. Only the WATS line in Scrivner's office was working, and that was already in use to summon help.

The town's brick buildings were gone, the downtown section destroyed, and hundreds of homes were badly mauled. As a contractor, Keith Scrivner understood such things very well. The image of his own home had been shoved to the back of his mind as his family had been dispatched to a relative's ranch outside town. He would worry about it later, he told himself, but there was no question about it structurally. From one brief glimpse it was obvious that the Scrivner house had been destroyed.

Fortuitous timing—traditionally the only salvation for unprepared Californians—had saved the people once again. The massive waves had torn into Coalinga at 4:42 P.M. The shops had been in the process of closing, and the post 4:30 P.M. time meant that downtown restaurants and bars were between crowds. There had been few people left on the streets, exposed to the potentially deadly rain of shattered masonry that began with the first shaking, a downpour of heavy missiles from the fragmenting walls of unreinforced, unreconstructed, uninspected, and uncontrolled ancient masonry and brick buildings, which, because they had been untouched

278

by modern seismic engineering codes and standards, had always been seismic bombs waiting to explode.

Indeed, in that sense, a deadly string of bombs had gone off in Coalinga—but they had been internally generated—as well as internally detonated by something mysterious beneath the surface only a few miles distant.

Dr. Karen McNally had been in her small office in Santa Cruz at 4:42 P.M. The beauty of a shady Pacific Coast forest scene outside her window—adjacent to the Charles F. Richter Seismological Laboratory at the new University of California at Santa Cruz—gave the office an almost stereotypical look, as if to certify that here was the lair of a working professor.

She was bending over in her chair to retrieve something from one of the endless stacks of papers and studies arrayed on the floor behind her desk when her chair began to move, the little wheels coming alive in response to a linear motion of the floor, as a rather sickening dizziness overcame Dr. McNally.

A woozy thought shot through her mind as she realized she was moving involuntarily: *Either I'm getting sick and disoriented, or someone's having an earthquake.*

A quick trip to the seismographs provided the answer. It was a quake, and in the middle 6.0 magnitude range. The epicenter, however, was uncertain.

At first it appeared to be to the southeast, and that was somewhat chilling. The main trace of the San Andreas Fault in middle California was to the southeast. Parkfield—a community which was expecting a moderate quake, and for which the first formal USGS earthquake prediction was about to be issued—was also to the southeast.

As they refined the data and listened to the radio, the usual checklist of questions ran through Karen's mind: *Should we go? Who else is going? What data can we get that we need? Who in the department can go? Are we field-ready? Do we have enough money?*

When the small town named Coalinga emerged as the epicenter in the constant calculations of fellow professors and excited students, the fact that there were no known faults in that location which could produce a Richter magnitude M_L 6.7 quake beneath the adjacent oilfield pressed in hard. What, indeed, was down there that had caused this? And why hadn't the seismological community known about it?

By evening, the decision had been made and acted upon, and McNally had a team assembled and in motion, planning to rendezvous with members of the California Division of Mines and Geology as they drove down from Sacramento that evening. There would surely be a host of aftershocks, and McNally's seismographs would be needed in the field to capture the wave forms. The seismic, near-field record was absolutely vital if they were to figure out what, seismologically, had occurred. And, of course, whether whatever had occurred, could occur again.

By 8:00 P.M. Monday—within four hours of the earthquake—a veritable army of rescue and relief forces was in motion. A fleet of ambulances from all over the state had been dispatched, unaware of the light casualties; a convoy of fire trucks from adjacent fire districts had been scrambled; state officials from the governor's office to the Office of Emergency Services as well as the Division of Mines and Geology were in motion; commanders of the California Highway Patrol had joined with officials of Fresno County (several of whom had flown in by private plane) to head for the stricken town; and troops of the National Guard, representatives of the American Red Cross and the Salvation Army, Federal Emergency Agency (FEMA) officials, the USGS, Karen McNally's team, and others all had gone into action, converging from the four points of the compass on the small town of Coalinga.

In addition, the news media had responded in force as soon as it became clear that the quake was very significant, and that the town of Coalinga was the victim.

"Where?"

"Coalinga. About halfway between San Francisco and Los Angeles, just west of Interstate Five, and twenty miles east of the San Andreas Fault."

"Never heard of it."

The same conversation was repeated in many California newsrooms. In many others nationwide there was no one to provide the answers, and many a dash to the nearest interstate map was accompanied by the whistled realization that Coalinga was a remote community. Within hours an incoming tide of reporters, photographers, television news teams, television helicopters, and other journalists

280

began rolling toward Coalinga as well, flowing in from Southern California and Northern California to converge at the outskirts of Coalinga—where they all ran into a brick wall, so to speak.

Mayor Scrivner and his fellow city officials had made the unprecedented decision to cordon off the entire town. Roadblocks were set up on all roads in and out, and within an hour, Coalinga was sealed off as effectively as if the military were veiling a secret testing site.

With immediate arguments and angry words, threats of resort to superseding state officials countered by threat of arrest from those maintaining the roadblock, and a growing line of vehicles stretching to the horizon, all of which had been denied entry (a line which included ambulances, fire trucks, and the cars of relatives of Coalinga residents, who, finding the telephone lines out, had dashed in to locate loved ones), the decision was an instant debacle. When the press joined the fray, however—smashing into the municipal wall on the outskirts of town—the level of fury and outrage at the denied entry reached new levels.

It was to be the start of a secondary and self-induced crisis that would echo all the way from a critical postmortem hearing (held months later by the Office of Emergency Services) to various threatened legal actions. Keith Scrivner had been instantly worried about looting. That was the traditional first thought of government officials whose jurisdiction lay exposed and bleeding at the hands of some disaster. That was the primary motivation for sealing off the town. Just like his counterparts in many other cities at many other times facing many other disasters involving shattered storefronts and spilled merchandise, Scrivner was equally unaware that in such crises looting is rarely, if ever, a problem—certainly not a problem requiring the instant quarantine of an entire town from many of the very people sent to help it. The young mayor was to take much political and personal heat for his decision, but in the growing darkness of Monday evening, the leaders of the bleeding town refused to budge.

There was no sleep for Scrivner or other city officials through the night as everyone worked to secure the town, reestablish essential services, and calm the people (many of whom had moved onto their front lawns for safety from aftershocks). By midevening, they were sure of the happy news that there was only one serious injury, no deaths, and no one left missing, despite the large number of collapsed buildings. Fifty-one major structures had made up the downtown area—forty-five were now either effectively demolished, or would have to be condemned and bulldozed within weeks. In the meantime, Scrivner and the others knew they had to keep everyone out of the damaged buildings which still stood in whole or in part. Aftershocks were occurring constantly, and if another heavy jolt hit while some store owner was picking through a perilous building, Coalinga could yet end up with a fatality. In addition to helping with the roadblocks on the edge of town, the Fresno County sheriff joined the city's efforts to prevent further injury and ordered the downtown area fenced off (first by officers, later with a rent-a-fence from another city).

By morning, media helicopters buzzed around the downtown area like angry hornets, taking pictures of an area made off limits to them. The idea that some city official could stand in the way of an American newsman was too much—especially since the city was (in the terminology of one TV reporter), "essentially bush-league." Pressure had built through the previous evening to do something, and under the gun of a strange reality, the sheriff stepped in to defuse the anger by arranging guided bus tours for the newspeople through the center of town. (The newsmen, however, were decidedly not satisfied.)

Sometime during the darkness of Monday night, Keith Scrivner and the city manager retreated to a back room at City Hall, closed the door, and looked at each other's weary faces. The scope of the disaster was now clear, and it was painfully obvious that little Coalinga was going to need a lot of help in the form of dollars from the outside. Material help was on the way, or already there, but to survive as an operating community, there would be millions needed for demolition and rebuilding of water and sewer systems and streets and a myriad of other city responsibilities. To complicate the matter, citizens were sure to leave (a move that would progressively reduce the tax base), and property values were sure to decline (further reducing the tax base). And, the citizens were sure to have problems financially in just paying the taxes they already had. New levies and bond issues would be out of the question—Coalinga simply couldn't recover on its own.[1]

Here they were, though, an isolated community with no significant impact on anyone else but themselves. The only way to get federal help for the city government and for the people was to be declared a national disaster area, but that would take some fast political footwork. First the county had to declare Coalinga a disaster area—a relatively easy step. Then California's governor would have to make a similar declaration, and further agree to ask President Ronald Reagan (himself a former California governor) for the national declaration.

But there had to be political momentum and public sympathy for President Reagan to commit additional federal funds to anything, even a disaster. Thus, agreed Scrivner and the city manager, the nation had to *want* federal aid for Coalinga, or Coalinga wouldn't get federal aid.

And, the media people who could get that message out—the people who would be the key to that strategy—were the very ones who had been storming and fuming just outside the roadblocks of the town and later at the edges of the cordoned-off downtown area.

The city manager and the mayor were similar men in their distaste for publicity. Both were independent people who cared little for public speaking, and even less for people who tended to grandstand on issues politically or otherwise. Yet what they were going to have to do was exactly that: play to the media—use the media— "play on the mercy of the media and use them to get the word out to the rest of the country as fast as possible."

Scrivner, with gritted teeth, immediately began talking into whatever microphones were pushed into his face, granting seemingly endless interviews to newspeople for whom he had little regard, and to whom he would never have given a moment of time were Coalinga not in need of what they could provide.

But by Tuesday night, he'd had enough. Exhausted, unshaven, and feeling gamey, Scrivner had accepted the invitation of a friend to retreat for dinner and a warm shower (impossible in Coalinga) at the man's ranch outside the city. Half dazed from lack of sleep, "a walking zombie" by his description, the mayor knew he had promised ABC Television News that he would be in the driveway of his parents' home in Coalinga that evening (where they were setting up a direct satellite link with New York) to appear live on Ted Koppel's *Nightline.* But after a hot shower and an extensive dinner prepared by his friend, Scrivner decided he didn't want to deal with the media any further until morning. Promise or no promise, expensive satellite equipment and staff time or not, they could live without him, and despite amazed, desperate, and indignant pleas from the network, it was Coalinga's equally harassed police chief rather than the mayor who appeared on TV screens nationwide from Coalinga, as correspondent Steve Bell (sitting in for Ted Koppel) began the interview. Scrivner, it seemed, could be pushed only so far (though his decision would net him another round of bad reviews from the press and the community alike).

Despite the affront to ABC, the cascade of media attention worked, as newspapers, radio, and television all across the country carried the images and the stories of the shell-shocked residents of the small, California community that had been suddenly walloped by a devastating earthquake resulting from sudden breakage of a fault no one knew existed. American opinion was fast to form, and genuine, deserved sympathy for those who had lost so much penetrated the political consciousness of the White House as well: Within forty-eight hours, President Reagan had declared Coalinga a federal disaster area, making it eligible for a variety of federal programs.

To the newspeople, the story was rich in human dimensions: stunned citizens moving into pitiful tents on the front lawns of damaged or mauled homes, the downtown area destroyed, the city government's "strange handling" of the situation, and the huge influx of fellow Americans coming to help. A giant circus tent was erected by the National Guard on Tuesday with an impressive field kitchen that began serving meals each hour to hundreds (including some reporters). The Red Cross was present, too, as were amateur radio operators (hams) who had provided the vital and unheralded help in the first few hours, and who stayed on, putting families in touch with worried out-of-town relatives with selfless use of their sophisticated gear.

And within weeks, the various government agencies had set up a unified, one-stop center at the Elks Lodge, where people were supposed to flow through one by one, table by table, in order to receive everything from low-cost Small Business Administration (SBA) loans to emergency cash from the Fresno County Economic Development Agency. Federal Housing Authority (FHA) people were there, as were the representatives of FEMA, the California Office of Emergency Services, and more. The range of offered help seemed too good to be true—and in too many cases, that's precisely what it was.

The federal official leaned against a Coalinga building and gestured in the general direction of the shattered downtown area.

"There is a standard myth to modern American disasters, born of our generosity as a people and our emotional commitment to each other—a generosity which erases [boundaries between us] most effectively when someone, or some community, gets trounced by a disaster. I see this all the time, and it can be very sad."

The veteran of many floods and tornadoes shook his head as he talked about the fact that Americans cannot stand the image of fellow countrymen standing beside ruined homes, their lives and hopes assaulted. "We use our tax dollars to help, we send donations and care packages, and we nod with profound approval when our presidents use their power to send in our tax dollars to help put our neighbors back on their feet.

"The myth, however, is that disaster relief can put Humpty-Dumpty back together again," he said. "In a phrase, it cannot!"

The wreckage of Coalinga's downtown, visible behind him, had already come under the bulldozer. As he spoke, vacant lots now marked the spots where numerous downtown buildings had stood for seventy years.

"People emerge from the wreckage of their homes after a tornado, or hurricane, a flood or earthquake, and make the disastrously wrong assumption that government aid will lift them back to parity, repair their home, restore their possessions, and make them whole again."

One of the reporters nodded, recounting the story of the wealthy owners of major San Francisco condominiums who had recently dropped earthquake insurance on their buildings because the premiums were too high. "When they were asked why by a professional municipal planner, they said they could get government aid if they got wiped out. Therefore, there was no point in the insurance."

"And so do homeowners." The federal man agreed. "'Why should we worry? The government will help us!' Well, look around. Look at the residential area here. The United States government isn't equipped to help beyond a certain point. These people have got to help themselves. And unless they've got insurance or deep pockets, they're wiped out and have to start over."

285

*　　*　　*

The shock which had slowly, progressively accompanied the realization that the man's words were true had crept in during the first few weeks after the quake, as slowly the people of Coalinga realized that they could be fed and temporarily housed, given some small amounts of money and medically cared for, but that the government would not rebuild their homes, repair or replace their businesses, or restore their economy. Such realities had begun to sink in with the trek through the Elks Lodge, where proud people were told at one of the first tables that they couldn't talk to representatives at the next table unless they accepted food stamps— whether they needed them or not. The reaction of many was simply to turn and leave in confusion and upset. Businessmen such as Scrivner himself were asked whether they had credit available, and, if the answer was yes, were told they didn't qualify for low-cost government loans from the Small Business Administration.[2] And those who did qualify were horrified to find out that such loans would bear 8 percent interest rates, only four to five points below the prime rate.[3]

And there were promises broken—promises which had been made with the purest of intentions by well-meaning government people who found later they had overstated their capabilities.[4]

Such problems prompted Keith Scrivner to make a small but significant—and profound—point in a speech some days after the quake. Standing in one of the town parks, addressing several hundred people, complimenting their spirit and their determination, Scrivner had told them the ultimate truth:

"Don't expect the government to do it for you. If you're going to rebuild and recover, you'll have to do it yourself. Don't sit and wait for a handout. That isn't what all of this government aid is about. That isn't what all these people roaming around here can do. You must do it on your own, or it won't get done."

A slight wind rippled through his hair as Keith Scrivner paused, took a deep breath, and continued.

"Government aid is to give you a hand up, not a handout. Remember that. Please."

Scrivner himself had lost over a hundred thousand dollars. But as he had watched his friends and neighbors, fellow businessmen and constituents, and members of his own family try to regain their bearings, it was obvious that there would be another victim of the Coalinga quake: public faith in the insurance industry.

286

Paul Lopez's new, earthquake-endorsed, replacement value policy did pay off. Within a month, plans were under way to build a new house for the family, this one worth far more than what he had paid for the original home so many decades ago—a home on which he had one, single remaining payment left to make on the day of its destruction.

But Lopez was one of the few, clear winners. Throughout the remainder of Coalinga, the performance of the insurance industry had ranged from amazing to scandalous, friendly and sympathetic to cynical and hateful.

State Farm had been first on the scene. A major court battle had been lost the previous year, when a California court ruled that a homeowner's policy which said "all risk" meant exactly that. Small-print exclusions on the inside were ruled ineffective, and the company was forced to pay on claims it had tried to deny.

State Farm's people, therefore, knew what was coming at Coalinga as soon as they heard about the disaster. Within days of the quake, their claims adjusters were visiting their "all risk" policyholders one by one, assessing the damages, and simply writing checks then and there, on the spot.

At the same time, however, other insurance companies with "all risk" policies informed their policyholders (some within forty-eight hours, while their clients were still sleeping on their front lawns) that if they had not paid for specific earthquake coverage, they could forget about getting any money for their damages (other than coverage for broken glass or fire).

And there were those in between, companies which would pay off a huge claim on one home in a development of identical and similarly damaged homes, then because of appraisals by a different adjuster, deny coverage to the one next door, even though the policies were the same. Lawsuits became a growing bank of storm clouds on the horizon as families with unoccupiable homes and defiant insurance companies wondered what to do: walk away from the mortgage and default (some banks permitted devastated homeowners to simply sign over the deed; other tried to sue), or try to rebuild without insurance.[5]

Homeowners who owed very little on their damaged or destroyed homes—many of them retired residents whose life savings were the equity in their houses—were faced with taking out new mortgages during a period of 12 percent interest rates in order to

287

raise the necessary money to rebuild or repair. People on fixed incomes were suddenly realizing that to get back in their houses, they would be saddled with an extra payment of five hundred dollars per month or more for decades—provided they could even qualify for a loan.

In many instances, damage to the homes of those who did have earthquake riders was in the thousands, but not expensive enough to get beyond the deductible. Seven thousand dollars in collapsed chimneys and ruined walls against a ten-thousand-dollar deductible on an earthquake-endorsed policy meant no payment, and no help.

And businesses with standard policies and no specific earthquake coverage—especially those with ruined, bulldozed buildings in the downtown area—faced a bleak future with no financial help. Some who complained, often and loudly, eventually reached settlements with insurance companies that were not inclined to pay otherwise. Others—longtime merchants such as John and Florence Bunker, whose building had been condemned and bulldozed after the quake—received nothing.[6]

John Bunker had invested much of his life in his business. Suddenly it was rubble, and through the first few weeks of trying to salvage what he could from the debris and stay ahead of the bulldozing of the building which had been ordered by the city, John Bunker knew he couldn't rebuild. The physical labor, the stress of losing so much, and the heartbreaking hollowness of realizing that there were no magic solutions for recovery pressed on him like a lead weight. More than a few fellow residents began worrying about him, spotting John one afternoon several weeks after the quake as he sat on a curb and stared into space, oblivious to greetings, oblivious to a future, his world in tatters.

And within days, he was dead—felled by a heart attack, as were numerous others in Coalinga, which had been a city heavy with retirees. For Florence Bunker, of course, the loss of her husband made discussion of the monetary loss emotionally insignificant— but that monetary loss was anything but financially insignificant: They had accumulated more than two hundred thousand dollars of hard-earned equity in the store in thirty years. But with the utter rejection of their insurance claims, not a penny of it survived.

"The thing that really got us during that summer was the uncertainty." The Coalinga resident, a man whose home had been catapulted from its foundation and condemned while covered by an "all risk" policy (which the insurer at first refused to honor), gestured to his rebuilt home as he spoke.

"Two years of hell to get them to pay. Two years of uncertainty. Would we be able to rebuild? What would we do without an insurance settlement? Could we afford a new mortgage?"[7]

He talked about the uncertainty of the city itself over the deteriorating tax base, the deepening oil depression, the flight of Coalinga residents to Fresno to do their shopping (in the absence of Coalinga merchants) in the first months, and the inability to get them to start trading again with reestablished local shops. And he talked of the overall reality that Coalinga had still not recovered— might never recover. Vacant lots still bordered Elm Street, several new retail businesses were on the verge of closing for lack of patronage, and real estate values had dropped so far that many people were now, as the man put it, "prisoners of our own equity. We can't sell; therefore, we can't leave."

And he talked of the irony that despite the good intentions of those who came to help, and the good intentions of the government agencies and representatives, in the end a tremendous amount of tax money was spent with little long-term benefits to show for it. It had been a very uneven, and inequitable, recovery, with some Coalingans going bankrupt, some walking away from mortgages and homes, others collecting full insurance settlements and rapidly rebuilding. Some SBA loans went to people who didn't need them, while some people who needed them, couldn't get the so-called low-cost money. The government couldn't repair the economy of Coalinga—not even Coalinga seemed able to do that—nor could they end the recession in the oil industry, which had hurt the city further. Recovery programs, in other words, might help some, but they were obviously not the answer.

The Coalinga native smiled again, raising his index finger as he raised his eyebrows, eager to press home an important point.

"I'll tell you what the lesson of this disaster was. The lesson is that the only way a devastated community can get itself back together, the only way people will be able to carry on and put their lives in order with any degree of assurance, is if they know their losses are going to be covered. I don't mean every cent. I don't mean everything's going to be exactly as it was. But to know for sure as you wobble out of the wreckage that, hey, we're going to

289

rebuild—to be able to tell your kids that with firmness and know you're not lying—that's what we need. How do you do that? Insurance. Good, low-deductible policies which cover earthquakes in full. We have to have fire insurance for a mortgage, why can't they require earthquake insurance? In my opinion, we need that right now, nationwide, for all natural hazards. A way to equitably—evenly—distribute recovery funds without using tax money."

"And I'll tell you," he continued, "a national insurance program giving better rates to those who built buildings and houses to withstand quakes would be a double-barrel benefit."

Indeed, it isn't the noble efforts of recovery and emergency aid that hold the greatest societal promise of taming the specter of earthquake disasters; it's the incentives that can be created to prepare our buildings and our cities, coupled with a national sharing of the risk through insurance which becomes the ultimate safety net beneath the high-wire act of life on an earthquake-prone continent.

Chapter 21

Michoacán, Mexico—September 21, 1985

The road ahead seemed to disappear into nothingness, the sudden curve to the left around the flanks of the mountain invisible in the pitch-darkness of the moonless night, the twin beams of the Travelall's headlights soaring off into infinity over an unseen abyss. David Smollar, a reporter for the Los Angeles *Times,* gripped the armrest even harder as he watched the driver for some comforting indication that she was going to follow the road, and not the headlights. Dr. Karen McNally had been gesturing energetically for the past half hour, her hands describing compression waves and surface waves, subduction zones and seismic gaps in the dark, humid airspace above the dashboard as they roared through the hot Mexican night, bound toward the Pacific coast north of Acapulco—a retinue of other rented vehicles behind them carrying a joint Mexican and American team of seismologists.

"You really shouldn't be asking me these things while I'm driving, David," she had volunteered thirty minutes and several hair-raising curves back.

"I know," he had responded—followed by another round of questions.

As Karen smoothly negotiated the curve on the rough, remote highway, the surrealistic aspect of their mission was not far from her thoughts. It was now late Saturday night, but it had been two days before—Thursday morning September 19th, around 6:30 A.M. on the U.S. Pacific coast—when the USGS earthquake-monitoring center in Golden, Colorado, had dialed her number in Santa Cruz, California. Minutes before the call, the seismic gap she and so many other scientists had studied and warned about in the Mexican state of Michoacán had rumbled to life in a great quake exceeding a surface wave magnitude of M_s 8.1, flattening several coastal towns and

291

radiating monstrous seismic wave trains throughout Mexico. The seismologists at Golden were waiting for word from Mexico, but in the meantime, they needed help. Would she go back to the university lab to read her seismograms and help locate the epicenter exactly?

Mexico City couldn't respond. Not yet, at least. Its central communications microwave link was in shambles, as transmitters and antennas had slammed back and forth inside their concrete communications tower until they had been reduced to useless junk, the long-distance systems and satellite relay systems going down at the same time. Without it, the rest of the world had no idea of what had happened—what was happening—in the world's most populous city of eighteen million people.

It had started 47.6 seconds after 7:17 in the morning, when the snag holding back the accumulated tectonic energy in the subduction zone northwest of Acapulco had shattered without warning, the Cocos Plate and North American Plate rumbling past each other at the northwestern end of the Michoacán gap, creating huge seismic waves, which traveled outward at 4.3 miles per second, shuddering the foundations of Mexico City 230 miles away 53 seconds later just as the capital city was awakening to another business day. The initial shudders of the P waves, and the beginning undulations of the S waves did little to upset the populace in the first few seconds—the memory of another minor tremor several days before was very fresh. It had passed harmlessly. So would this.

As the initial seconds ticked by and the surface waves began to move the foundation of Mexico City back and forth laterally, the amount of energy contained in one particular frequency of waves began to build up to unprecedented proportions, relaying incredible pulses of energy to the rock beneath most of the Mexican capital, and to the deep lens of alluvial, unconsolidated muds and clays and sediments which had filled the northwestern corner of an old, drained lake known as Texcoco.[1]

The ground began to move first to the left, then to the right, passing back through the starting point every two seconds as the undulations increased in amplitude (the degree of displacement from the center). The buildings and houses and structures of Mexico City followed, their foundations moving in the same directions on the same time scale, the upper levels of multistory structures following, but just a bit behind their foundations as the structures of

292

the buildings themselves flexed and bent, protesting the sudden movements. In buildings on bedrock (the majority of the city) the structures moved with enough acceleration to knock over filing cabinets and empty shelves, shuttling tables and chairs and other furniture across thousands of rooms—but the structures themselves remained intact. But the buildings whose foundations sat on the ancient bed of Lake Texcoco were feeling something different. Within ten seconds of the first S wave arrivals, those structures began to come alive, swaying with the rhythm of the quake, the upper stories of buildings up to fifteen stories high rumbling to the limits of a cycle to the left just as the foundation began traveling back to the right, each cycle building the amount of displacement.

Within seconds of their arrival the two-second-cycle seismic waves had begun to vibrate the spongy clay of Lake Texcoco's dry lake bed first to one side, then to the other—back and forth—each cycle causing greater side-to-side undulation of the resilient mass like Jell-O, responding to a shaken bowl with increasingly violent wobbles. With each cycle the alluvial Jell-O amplified the waves even more, transferring that amplified motion to the foundations of the buildings on its surface, those foundations in turn whipping the upper levels of multistory buildings back and forth, each cycle increasing the displacement like the increasing arc of a child on a swing set going farther and farther from the vertical position but powered only by a gentle nudge from someone on the ground at the start of each cycle—a phenomenon known as resonant motion.

In the first thirty seconds, hundreds of reinforced concrete buildings took the frightening undulations in stride, walls breaking and buckling, concrete cracking around joints where floors were attached and walls were bonded, but holding together with the glue of a thousand steel reinforcing rods embedded in the poured concrete. In buildings such as the Hospital Juárez where nearly a thousand patients and staff had been panicked by the first violent undulations) each floor was a heavy slab of steel-reinforced concrete supported by slim columns also of reinforced concrete—the reinforcing rods welded together haphazardly throughout the structure. The building might end up fatally damaged, but at least in theory the strengthening would keep it from collapsing. Most contemporary buildings had been designed (and supposedly built) to meet Mexico City's stringent earthquake building code standards, but those were standards which called for the ability to withstand ground shaking only one-quarter as severe as that which had begun to happen to the structures of the southeastern section of the city.[2]

And as the hospital—along with hundreds of other buildings like it began to accelerate with each sideways lurch, a second snag on the southeastern end of the Michoacán gap fragmented, some twenty-six seconds after the first (at 7:18:14). An adjacent section consisting of hundreds of square miles of rock surfaces twelve miles deep rumbled past each other, radiating out more waves of many wavelengths—but especially the same monstrous pulses in the two-second range—additional pulses which bore in on Mexico City at eighty-eight hundred miles per hour, arriving just as the first-wave trains were diminishing, picking up the undulations of the lake bed and the buildings on top of it where the other had left off, whipping the foundations of buildings which had started with a natural resonant frequency of less than two-second cycles, but which had loosened up with fragmenting walls and breaking joints, their resonant frequency increased now into the same range as the worst of the waves undulating the alluvial muds.

And with fewer than sixty seconds of shaking past, the reinforced concrete buildings of Mexico City which stood between seven and fifteen stories high began to tear themselves apart.

Dr. José Hernández Cruz, an intern at the twenty-five-year-old Hospital Juárez, had joined five other doctors in laughing at the startled looks on the faces of his patients in the orthopedic ward when the building began to move. Moment by moment, however, the motions had become more violent, canceling the laughter, drawing veils of serious apprehension over the faces of the medical men as they listened to the sounds of a thousand items hitting the floor, the roaring and squealing of concrete and steel being forced into motions never contemplated by the design. The entire building would accelerate to one side, taking everything and everybody with it until building and occupants all had reached the same lateral speed—at which point the hospital would suddenly stop and reverse direction, leaving the people, the beds, the furniture, and anything else loose crashing toward the walls as the hospital began accelerating in the opposite direction. With each cycle the force of the reversals became greater, and it became obvious from the horrendous noise that the building couldn't take this for long.

Suddenly there was an absence of light, accompanied by a horrible sinking sensation amidst unbelievable noise and dust and thundering motion as something hit the doctor on the head, forcing him down in a microsecond on top of one of his colleagues. Several blocks away hundreds of people in the Nuevo León apartment complex (fifteen stories, three wings, four hundred units) had felt the same motion, as had the occupants of the huge Hotel Régis. Floor by floor the various structures pancaked, leaned, and crumbled, hundreds of tons of concrete and steel rubble crushing many of those within, trapping many others deep inside spaces barely high enough to survive—spaces which moments before had been rooms eight feet high.

The motion continued, but the world was pitch-black, filled with choking dust and strange odors of spilled liquids and gas. Dr. Cruz realized that the doctor beneath him was not breathing, and that he was trapped—pinned by wreckage, cut off from light, and obviously in mortal danger. Exactly how bad it was, he didn't know, but the fact that the orthopedic ward had collapsed was as obvious as the fact that he physically could not move.

But the sounds from all around him were more chilling than his own worries for safety. There were cries of terror and moans of pain, and chilling screams from the trapped, the hurt, and the dying. Sounds from fellow humans entombed in a district of heavy wreckage which in the space of three minutes had taken more than five thousand lives—a toll which would increase as the hours to come ticked by.

Her reporter companion had grown quiet for a while as they reached the lower levels of the mountains, still seventy miles or more from the coast. Karen McNally's mind had begun to race past her growing fatigue into a host of subjects: the task which lay ahead of placing the portable seismographs; the logistics problems of getting the team fed and bedded down later on; and the hope that any more serious aftershocks would have the courtesy to wait for her seismograph network to be installed and activated. Other members of her University of California at Santa Cruz team had left for Mexico within twelve hours of the quake. Karen had departed a day later, on Friday. All of them were to rendezvous on the coast on Tuesday after installing the portable network. In the meantime, there would be nonstop, backbreaking effort required if they were to capture more of the telltale signatures of this subduction zone.

There were so many overtones from past, last-minute expeditions—unexpected phone calls followed by sudden scrambles to field a team of experts in search of aftershocks. The Coalinga earthquake two years before, for instance, also had been a rushed affair—and a fascinating one. The remembrance of that late-night trek into very familiar territory was quite a contrast to the current one: racing through the wilderness of rural Mexico in the middle of a tropical night.

Karen had grown up in California's San Joaquin Valley, adjacent to the town of Coalinga. Her father, who had really expected his firstborn to be a son, had ideas and plans of what a father and son would do together when Karen had arrived. The realities of the business world and the working world were things he wanted to teach his heir. When he found himself with a smart and energetic daughter instead, the highly educated inventor and manufacturer of farm machinery had decided to keep the same script, and Karen was treated accordingly. A childhood replete with hard work and early responsibility coupled with expectations for superior achievement in a happy family environment was the result. She had driven a tractor by age three (and been run over by one, escaping uninjured, by age five). She had helped with her father's business, and she had traveled with him many, many times through the rural fields and farms of the San Joaquin, her mind etching the sights and the smells of the fertile farmland and the adjacent oilfields of Coalinga along with the memories of her father's endless negotiations and conversations with the farmers who owned and tilled the land. She knew the people, she knew their temperament and their outlooks and their hopes and dreams, and she had experienced a profound feeling of déjà vu to be back among the same farms and fields as they had approached Coalinga in the predawn hours following the 1983 earthquake.

The subsequent days of dealing with those same farmers, gaining permission to install seismographs, asking questions about the earthquake, and keeping an exhausting schedule as the aftershocks continued to rock the shattered town, had been a combination of pleasant memories and confusion. Her father had expected her to be a doctor, an M.D. who might, perhaps, return to the valley to practice as a country physician someday. She had always thought being a doctor meant earning a Ph.D. as a scientist, and seismology had been her ultimate interest. As a seismologist, however, Karen

McNally had somehow never expected to "practice" near her childhood home. Coalinga's agony and the ensuing weeks of field research had changed that.

And Coalinga had changed something else. Not that she had been smug about the abilities she and her colleagues had acquired to identify seismic gaps and pinpoint the locations of upcoming earthquakes, but the sudden eruption of seismic energy from two previously unknown faults (eventually identified and mapped by Karen and others from the aftershock seismograms) had been a warning against smugness. No one had known that those faults lurked beneath the Coalinga oilfield. No one had suspected. Yes, they had come very far in understanding the earthquake mechanisms and identifying potential hazards, but it was painfully obvious that it was only the beginning. Decades of expensive research efforts were vital. Even on the West Coast, it seemed, there were many seismically active cracks beneath the surface which no one had yet discovered, and to that extent, Coalinga had been a profoundly disturbing reminder of how far her science had to go, and of how much there was ahead to discover. It was a feeling and an excitement she tried to convey to her students as a professor, a belief that any of them could make a profound difference in advancing our knowledge and our ability to keep earthquakes from being the killers that this current monster in Mexico City was turning out to be.

They were within fifty miles of the Michoacán coastline now, almost to the area where the first portable seismograph should be placed amidst jungle grasses in the sweltering temperatures and sopping humidity. Karen chuckled quietly at the fact that her resident reporter was going to have to earn his keep. Like it or not, David Smollar was going to be lugging heavy car batteries and other equipment into the jungle in an hour with the rest of them.

Small clouds of mist passed into and beyond her headlights as she thought about the next moves, and about what was going on back in the Mexican capital. Karen was acutely aware that hundreds—perhaps thousands—of fellow humans lay trapped and dying beneath tons of crumbled building materials in the Mexican capital city some two hundred miles to the east of her. There had been a massive aftershock on Friday—an M_s 7.6 monster which hit the city at the exact moment she was standing in the terminal at Los

297

Angeles International Airport telling David Smollar that such an aftershock might be imminent.

In Mexico City the shifting rubble and precarious structures of critically damaged buildings had collapsed further, extinguished more lives, including those of many trapped people who had been hanging on by a thread of hope and prayer since Thursday morning, many of them deep within the artificial tomb which so many downtown buildings had become. But there were many hearts still beating under the tons of rubble. Karen and the other members of the team, especially those from Mexico City, had heard much of the rescue efforts while they worked feverishly in Guadalajara, preparing for this dash to the sea. Obviously some people would be pulled out in time, and some would not. The television clips of the pancaked horror that had been the Benito Juárez Hospital, for instance, made that reality all too clear. The citywide death toll was already estimated at near ten thousand people, with thirty thousand injured, more than a hundred thousand homeless, and more than seven thousand buildings badly damaged or destroyed. And that toll was likely to grow—especially if more major aftershocks hit the municipality.

But the Mexican capital was a city of more than one million buildings and eighteen million people. Most of Mexico City still stood intact. Unreinforced masonry buildings in the areas of worst shaking had all but exploded, and some reinforced concrete towers standing too close to other similar buildings ended up beating each other to pieces, but older structures such as the Metropolitan Cathedral and very modern skyscrapers, such as the fifty-two-story headquarters of Pemex (the Mexican state oil company and the tallest building in Latin America), still stood effectively undamaged. Even Mexico City's airport, located entirely on the old lake bed, had come through intact. While it was a horrendous tragedy—while the price in human lives and human suffering would stagger the imagination—it was obvious even in the early stages of recovery that the seismic building codes had worked to save lives and property.

It was also obvious, Karen knew, that the monstrous destruction which had occurred over 230 miles from the epicenter of the coastal quake validated what Dr. Otto Nuttli of St. Louis University had been warning of for so long regarding the East Coast of the United States: Great earthquakes could cause massive damage hundreds of miles away. The New Madrid Fault, for instance, could collapse buildings in Chicago and Kansas City, Dallas, Little Rock, New Orleans, and Memphis all in the same cataclysm if it produced a future M_s 8.0 or greater earthquake. Many seismologists and seismic engineers had winked indulgently at Nuttli's theoretical worries in past years. Now, of course, they would have to take him more seriously. If Mexico City produced no other lessons, it would drive that one home.

As Karen began braking the Travelall to a halt to drop the first seismograph, 210 miles to the east in Mexico City Dr. José Cruz had felt his heart nearly stop as he recognized the words in Spanish from a rescuer somewhere in the darkness above him:

"*Demasiado personas son muerte ahora, un otro no está importante.* [Many people are already dead, (if another dies) it doesn't matter]."

The chief of a rescue squad which had been trying for hours to tunnel through to him had been told to give up. But they had argued vehemently and successfully for more time. Now the time was gone, the rescuers were many steel rods and concrete chunks away from where Dr. Cruz had been imprisoned, and once again they were being told to give him up for dead and move on.

José Cruz had heard the sounds of other people being pulled joyously into the sunlight in the previous hours, escaping the prison that the pancaked floors of the hospital had become. He had longed to join them—he had yelled and screamed for help until hoarse—but now he would surely die.

An argument flared outside, the boss relented again, and once more the digging began—one of a thousand Herculean efforts across the damaged city.

And once more the young doctor had a chance.

On Monday morning, while Karen McNally slept through the last few minutes of a short night on the Michoacán coast, Dr. José Cruz was finally pulled into the morning light, bruised, dehydrated, emaciated, traumatized, and shaking—but alive, two days past his twenty-third birthday. Behind him, however, in the rubble, were over five hundred patients and doctors and nurses who had not been so fortunate. Even as Cruz was being loaded into an ambulance before waiting TV cameras, those trapped within tried to hold on still longer, clinging to a last few hours of life while frustrated rescuers practiced the art of the possible.

And as Karen McNally and her team punched off portable alarm clocks and prepared for another exhausting day of tending remote portable seismographs along the coast, the knowledge that the Michoacán seismic gap had been filled by the great quake was replaced by the more ominous reality that the Guerrero gap—adjacent to Acapulco and right between the site of the Oaxaca quake and the Michoacán (Mexico City) quake—was next. The seismic gap method obviously worked in providing the answers to whether and where—the only remaining question was when. And answering that one would take a lot more time, and a lot more research—the financing for which would ultimately have to come from the Congress of the United States.

Washington, D.C.—Thursday, October 3, 1985

Senator Slade Gorton of Washington State took his seat at the head of the hearing table in the second-floor room of the Russell Senate Office Building, aware that as he prepared to gavel the proceedings into session, the cleanup continued nearly two thousand miles distant in Mexico City. The official death toll was above five thousand now, the unofficial toll over ten thousand, and damages were being estimated in the range of four to five billion dollars. Gorton's subcommittee (on Science, Technology, and Space) of the Senate Committee on Commerce, Science, and Transportation had hurriedly asked a group of distinguished scientists and professors to come to Washington to begin building a graphic record on exactly what had occurred in the Mexican capital. To Gorton and the only other senator present, Al Gore of Tennessee, the exercise was urgent and very important.

Slade Gorton, a tall and distinguished-looking lawyer and former Washington State attorney general, was well aware that his own home state of Washington was earthquake country. Thus the subject was doubly important to him, especially since there had been indications lately that Washington, Oregon, and Northern California might be subject to the same magnitude of great subduction zone earthquake which had just occurred in Michoacán.

The previous March, Gorton had dealt with the reauthorization of the Earthquake Hazard Reduction Act, which President Reagan had just signed. That had helped open his eyes to the problem, but

300

Mexico City had ushered in a higher magnitude of sensitivity. There were obviously profound lessons the United States needed to learn from this great earthquake, and perhaps this early hearing record would be a beginning.

Slade Gorton noticed the clock standing at 10:25 A.M., the appointed time for the hearing, as he looked at the different people now taking their seats. Representatives from the Federal Insurance Administration, the Federal Emergency Management Agency, and the USGS were off to one side, along with a friend of Senator Gore's, Dr. Arch Johnston, director of the Tennessee Earthquake Information Center in Memphis, and a professor at Memphis State. Johnston had been almost alone for many years in his attempts to alert his hometown to the fact that the New Madrid Fault could bring the city of Memphis to its knees in any future great quake. He was making progress, but it was slow going.

And near Dr. Johnston was a familiar face from Gorton's home state, Dr. Linda Noson, a seismologist from the University of Washington in Seattle who also served as the state seismologist in an even lonelier quest to alert Washingtonians about the dangers of future earthquakes.

Gorton banged his gavel and began, making a brief opening statement before turning the floor over to Al Gore.

"Two weeks ago today," Senator Gore began, "the world witnessed one of the worst natural disasters of recent years. On September 19, an earthquake registering 8.1 on the [surface magnitude] scale struck the western coast of Mexico. . . .

"The tragedy of Mexico City's earthquake illustrates all too starkly the devastation that can result when a city is prepared to cope with neither the eventuality of an earthquake nor the tremendous damage that can be caused by one.

"Indeed, the city lay vulnerable to the earthquake that struck it like a sad, helpless giant. Many of the buildings were structurally incapable of withstanding an earthquake, and the ground upon which [a portion of] the city stands actually amplified the shockwaves.

"Even worse, once the disaster had occurred, the city proved incapable of responding quickly to the disaster. . . .

"There are many lessons that we in the United States should learn from the earthquake. . . . [F]oremost among these is that we

301

must do everything within our ability to assure that no city or area in this country suffers like Mexico City because of an earthquake. We must take every step to make certain we are prepared for the eventuality of earthquakes, and that we are capable of responding swiftly and effectively to them when they occur.

"Earthquakes are not a possibility," Gore continued. "They are a certainty. . . ."

Nevertheless, as the hearing progressed, the specter of a legislative measure known as the Gramm-Rudman-Hollings amendment continued to spread its inexorable shadow over the federal budget, threatening even the newly reauthorized Earthquake Hazard Reduction Act, and threatening to reduce, rather than expand, the lifeline of federal funding which had already dried to a trickle for far too many university researchers, such as Dr. Karen McNally, who depend on federal grants through the USGS to keep going.[3] Funds for other vital programs—efforts such as Dr. Arch Johnston's Earthquake Information Center activities in Memphis—were also tight to nonexistent. It was obvious to many in the hearing room that until the issue became a sufficiently significant national priority—until people realized that not only Los Angeles, but Memphis, St. Louis, Chicago, Buffalo, or even New York City could be transmitting those horrific television images of crushed humanity and destroyed lives—the momentum and the money would remain ridiculously insufficient.

302

Chapter 22

Charleston, South Carolina—1987

The last of the tourists—a man and a woman walking arm in arm—moved silently past the imposing gazebo of the elegant old waterfront park, seemingly lost in their enjoyment of the lyrical setting under the starlit canopy of a South Carolina summer night.

The south side of the park called White Point Gardens was bordered by Murray Boulevard at the southern point of old Charleston—overlooking the confluence of the Ashley and Cooper rivers and the lights of historic Fort Sumter farther south toward the Atlantic.

The north side, however, held a wall of American poetry in brick and mortar on the other side of South Battery, a picturesque street adorned with expensive, historic residences rich in American history and the tapestry of life in nineteenth-century South Carolina—and rich with the promise of instant disaster if what happened beneath the alluvial muds of Charleston in 1886 were to occur again.

"It's the same old story," the Charleston city engineer had said. "Mortar reduced to virtually nothing but sand and powder. As long as nothing moves it, it's all right."

Charleston had been warned for most of the summer of 1886, but no one really knew what the warning meant. Residents of the elegant American city had heard constant tales about swarms of small earthquakes occurring just to the north of Charleston in the farming community of Summerville, but few paid any attention. There was no one in 1886 who had any reason to suspect that what the Low Country (as the Charleston area was called) had felt might be the low-volume overture to an impending symphony of seismic waves.

At 9:51 P.M. on the 31st of August, however, an unseen and unknown fault somewhere beneath the thousands of feet of sediments underlying Charleston rumbled into motion, great rock faces suddenly moving past each other, breaking whatever snag had been holding back a torrent of stored energy. The city shuddered with the first P wave arrivals, then began to whip and shake horrendously in the grip of what would be identified decades later as probably a surface magnitude M_s 7.7 earthquake. For thirty-five to forty seconds the ground beneath the city (an alluvial aggregate thoroughly saturated with water) lurched first to one side, then to the other, the multistory brittle, unreinforced masonry buildings trying to follow their foundations, but fragmenting into a million flying pieces amidst dust and falling timbers. Stucco, masonry blocks, and bricks were presumed glued together by mortar, but the high-lime mortar had turned to sand over the years, leaving much of Charleston's elegant brick buildings intact only through the grace of gravity and the audacity of weight.

Now in the grip of a great quake, they began collapsing like an unsupported wall of canned goods in a grocery store, fourteen thousand chimneys crumbling, walls and entire houses fragmenting and falling on a population which would lose sixty lives and hundreds of destroyed homes to the deadly rain of ruined building materials. As the worst of the shaking took hold of Charleston, a spherical wave of seismic energy fanned out to neighboring communities, spreading like the ripples from a rock thrown in the middle of a quiet pond, wreaking havoc and shaking apart man-made structures as far away as a hundred miles.

And what the main shock didn't disintegrate, a hard aftershock eight minutes later would finish off.

Charleston lay badly damaged, with over twenty-three million dollars in destruction. And Charleston's population, both black and white, was traumatized. As aftershocks continued, people moved onto lawns and common areas, some vacating perfectly sound houses for weeks in fear. Prayer meetings became thoroughly interracial as a shocked community of fellow humans shuddered at their vulnerability in the face of such power.

But as has been American tradition since the earliest days, Charleston dove into the task of rebuilding itself. Within a year the city's reconstruction effort had reached significant milestones—not the least of which was an inadvertent legacy of vulnerability to future great quakes: many seriously weakened buildings were rebuilt with little more than cosmetic patching.[1]

Most of the homes which had been standing in 1886 had suffered major damage, but the majority were repaired too superficially, with grave structural weaknesses hidden beneath a veneer of fresh mortar. Now they sat in endless ranks, these elegant mansions, looking permanent and timeless, bathed in the soft light of sodium vapor lamps from the southernmost park in the city, sitting like stately ghosts along the margin of the treelined South Battery Street in the cool, humid breeze blowing up the bay from the direction of Fort Sumter, mansions at once elegant and imposing and dangerous as hell.

How do you get people to rebuild fantastically expensive old classics like those? The question had haunted seismically knowledgeable engineers for years. And in other American cities thousands of buildings which had little or no historical value and were verified seismic bombs remained standing with the same financial momentum. Passing new, stringent seismic building codes and requiring new buildings to conform is many times easier than forcing people to tear down or completely rebuild existing structures which may be worth millions.

Charleston in particular was merely waiting for disaster, the entire southern end—the classic, historic, beautiful section which drew tourists each year by the tens of thousands—barely held together by powdery mortar. In 1981, for instance, the front of one old building at 64 Beaufain Street simply collapsed spontaneously, the stucco and brick cascading down onto the sidewalk in front of startled pedestrians (none of whom was hurt). The collapse prompted Charleston's chief building official, Doug Smits, to order it vacated—and rebuilt. But the thing that had chilled Smits and many others was the apparent cause of the collapse: mere traffic vibrations.[2] The three-story house had been built before the Civil War, and though the great quake of 1886 had not demolished it, the masonry structure apparently had cracked and fragmented in places which remained hidden for the next hundred years behind freshly applied—but structurally useless—masonry veneer.

"The only thing that held that part of the facade [at 64 Beaufain] together," Smits had said, "[was] the stucco."

There was no easy answer, of course. It had taken Los Angeles sixteen years to rebuild or tear down only a third of its dangerous masonry buildings—their "seismic bombs"—and few, if any, of those had historic value. Charleston was awash in multimillion-dollar structures of considerable historic value which had been significantly weakened in 1886, and which would probably explode into fragments of walls and bricks and chimneys and rubble the next time the unknown fault which had snapped in 1886 lurched again.

If it was a difficult proposition on the West Coast, it was many times more problematic on the East. The challenge of getting people east of the Rockies to believe a major quake could occur beneath their real estate seemed to bedevil all the experts. Even in Charleston that was true. Even in a city of proven vulnerability where a seismic catastrophe had happened before and so clearly could happen again, people wanted to ignore the possibility.

Most Charlestonians seemed well aware of their earthquake heritage, but they were equally convinced they had little to worry about in the future.

"We won't get another like that for three hundred to a thousand years!" another city official said, ". . . and most of the dangerous homes won't last that long anyway without a complete rebuild."

Yet there were some valiant efforts under way by some energetic pioneers in earthquake mitigation—people such as Professor Joyce Bagwell of Baptist College at Charleston. An enthusiastic educator, she was one of the first in the nation to attack the problem from the ground up—concentrating her efforts on teaching schoolchildren about earthquakes, involving them in classroom exercises, finding hazards, drawing up lists of repairs, and even making out school requisitions for needed materials.

"We get them involved," she explains to visitors; "then they teach their parents."

It had been the joint interest of Joyce Bagwell and another Charleston educator, Dr. Charles Lindbergh (a professor of civil engineering at the Citadel), that had prompted them to attend a pivotal conference on eastern earthquake potential held in Knoxville, Tennessee, in 1981. The recognition of just how unprepared their area and the entire eastern seaboard was for major earthquakes had launched both of them into the mainstream of hazard mitigation.[3]

Hazard reduction means establishing realistic seismic building codes nationwide—stringent codes based on assessment of potential ground shaking which would require seismic engineering precautions which, on average, would add less than 20 percent to construction costs (even in the most deadly seismic zones such as Charleston, South Carolina, or Redwood City, California). Putting such codes into effect to cover future construction, as well as mandating the teardown or reinforcing of the seismic bombs—the buildings and structures which will unquestionably collapse in a significant earthquake—must become high priorities in New York, Boston, Chicago, St. Louis, Dallas, Kansas City, Louisville, Charleston, and many other cities.

But these recognitions are slow in coming. In the case of Memphis, for instance—a city which sits on the same grassy bluff which had wiggled like a bowl of possessed Jell-O during all three of the New Madrid quakes—the community has yet to enact a single seismic building code. Unbelievably blasé in the face of cataclysmic danger, Memphis, Tennessee, stands exposed and ready for destruction—and reluctant to face the facts.[4]

Yet beneath the runways at Memphis International Airport, beneath the massive facilities of the Federal Express Corporation's headquarters on the northeast shoulder of the airport, beneath the corporate headquarters of the Holiday Inn Corporation, and beneath the tourist-infested entrance to Elvis Presley's Graceland, the unconsolidated soils covering the soft sedimentary rocks beneath Memphis stand ready and able to massively amplify the monstrous seismic waves that a new lurch of the New Madrid Fault (which runs as close as forty-four miles away) could send out.

Unreinforced masonry buildings sitting on shaky foundations atop soggy, water-saturated ground; blocks of city buildings built on well-engineered fill but resting on top of weak and saturated layers of clay and sand which could fail just like the Bootlegger Cove Clay of Anchorage; and tens of thousands of residences and other buildings heavily adorned with bricks and cinder blocks and masonry walls of inadequate reinforcement—all stand ready to collapse in the violent shaking of another 8.0 magnitude quake (or even a lesser quake).

Damage estimates of more than fifty billion dollars and carnage in excess of eight thousand deaths are considered realistic—yet the members of City Council and the county government had spent the previous two years hemming and hawing and scratching their heads over whether the political risk of passing new codes and slightly

307

increasing building costs might be too great a price to pay for getting their community ready to survive what someday is going to happen. In the particular case of Memphis—sitting astride a seismic bomb of nuclear proportions—the municipal foot dragging is quite obviously madness.

Paul Flores sat behind his desk with downtown Los Angeles visible over his shoulder considering the long distance his organization had come in six years. The Southern California Earthquake Preparedness Project—known far and wide in Southern California as SCEPP—had no power. Neither Flores, as director, nor the SCEPP itself could make any new laws, compel any city to change its building codes, or force anyone to tear down dangerous buildings. All SCEPP could do was urge and educate people and community leaders about the dangers they all faced in the valleys of the shadow of the San Andreas.[5]

"I think we're more of a catalyst," he said. "Our trick, our primary means of survival [in demonstrating] that we're worth the taxpayers' money, is how successful we are at convincing target groups to take action."

SCEPP was the very first "before the disaster" earthquake hazard reduction program in the nation to be sparked by the funding and the momentum of the 1977 federal Hazard Reduction Act. Now there was a similar program in the San Francisco–Oakland Bay area (Bay Area Earthquake Preparedness Project, or BAREPP for short). Both used very small amounts of federal and state funding to push along community awareness and municipal governments.

The problems had been overwhelming at first, many of them revolving around communications. While SCEPP's initial focus had been to prepare the L.A. area for responding to a short-term earthquake prediction, the Project quickly began to evolve into a nucleus of people who tried constantly to get various agencies of city and county governments, building departments, fire departments, police and sheriff's departments, water departments, emergency response coordinating agencies, and the university seismological community simply to talk to each other.

"The problems just in emergency radio communication were unbelievable. We had over a hundred and forty police and fire jurisdictions all with different radio systems. If there had been a city-wide emergency, none of them could have talked to each other."

The focus, however, rapidly broadened to the questions of how to get rid of L.A.'s seismic bombs—the thousands of unreinforced masonry buildings—and how to upgrade the building codes in all the communities around L.A., not just the city itself. With no power to compel anyone to do anything, SCEPP could actually operate more effectively and with much greater freedom by talking, cajoling, urging, informing, pleading, and sometimes building public pressure through public exposure of hazards or local municipal foot dragging. With energy, logic, and the ability to spark action by the myriad of city and county governments throughout the L.A. area, SCEPP began to have an effect, and things began to change.

Even with substantial progress, and even with all the accomplishments and meetings and coordination, by midyear 1987 SCEPP was just beginning to grapple with the first vestiges of what would be a many-decade battle to put the public safety ahead of the short-term public and private interests.[6]

But in Portland, Oregon, and Seattle, Washington, no equivalents to BAREPP or SCEPP have been formed. Nor are there such organizations in New York, Boston, Chicago, St. Louis, Washington, D.C., or even Salt Lake City (where only a few dedicated people who understand that their home-on-a-fault at the base of the Wasatch Range will shake again violently someday work to educate their neighbors about the reality of seismic hazards).

By 1987, though, there was at least one place outside California where the populace and the politicians had a responsibility to know better. It is a place where the seismic hazards are more than well known, where the potential for ground failure and massive shaking is well established. It is a community where seismic buildings codes and intelligent zoning should have been coupled with constant earthquake education and hazard mitigation in providing the basis of every act of every building department, city and county government, and zoning commission in the region.

Yet it is a great American community which has no BAREPP, no SCEPP, no Dr. Lindberg or Dr. Johnston, and no USGS presence of sufficient import to influence or affect community thinking. It is an area which seems to have forgotten its past within months of a cataclysm which had been, in seismological terms, the greatest in North America since the New Madrid quakes.

That city, in fact, is Anchorage, Alaska.

Chapter 23

Anchorage, Alaska—1987

"The 1964 earthquake? Good grief, that's ancient history!"

The Anchorage man paused for a minute, searching for a name.

"I'm sure there are a lot of people still around who lived through it, but I didn't come up here till later."

Anchorage, in many ways, has forgotten the past—relegating the experiences of the Good Friday disaster to the category of quaint and colorful local history and forgetting any lessons that might have been learned.

But in truth, that process had begun almost as soon as the ground stopped shaking in 1964. Anchorage residents were hearty and self-sufficient. They wanted no one standing in the way of rebuilding their city.

Former Alaska Governor Walter Hickel had set the tone himself, within months of the quake, during the summer of 1964, when he broke ground for a new hotel (the Captain Cook) by the site of the L Street slide—running full speed against the professional advice of seismic engineers and municipal planners and federal reconstruction task force officials. Hickel had effectively looked the city and the scientific community in their collective eyes and said, "No damn scientist is going to stand in the way of this city's progress!"

And his opponents blinked.

Anchorage may have traveled chronologically twenty-three years forward by 1987, but in terms of seismic safety, in some respects it was as vulnerable as it had been in 1964. Now 180,000 Anchorage residents live in the crosshairs of future great quakes, yet most were not around that particular Good Friday. Even those who are survivors of the quake—many now wealthy leaders of the community with a heavy responsibility for the public's safety—have

311

long since begun to wink at the reality that Anchorage has the potential to be a seismic bomb if its houses and buildings and institutions fail to incorporate the lessons of the recent past.

Yet, as Governor Wally Hickel made very clear within a few months of the cataclysm, the "progress" of Anchorage has always involved the process of calculated and assumed risks, a process that came into nose-to-nose conflict with the honest efforts of concerned geologists, seismologists, politicians, bureaucrats, city planners, and humanitarians in the days and weeks and months following Good Friday, 1964—a cadre of concerned fellow Americans who wanted nothing more than to help their brave frontier neighbors rebuild, but at a lower, more reasonable level of risk.

But that sparked an inevitable clash between private rights and public interests—an inherent contradiction between the very American desire to decide for yourself how much risk is enough from a particular hazard, and the responsibility of the society (acting through government) to minimize the public's risk of physical and financial harm from the same hazard. It is, in other words, merely a scaled-up version of a familiar debate: that of the motorcyclist who rages against a state law requiring him to wear a helmet, yet who will become an expensive ward of the state if his failure to wear a helmet should metastasize through an accident and paralysis into the need for lifetime public assistance. In the final analysis, there is no standard answer—only the need for constant, intelligent discussion and decision by the populace and their leaders who must first face the fact that there *is* a significant seismic risk, and who then must decide how much damage and carnage that same subdivision of society is willing to accept when the inevitable happens. And those subdivisions of society begin with the smallest of governmental units: cities, towns, and communities, and their city councils, county councils, zoning commissions, and any other gathering of two or more citizens concerned about the common good.

Warren Hines and his wife had been walking their bicycles along the beach below Turnagain when Warren saw the plate. It was a piece of porcelain in the mud. They had passed the same spot before over the years, cycling along the waterline westward from the downtown area toward the city's Earthquake Park (where the torn and jumbled landscape had been left just as it had settled on March 23, 1964). Year after year the waterline had moved closer to the new Turnagain bluff, the waves eroding the tongue of dirt and clay and sand which had flowed into the inlet on the slippery layer of Bootlegger Cove Clay during the great quake, carrying his neighborhood—and his family home—with it.

Warren leaned down and began digging for the rest of the object, startled to see the familiar pattern of apples appear as he pulled it free from the sand and mud.

What on earth?

At first his mind rebelled at the idea, but the object was unmistakably part of a plate—a set of plates from which the Hines family had eaten many a meal more than twenty years before. Of the many personal possessions that had submerged with the wreckage of their home in 1964, his mother's china had been one—and here it was again.

He began clawing at an adjacent clump of sand, uncovering bits of green and pink tile from their downstairs bathroom wall, and then found the carcass of a little red plastic radio, one that had sat on the family refrigerator, and one to which he had listened many a morning before school. Obviously the ground beneath his feet had become the final resting place for the broken pieces of his family home, but for some reason he wasn't compelled to keep digging.

The erosion of the "new" shoreline had been exposing more and more wreckage during the past decade. Hines had seen an article in the Anchorage paper about that—accompanied by a picture of cinder blocks and bricks and other rubble appearing at low tide. But somehow Warren had never expected the erosion to come back this far; their home had glided only halfway to the water when it disintegrated. These bits and pieces were now *on* the waterline.

Warren Hines replaced the objects at first. They belonged to another time placing, and they belonged to the beach. It was only to appease his wife that he finally, reluctantly, bent down and scooped up the familiar little radio, brushing off the sand and silt, placing it unceremoniously in the basket of his bike. Even then, it seemed almost a sacrilege. What was past, was past, and best forgotten.

Or was it?

Warren had followed his father into the land development business, learning to live with seismic engineering statistics. But this land, this beach, this graveyard for scores of homes (and two little boys—the Mead children)—had never been made into a park or a greenbelt as the Corps of Engineers and the Alaska State Housing Authority and many others had intended. And now, as Warren knew well, debates and lawsuits were raging over a new subdivision plan laid out by those who wanted to build new houses and apartments *between the new bluff and the beach,* on the rubble of the old Turnagain Heights, where he had grown up.

"Part of the reason for this, is that the state never demanded title to those ruined lots!" Dr. Lidia Selkregg sat in the coffee shop of the Anchorage Westward—now the Anchorage Hilton—and gestured toward the western wall with infectious enthusiasm.

"They gave the people new land free in a place called the Zodiac Manor, but they never demanded title to the Turnagain lots in return. For ten years Anchorage keeps the ruined land off the tax roles. Suddenly they decide to assign a value and tax it, and these people say, 'Hey, if this land has value, I want to sell.'

"Then, the people whose houses didn't go over the edge, you see, those people never had view property, but after the earthquake and the Turnagain slide, now they do—and they don't want someone building new houses below their new bluff and blocking their view. So when the lot owners start to sell and builders begin trying for building permits, the people on the new bluff start suing.

"But when the next big quake comes, Turnagain will slip again, especially the area below the bluff that collapsed in 1964."

In the months after the quake the Corps of Engineers had tried in vain to find ways of stabilizing Turnagain, and as Lidia Selkregg herself had reported in later publications, the engineers agreed that the only thing that would keep Turnagain usable *above the bluff* was the presence of the approximately thousand feet of ruined ground between the bluff and the waterline—"provided the [natural] buttress is protected against beach erosion. The buttress itself, however, will be subject to substantial differential movements for some time to come, and may experience large distortions in future earthquakes. Therefore, construction upon [the ruined area] should not be permitted."[1]

Nothing, however, had been done by the city in the following years to forever prohibit new construction in the very ruined area of Turnagain Heights that the engineers had warned about. (In fact, by 1985, one new house had been built in the slide area below the bluff before the city suspended further construction.)

And the reemerging bits and pieces of a former life which Warren Hines had found bore mute evidence to another major failure: Nothing had been done to prevent the erosion of the very material which was to stabilize the hundreds of houses which now sat on the edge of the new bluff, and which, in the absence of that "natural buttress," would likely suffer the same fate in the next great quake.

"It is amazing, but they don't want to think about it. It will never happen again in their lifetimes, they say." Dr. Selkregg sipped her coffee for a second, oblivious to the restaurant sounds around her, concentrating on twenty-three years of postearthquake history with the intensity of a university professor—which she had been for as many seasons at the University of Alaska's Anchorage campus.

Lidia Selkregg had become a part of municipal planning in Anchorage before the quake, and before she had joined the Alaska State Housing Authority (ASHA). Her training as a geologist, her deep love for Alaska (she had come to the state in the 1950's with her husband, Fred), and her boundless energy mixed with a distinctive accent from her native Italy, had made her a dynamic and memorable part of the equation in the hours and days following the 1964 convulsion. She had immediately organized a large team of local geologists and engineers into the volunteer Engineering Geology Evaluation Group, which in two weeks had mapped most of the cracks and fissures and landslides in the Anchorage area in great and precise detail—work that was of immeasurable help to other groups ranging from the USGS to the Corps of Engineers. Selkregg had also done much of the tremendous volume of work of getting the population of Valdez prepared to abandon the old townsite completely and move to a new location along the bay—a project partially controlled by the ASHA.

She had known of the studies by Ernest Dobrovolny and Robert Miller in 1959, when they predicted future problems for anything built on the Bootlegger Cove Clay and identified the Turnagain and L Street areas as having suffered major landslides at least several times in the past. And it had been Dr. Selkregg, working in the Anchorage City Planning Department, who had overheard Wally Hickel five years before the Good Friday quake when he brought in his plans for a hotel to be constructed on a plot of ground to the north of Third Avenue—a section of earth which would subside and buckle when the earth began to shake in 1964. It had, in fact, been Lidia Selkregg's recommendation that the site be tested (based on Dobrovolny and Miller's study), a test sequence that found sufficient dangers to change even Hickel's mind—and the hotel's eventual location.

"When the [Captain] Cook eventually opened in 1965 at the west end of downtown, he even invited me to the opening ceremonies—me, one of those damn scientists that tried to stand in his way! That was nice. I congratulated him." Lidia smiled broadly, the remembrance of that and many other civilized clashes with the established movers and shakers of Anchorage intertwined with years of service on the Municipal Assembly (city council).

"There was this editorial cartoon in Bob Atwood's paper [the Anchorage *Daily Times*]," she said, smiling again, ". . . which ran in regard to my constant involvement with earthquake safety issues and building locations. Here I am as a chicken running down the street yelling, 'The ground is falling, the ground is falling!' I thought that was wonderful, good satire, and the cartoonist sent me the original, which I framed.

"But"—she held up an index finger, wagging it in remonstrance—"but there are still buildings in the wrong place!"

"The point Wally was making," Bob Atwood had said, ". . . was that this is valuable land, and until another quake comes, why shouldn't we use it? Use it safely, of course, but use it." Atwood, the newspaper publisher whose memories of losing his elegant home (and his trumpet) at Turnagain were still fresh, described the way the business community and civic leaders had rebelled at the initial ideas of the scientists and municipal planners who had identified most of downtown Anchorage as high-risk and even recommended relocating the business district. As geologic and soil studies continued into May and into summer, the area labeled "high-risk" shrank, until the downtown section included the Forth Avenue area (adjacent to the surviving Anchorage Westward Hotel, of which Atwood had been a part owner), and the west end of the downtown area, the L Street slide—on the eastern edge of which Wally Hickel was determined to place the Captain Cook.

"He had some method of removing enough soil to equal the weight of the building, and used other methods to anchor it, but he couldn't get [the federal government] to take the lot out of the high-risk classification."

316

Bob Atwood had alternated between stories of worrisome overdevelopment of high-risk zones and his concerns over the quality of contemporary Anchorage building inspection and compliance standards, to prideful remembrances of his fellow business friends who had pushed ahead against all odds—and against much advice.

"There were many of us around here who felt, a year after the quake, that the plague of scientists had been harder to deal with than the quake itself."[2]

That line had been used many times around Anchorage in the years after 1964, along with the rather common attitude that the task force and the invading scientists had overstayed their welcome the moment they began to close their checkbooks and open their mouths.

As another Anchorage earthquake veteran put it, "We wanted their [federal dollars], but we didn't want their goddamn dictatorial advice. We'll rebuild where we want to rebuild, and take the risks ourselves."

But, with hundreds of millions of federal money spent after such a disaster—our tax money—there is a legitimate question whether the rest of us who pay the bill have the right to say to any community: "If you want our help, you need to be more careful how much risk you take." Americans will always provide federal aid, no matter how negligent a community has been in permitting dangerous building practices. And in 1964, Alaskans welcomed federal aid. Coalinga—at least the city government—welcomed federal aid. San Fernando wanted low-cost loans and federal highway funds and disaster relief. But there is good reason for the argument that such help should not become a substitute for careful hazard reduction efforts.

There is also a substantial difference between one homeowner's accepting a major risk for himself and his family, and a developer's "accepting a risk" for the future occupants of a condominium, or the unknowing, transient occupants of a hotel, or the workers in an office building. And in the case of the so-called L Street slide, that was precisely the issue.

The block Wally Hickel chose for his new Captain Cook Hotel sat just to the east of the graben—the trench—which had opened between the rest of the downtown area and a crescent-shaped, thirty-square-block chunk of the city's western edge when that chunk moved as a unit up to fourteen feet toward the water. In

317

1964 there were mostly houses among the single high-rise apartment buildings and the few businesses, and the majority had not been extensively damaged—merely relocated involuntarily. The governmental task force of engineers and geologists (called Task Force 9) quickly classified the area as high-risk, blocking all federal assistance to property owners for repair or reconstruction. Nevertheless, disaster relief funds were spent immediately to restore water, sewer, electrical, and natural gas services as well as streets, and that restoration of utilities to expensive buildings on view property which were more or less structurally intact gave the owners the unforeseen ability to hold out against any attempt to condemn, relocate, or rezone. Several geologists were convinced that the L Street slide was incomplete, and that with the slightest seismic provocation the movement would start again as the upper blocks of building-laden ground rolled toward the bluffs on the tiny waterlogged "ball bearings" of the Bootlegger Cove Clay. The result would be measurable in smashed buildings and perhaps smashed occupants on the beach below, with buildings to the rear of the leading edge treated much the same as the houses in Turnagain Heights.

The political pressure on the municipality of Anchorage was instantly at a fever pitch to leave the L Street slide out of any apocalyptic land use planning. The idea had been floated—and just as quickly sunk—that the entire area should be razed and made into a daytime-only park or greenbelt. But in a city which had already lost far too many buildings and far too much business, the idea of tearing down more—especially with government compensation based on postearthquake values—was unacceptable. In addition, there was no support for any extensive economic or engineering study of how the L Street blocks might be stabilized, and the task force, as a result, sidestepped the issue. In fact, within a year the Municipal Assembly had gone entirely in the opposite direction, and amazingly enough voted to approve rezoning to increase the residential densities in the slide area. By 1987 the L Street slide district had been adorned with many new high-rise office buildings, condominiums, businesses, and a few houses, and had progressed from merely an area of accelerated risk to its present-day position as a potential major disaster waiting for the pull of a seismic trigger.

And below the bluff of the L Street slide area—in a location where some attempt at stabilization might have been attempted—nothing but the restored rails of the Alaska Railroad are anchored.

318

As the authors of the National Science Foundation—sponsored study *Land Use Planning After Earthquakes* pointed out, "No restrictions on development have been imposed in the area to reduce seismic risk, and the zoning changes have certainly increased the potential for casualties and property damage in future earthquakes."[3]

In Seward, the recommendations of scientists and geologists and municipal planners had been followed primarily because the ruined economy had never recovered, and there was never the financial pressure on the city to relent to new and dangerous waterfront development in areas where the San Juan dock and the Standard Oil docks had been.[4]

In Valdez, however, the recommendations had been followed to the letter because the solution was wrenchingly simple: Since the site of the pre—Good Friday Valdez was patently unsafe and now many feet lower than before (the lower streets washed by seawater at high tide), the entire site had to be abandoned.[5]

Even so, with the prosperity which the southern terminus of the Trans-Alaska Pipeline brought to Valdez, there has been considerable pressure on the city to relent and permit some new development at the old site—attempts largely by newcomers who look at unused land and ache, ignoring the deeper human aching of twenty-three years before when twenty-eight Valdezians died at the end of John Kelsey's dock.[6]

But in Anchorage, the momentum of the business community and the financial interests of the citizenry in the impassioned rush to rebuild and return to normal had shrunk the well-intentioned seismic planning of various agencies to a small section of the Fourth Avenue slide area, and in the opinion of many downtown merchants and city leaders, even that was too much governmental involvement.

"We gave [the scientists and bureaucrats] a little area around Fourth Avenue to play with, so they could play their renewal games, justify their jobs, and leave the rest of us the hell alone!" one former city official explained.

With the scope of federal redevelopment massively curtailed under the boot of political pressure and economic protest—with the map of high-risk and provisional high-risk areas shrunk to the smallest possible size—and with the scientific community's being made to feel like a roadblock in Anchorage's highway to prosperity, the bright hope of making the city a seismically safe, model community evaporated. Worse, the redevelopment failure left the huge chunk of L Street and the ruined landscape at Turnagain wholly vulnerable to forgetfulness, rationalization, and the profit motive.

The problem wasn't an absence of codes or standards in Anchorage. In fact, the city had a strict seismic building code which was carefully updated to even more stringent levels in the years after 1964. Requirements for careful design of foundations and structures, plus requirements for appropriate grades and quantities of structural steel to make buildings truly earthquake-resistant, insured that whatever was built in Anchorage would be far better prepared for major earthquakes than buildings in most American cities. The quality of such buildings was seldom in question—the location, on the other hand, often was.

In addition, the survival of the Anchorage Westward Hotel—and all the slide-prone ground beneath and behind it—proved that not only the buildings could be designed to stay together, but in certain cases even an otherwise unusable location could be sufficiently anchored to withstand the combined effects of the Bootlegger Cove Clay and a magnitude 9.3 earthquake. But to use that capability and knowledge properly, strict control of building standards *and* development location had to go hand in hand. That was the aim of the starry-eyed government municipal planners. And that, ultimately, was the area in which Anchorage's eagerness to recover and forge ahead would push the lessons of 1964 aside.

By 1976, when the newly combined city-county Municipality of Anchorage finally adopted a Comprehensive Development Plan, Dr. Selkregg and others who knew what was needed and what was not being done in terms of seismic safety were shocked to find that several telling changes had been made in the language of the preliminary draft. Language which sought to bind the Municipality to follow the no-development recommendations of Task Force 9 concerning Turnagain and L Street had been removed. But more amazingly, so had literally all use of, or references to, the word "earthquake" itself! Just as the city of Mammoth Lakes, California, would later do with their cynical labeling of their emergency escape road as the "Mammoth Scenic Loop," Anchorage seemed determined to chase the seismic devil away by refusing to speak its name. It was a tawdry and essentially stupid deletion, to say the least, but it tacitly reflected the will of a community which had—as newsman Larry Makinson wrote—"largely forgotten the Great Alaska Earthquake of 1964, except as history."[7]

320

Also forgotten, apparently, was the oft-repeated and increasingly profound warning to mankind written by philosopher George Santayana many years ago:

"Those who cannot remember the past are condemned to repeat it."

With precise earthquake prediction still an unrealized goal, the fact of Alaska's vulnerability should be all the stimulus required, because as Anchorage continues to build—devoid of a seismic safety commission or an earthquake hazard mitigation agency—so do the tectonic pressures below.

Chapter 24

Parkfield, California—1987

It was amazingly hot, the merciless sun blasting through a clear blue sky to assault the small group of sweating scientists where they stood around a three-foot-tall rack of electronics in ninety-degree temperature. With a two-way radio microphone in one hand (its cord disappearing into the cab of a U.S. Geological Survey pickup truck), and a small screwdriver in the other, one of the seismologists labored to adjust a relay hidden in the electronic maze, carrying out the vocal instructions of another scientist who had designed the new instrument—instructions coming in live through a patched satellite phone call originating in Australia.

Donalee Thomason shaded her eyes against the sunlight and watched the seismologists intently, standing next to the plaque which proclaimed the small, fenced-off enclosure of seismographs, strainmeters, and creepmeters the "Donalee Site"—part of the survey's Parkfield network. True, it was on her land, a few miles from the main trace of the San Andreas Fault, but she enjoyed being a part of a bold experiment in her own community—an experiment which, if successful, might give seismologists new tools for short-term prediction of earthquakes.

The summer months can be brutal halfway between San Francisco and Los Angeles. For the tiny collection of farms and ranches known as Parkfield—nestled between ridgelines and rolling hills and grassy meadows amidst terrain shaped for thousands of years by the periodic upheavals of the two great tectonic plates—life was often hardscrabble and tough. Even with the sudden infusion of scientists in 1984 along with the steady stream of writers, television journalists, and newsmen who followed them, the end of the month too often came long after the end of the money for families dependent on agriculture or seasonal incomes. Yet there was a peacefulness to the valley which helped to keep life tranquil for the locals—even as the newcomers became more excited over what was about to happen.

An earthquake was due in Parkfield, according to the survey. Sometime before 1993 (and most likely in 1988), the San Andreas Fault was expected to break just northwest of the tiny community, sending the seismic waves from a Richter magnitude $M_L6.0$ quake through the region. The forecast was the first one approved by the USGS and validated by both the National Earthquake Prediction Evaluation Council and the California Earthquake Prediction Evaluation Council. In some respects, however, the prediction wasn't much of a risk. For over a century Parkfield had been no stranger to magnitude 6 earthquakes, each of which seemed to occur on something resembling a regular schedule.

And as a lifelong resident of Parkfield, Donalee Thomason knew the propensities of the fault very well. Not that she and the other one hundred seventy-five residents of the community spent their days watching the main trace of the boundary between the North American and Pacific plates, but the presence of that great boundary had been no secret.

She had been only nine years old on June 7, 1934, standing in the darkened hallway behind the small "stage" of the Parkfield Community Hall when the ground began to shake around 8:00 P.M. White gas lanterns began swinging overhead in the nonelectrified wooden building, and the progress of a year-end school program froze in mid-sentence as a small segment of the San Andreas northwest of the town lurched slightly—an initial break along a one-mile stretch of the fault that seismologists would later call the preparation zone which sent shivers through Parkfield.

The first jolt, however, was merely the feeling of the seismic trigger being pulled. Seventeen minutes later the charge went off, stored energy in the form of seismic strain causing the west side of the fault to lurch northwestward as the almost simultaneously arriving P and S waves shook the Community Hall, sending the residents fleeing outside into the night—scaring people profoundly, but doing very little damage to the sturdy wooden buildings in town.

It had been young Donalee's first close encounter with such seismic energy, though her parents and many of her neighbors were far less startled. The Parkfield section, they knew well, had been shaking like that at intervals for 130 years.[1]

324

By the time the Parkfield segment broke again in 1966, Donalee Thomason was a wife and mother standing in her wooden frame home north of town, recalling instantly the one most intriguing fact about the small lurch which had startled her so at the back of the Community Hall: The big one had followed seventeen minutes later.

Suspecting it would happen again the same way, Donalee began pulling breakables from her shelves and wrapping them in towels, securing her Hummel figurines, and trying to anticipate what could be saved from impact with the floor—before taking up a position in the doorway of her home to wait.

Exactly on schedule the seismic waves slammed in from four miles away to the northwest, pushing the house into unbelievable contortions for half a minute, cascading the contents of her kitchen cabinets onto the floor, but doing no serious structural damage.

Now, twenty-one years had passed since the 1966 episode, and in the intervening period—as the seismological community had become aware of plate tectonics and the steady slip rate between the two great plates—it had also become aware that Parkfield's quakes seemed to occur with clockworklike regularity.

The local historical record was clear: Jolts of approximately M_L 6.0 had occurred in 1857, 1881, 1901, 1922, as well as 1934 and 1966. Those were, therefore, separated by 24, 20, 21, 12, and 32 years. But if they considered the rate of slippage of the plates to be constant many miles below (where the temperatures were high enough to make the rocks almost plastic), and if they took into account the fact that the 1922 quake was considered significantly weaker than all the others (and thus had not released all the built-up energy), the 1934 quake could be seen as having occurred ten years before the normal breaking point for that segment of the San Andreas, and the overall average would then be twenty-two years, plus or minus five years.

With the passage of the Earthquake Hazard Reduction Act of 1977 and the growing confidence in the geophysical community that earthquake prediction might be just around the corner (especially if seismologists knew what premonitory jolts, lurches, movements, or other phenomena to look for just before a quake), the crosshairs of USGS research began to center on Parkfield. With scientists such as Dr. William Bakun and Dr. Tom McEvilly, Dr. Alan Lindh, and Dr. Wayne Thatcher, and others of the USGS all signing

325

on (and with a certain amount of financial participation from the state of California), the process of wiring Parkfield with an unprecedented network of instruments began in earnest. By 1987, the San Andreas Fault was incapable of stretching, creeping, lurching, or slipping without setting off a network of alarms and portable beepers back in Menlo Park through telemetrically monitored sensing equipment. If there was going to be another Parkfield quake (a probability rated at 95 percent), the USGS was determined to capture it alive.

The crunch of gravel and rocks beneath the tires of the pickup rose above the gentle sounds of crickets, wafting on a soft breeze in the relative cool of early evening. The headlights of the truck cut through a slight veil of dust as the vehicle crawled up to the saddle between two rolling hills, turning left then, following the dirt road as it flanked the V-shaped draw which marked the main trace of the San Andreas Fault, then climbed to the top of the westernmost rise and onto the crest of Car Hill, which was capped by a small wooden structure known locally as the laser house.

The tall, youthful-looking driver bounced out of the cab, unlocking the building and flipping on lights in a practiced, fluid series of movements. Amidst the hum of microwave transmission equipment and the chattering of computer disks loading their programs, he began opening the wooden shutters on each of the building's four sides—shutters which normally covered the path of a *Star Wars*-style two-color laser (called a theodolite) which sat on a pedestal in the middle of the small, instrument-packed room. With the laser, the relative motion of the Pacific plate and the North American plate as they grind past each other in the deceptively beautiful setting of Parkfield could be tracked to within a millimeter.

Some three nights a week, after teaching the schoolchildren of Parkfield and joining his family for dinner, Duane Hamann repeated that ritual trek, spending several hours putting on a semiprivate laser show over the pastoral countryside, and gathering data which just might help predict the next quake. That was the aim of the Parkfield project: to attempt to identify enough preliminary changes along the fault to justify a short-term earthquake warning (of days or even hours), and to gather as much knowledge as possible about what happens to the fault before an earthquake.

Duane Hamann had helped build the laser house, and had signed on with great enthusiasm as the plans of the USGS scientists and the Colorado team garnered enough funding to build the structure. Hamann, it was decided, would do the nightly work of pointing the gun at a network of eighteen reflectors mounted carefully on distant hilltops in all directions, measuring with great care and repeated practice the exact distance between the center of the laser house enclosure and each distant point—measurements precise enough to detect movement of half a millimeter.

"We think of the ground as solid and stable," he explained, "yet I sit up here and take these measurements night after night and see the different points move for weeks slowly in one direction, then reverse course and move the other way for awhile—movements only a fraction of a millimeter in length, which are better described as trends. Anyway, sometimes it's instrument error—which is why I take so many repeated readings—but most of the time it's because the surface out there is more fluid than we think. It almost undulates." [2]

With boundless enthusiasm Hamann spends his hours on the hill carefully adjusting the laser, entering data in the computer, swatting at a squadron of determined summer insects attracted by the incandescent lights, then bounding outside to adjust something. Returning inside, he begins aiming the laser with meticulous precision at a dark point marked only by a reference line on the interior of the laser house shutters. Gently massaging the small knobs which turn the laser housing, barely moving them as if adjusting an unsteady telescope, he works at it until a sudden, pulsating flare of red and blue light erupts from a previously dark spot on a distant hill— light easily visible from within, yet as much as five miles distant. [3]

Within seconds the oscilloscope behind Hamann begins to show a three-peak wave form indicating a good reading, and the digital counter begins measuring the time it takes the pulses of laser light to make the round trip at approximately 186,000 miles per second. Smiling at the steady data, he makes notes on an emerging printout before turning back to the laser to find the next reflector.

Night after night, always looking for changes reading after reading, Hamann has maintained one of the basic monitoring networks across the fault.

And from the valley—across the Van Horn Ranch toward Turkey Flat, to the east, or northward toward Parkfield itself—the occasional sight of the low-powered laser light describing thin lines overhead on misty nights has been as familiar a part of life since 1984 as the sight of green government vehicles and antenna-festooned plastic igloos (housing more seismic monitoring equipment) has become an accepted part of the Parkfield landscape.[4]

To anyone who visits Hamann and the laser house and gets to know the equal enthusiasm of Bill Bakun, Alan Lindh, Bob Burford, and the rest of the cadre of USGS scientists who have focused their professional attention and their reputations on Parkfield, it is obvious that there is an element of chance in the Parkfield project.

"The worry all of us have," a senior seismologist in the university community pointed out, "is that the USGS is putting all of their eggs in one basket on prediction. Parkfield is very necessary, and the project must be done, but that's not enough. What happens if the quake doesn't come in by 1993? Will the scientific community and Congress lose interest in prediction? What happens if the precursory indications don't happen anywhere else, or can't be scaled up to larger earthquakes? Do we give up? I'm afraid a failure could damage the whole prediction program."

The lesson, though, is that Parkfield is only one element of a vital program of government and academic research looking for the methods of bringing short-term and intermediate-term earthquake predictions to the point that they can be expressed in terms of probable date, time, place, and magnitude.[5]

Long-range prediction is already here, and intermediate-range predictions are approaching the viable stage with seismic gap theories and numerous other observations of changes that occur in the area of an expected earthquake in the weeks and months before the event. While some seismologists such as Dr. Bruce Bolt of Berkeley feel that precise, worldwide short-term predictions will probably not be possible for many decades, if ever, the search for more information must not fall victim to cost cutting and the loss of federal funding. Such projects as the deep drilling probe of Dr. Mark Zoback of Stanford on the southern San Andreas near Cajon Pass east of Los Angeles, and the continuing research of Dr. Kerry Sieh, along with many other programs, are too important to surrender to the Gramm-Rudman-Hollings budget-cutting act or any other federal cutback.[6] And there is a very profound reason: On the way to the ultimate goal of short-term prediction, a project of scientific research will usually discover many new things not directly antici-

328

pated. And some of those discoveries may be extremely important. The ability to detect not only what faults underlie the city of Los Angeles, for instance, but to have some idea when they'll move and what magnitude of seismic waves they'll produce, could have prevented deaths and the imperilment of thousands in 1971.

And, it would turn out, the same would be true in the fall of 1987.

Chapter 25

Whittier, California—
Thursday, October 1, 1987

On Tuesday, the county building inspector had closed his notebook and looked at the young priest for a moment before speaking, his inspection of the sixty-four-year-old Catholic school complete for another year.

"Y'know," he began, "if your school building was in Los Angeles, I'd have to condemn it." He let the words sink in before continuing.

"But, since you're here in Whittier, and you don't have a stringent seismic building code in this town, you can keep on using it." The inspector shook his head slightly and rose from the table, extending his hand.

It had been a passing curiosity to Father Tony Ross. Only sixty-two days had gone by since his posting at this new assignment. While he was quite aware of earthquake potential in the Los Angeles region, the full meaning of the inspector's words had not penetrated.

Until now.

The sudden shudder, the rattling of the windows in the rectory chapel had caught him in mid-sentence while officiating with the other clergy and staff members of St. Mary's Church at morning prayer, two days after the inspector's visit. The school day was scheduled to begin in less than twenty minutes in the old masonry two-story building fifty feet to the west of the chapel, across a small alley through which garbage trucks sometimes rumbled in the mornings about this time. Tony Ross figured that was the explanation: A heavy truck passing by.

But the altar had begun to move within a second, bouncing and vibrating as the entire building came alive, shaking with an east-west motion, the overhead lights now bouncing wildly, as he pre-

331

pared to speed up his conclusion of the devotional service and shifted instead to a half-shouted, half-bellowed command to the others in the chapel:

"Everybody out!"

As their feet began propelling the group toward the one side door, Tony watched in shocked fascination as the eleven-hundred-pound marble altar rose up off the floor in what appeared to be a slow-motion, vertical levitation, then pitched forward six feet, rotating as it went, wine and hosts and chalice scattering in all directions, throwing itself away from where he and his fellow priests were standing, crashing to the floor of the chapel as they maneuvered to escape.

Plunging into the smoggy morning air hanging over the courtyard and noting the wildly swinging power lines that were threatening to fall on his new, tiny compact car, Father Ross ran headlong into a new sound, clearly audible above the thunderous rumble and growl of what was obviously a serious earthquake.

Voices were coming from the direction of the school, across the alley. Voices of children. Voices screaming in terror.

Oh, my God! he thought. *They've been hurt.* The memory of the building inspector's words, coupled with the image of several hundred students assembled in the passageways around and between the walls of the old school flashed through his mind as he lunged through the gate and into the alley. If the side wall of the unreinforced masonry building collapsed, it would descend on anyone below—and parents usually dropped the kids off in that exact spot on such mornings. As he rounded the corner of the school, a huge crack in the east wall opened and closed again as the vibrating of the quake continued—then, suddenly, stopped.

The alley was full of students; but the walls had not fallen, and the children were being led away to the safety of an open area to the south by the assistant principal as Father Ross reached them.[1]

As the priests, nuns, and staff of St. Mary's School swung into action, fearful of immediate aftershocks, their 1923 school building of brittle masonry—a building barely held together by ancient mortar—stood fatally wounded. Within twenty-four hours it would be condemned, even under Whittier's relaxed codes.

Somewhere beneath the Montebello section of Los Angeles, about nine miles south of Pasadena and about six miles east of the downtown district, a previously insignificant snag had for many years held back the slippage of one of the many complex fractures which underlie the Los Angeles basin. The fault had reached its breaking point at 7:42 A.M. by lurching slightly, readjusting pressures placed on it at odd angles from other subsidiary faults over untold years, all driven indirectly through the pushing and jostling of many tectonic blocks and "flakes" by the inexorable movement of the great tectonic plates past each other thirty miles to the north along the San Andreas Fault.

Montebello, however, is five miles northwest of Whittier. Somewhere beneath the surface, the alignment of the fractures included a break which dipped from the town of Whittier to the northwest, intersecting the portion of the fault which snapped. Instead of throwing the brunt of its seismic convulsion up and out in a unified spherical fashion, the energy released at 7:42 A.M. channeled itself inordinately to the southeast, angling upward and toward Whittier, ripping into the town in a northwest to southeast swath, shaking brick chimneys apart, escalating nine hundred houses into major repairs or eventual abandonment, knocking down seventy-year-old plaster walls and younger stucco facades, shattering unreinforced brick walls and cinder-block foundation supports, destroying a new city clock, collapsing a parking garage, and raining down bricks and ornamental debris with fury as its shaking threw personal possessions, fixtures and furniture, pictures and pots to the floor in a thousand area residences.

Gary Strait had been sleeping when the lurch threw him to the floor in his rented house just to the west of the downtown section. There had been no warning, just a sudden "whooom!," and instantly all the objects in the upstairs shelves and cabinets were throwing themselves out into the room as if propelled by some poltergeist from a Steven Spielberg movie. Strait tried to struggle to his feet, fighting the rain of objects, stumbling over debris on the floor as he almost threw himself onto the gyrating stairway, stumbling down to the first floor in time to see the plaster raining off the walls and the bricks of the fireplace exploding outward, daylight visible beyond. By the time he reached the front door, stunned by the crashing sounds from behind, the 1912 home had come apart internally. Beneath—as with so many other ill-supported residences in the area—the house had jumped the foundation blocks.

As Gary fled through the door and the fireplace collapsed, a delicate, crystal bud vase which had sat daintily on the now-shattered mantel, flew, unseen, through the air, catapulting off its perch. As the seismic waves subsided and the creaking, groaning house became still once again—shafts of morning light cutting ineffectively through the heavy pall of dust like spotlights through a smoky auditorium—a small object was barely visible in the middle of the ruined Oriental carpet now covered with broken bricks and plaster. The crystal bud vase—flowers still intact—sat upright in a tiny clear space, as if placed there in requiem for the fragile, ruined home.

Twenty-three-year-old Lupe Exposito and her twenty-two-year-old sister, Rosa, had been walking toward their 8:00 A.M. classes at L.A.'s California State University when the seismic waves from beneath Montebello began gyrating the campus. Their car behind them in the underground parking garage, they continued up the pathway, bordered on one side by a retaining wall made up of individual slabs—a design which had escaped the requirements of good seismic engineering. As with the inherently dangerous tile and concrete facades on the J. C. Penney Building in Anchorage (which descended like battering rams during the 1964 Alaska quake), the first few seismic waves from Montebello shook one of the slabs loose almost instantly, gravity taking over at the acceleration rate of thirty-two feet per second/per second, causing the multi-ton mass of unyielding artificial rock to gain enough speed to impact the pathway beneath in a thunderous roar, shattering one corner as it struck, then flopping over.

Rosa Exposito had seen the blur of motion and felt the impact. It startled her mightily, but it was microseconds before she realized that Lupe no longer walked beside her. Turning in terror—her path of vision followed by one other student to the rear who had watched helplessly as the slab descended—Rosa could see only the slab of concrete flat on the sidewalk.

But where was Lupe?

The student fifty feet behind had already seen too much. As Rosa Exposito looked around in confusion and growing horror, her heart leapt to her throat as she fought with her mind's offered explanation of where her sister might be. George Torres already knew. He had closed his eyes in horror as the slab fell, but now he had spotted Lupe's blue book bag at the edge of the concrete monolith, and a portion of Lupe's arm protruding from beneath it, already encircled in a crimson stain. The ground was still shaking, but it was not noticeable in the enormity of what had just happened.

"My sister! My sister is under there!" Rosa began screaming, suddenly aware and determined to get help, determined to find some way to lift the weight from Lupe, lift her back to her feet, deny that this horror had ever happened. She had to be all right. Despite appearances, she *had* to be okay!

Rosa, a popular medical technology student at California State, struggled to get someone to listen, to help, to pull her sister out while there was still time.

Which, of course, there wasn't. It was too late, as those who tried to comfort Rosa and lead her away knew instinctively.

Lupe Exposito had been three years old when the slab of inadequately anchored concrete that would cut her life short had been raised into position along the pathway. It, and tens of thousands of structures like it (especially those which predated the 1971 San Fernando quake), stood like seismic time bombs throughout the metropolitan area, always primed to be torn loose in even moderate earthquakes—bricks and blocks and walls and concrete structures which man can build, but whose impact no human can survive.[2]

Just above Altadena in the San Gabriel Mountains north of Pasadena the first jolt from the quake had caused a cave-in in a six-foot-wide excavation being prepared by a construction crew for a new electrical transmission tower. Several men at the intermediate level of the thirty-three-foot deep shaft scrambled out, but for forty-one-year-old Antonio Bernal, the dislodged tons of dirt and rocks which caved in on his position at the very bottom pinned and suffocated him within minutes.

Juan Herrera had lived through a killer quake in his home country of Guatemala in 1976, a quake which killed twenty thousand people and left his family homeless and destitute. Looking for better income to send home, he had worked in Los Angeles for ten years, finally becoming a legal alien one week earlier, living in a tiny second-story apartment over the meat market which employed him in Maywood, a part of east Los Angeles. The seismic waves that lashed out from the focus of the quake beneath Montebello traveled fewer than five miles before reaching the building at 7:42 A.M., where Juan was taking a shower. With the memory of collapsing adobe buildings in 1976 vivid and fresh in his mind, Herrera reacted instantly, throwing open the bathroom window and propelling himself through it in an instant, perhaps helped by the lurching of the quake. Wet and naked, he landed at the foot of the still-intact building, seconds before the shaking stopped. Exactly what had gone wrong with his attempt to break the two-story descent was not clear to his friends at first, but Juan Herrera had miscalculated his chances with American buildings, and had paid an ultimate price. Having landed on his head, he lay severely injured and bleeding in front of the shop. Herrera would be dead by late afternoon, the third fatality in what would be called the Whittier quake.[3]

By 8:00 A.M. the shocked residents of Los Angeles began picking themselves up and taking stock of the damage, bracing for aftershocks, and wondering what would happen next. Was the quake a precursor? Would something worse follow?

As excited seismologists poured over the wild tracings of the seismograph record at Caltech (and the USGS monitoring center in Golden, Colorado, calculated a Richter magnitude M_L 6.1), an aftershock of M_L 4.4 rumbled through the area, its epicenter only slightly removed from the main break.

Los Angeles was indeed stunned. Nothing had rocked the area with that much force since the 1971 Sylmar quake in San Fernando. Cracks had appeared in L.A.'s City Hall, offices and homes were littered with items thrown from shelves, and windows in various places were in pieces. The glass windows of the control tower at Hollywood-Burbank Airport had exploded outward, closing the airport for twenty minutes as controllers tried to slow their heartbeats and regain control of the traffic situation. And, of course, Whittier lay bruised and bleeding.

"This," said one breathless television newsman at NBC's studios in Burbank, whose image had been substituted suddenly for the western time zone transmission of the *Today* show, "may be the big one."

But it was not the "big one." In fact, said one seismologist at Caltech within hours, it was merely a seismic "fender bender compared with what's still out there to the north in the San Andreas." The quake had been a rather insignificant readjustment in one of the smaller faults beneath eastern L.A., but with no ground breakage

336

apparent at first, seismologists couldn't quite figure out why the epicenter of the quake was located more than five miles from the spot where most of the damage had occurred. Perhaps, said one, we have a dipping fault plane here rising toward Whittier.

By 9:00 A.M. it was obvious that L.A. was neither burning nor heavily damaged. With the exception of widespread shock and seven deaths (and about a hundred injuries), and, of course, the destruction centered around Whittier, there was a cautious feeling of euphoria in the city. At M_L 6.1 it was less than a third the magnitude of the 1971 quake. Nevertheless, it was also apparent that steps taken since 1971 to reduce hazards had worked: No freeways collapsed, even those adjacent to Whittier, due in part to retrofitting of all bridges and overpasses with metal strap restraints to prevent the type of disconnection collapse that had occurred in 1971. The Southern California Earthquake Preparedness Project's influence could already be seen in both the efficiency of the emergency response from all over L.A., and the performance of buildings throughout the area. Newer buildings and many refurbished buildings throughout the city performed well, while many newer buildings in Whittier, even in the absence of a stringent seismic code, responded adequately with minimal damage. Water systems, electrical systems, and sewers for the most part came through intact (with some exceptions), and communications—especially for emergency response services—came through beautifully. Even the satellite dish antennas connecting the big three networks, the Cable News Network, and others with the rest of the world joined the majority of the phone system in continuing to work.

Angelenos had indeed survived an earthquake—but not much of an earthquake. Whatever euphoria existed flew in the face of the reality of what was coming, as the media quite properly began reminding their audiences. However well their metropolis had performed this time, they had yet to be tested by *the* earthquake which was still in the future.

There was a good news/bad news air to the analyses which began by late morning. L.A. had survived far better than expected and reacted in terms of emergency services far better than in 1971 because strict seismic codes had been enacted years earlier, freeways had been strengthened, a generation of children as well as adults had been exposed to earthquake preparedness information, and more than a third of the hard-core dangerous unreinforced ma-

337

sonry buildings scheduled to be destroyed or rebuilt by 1990 had been finished off, one way or the other.

But the bad news included some sobering realities, such as the fact that seven thousand targeted buildings still remained occupied and unreinforced, and outside Los Angeles proper, wholly inadequate or nonexistent seismic building standards permitted many tens of thousands of other marginal buildings to stand unchallenged. Then too, there was the reality that L.A. had not really been tested. A M_L 6.1 event was a puny nudge compared to the nearly one thousand times increase in the energy and more than a hundred times increase in the magnitude of the great quake which Dr. Kerry Sieh's research had proven occurs along the southern San Andreas on the average of every 140 years.

"Nature," said a Los Angeles city councilman, "has merely issued us a warning."

By Friday damage estimates had risen to sixty million dollars as the aftershocks continued, all of them minor, but very upsetting. By Saturday morning, one seismologist at Caltech was warning that the aftershock sequence wasn't right. Kate Hutton told reporters that the aftershocks were migrating deeper into the ground beneath L.A. and migrating in a northeasterly direction. While it appeared, she said, that there was "less than a one percent chance of a bigger quake coming out of Thursday's earthquake," the absence of a hard aftershock was puzzling.

To the residents of Whittier, it was also nerve-racking. Many of the damaged buildings and houses had cracks snaking through masonry in chimneys and walls and foundations that could ill afford another hard shock. The partially collapsed parking structure on the south end of town would go down completely with another jolt, as would, it seemed, the rest of the St. Mary's school building. With hundreds sleeping on their front lawns, in the parks, or in community shelters—children and adults alike traumatized by the disruption and uncertainty—Whittier picked at its wounds and waited.

And then came the twenty-second aftershock, a jolt that struck out once again from beneath an area six miles northwest of Whittier at 3:59 A.M. on Sunday morning, ripping up at an angle toward much of the same area, jolting the ground beneath Whittier and Alhambra alike, and delivering a coup de grace to scores of damaged buildings. As jittery residents awoke in now-familiar fear, the sudden jolt completed the job begun Thursday on the Whittier parking garage,

338

sent a bell tower crashing through the roof of the San Gabriel Civic Auditorium, shattered many of the remaining masonry joints in St. Mary's School, tumbled chimneys and walls throughout the area, and launched the newly repositioned contents of a thousand bureaus and tables, shelves and bookcases toward the floor once again with a seismic magnitude measured at M_L 5.5. There apparently *had* been a deficit in the aftershock sequence, but it was now resolved.

"It was the oddest thing," the man said, standing in the shattered front room of his rented house in Whittier, a house damaged now beyond hope in the aftermath of Sunday's aftershock. "I was forty miles away when it hit Thursday. I had no idea what had really happened."

Ron Reader shook his head as he watched his neighbors across the way, stumbling in shock around a little house they had spent three long, hard years remodeling and polishing. They had finished just two weeks before. Now it stood in ruins, the foundation shattered, the chimney gone, an ominous red warning sign posted on the front door by the building inspectors, who had declared it too dangerous to occupy. Next door a rental moving van sat at the curb, watched by an elderly lady in an easy chair, sitting incongruously in the street and watching the efforts of her son and daughter to pack her things. Her shattered home of thirty years lay broken and slumped, her pictures of a lifetime strewn about the cluttered living room, her furniture bearing the scars of fallen plaster. The lady watched without tears. "I have earthquake insurance," she had said. "I just don't know what I'm going to do in the meantime." On her front porch, too, was the telltale red warning sign, as with the next house down, where a tearful couple poked in desultory fashion at a growing pile of their furniture arranged on the front lawn.

Reader shook his head again. "I didn't know [at first]—they said 'Pasadena' on the radio—so I'm just coming home, and I thought we would have some damage here; but I didn't expect anything like this. But what kind of brought me up to the point where I knew it was [going to be] worse was the physical posture of people in the street.

"About four miles away in Norwalk—I grew up there—there was some stucco down, but there were people standing in the street and just talking. As I came this way, there were people just standing in the street, talking and waving their arms and pointing, y'know, look at this! I got closer, and there were people standing and staring into nowhere, then people sitting on the curbs with their heads in their hands. Then I got within a few blocks and I saw people standing and crying openly, pitifully, and I thought to myself, *Oh, Lord, this is serious!* Then I get here, and, well, it's a total loss."

The man paused again, looking once more around the shattered neighborhood and shaking his head in solemn disbelief.

"If this was just a little one, I can't imagine what the big one will be like."

Chapter 26

University of Washington, Seattle—April 1988

It was hard to believe such tranquillity could be shattered suddenly. The stately campus of brick and masonry buildings set amidst tall trees encouraged the uniquely human delusion of permanence, as if the endurance of the works of man is superior to the destructive potential of nature.

Dr. Brian Atwater paused for a moment, looking to the south through the windows of his third-story office in Johnson Hall at the campus and the city beyond, acutely aware of how unprepared it all was for the type of cataclysm which had struck this ancient meadow many times before these buildings had risen—a type of great earthquake which could (and would) strike again someday.

He had found the smoking gun: evidence in the muds of streams and estuaries along the Washington coast—evidence of sudden drops of the landscape which had probably occurred during periodic great subduction zone earthquakes in past centuries—evidence that the Pacific Northwest was indeed at extreme risk.

Yet his descriptions had to be carefully worded, professionally at arm's length with the increasingly compelling nature of the evidence, and his words properly restrained. "The great-earthquake hypothesis," Brian had said, ". . . is hanging together very well."

The remnants of suddenly inundated marshes he had found, and the dark, decayed material (peat) he had so carefully carbon-dated during the past summer told a frightening tale of massive tectonic upheavals off the Pacific Northwest coast, the last one occurring only three hundred years before. Yet this city, this state, and indeed the entire region were unprepared. The building codes were based on a seismic zone 3; but zone 4 was both the highest level of risk classification, and the one more appropriate for the Pacific

Northwest if he and a growing cadre of other scientists were right, and the Pacific Northwest faced an earthquake far greater than anything California's San Andreas Fault could ever deliver.

And he was becoming convinced that the only real question was when, not if.

"What impressed me the most," Brian had said, ". . . even more than the radiocarbon evidence of the various events, was seeing similar sequences of suddenly immersed marshes at a wide variety of places."

Those black layers were not elements of conjecture, or convoluted technical descriptions in the form of cold words in a professional paper. They were black layers of decayed material in three dimensions exposed by the shovel blade at various places, interlaced with ancient seeds and the roots of certain marsh grasses, exhumed and explained by Atwater. They were remains of grasses and plants which had died when their meadow or marsh had suddenly dropped in elevation four to six feet perhaps on some ancient evening, plunging them below sea level (in the intertidal zone). And some were layers coated with a sand which could have only been transported there on the back of a raging tsunami.

As the summer of 1987 passed and fall brought Dr. Atwater and the samples back to his tiny USGS "encampment" at the University of Washington, the results were compelling.

"What I was testing," he explained, "was whether the jerks [of marsh submergence] had sufficient regional extent to represent magnitude 8 earthquakes. In other words, did the ages of the buried marshes at one place reasonably match those at other places in a coastal strip eighty-five kilometers long and thirty kilometers wide. In the summer of 1987 I learned that at least two of them do. A large stretch of the southwestern Washington coastal area sank suddenly seventeen hundred years ago, and again just three hundred years ago."

There had been similar findings by other geologists in Oregon in the meantime—findings which indicated that the jerks may have resulted from earthquakes of magnitude 8.5 or even larger.

In addition, there had been another large event sixteen hundred years back (perhaps a hundred years after the one that carbon dated at seventeen hundred years), evidence of which Atwater found in the strata of Willapa Bay and Grays Harbor, Washington.

And there was a jerk a thousand years ago which produced the dark line in the stream bank near Neah Bay that had been Atwater's first clue.

There had been widespread jerks twenty-seven hundred years ago and thirty-one hundred years ago at Willapa Bay and Grays Harbor, and also thirty-four hundred years ago (dated thus far only at Willapa Bay).

"It's a repeat time average of about six hundred years, and the last time southwestern Washington was hit was three hundred years ago. But does that mean we're safe for another three hundred years? Not necessarily.

"Though the average is about six hundred, the radiocarbon ages indicate that the jerks can occur as little as one hundred years apart, or as much as a thousand years apart. There doesn't seem to be a lot of regularity in the repeat cycles.

"In other words, the next jerk conceivably could happen tomorrow, or it could be in seven hundred years in the future."

Brian knew that the seismological community had yet to come to grips with the growing evidence. He had not yet presented his research formally, so the rest of the geophysical community had yet to review it, let alone draw conclusions of repeat cycles.

But that review was about to begin. As Brian Atwater stood at the window, the abstracts of twenty-two professional papers that had been presented at a December 1987 meeting of the American Geophysical Union in San Francisco sat on the desk before him. His preliminary findings were there, too, along with abstracts from supportive papers of research just completed in Oregon, which had found evidence of the same types of sudden dropping of coastal areas, and of similar dates for the events.

And there were papers by seismologists who sought to argue with the original, theoretical conclusions of Dr. Tom Heaton of USGS at Caltech that the Cascadia subduction zone parallel to the Washington-Oregon coast was a seismic time bomb.

Heaton, in many respects, had started the whole thing. It had been his presentation which had drawn Brian Atwater and others into this increasingly exciting investigation. It had been Heaton (and colleagues) who had argued several years before that the subduction zone off the Pacific Northwest coast was too similar to the great earthquake-producing coastal areas of southern Chile and southern Japan to be quiet (aseismic). Many other seismologists had taken on Heaton with theory-to-theory arm wrestling over interpretations of seismographic tracings, trying to deduce what was really down there and whether the Cascadia subduction zone could indeed produce great quakes.

But those arguments had been based on broad theories, not physical evidence. And the December conference had included more theoretical arguments that the Pacific Northwest was not subject to great earthquakes from the subducting of the Juan de Fuca tectonic plate beneath the North American plate.

"What *else* could [cause those layers]?" Tom Heaton had asked Brian on the phone. While the conclusion that great earthquakes were responsible had not been formally established, it was difficult to see how anyone could come up with any other credible explanation.

The subject had hung in the very air of the San Francisco conference, yet the process would have to proceed as a steady trek through the jungle of scientific caution and professional skepticism designed to weed out insubstantial theories and conclusions. Brian would have to defend his position, describing his evidence and his methods in scientific journals (as would the other geologists who had found similar evidence in Oregon). Provided no great quakes erupted in the Cascadia subduction zone in the meantime to make the debate academic, and provided Brian's paleoseismic inferences would withstand the scrutiny of his peers, it might still take years before the paleoseismological, geological, and seismological communities would be sufficiently convinced to stand as a group, square their collective shoulders, look the people and the political leaders of the Pacific Northwest in the eye, and deliver the frightening news: "The possibility of a future great earthquake as large as M_w 9.2 has been confirmed. We just don't know when to expect it."

Yet the process of getting a population and its buildings ready for such a quake would take decades, and every second would count. Within a week he would be presenting the evidence once again, this time to a major earthquake preparedness workshop organized by the USGS in Olympia, Washington. It would be a meeting of scientists, emergency preparedness experts, engineers, politicians, and insurance company representatives, all of whom would be starting the arduous process of coming to grips with a growing reality: that the Pacific Northwest is subject to a far greater seismic danger than ever before believed.

Two floors beneath Brian Atwater's office, the state of Washington's unofficial "state seismologist," Linda Noson, sat at her desk and considered the questions.

344

If the people of the Pacific Northwest were convinced a great earthquake could strike their homes and businesses, would they get busy and start reducing their exposure? Would they support programs to make school buildings safer, educate the population on what to do if the ground started shaking, and support more stringent seismic codes?

For ten years Linda had been seismologist at the University of Washington, and working on hazard reduction programs and public education under USGS and FEMA contracts. She had become known as the state seismologist from such work, but the fact that it was an unofficial title pointed up how little was being done officially. And with the Seattle-Tacoma area's massive seismic exposure, what was being done was ridiculously insufficient.

And for as many years she and a few other volunteers had crisscrossed the state, giving programs and talks to schoolchildren, trying to convince uninterested school district administrators of the vulnerability of their buildings and their students, and generally fighting a very lonely, largely unsupported battle.

All of the Puget Sound area (containing Seattle and Tacoma and many smaller communities) was built on a known seismic danger zone. For decades it had been common knowledge that deep-focus earthquakes as well as shallow earthquakes greater than M_L 6.0 could shake the area at any time (and had many times before), yet in 1987 there were still no BAREPPs (Bay Area Earthquake Preparedness Project as in San Francisco) or SCEPPs (Southern California Earthquake Preparedness Project as in Los Angeles), no organized hazard mitigation efforts or public education drives, and no major emphasis on upgraded land use planning.

There was only Linda Noson—and a few friends—standing between Washington's western cities and complete ignorance.

"What will it take to get them off their tails and shake their complacency?" she was asked.

Linda sat back and smiled, almost wistfully.

"Even if [the population is] convinced, I don't think everyone will suddenly start preparing for a magnitude nine earthquake. We had major, killing earthquakes here in 1949 and 1965. We know we're subject to major quakes even without a subduction zone, and there are many things we have long needed to do to prepare which just haven't been given any priority.[1]

"We had a seismic safety bill which passed 2 years ago, but it was vetoed by the governor. He thought it was better to give that function to the existing Department of Emergency Management, which would then form a Seismic Safety Council.[2]

"I can't say nothing is being done, but there's not enough. The state of Oregon is in far worse shape, though. Portland has had large earthquakes before—is subject to the same great quakes Brian Atwater is documenting—and yet they only have a seismic zone 2 building code, with much of their city built on alluvial Jell-O, and virtually no hazard reduction programs. At least Seattle is a seismic zone 3."

Noson fell silent again for a minute, seeming almost physically overwhelmed behind a desk piled high with reports and papers, flanked by an impressive stack of bookshelves bearing hundreds of pounds of seismological and technical information. While her role at the university would be ending from lack of funds; she would be transferring shortly to the Federal Emergency Management Authority as a natural hazards specialist, and her struggle for earthquake education would continue.

"I guess I get the most frustrated at not being able to provide the resources—the money and the materials and the assistance—to the people who want to push hazard reduction programs forward. There is so much to do, and so little to do it with. Getting people motivated to change that will be a monumental task. . . ."

Linda Noson tapped a pencil on the book in front of her for emphasis.

"But it must be done! We're vulnerable—*very* vulnerable—yet we have the power to protect ourselves if we'll just do it!"

From the viewpoint of a low stone wall at Kerry Park atop Seattle's Queen Anne Hill, the Space Needle, the proud centerpiece of the 1962 Seattle world's fair stands in the foreground like a metallic exclamation point emphasizing the growth and success of the Seattle downtown district. On the evening of March 27, 1964, the Needle rocked harmlessly through the massive P and S waves coursing in from Alaska (as a group of eminent seismologists looked up from their dinners in the rotating restaurant on top).

The following year a mighty M_L 6.5 quake beneath the Puget Sound region had rocked the Needle again, once more without significant effect—though many buildings in the area were damaged.

But what will happen when monstrous seismic shaking of many

seconds' duration from a cataclysmic subduction zone quake a hundred times more powerful and nine hundred times more energetic than the Puget Sound quake of 1965 ripples and roils Seattle's foundation with a magnitude of 8.5 or higher?

Moreover, what will the public response be when the people of the Pacific Northwest realize the monstrous seismic threat in the subduction zone beneath them? Will there be the sort of denial with which the people of Mammoth Lakes used to cloak themselves from the truth? Will there be a forced ignorance—a laissez-faire refusal to acknowledge the threat, such as that exhibited by Anchorage? Or will this community face up to what needs to be done? With that very challenge facing the entire Pacific Northwest, it will constitute a fascinating study in the psychology and sociology of the process of applying the real-time discoveries of science to the real-time lives of people in a complex social and economic system.

Just over a mile south of the Space Needle sits the new seventy-six-story Columbia Center, Seattle's tallest skyscraper—the tallest building west of the Mississippi. To the right, peeking over another rooftop, is the Smith Tower (which once held the same title), very, very vulnerable with its heavy use of masonry throughout. Just behind the tower sits the gigantic concrete roof of the Kingdome sports stadium and municipal arena, a structure which can hold more than seventy thousand human beings at one time—perhaps at exactly the wrong moment in time. And farther to the southwest, along the mud flats, sits a garrison of more than a dozen giant containerized cargo cranes, each of them many times larger than the crane that "walked" into the bay at Seward in 1964 from the Alaska Railroad dock (almost taking its operator with it). The Port of Seattle's facilities are located largely on the soft mud and sand of the Duwamish River—much as Tacoma's port facilities and cranes and buildings sit on similar risky muds deposited in the past several thousand years by the Puyallup River, which enters Puget Sound some thirty miles to the south of Seattle. The effects of massive seismic waves on such soils might well parallel Mexico City—yet little has been done to examine the hazards, let alone reduce them.

Unreinforced masonry structures sit on suspect real estate throughout the Pacific Northwest, from Canada's Vancouver in British Columbia (a little over 120 miles north of Seattle), through Portland, Oregon, 180 miles to the south. Millions of people and billions of dollars of property values remain in the valley of the shadow of seismic cataclysm, yet almost no one pays any attention to what could happen—what will happen—someday.

The impressive sight of Seattle's prosperous downtown skyline in stark contrast to the reality and the magnitude of the seismic threat is typical of cities throughout North America. But as one USGS scientist put it, "Believe me, once you visit the site of a major earthquake where thousands have died and see a few arms sticking out of a few collapsed apartment buildings or hospitals, you become very motivated to recognize the hazards, and to do something about them before that disaster area is your own community."

Even California scientists and hazard mitigation workers have a hard time convincing their people (and their municipal leaders) that preparing for the coming southern San Andreas great quake—preventing the loss of thousands of lives and billions in property damage—will take years of preparation and millions of dollars. Everywhere else in the country—a nation in which fully thirty-nine states have been declared significant seismic hazard zones—the danger of earthquakes has always been passed off as a "California problem" or a "West Coast problem."

But as is very clear, the East Coast of the United States in general and places such as Buffalo, Charleston, and Memphis in particular are highly vulnerable to earthquake damage even from a smaller quake, yet too little, if anything, is being done anywhere in the nation.

"It's a good news/bad news list," as one seismologist put it. "The bad news is we're vulnerable; the good news is we can do an awful lot about it."

Another knowledgeable scientist, Dr. Arch Johnston of Memphis, has presented in more eloquent terms the very same thing before several congressional committees. "We can't do anything about the hazard, we can't prevent earthquakes for the foreseeable future, but we can do something about the degree of risk!"

There are answers. Straightforward, logical methods of realizing that the United States is among the nations of the world with major exposure to ruinous earthquakes, and that we have it in our power to reduce the potential damage of such monstrous episodes of ground shaking to very handleable proportions. Many suggestions can be formulated, but there is a list of basics for the entire nation:

348

1. Admit that a hazard exists. Force public and governmental leaders to admit the reality of the seismic hazard, and the scope of the seismic risk (or exposure).
2. Fund and support continuous research, nationally and at state level, to map and identify specific risk areas in each locality, and to provide strong national funding and direction for continuous research into basic seismological, geological, paleoseismological, volcanological, geophysical, and prediction efforts along with their sociological effects.
3. Defuse the seismic bombs.

   a. Change and upgrade building codes to reflect rational seismic threats.
   b. Require reconstruction, reinforcement, or destruction of seismically dangerous buildings and structures of all types, public and private (especially schools, whether public, private, or parochial).
   c. Limit the use of dangerous or seismically vulnerable land; prevent the Turnagain Heights syndrome.
   d. Establish programs of education (especially for schoolchildren) to inform everyone on what he or she should do to prepare for an earthquake, what to do in an earthquake, and what to do immediately after an earthquake and, on what to insist that our governmental leaders do to support and fund earthquake hazard reduction programs.

4. Immediately pass a National Natural Hazards or National Earthquake Hazards Insurance Program providing required, standardized earthquake insurance with very low deductibles for everyone—homeowners, business owners, and cities alike—spreading and minimizing the risk through a government reinsurance corporation (or similar plan).
5. Establish and fund programs similar to SCEPP and BAREPP throughout the United States.

And, of course, there is the pipeline into the future of seismological knowledge—the graduate students and would-be graduate students being starved nationwide of opportunities for funding and chances for employment as professional scientists. It is entirely possible that had Kerry Sieh come along in 1987 instead of 1972,

349

there would have been no student program money available for the pivotal research that catapulted him into graduate school, fixed the idea of trenching across faults to gather historical seismicity information, and gave us invaluable knowledge of the southern San Andreas Fault's history and future. Without a major national rededication to scientific research, there might be too few jobs available for bright, dedicated, excited young scientists such as Karen McNally, Tom Heaton, or Brian Atwater in the upcoming generation of graduate students.

There is so very much to discover in an area of science that is in its infancy and is wide open to the bright minds and dedicated, impassioned researchers of tomorrow.

But it is also very obvious that the scientific breakthroughs of tomorrow—the possibility of accurate, lifesaving short-range prediction of earthquakes, the expanded understanding of exactly what is in store for the eastern United States, Utah, Tennessee, Washington, and unprepared Anchorage, Alaska, and American leadership in the geophysical sciences—depend on the progress of students, which in turn depends on funds that seem to be evaporating and employment possibilities which seem to be contracting. Indeed, it will be our future scientific knowledge and scientific leadership which will end up imperiled and shortchanged if we're too budget-conscious today to pay the minimum bill for tomorrow.

"I am an idealist with no illusions!" John F. Kennedy once proclaimed. The phrase seems a perfect balance to so many of the challenges facing mankind and especially this one. It may take a degree of idealism to think that our cities and homes and lives can be adjusted to ride through great earthquakes with minimal damage—our insurance programs guaranteeing the recovery of our personal lives and our economy from the effects of damage we can't prevent—but it is merely realism to apply a known set of solutions to a known hazard so as to minimize the risk.

And, conversely, it is stupidity to do nothing but wait for preventable disasters.

Throughout mankind's tenancy on earth, natural hazards—including earthquakes—have formed an unmodifiable clause in our contract with nature.

"Civilization exists by geological consent," wrote historian Will Durant, ". . . subject to change without notice."

At long last, though—after thousands of years of helplessness in the face of such disasters as earthquakes—we have the means, and the license, to amend that clause. Our scientific understanding can provide us with notice, and our hazard reduction efforts can render many aspects of "geologic consent" immaterial.

The only question is, *will* we get around to doing it, while we have time?

Footnotes

Chapter 1

1. The problem was a classic one in modern seismology. The task of convincing people that damaging earthquakes can occur is very difficult, even though thirty-nine states containing cities such as Memphis, St. Louis, Chicago, Pittsburgh, New York City, Washington, D.C., Salt Lake City, along with large communities such as Buffalo and Charleston, South Carolina, are clearly in harm's way. The active, dangerous faults are hard to find east of the Rockies, not because they don't exist, but because they're buried under thousands of feet of younger layers of rock which obscure the deep cracks in the continental crust—the principal material of the massive, ever-moving North American plate. But, because they are hard to find, too many people erroneously believe they don't exist.

2. Juan de Fuca, a Greek sea captain of dubious accomplishment whose real name was Apostolos Valerianos, claimed to have found the entrance to "a broad inlet of sea" on a mysterious voyage for the Spaniards in 1592—a hundred years after Columbus sailed to North America and two hundred years before British Captain George Vancouver entered the region. The Spaniards called him Juan de Fuca, and a book detailing his claims circulated for two centuries before fur trader Charles Barkley found the wild and beautiful inlet between what are now known as the Olympic Peninsula and Vancouver Island. About the time that Spanish and British expeditions were sailing in and out of the Puget Sound region (from 1775 on), Barkley gave the strait the name of the long-dead Greek, Juan de Fuca—whose claim is widely disputed by historians. (An excellent discussion of this comes from the locally published book *Magic Islands: The San Juans of Northwest Washington,* by David Richardson [Orcas Publishing Co., 1964, 1973], p. 13.)

3. This is from Dr. Tom Heaton and Dr. Parke Snaveley's paper, "Possible Tsunami Along the Northwestern Coast of the United States Inferred from Indian Traditions," published in the *Bulletin of the Seismological Society of America,* in 1985 (vol. 75, pp. 1455–60).

Chapter 3

1. This was a study done by Ernest Dobrovolny and Robert Miller in 1959 entitled "Surficial Geology of Anchorage and Vicinity, Alaska," which was published in the *U.S. Geological Survey Bulletin 1093* (1959).

Chapter 4

1. The epicenter of a seismic event—an earthquake—is a point on the surface of the earth directly above the location where the principal point of breakage is located. The point

353

of breakage itself, sometimes scores of miles beneath the epicenter, is called the hypocenter, or the focus.

2. When rocks break, they produce two types of seismic waves: compression (or P, for primary) waves and body waves (S for secondary), which in turn produce long wavelength surface waves. P waves travel faster than S waves, but the ratio of the speeds of the two kinds of waves is a constant; which is why the simple measurement of P and S arrival times in distant locations on the earth can reveal the distance the waves traveled and where the quake is located.

Hitting a long board on one end produces compression waves; the molecules move out and back when viewed from the source. S waves, however, move from side to side or up and down when viewed from the source (transverse motion at right angles to the point of origin). It is the S waves and the surface waves they create in the ground that begin yanking foundations out from beneath houses and buildings or creating sympathetic vibrations in tall structures that can cause collapse. It is the S waves and surface waves that cause water-saturated sandy soil to liquefy and flow like a viscous liquid. It is these transverse waves that shake unreinforced masonry buildings into rubble, cause cracks in the ground, and shatter glass windows.

3. To understand this, think of trying to drag a heavy pallet of bricks across a field by pulling on it with a huge rubber band. You would have to put great tension on the rubber band at first, pulling very hard, before the stored energy in the taut rubber band could break the frictional tension between the bottom of the pallet and the ground. When that happened, when that singular moment came, the pallet would leap forward, propelled by all the energy you had stored in the rubber band by pulling it so taut. Once freed from the ground friction and with momentum imparted to it, the pallet of bricks would move forward to a point where the now-decreased tension on the rubber band could no longer move it. Once again the friction between the pallet and the ground would be far greater than the force you are imparting with the rubber band, until once again you pull it tightly enough to cause the same cycle to occur over again. This is basically the same sequence "mechanism" which works in seismic strain, where rocks "snag," or develop too much friction between them, to be overcome by the normal forces pushing them past each other. The pressures—energy—stored in those rocks have to· grow sufficiently over time to large enough values to overcome the friction. When the breaking point comes and the rocks snap to a new position, the friction will once again exceed the newly lowered levels of stored energy. If snags are sufficiently large and strong, the resulting breaks produce large earthquakes. If the snags cover a small area and are weak, the seismic waves created when the inevitable snap occurs are minor. Keeping this system in mind will explain much of what the past twenty-three years of discovery in seismology have validated. But please keep in mind as well that in 1964, this type of system as applied to earthquakes was little more than a distant theory in a few brilliant and inquisitive minds.

4. *Tsunami* is a Japanese word meaning "great wave." Normally, though, it is used only to describe massive waves in ocean areas which are caused by sudden movement of the ocean floor. Waves which occur inside a harbor or lake that resemble water sloshing back and forth in a tub are given a French name: *seiche* (pronounced "saysh").

By the way, contrary to popular belief, there are no such things as damaging "tidal" waves. With the exception of small tidal rips and waves created by tides flowing in or out in places of extreme tidal variations such as Puget Sound and the Bay of Fundy in Nova Scotia, tidal waves are a myth as amusing to scientists as mythical "air pockets" (which don't exist) are to aviators.

Chapter 8

1. It was estimated that the seismograph needles at the Lamont-Doherty Geological Observatory at Columbia University in New York would have traveled an additional foot beyond their mechanical stops if not restrained. The reflection and refraction of the saturated wave

354

trains coursing through the planet made interpretations of magnitude and epicenter very difficult in the first few hours, as well as during detailed analysis in the following months and years.

2. In fact, Cordova was not wiped out. Some damage to buildings occurred, but very little physical damage to the city resulted from the ground shaking or the seismic sea waves which arrived later. The Cordova waterfront, however, was devastated economically by a simple and catastrophic gain in altitude. The tectonic uplift in the region thrust all of Cordova 6.5 feet higher than before in relation to sea level, rendering the commercial waterfront facilities unusable. All the dock structures were left too high to be reached at anything other than high tide, and the entire fishing industry was severely hurt. Cordova would recover, but it would take many years.

3. It was the third and fourth waves which trapped and drowned some of the people at Crescent City when they made the fatal mistake of returning prematurely to their homes and businesses, thinking that tsunamis only come as one wave. To the south, in an amazing act of mass misunderstanding of the potential forces involved, some ten thousand Californians streamed down to the ocean beaches in San Francisco to watch the wave come in. In fact, this sort of tendency can be found in almost all natural disasters in the United States in which there is a stated threat but no visible sign. Even in hurricanes, such as Hurricane Camille in August 1969 at Gulfport, Mississippi (the most powerful hurricane to ever hit the United States, with winds above 235 knots), some of the 139 people lost were killed while having a blasé "hurricane party" in a beachfront motel. The tendency to "go down to the beach to watch incoming tsunamis" accounted for loss of life in Hilo, Hawaii, in the late forties, and could have resulted in massive deaths in many other locations.

Chapter 9

1. Not that the earth beneath New York City has never shaken. It has, with many small tremors from epicenters of unknown origin connected to little-understood faults. Faults run beneath the city as well as nearby. Cities as close as Buffalo, New York, are proven high-risk seismic zones, as is much of the St. Lawrence Seaway.

2. Bryce Walker's excellent book *Earthquake* (Time-Life, 1982) presents an entertaining rendition of the Boston quake which was a source for this paragraph. It maintains that Benjamin Franklin, "who had left his publishing business in 1748 to devote more time to science, had proved the existence of electricity in storms with his famous kite experiment. Soon after, he had invented the lightning rod and promoted its widespread use." Since the popular "scientific explanation" for earthquakes in Boston in 1755 was that they were somehow related to static electricity, Franklin "believed that electricity had a role in causing earthquakes," and the idea was accepted even by the formidable Reverend Thomas Prince, who had been preaching since the tremors of 1727 that such events were, as he titled a famous sermon, "The Works of God and Tokens of His Just Displeasure." In a 1755 revision of the sermon, Prince suggested that God's displeasure might be electrical in nature, and might be affected by the forest of Franklin's lightning rods atop Boston's roofs.

The Lisbon disaster in the same year of 1755 was a watershed in European history and philosophy as well as in seismology. More than sixty thousand people died in the Portuguese capital, which had been the self-appointed bastion of Catholic piety and a stronghold of the Inquisition. It was the *Age of Reason,* and philosopher-writers such as Immanuel Kant and Jean Rousseau formed a school of optimists who argued that theirs was the "best of all possible worlds" in which everything that happened, happened for a beneficial reason. The Lisbon quake wounded the philosophy badly, and gave pragmatists such as French philosopher Voltaire the impetus to lampoon the optimists' rosy philosophical ideas with his bitingly sarcastic novel *Candide.*

3. Although the Richter magnitude scale is the one used principally by the media in reporting the relative sizes of earthquakes, there are other scales of similar logarithmic progression now in use which better describe the full range of power of major and great earth-

quakes outside the California area (which was Richter's intended application area for the scale that bears his name). When an earthquake is described as being above 9.0, for instance, the scale being used is most likely called the moment magnitude scale. Although it works exactly the same as the original Richter scale in terms of showing each tenfold increase in ground amplitude as an increase of only 1.0 in magnitude, it takes into account a measure of the energy released as well as the size of the seismic waves produced. A straightforward explanation of all this may be found in Appendix 1 of this work, and for clarity and precision through the rest of the test, the magnitudes of different earthquakes will be presented with the designator for the scale used in accordance with Appendix 1. Therefore, you may see a reference to a Richter magnitude 5.6, or a $M_m 7.5$ (for moment magnitude), or an M_s 6.6 (for surface magnitude). The scales are sufficiently similar, however, for you to disregard the subscript ("S" or "Wc" or "L") and consider only the number. An $M_W 9.5$, for instance, is still approximately one hundred times as great as an $M_L 7.5$, or ten times as great as an $M_S 8.5$.

Chapter 10

1. Bradbury had a commission from the Botanical Society of Liverpool to study and collect specimens of North American plant life.

2. The islands south of the confluence of the Ohio with the Mississippi were simply numbered in sequence downriver.

3. The journals of John Bradbury can be found in several locales, along with at least one letter to a friend in New Orleans. Perhaps the most detailed glimpse is from a book entitled *Voices on the River—the Story of the Mississippi Waterways* by Walter Havinghurst (New York: Macmillan, 1964). The quoted material in these paragraphs are from this source.

4. Elizabeth Bryan wrote these words in a letter to the evangelist Lorenzo Dow several years after the quakes (dated March 22, 1816). The letter has been quoted and reprinted many times, but the literacy of the lady, and the corroborating writings of so many other literate and well-educated people (such as botanist John Bradbury) who were in the area at the time, have given us a rare insight in substantial detail to a series of events which occurred, essentially, in the middle of nowhere. So detailed were the reports and the subsequent newspaper articles that 150 years later Dr. Otto Nuttli was able to draw up a detailed map and analysis of the intensity of ground shaking from the December 16 and February 7 shocks.

Bryan (sometimes spelled Bryant) is a figure of some mystery. Author Harry Harrisson Kroll in his early historical novel *Fury in the Earth: A Novel of the New Madrid Earthquakes* assigned her the profession of schoolmarm. But as New Madrid earthquake scholar and authority Professor James Lal Penick, Jr., points out in his definitive work, *The New Madrid Earthquakes* (Columbia, Mo.: University of Missouri Press, 1981), ". . . while this additional information cannot be refuted absolutely, neither can it be confirmed."

5. One young settler who later became a colonel in the U.S. Cavalry, John Shaw, returned to the shattered remnants of the town amidst the constant aftershocks to help young Betsy Masters. With her leg broken below the knee, she was unable to move. Shaw cooked some food for her and tried to make her more comfortable before returning to the "grand encampment" with the others.

6. Otto Nuttli originally estimated the three principal shocks at 7.2, 7.1, and 7.4 respectively in M_b values on the Richter scale but later revised those values upward. On the Modified Mercalli Intensity Scale, which is the principal measure of how intensely earthquake waves of *any* magnitude earthquake affect particular areas, the waves ranged from a high of XI at New Madrid on February 7, 1812, to values as high as V for Washington, D.C. Please see Appendix 1 for an explanation of the various magnitude scales and the Mercalli Intensity Scale.

Chapter 11

1. This Chilean quake would, in fact, be called the largest earthquake in recorded history.

2. The World-Wide Standard Seismograph Network (WWSSN) is a network of approximately 110 seismograph stations similarly calibrated and distributed throughout the world. The network was originally established in the early 1960's to help monitor Soviet nuclear tests by reading their seismic waves, and the USGS now coordinates its activities. Six seismometers at each station measure vertical and horizontal ground motion in two fixed frequency ranges, and transmit that information to the USGS center in Golden, Colorado, twenty-four hours a day.

3. One model of the earth's crustal structure at that time held that the Pacific basin was rotating slowly counterclockwise, and thus was ringed by steeply dipping (not necessarily vertical) faults which would periodically break at various points, causing slippage, some variations in coastal levels, and earthquakes up to the level of great quakes. The model considered the entire Pacific to be ringed by the very same type of strike-slip fault as the famed San Andreas in California. There were many flaws with that model, and in fact, the subsidence and emergence Plafker was documenting could not be explained even in gross terms by the theory. In addition, with what we now know about hot spots in the crust (a hot spot is basically a flume of intense thermal activity from deep within the planet which punches a hole through any crust that passes over it, causing volcanoes and, in the ocean, island-building activity), if the rotating-basin theory were true, the Hawaiian chain from Midway and the French Frigate Shoals through the big island of Hawaii would be arranged in a circle—an arc—instead of a relatively straight line, since the "turntable" of the Pacific floor would have rotated for millions of years over that same hot spot. In fact, the Hawaiian chain provides a graphic trace of the direction and extent of movement of the mid–Pacific Ocean for the last few hundred million years. By the same token, the historic path of the hot spot which now underlies Yellowstone National Park in Wyoming can be traced with great ease from the West Coast of the United States to its present position, forming the strange features of eastern Idaho all the way back to the Pacific coastline.

4. The article was entitled "Science: The Earth's Upheavals," by Walter Sullivan on page 6E of the *New York Times Sunday edition* on July 11, 1965.

5. Certainly with eminent scientists such as Press, such disagreements are minor career glitches and are handled in gentlemanly fashion.

6. Wegener wrote: "The continents must have shifted. South America must have lain alongside Africa . . . the two parts must then have become increasingly separated over millions of years." (Quotation selected by Samuel Matthews in his *National Geographic* article "This Changing Earth," January 1973).

"Utter, damned rot!" raged one scientist in 1920. The reaction, of course, was as old as science itself. One constant of human behavior is the tendency to institutionalize, then nearly deify, "established" conclusions or answers, and then to be outraged and threatened when at some later date or age someone comes along with a new way of viewing things and with the temerity to question the established order. From the outrage and indignation which greeted Aristotle's ideas to the fury with which medieval religious leaders rejected any question of the church's view of the cosmos, the definition of "heresy" has historically included any radically new scientific idea.

The history of western civilization is full of incredible discredited "truths" which were once sacrosanct. (For instance, there must have been a radical change in the orbits of the sun and the planets in our solar system during the past several hundred years, since in the Middle Ages it was an unquestioned fact that they revolved around the earth—which itself was quite flat at the time.)

The longer a theory goes without serious challenge, the more it tends to be regarded as the natural order of things—the ultimate answer—the final word.

It is right and necessary that once a theory is established, a high standard of proof should be required to change scientists' minds about how nature really works. Once erected like an alabaster citadel, the "established theory" on any scientific subject should enjoy a certain presumption of correctness. New ideas and theories should be forced to approach the gates of the citadel cautiously, lest their lack of preparedness or lack of proof leave them vulnerable to fatal attack by those who reside within the comfortable confines of the accepted theory.

Time and time again the scientists of the day have clung tenaciously to an accepted "reality" whose foundation of legitimacy is being eroded with each succeeding scientific paper. The battles which develop between the warring men and women of science have often gone far beyond the bounds of careful skepticism and ended up holding back the advance of our scientific understanding.

In the final analysis, of course, it is merely human nature at work: our human tendency to want to know what is true and once "known," to cling to that belief, as well as our tendency to put protection of reputation above the greater good of scientific gain.

Such was the treatment of Wegener and his prophetic (if ill-supported) theory. As his detractors pointed out, the idea that continents somehow plowed through the earth's crust in constant motion, and that they all had once been a part of a single supercontinent in the dawn of geologic time, was based as much on artful leaps of his prophetic mind and imagination as on hard supporting evidence. While it was true that the geologic evidence for separation of Africa and South America was fairly substantial (plants and microorganisms from each side matched amazingly well), the "mechanism" Wegener proposed to explain the drift was unsupported by fact, and therein lay the controversy, and the conflict with the scientific method, which demanded a much closer connection between known facts and proposed theory.

Nevertheless, it was basically right—a fact which would take earth scientists more than a half a century to discover.

In the meantime, any graduate student who expressed a serious interest in the theory of continental drift could be sure of harpooning his career as certainly as if he opened his oral exam for a Ph.D. by expressing support for the "science" of alchemy or witchcraft.

7. As molten rock cools and solidifies after a volcanic eruption, bits of ferrous metal in the rocks are left aligned magnetically with the earth's magnetic field as it exists at that time. Many years ago geologists discovered that the earth's magnetic field reverses at intervals over millions of years in rather regular cycles, and that drifting of the earth's magnetic poles or periodic reversals can be dated because the changed orientation becomes locked in the magnetic alignment of volcanic rocks whose date of origin can be determined through carbon dating techniques.

With the voyages of the research ship *Vema* in the Atlantic in the fifties, scientists began to notice that bands of the ocean floor running north-south all reflected one magnetic alignment, while an adjacent band (either the next one to the east or west) had the opposite magnetic alignment. Eventually it was discovered that as each of the bands were extruded as magma along the mid-Atlantic rise, the existing alignment of the earth's magnetic field was "recorded" in the rocks as they cooled and hardened. The discovery became one of the keys to validating the constant extrusion of magma in the mid-Atlantic rift and its conveyorlike progress both east and west of the rift. The phenomenon was called magnetic reversal.

8. A zone of extension is an area of the ocean floor in which new magma is coming to the surface and creating new seafloor, which is constantly creeping away from the zone in both directions. The mid-Atlantic rise is a zone of extension.

9. Benioff believed that the dipping, hypocentral zones marked major faults, but that movement was now horizontal (strike-slip) rather than dip-slip thrusting.

Chapter 12

1. Wallace's insight ran to greater questions as well. It had occurred to him that since the fault slipped, it would be helpful to society and science to know the rate of slippage per year. That, he reasoned, might enable some calculations on how fast strain might be building in the fault. It was a small point in an already excellent paper, but it would prove to be the first time anyone had suggested looking into such a question.

Bob Wallace has always professed to be embarrassed by his thesis, because it is not as extensive as the style and manner of such doctoral dissertations today. It was, he protests, "quick and dirty," and limited by the war. Nevertheless, it has, by his own admission, stood up well enough with prophetic conclusions and postulations which turned out to be true.

2. Dr. Charles Richter was actually one of the best observational seismologists around, and, indeed, was first to report many "paleoseismological" and geological observations in his 1958 book *Elementary Seismology,* a work that still serves as the basic bible of beginning seismology courses worldwide.

3. Gilbert's comprehensive reports on the great earthquake which damaged San Francisco so badly in 1906 were reported formally by G. K. Gilbert and others in 1907, "The San Francisco Earthquake and Fire of April 18, 1906, and Their Effects on the Structures and Structural Materials," *U.S. Geological Survey Bulletin,* no. 324 (1907), pp. 1–170.

4. The quote comes from an excellent paper written by Dr. Robert Wallace in 1980 for the centennial celebration of the USGS (Geological Society of America Special Paper 183) on Gilbert's contributions, in which he chronicled the almost precognitive ability Gilbert showed to construct theoretical models and theories that are still, in large degree, valid:

". . . Gilbert's observation of small, fresh scarplets at the base of fault-generate range fronts indicated to him that:

"'A mountain is not thrown up all at once by a great convulsive effort, but rises little by little. When an earthquake occurs, a part of the foot-slope goes up with the mountain, and another part goes down (relatively) with the valley. It is thus divided, and a little cliff marks the line of division. This little cliff is, in geologic parlance, a "fault scarp," and the earth fracture which has permitted the mountain to be uplifted is a "fault" ("A Theory of the Earthquakes of the Great Basin, with a Practical Application" [from the *Salt Lake Tribune* of Sept. 30, 1883]: *American Journal of Science,* 3rd series, Vol. 27, pp. 49–51).'

"In a popular article in the Salt Lake Tribune, Gilbert carried the readers through the sequence of logic that:

"'(1) mountains of the Great Basin are uplifted along faults, (2) mountains "rise little by little," (3) alternate cohesion and sliding characterizes the motion, and (4) the instant of yielding is so swift and so abruptly terminated as to constitute a shock' [1884, p. 50].

"This line of reasoning is so modern that, in 1980, it is difficult to understand why, once stated, the concept would not have been generally accepted and become a firm part of the working base of geologists and seismologists.

"In the nineteenth century, however, the sciences of geology and seismology were unprepared to acknowledge the verity of several major facts that formed the foundation for Gilbert's hypothesis.

"Seismologists were preoccupied with the shaking phenomena, not with field observations. . . ."

5. The report was entitled: "Earthquake Prediction: A Proposal for a Ten Year Program of Research," Ad Hoc Panel on Earthquake Prediction, prepared for the Office of Science and Technology (May 1965).

6. The engineering report—"Earthquake Engineering Research," National Academy of Engineering—was not formally issued until 1969, though rumbles of its preparation and the upset which was driving its formulation were certainly no secret in Washington or in the seismological community in the years between Dr. Press's effort and its issuance.

7. The USGS-driven effort was entitled "Proposal for a Ten Year National Earthquake Hazards Program: A Partnership of Science and the Community," Ad Hoc Interagency Working Group for Earthquake Research, Federal Council for Science and Technology (December 1968).

8. The challenge facing Steinbrugge and his copanelists was formidable. There were intense seismological interests in basic research (and the funding to fuel it); geology's increasing role and need for funding as a dynamic supporting actor on the stage of advanced earthquake research, prediction, and threat assessment efforts; the concerns of social scientists over what earthquake predictions could do to the society at any given point, and how the problems could be turned into advantages; and, the serious concern of engineers that those advances in engineering research and heightened standards for earthquake-resistant building design already realized, and those that could be realized, not be lost in a flurry of "misplaced" excitement over prediction. In addition, they had to deal with (and incorporate)

the sensitivity of political leaders and economists who saw prediction attempts and large-scale hazard mitigation programs of changed building codes and standards as a loose economic and political cannon on a rolling national deck. And that, in turn, raised an issue which was squarely in the professional center of Karl Steinbrugge's expertise: the ability of society to spread the financial risk of major natural disasters such as earthquakes through the operation of private enterprise: the insurance industry. Earthquake insurance existed, but the concept and the future of the nation's involvement as a whole were not even embryonic in 1969 (though they would grow to form a major legislative challenge for the nation twenty years later).

9. This quote is from the introduction page of: "Report of the Task Force on Earthquake Hazard Reduction, Executive Office of the President, Office of Science and Technology," (September 1970).

Chapter 13

1. Dr. Charles Richter was a world-class scientist. Along with Dr. Beno Gutenberg, Richter had invented the unified magnitude scale (used for a particular wavelength of seismic energy) which permitted at long last a comparison of apples and oranges—different earthquakes at different depths the waves of which were read on different seismographs in different parts of the world. With the Richter scale, they all could be compared as apples to apples, giving at least an initial indication of size (please see Appendix 1 for a comparison of the different types of magnitude waves). Richter, who had received his doctorate from Caltech in 1928, never failed to give the lion's share of credit to Gutenberg. But the world had already made its decision on how to refer to the method and the scale, making the name Richter and the phrase "Richter scale" extremely familiar to millions. And in the fifties Professor Richter had published the bible of modern seismology, titled simply *Elementary Seismology*, which became required reading for any serious student.

Charles F. Richter, professor emeritus of Caltech, had retired eight months before (in June 1970), but even at the age of seventy he was still fully engaged and active, going to Caltech almost every day, serving as a consultant on many advisory committees and boards, and monitoring endlessly the seismograms that his efforts had helped so much to standardize and improve.

"He's supposed to be retired," Mrs. Lillian Richter told a *New York Times* reporter, ". . . but mostly it's just his salary that's retired."

2. The elastic rebound theory was first developed by Harry Fielding Reid following his extensive study of the 1906 San Francisco earthquake and the effects of fault slippage on Marin County to the north.

3. The San Gabriel Mountains, which form the northern flank of the San Fernando Valley and run eastward as the bordering line of ridges and mountains north of Los Angeles and San Bernardino, sit just south of the San Andreas Fault, and have been moving northwestward relentlessly for thousands of years with the western side of the fault. The mountains themselves are an upthrust core of Precambrian metamorphic and Mesozoic plutonic rocks flanked by thick sections of sedimentary strata.

4. A comprehensive (and highly technical) examination of the seismographic tracings and the interpretation of the results which validated the accelerations greater than 1 G are contained in the professional paper, "Stress Estimates for the San Fernando, California, Earthquake of February 9, 1971 . . . ," by M. D. Trifunac, as published in the *Bulletin of the Seismological Society of America*, Vol. 62, No. 3, pp. 721–750, June, 1972.

5. The faults which caused the quake were quite complex, it turned out, but had no direct connection to the San Andreas to the north, and, in fact, ran more or less at right angles to the San Andreas. There was some confusion at first over whether the slippage in San Fernando's faults had increased or decreased the pressure on the San Andreas, or had had no effect at all. There is a technical but readable article on the preliminary conclusions regarding

this subject written by D. F. Palmer and T. L. Henyey and published in the May 14, 1971, issue of *Science* magazine.

6. As Professor Richter pointed out to newsmen in the following days, there is no such thing as an "earthquake-proof" building. Nor is there ever likely to be such a thing. Earth-quake-resistant, certainly. But not earthquake-proof.

7. The Field Act did change the construction of new schools, and caused the abandon-ment of damaged, unsafe structures, but it took other laws in later years to force abandon-ment of marginal school buildings. Even then, this affected only public schools. Many of the buildings abandoned by the school districts as a result of the new laws were sold to private or parochial school systems, and remained in use, a few to the present day—all of them as dangerous and as potentially lethal as ever.

8. In a February 12th article printed three thousand miles away in *The New York Times* ("Threat of Flooding Eases in California; 57 Now Dead in Quake," Section 1, p. 16), Curt Gentry, an author who had written a popular novel about the supposed slide of the western side of the San Andreas—and much of the state—into the Pacific Ocean (an impossibility), complained bitterly to reporter Steven Roberts that "We've played ostrich in California with the earthquake hazard for too long." It was ironic that Gentry's novel had inadvertently retarded popular understanding of the level of threat from the San Andreas, but following its publication, seismologists' efforts to refute the idea were often misinterpreted by the public as assurances that the fault could never cause widespread destruction. The truth, of course, was that California is destined to shake violently, not to split in half and sink. (Even the popular movie of the late seventies *Superman I,* repeated that same geologically improbable theme in the nefarious plot of archcriminal Lex Luthor. He didn't succeed, by the way.)

9. Once again, Dr. Karl Steinbrugge became involved, joining a score of other eminent scientists on a panel formed by the National Research Council to do a rapid evaluation of the lessons of San Fernando. Dr. Clarence Allen chaired the group, which published "The San Fernando Earthquake of February 9, 1971—Lessons from a Moderate Earthquake on the Fringe of a Densely Populated Region" two months later in April. The panel knew well the short memory of people and their government leaders. They knew that recommendations and ideas needed to be in front of a wide variety of officials asking for action on earthquake hazard mitigation, and that any such report would need to be issued rapidly.

10. This is from the News and Comment article "San Fernando Earthquake Study: NRC Panel Sees Premonitory Lessons," *Science* Magazine, Vol. 172, page 140–143, (April 9, 1971).

Chapter 14

1. A "sandblow" is an ejection of sand and water in a pressurized stream which punches through upper layers, usually all the way to and above the surface. Sandblows are caused by moderate to severe earthquakes, and occur when a layer of water-saturated subsoil takes on the characteristics of a liquid upon being shaken and compressed. The pressure drives the waterlogged sand and silt up through a fissure (or opens a path through homogeneous layers of soil above), leaving in many cases a mound of sediment on the surface that geologists can use to identify and later date the causative earthquake.

2. Caltech, in fact, has to some extent institutionalized an atmosphere of controlled pranks and creative jokesterism on campus as a means of breaking the tension of intense academic competition at what has become one of the world's best universities for the sciences.

3. Jahns was considered a true genius by most who knew him. Indefatigable, ambidex-trous, and charming, he had begun his career at Caltech by switching during his senior year from chemistry to geology and doubling up on his courses while serving as captain of the basketball and baseball teams and president of the student body, all the while maintaining a straight A average. According to Bob Wallace, Jahns once came into their dorm room at 1:00 A.M., sat down to do a term paper on a highly technical subject, and finished it two hours later at 3 A.M. When Wallace looked it over, the paper was perfect on the first draft. "It was," said

Chapter 15

1. In fact a type of poison later banned by the federal government had been used in the area. 1080, as it was called, was used to increase crop yields, but it killed several times over. Any animal that ate prey which had died or consumed the poison, was itself killed, and that meant the effective eradication of all animal life in an area. Kerry Sieh discovered these facts months later.

2. The Carrizo Plain is a desolate piece of landscape, but it contains the most photographed segment of the fault. Located roughly forty miles west of Bakersfield, geologists have recognized for decades the stark clarity of the San Andreas' path as it cuts from north-north-west to south-southeast across the landscape like a giant zipper (as seen from the air)—wrinkled foothills and offset streams bisected by the fault scarp itself. The theory of plate tectonics had shown that all the land to the west sat on the Pacific plate, and that the western California edge of that plate was moving northwestward at an average rate that had been measured by marine geologists out on the ocean floor at 5.5 centimeters per year, but was later found to be 3.4 centimeters per year. To the east of the San Andreas Fault, the entire continental United States (and the floor of the Atlantic Ocean eastward all the way to the mid-Atlantic rise) sits on the North American plate. The dividing line—the seam—is the San Andreas Fault itself, which runs between the two crustal plates almost the length of California, producing earthquakes whenever the two sides of the fault suddenly slip past each other.

3. A 1955 paper written by a Caltech seismological laboratory professor, Dr. Harry Wood, had already examined the historical accounts of the 1857 Fort Tejon quake, providing a wealth of human history on the event. But there were no seismograms available, or standard instruments in operation to record the waves anywhere near California at the time, so the usefulness of the reports was limited to measurements of the intensity of ground shaking.

4. There was a reason for dividing the project into three semiindependent projects. If any one of the questions proved unanswerable, he could still finish his thesis—and his doctorate—with the remaining two.

5. It was the basic strain-release cycle at work. Somewhere beneath the surface, perhaps forty to fifty miles below, the rocks are hot enough and plastic enough so that the two great plates could almost ooze past each other at a steady rate without causing earthquakes. However, the cooler crust at the top (the land that *is* California on either side of the fault), cannot slip at a steady rate (except, apparently, in the San Juan Bautista area). Snags develop between the upper levels of the two plates, locking them together at the top while at great depths they continue to slip past each other. That puts increasing pressure on the snags holding the top sections together, until at last a breaking point is reached. Then, if the bottom sections (many tens of miles beneath) have oozed past each other as much as 3.5 meters (for instance) in a hundred years while the surface level never slipped at all, when the breaking point comes, the upper surface level will snap back into equilibrium, and the west side of the San Andreas will suddenly slip up to 3.5 meters to the northwest, releasing enormous amounts of stored energy in the form of seismic waves.

6. Free-lance surveyors were a common feature of the expanding frontier, and in fact, a majority of the older surveys in the West were done by such people under contracts of one sort or another to the government. Hancock and his son later acquired title to most of Rancho La Brea—the site of the famous La Brea tar pits, which now sit in downtown Los Angeles.

7. Since the 1857 quake apparently resulted in movement of the fault through the Carrizo Plain and the Fort Tejon segments—and may have been triggered by the Parkfield segment to begin with—it is reasonable to assume that all three segments were fully strained and ready to break at the same time (although the Carrizo might have been somewhat short of the full amount of slip-deficit strain which would have been needed to cause it to break in

the absence of a pulse from the Parkfield section to the north). Like the second, minute, and hour hands of a clock all coming together twice every day at the 12, the segment of the fault with the longest period—the Carrizo Plain—may occasionally be sufficiently "ripe" for a break at the same time the Fort Tejon segment to the south also comes into readiness for a break. When such a conjunction occurs, an initial pulse on the Parkfield segment (which itself is probably triggered by a small preliminary lurch in the so-called preparation zone north of Parkfield) may trigger the Carrizo Plain, which in turn triggers the Fort Tejon segment, creating a massive and monstrous release of pent-up seismic strain over a distance of several hundred miles, and causing a great quake in excess of 8.0 magnitude.

8. When Bob Wallace first used the term in a professional article, one of his colleagues complained: "Oh, no! Please don't clutter up the literature with still another term!" But Wallace was well aware that to rally fellow scientists around a new concept, it needed a name—a catalyst—without which a coherent momentum would not develop. It would be ten years, however, before the term gained official acceptance. By 1987 a new science called "paleoseismology" had emerged, and a major scientific conference had been held to validate the new discipline—a conference at which Bob Wallace gave the keynote address.

Chapter 16

1. For instance, on January 23, 1556, during the Ming dynasty, a great earthquake slammed into the city of Xiau in the Shoanxi Province, killing 830,000 Chinese (according to dynasty records).

2. The extensive apocryphal reports of strange animal behavior just before earthquakes have fascinated and frustrated seismologists and other scientists for decades. Dogs, cats, horses, cows, other barnyard animals and fowl, fish, and even insects at various times and places have been reported to have acted in some unusual manner hours or minutes before earthquake waves arrived beneath them. While the tendency was to regard such stories as folklore, many serious scientific studies have tried to find valid links and explanations. Even in 1988 the best state of scientific knowledge is that animals and insects at various times and places seem to have the capability of sensing *something*, but what those advance warnings are, we do not know. In some circumstances they may simply detect changes in the earth's magnetic or electrical field; in others, they may sense preliminary small earthquakes which humans can't feel. But serious and careful attempts to monitor animals (and even cockroaches in one experiment) as an early-warning system have not provided scientists with any reliable or consistent ability to detect earthquakes before they occur. While the rural Chinese watch their animals carefully as part of their earthquake prediction and monitoring effort, reports of odd animal behavior simply reinforce other indicators (such as well water level changes and radon gas emissions) rather than provide a primary indicator in and of themselves. "There is definitely something going on," according to one researcher, "but we're still groping in the dark for what it is, and how it works."

3. Earthquake lights, as this phenomena is called, are still a scientific mystery. There is no doubt they exist (there are even color pictures of them), but there is no certainty about what causes them—though various theories have been advanced. The lights seem to occur most often within seconds of great earthquakes such as those in New Madrid in 1811 and 1812, and various Chinese and Japanese quakes.

4. Dr. William Brace of the Massachusetts Institute of Technology did the primary experiments in the early 1960's, which also discovered changes in the electrical resistance (which decreased) and the porosity (which increased) just prior to the main break. Dr. Brace even predicted that the changed prebreakage properties of the rocks might be of use someday in earthquake prediction efforts, but he left it at that and went on to other unrelated research.

5. This really is a national problem, not a regional problem. The Pacific coast states, principally Alaska and California, are indeed especially vulnerable to earthquakes and related disasters, yet nearly every state in the nation faces some degree of risk from future earth-

quakes, and some seventy million people live in the thirty-nine states that are wholly or partly in areas facing a risk of moderate to major damage.

The earthquakes away from the plate boundaries are really infrequent, occurring perhaps every five hundred thousand years in some places, maybe every five hundred to a thousand years in others. But we haven't been around this continent long enough to know which states are subject to such quakes and which states might not be. With great quakes so unpredictably infrequent, yet catastrophic when they do occur (such as in Charleston, South Carolina, in 1886, and Boston, Massachusetts, in 1755), there is a strong possibility that the only reason we place certain states in the "no earthquake potential" category is that we are not historically aware of what really happened before our occupancy of this continent began.

But if every spot east of the Rockies is potentially at risk, which in fact, is true—then eastern cities are even more exposed than Los Angeles and San Francisco because too many of them are crowded with thousands of buildings raised with virtually no earthquake engineering or seismic design standards. Masonry buildings and brittle masonry facades, exterior gables and ledges, exposed bridges and saturated earthen dams, complexes of rail lines across saturated roadbeds, and a thousand other dangerously exposed man-made structures throughout the eastern seaboard make the thought of a major earthquake on an unexposed, unknown fault very disturbing. Could that type of quake be predicted? And if such a prediction were ever issued, how would the people respond?

As President Carter's science adviser Dr. Frank Press told a congressional hearing in 1977, ". . . we must remember that despite a considerable seismic history, the United States has been extraordinarily lucky. Less than 1,200 people have lost their lives in United States earthquakes . . . [yet] seventy-four million people have died in earthquakes [through recorded human history].

". . . In the Los Angeles area alone . . . estimates go as high as twenty-five billion in destroyed property and as many as twelve thousand lives lost if the so-called Palmdale Bulge is a warning that a major earthquake is forthcoming. . . . [Such] a catastrophe would certainly have national economic repercussions."

Chapter 17

1. A seismologist by the name of J. A. Kelleher had identified this gap several years earlier, but the University of Texas team began its level of interest and research where he had left off.

2. Inamura's work was discussed by several papers published in the eighties, those papers summarized by Karen McNally in "Variations in Seismicity as a Fundamental Tool In Earthquake Prediction," *Bulletin of the Seismological Society of America*, vol. 72, no. 6, (December 1982), p. S361.

Without the unifying principle of plate tectonics, no one could figure out why such great quakes seemed to occur at regular intervals. With Alfred Wegener's theory still considered a discredited joke, it was two decades before the constant movement of the continental plates as the engine of such seismic events became clear—and Inamura's work took on much greater significance.

3. There were two insurmountable problems: Allotting $250,000 meant that several other projects would go begging under available 1977–78 funding budgets, and, the Texas proposal concerned *Mexican* quakes, not U.S. quakes. Even though it was obvious that Alaska was subject to similar subduction zone great quakes, funding foreign projects had become a politically sensitive affair to the occasional congressman or senator who couldn't understand why the USGS (whose funding he had quite often voted to trim) could not afford to finance a research project in his own state. Though such pressures would become far worse as the years went by, even in 1977 they dictated their own priorities. Then, too, as broad-minded and scientifically sophisticated as he was, the USGS project officer who rejected the Texas proposal, Jack Everendon, was not convinced that there was any possibility of predicting earthquakes by interpreting patterns of seismic activity (seismicity).

4. Even the governor of the Mexican state had to get involved, trying to calm his relatively unsophisticated population on the day the quake was supposed to occur—but didn't.

5. This was the original definition of an earthquake prediction. In a report by the National Academy of Science-National Research Council (Panel on Earthquake Prediction of the Committee on Seismology, 1976), a prediction was defined as "[specific] expected magnitude range, the geographical area within which it will occur, and the time interval within which it will happen with sufficient precision so that the ultimate success or failure of the prediction can readily be judged. Moreover, scientists should assign a confidence level to each prediction."

The definition instantly created nearly insurmountable problems for a seismological and geophysical community which suddenly found itself committed by the 1977 Earthquake Hazard Reduction Act to finding the perfect way to satisfy this precise definition for each anticipated earthquake. It would be several years before the work of the Chinese and the force of reality weighed in on American attitudes, and forced a much needed broadening and refinement of the definition to take into account the art of the possible.

6. Karen McNally wrote these words in a paper published in the *Bulletin of the Seismological Society of America*, Vol. 72, No. 6, Page S351, "Variations in Seismicity as a fundamental Tool in Earthquake Prediction," December, 1982.

7. Of course, part of the credit for that came from the work of Karen McNally herself, whose efforts to understand seismic gaps had advanced the science in leaps instead of steps. Dr. Kerry Sieh (whom Karen McNally had met several years earlier at Caltech) had been one of the other pivotal factors, providing a major breakthrough in the paleoseismologic methods of finding seismic histories. This is not to suggest that these two scientists were the only ones pushing the frontiers of knowledge in earthquake prediction; but their contributions have been (and continue to be) seminal, and they perhaps best reflect the dynamic and exciting possibilities open to any bright, hardworking young man or woman who approaches geophysics, geology, or seismology with the attitude that he or she can make a major difference. That attitude is fact. This is a very young science examining a very old planet, and we are on merely the threshold of understanding the processes, developing the theories, finding the evidence, formulating the models, and building the equipment needed to gain greater control of our environment and hopefully secure an increasingly harmonious and safe place within it. Kerry Sieh and Karen McNally, Brian Atwater, Tom Heaton, and hundreds more are sterling examples of the limitless opportunities. Geology is anything but just looking at rocks in a dusty university lab. Seismology is anything but passively watching squiggles on a seismograph drum. And geophysics is far more than endless mathematical theorems or theoretical stagnation.

8. In the early eighties, Karen McNally invited Kerry Sieh along with several other researchers to examine the seismic gap area in Michoacán, Mexico (northwest of Acapulco), with the idea in mind of perhaps working on a joint approach of paleoseismological excavations complementing her seismological approach in determining as detailed a seismic history for the area as possible. Sieh, however, elected not to join the project because of other commitments.

Chapter 18

1. Liquid rock—magma—that contains heavy concentrations of silica becomes very thick and sticky and easily forms plugs which can block the throats of cooling volcanoes following an eruptive phase. When a huge hollow beneath such a mountain—a magma chamber—fills with molten rock at thousands of degrees Fahrenheit at the beginning of a new eruptive cycle, the magma is infused with gases and water vapor. As more magma enters from below, and more heat transforms more gases and steam into higher pressures bottled up by ancient plugs of cooled lava from previous eruptions blocking the deadly mixture's path to the surface, the entire mountain becomes a bomb. When such a bomb explodes, it does so in a monstrous occurrence very unlike the smooth and predictable lava flows typical of Hawaii's

volcanoes. Such mountains as Mount Pelée in Martinique (which blew up in 1902), Mount Krakatoa (which pulverized an island in 1883), and many others are of this explosive classification. By contrast, the volcanoes of Hawaii are very low in silica content, and rich in iron (a basaltic lava type), which results in easily flowing magma and little explosive potential.

2. After a Transamerica C-130 cargo airliner had lost three of its four engines to an ash plume embedded in instrument weather—solid cloud layers—(and not noticed by radar), air traffic controllers began taking great care to coordinate ash plume activity with rerouted air traffic over the northwestern skies. In the meantime, hundreds of emergency vehicles were found to have major engine damage from operations in the ash storm of May 18th, and farmers in eastern Washington were confronted with fields inches deep in ash that would destroy the engine of any bulldozer that attempted to move it. In addition to the very serious concern over what the thousands of tons of ash would do to the crops, the losses to machinery were staggering. There were, as well, respiratory problems with the ash, and quite a bit of uncertainty over just how dangerous it might be to breathe air containing suspended particles of ash. In eastern Washington and Idaho, especially, there was a run on dust masks at local hardware stores.

There were, of course, many humorous stories, jokes, and bumper stickers—some sophisticated, some not—which came out of the explosion. Perhaps the best was a simple bumper sticker with an image of the gigantic ash plume of the May 18th eruption and the words "Don't come to Washington—Washington will come to you!"

3. The San Andreas Fault is the boundary line between the North American plate and the Pacific plate, but unlike the Pacific Northwest to the north and all of Mexico, Central America, and South America to the south, the San Andreas is not a subduction zone. Instead of diving beneath the North American plate, the Pacific plate moves slowly northwestward, scraping and sliding past the presumed vertical wall of the North American plate along the San Andreas Fault. Given the current accepted estimates of the slip rate at 3.45 cm/year (approximately), some seismologists have illustrated the relative speed of the Pacific plate's northwestward movement by pointing out that Los Angeles (which is on the Pacific plate side of the San Andreas and is being carried northwestward with the plate) will become a suburb of downtown San Francisco in 18,663,000 years (while the Daly City on San Francisco's western flank will be little more than an underwater ridge four hundred miles north-northwest of San Francisco). In only 55.9 million years, L.A. will become an island hundreds of miles west of Puget Sound out in the Pacific, and within 100 million years the block of earth L.A. now occupies will dive under the Aleutian Islands in Alaska, subducting beneath that portion of the North American plate, only to be remelted 15 million years later and emerge in some distant future as magma in a volcanic eruption.

4. The Rainiers and St. Helenses and Krakatoas of the world consist primarily of rhyolitic lavas—magma rich in granitic, crystalline rock, which is, in turn, rich in silica. The Hawaiian type (shield volcano in terms of classification of cone shape) involves magma which comes more directly from the earth's mantle, and thus is primarily basaltic.

5. The location of the hot spot has not changed in millions of years, but its position beneath the North American plate has. In fact, looking at any surface relief topographic map of the western United States will provide a startlingly clear picture of the path of the Yellowstone hot spot from the Pacific coast across Oregon and Idaho to its present position beneath northwestern Wyoming—a process that has taken tens of millions of years.

Chapter 19

1. This was reported in the Sacramento *Bee,* August 1, 1982, and cited by George Mader and Martha L. Blair in an excellent book on the Mammoth Lakes affair entitled *Living with a Volcanic Threat,* written by George G. Mader and Martha L. Blair of William Spangle and Associates, Inc. of Portola Valley, California, and printed by the same firm in 1987.

2. The USGS was supposed to issue this level of alert when they were convinced that "a potentially catastrophic event of generally predictable magnitude may be imminent in a gen-

eral area or region and within an indefinite time period (possibly months or years)." This comes from the USGS 1977 "Warnings and Preparedness for Geologic-Related Hazards, Proposed Procedures," as published in the *Federal Register,* vol. 42, no. 70, April 12, 1977, p. 19292, and as cited in Mader and Blair's book mentioned previously.

3. The USGS men had promised—as had their new director, Dallas Peck—that all official discussion in the public arena would come from another volcanologist, Dr. David Hill. One of the major complaints of the publicity holocaust of the previous three months had been the diverse opinions from various scientists interviewed by various reporters under varying circumstances involving vastly different questions. The resulting chaotic mix of stories carried widely diverse quotes, some scientists seemingly stating that no danger existed, others apparently indicating concern that the town might blow off the map at that very moment.

4. Al Leydecker and Mike Jencks had refused to deny the volcanic hazard, or join in the attacks on the USGS. Both men had also refused to attribute the local economic crisis solely to the USGS action of issuing the notice, citing instead the national recession, gross overdevelopment, artificial inflation of real estate prices, and the effects of bad weather on both the summer season and the winter ski season during one previous year. Leydecker, who was technically conversant with geology (and had held formal slide shows and classes in Mammoth Lakes to explain the situation), was also, however, a rather aggressive nonconformist in his dress and his style of service on the county Board of Supervisors. Jencks, a local attorney, also had alienated himself from the political mainstream on several issues. With these public and political liabilities, it would be inaccurate to say that the two men were recalled simply because they advocated a more realistic response to the USGS warnings and the volcanic threat (or because they were willing to talk about it in public). There is little doubt, however, that their stand on the volcanic issue accelerated their political demise. In any event there was an unfortunate message sent by the voters to the other members of the Board of Supervisors: Recognition of the volcanic threat could be hazardous to your political health.

5. In a rather facetious effort to hide the real purpose of the road from the visiting public, however, it was labeled the "Mammoth Scenic Loop," though little more than a forest and a few distant ridgelines can be seen from its entire six-mile length!

Chapter 20

1. The final figure for city repairs subject to government assistance payments would come to $2,871,160, of which FEMA paid 42.84 percent, the state of California paid 51.84 percent, Fresno County Redevelopment paid 3.45 percent, private contributions picked up 0.79 percent, and the city paid 1.08 percent. It would require four years of constant staff work, however, to prepare and process the appropriate paperwork—staff time for which no reimbursement was allowed (as per Coalinga Earthquake Claims Project records).

2. Scrivner approached the Small Business Administration several months after the earthquake, assuming that lower-interest disaster assistance loans could help ease his $120,000 loss. Like many other businessmen, Scrivner had erroneously believed the SBA disaster loans were based on degree of damage, not degree of financial need.

Keith Scrivner had been the only licensed underground utilities contractor in the city at the time of the quake, and because the town had urgent need of his company's services (and his employees needed the business) which he could not provide under conflict-of-interest laws as long as he was the mayor, Scrivner resigned after much soul-searching, and after assuring himself that the first phases of the recovery were firmly in hand. In 1986 he again ran for—and was elected—mayor of Coalinga.

3. "We had all watched Grenada," Scrivner would say later, ". . . and how two days after we ran out the Cubans, we poured tens of millions of dollars into the place. Well, the people of Coalinga could have used just a fraction of that. But we're afraid to give each other federal dollars, while unafraid to give it to foreigners. That, to me, is ironic."

4. FEMA, for instance, brought in mobile homes for emergency housing, promising that those who occupied them would be able to purchase them later on. But the trailers had been

brought in from out of state and did not meet California standards, so the state would not permit the federal agency to sell them to Coalingans. In the meantime, even though the city had donated the land for the temporary trailer park, the authorities overseeing the site refused to allow any beautification or improvements. As a result, many moved out in disgust and left the area—some permanently.

5. Even some of those who did receive insurance policy payoffs ended up without the financial ability to rebuild thanks to fast-buck artists or dishonest contractors who took their insurance payments and left town.

6. The city of Coalinga, under its police power and ordinances and during its declaration of municipal emergency, had the authority to condemn and tear down buildings it felt were a hazard to life and property. The exercise of that power, however, was understandably controversial to people whose buildings seemed intact, though grievously damaged, yet were bulldozed within days. In one instance, a jewelry store was flattened to halt the fire from the Coalinga Inn. Though the owners were given some time to remove the stock, they later sued the city on the grounds that thousands of dollars of expensive jewelry items had been crushed in the rubble and sent to the dump. Other merchants were unable to remove possessions, stock, office equipment, records, and valuables before the bulldozers moved in. It was a heartbreaking exercise, but the specter of damaged buildings collapsing on owners engaged in recovering material items haunted the city officials and guided their actions. Meanwhile, the lack of insurance for many of the lost items—as well as for the buildings and business equity—haunted the owners and guided subsequent lawsuits and bankruptcies. The insurers of the jewelry store, for instance, denied coverage for their municipally ordered loss simply because the building was knocked down before it could be consumed by the fire its destruction was supposed to halt!

7. One of the Coalinga homeowners whose insurance claim had been refused hauled the insurance company into court on the grounds that a policy which was labeled "all risk" on the front could not exclude earthquake damage with the small print inside. Eventually, the California court agreed with the earlier State Farm decision, and ruled that the words "all risk" did indeed require payment. That led rapidly to the settlement of many "all risk" policy claims which had been previously denied in Coalinga. Business owners, however, did not have "all risk" endorsements on commercial policies, and therefore could not benefit from the ruling.

Chapter 21

1. Mexico City sits 7,300 feet high in a basin ringed by high volcanic peaks, the erosion of which over thousands of years has deposited many layers of alluvial silts and muds, gravels, sands, and clays into the natural basin which at one time was filled with water and known to the ancient Aztecs as Lake Texcoco. Four hundred years ago, when Hernando Cortez conquered the Aztec empire, the lake was still partially filled, but the Spaniards drained it to gain more land for building. Much of Mexico City sits on the high ground above the shore of the old lake, but the airport and parts of sprawling southeast Mexico City have projected onto the soft muds and clays—significant parts of the city center seated on soft sediments over 7,000 feet thick at some points.

2. These codes would be upgraded immediately after the quake with an emergency interim building code that went into effect on October 18, a code that contained higher seismic safety coefficients than the previous code adopted in 1976. The city's Public Works Department knew that the standards for the portion of Mexico City which sat over the lake bed would have to be upgraded significantly, and a final revised and much improved code was to be adopted by the end of 1986. Nevertheless, the department suspected that many repairs to large buildings and apartment complexes would be done with noncomplying techniques and standards while the revised codes were being written. Because of the very limited number of inspectors available to monitor the process, new seismic bombs would be locked into weakened concrete columns and beams and inadequately welded steel reinforcing mem-

bers in many locations—"bombs" which would probably go off the next time the capital city received massive pulses of long-wave seismic energy.

3. Indeed, before leaving for Mexico, Karen McNally was forced to withdraw eight thousand dollars of her own personal savings to finance the trip in the absence of immediate funding from the USGS Earthquakes, Volcanoes, and Engineering Office Chief John Filson. Filson, it seemed, was caught at the end of the fiscal year and could not help. Yet when McNally submitted a request for reimbursement later in fiscal 1986, she was turned down by the internal bureaucratic structure of USGS on the grounds that the expense had actually occurred in fiscal 1985. The National Science Foundation eventually came to her rescue, but the episode was a graphic reminder of how extremely difficult it is to expect global advances in geophysical science with sweeping planetary implications for the well-being of millions of people while restricted to K Mart budgets and bureaucratic hair splitting restraints.

Chapter 22

1. The aftermath of a destructive quake brings a heavy emphasis on returning to "normalcy," whatever "normalcy" really is. The focus is on rebuilding, not necessarily on rebuilding properly. There were efforts in Charleston to rebuild stronger structures which would have a better chance of weathering another great quake, but the methods used were woefully inadequate in most cases. Long metal bars were installed, for instance, through hundreds of damaged buildings and homes, anchored at upper-floor levels on each end with a circular metal plate (earthquake anchor) through which the screw-threaded bar would be tightened down with a large bolt. The anchors were destined to become as much an architectural feature as an element of earthquake engineering, but their purpose was to prevent walls from undulating out from under floor beams and braces during the wild waving of an earthquake—a phenomenon responsible for collapsing many of the buildings in 1886.

Interesting enough, the design was copied in various places up the eastern seaboard and as far away as California in the decades following 1886. There were, in fact, similar earthquake bars and anchors engineered into the unreinforced masonry buildings built around 1910 in Coalinga, California—the same buildings which collapsed in 1983. And it is true that some of the collapsed buildings in Charleston in 1886 had already been fitted with these ineffective devices. The anchors themselves have proven to be a "chicken soup" solution: They may not help—they may not prevent the floors or the building from collapsing—but they can't hurt. The major malady, of course, is always going to be seismically vulnerable unreinforced masonry construction.

The anchors, however, were often installed as a cure-all in brick-and-mortar buildings, which had been pieced back together with more brick and questionable lime-filled, sandy mortar. Thus by 1890, Charleston was replete with hundreds of brick-and-mortar buildings with great damage and deep cracks which had been merely "plastered" over externally, and within which the original mortar (which had already turned to sand) remained undisturbed—and incapable of holding anything together. With or without earthquake anchors, another large quake would mean another significant disaster. And so it would remain for at least the next hundred years.

2. A jackhammer had been used in the street nearby the morning of the collapse, but several hours of normal traffic vibrations passed before the wall fell.

3. The advent of a small seismograph network in South Carolina, and the development of the South Carolina Seismic Safety Consortium and later the Eastern United States Seismic Safety Consortium were direct results of their efforts. With Charleston a clear "ground zero" for a great quake, it was a logical place to begin. Whereas Joyce Bagwell has concentrated her efforts on education, Charles Lindbergh has focused on earthquake engineering technology. "The essential problem," as he puts it, "is that there is not even minimal earthquake engineering technology among our [eastern] communities sufficient to form sensible seismic risk awareness and safety policy. We need to place top priority on transferring the available excellent technology and experience from the west to satisfy this need at all levels, especially at

the grass roots. Technology and community commitment are the two basic keys to even minimal seismic safety in the Eastern U.S." With minuscule funding, endless energy, and support from the USGS, the efforts of both Bagwell and Lindbergh—and others—began to slowly, painfully push into the margins of public awareness. There were light-years to go, of course, but their efforts had been a start. Still, in all the eastern United States, their efforts constitute the only formal hazard reduction programs. Nothing is being done formally in New York City, Washington, D.C., Chicago, Philadelphia, or a host of other highly vulnerable U.S. metropolitan areas.

Residents of the eastern United States generally do not realize that the major rock formations which make up the entire North American continent are riddled with cracks—faults—even from the Rocky Mountains to the Atlantic coast. The complex tectonics of the mid-Atlantic states, especially in New York City, the vulnerability of Buffalo, New York (where a new Earthquake Research Center was established at the State University of New York under Dr. Robert Kettler), and the inferred and suspected faults beneath Illinois and Pennsylvania and most other eastern states, should provide a clarion warning for easterners to get their act together in terms of earthquake hazard reduction programs.

Yet with the exception of Charleston, South Carolina, and Memphis, Tennessee, there are few, if any, efforts being made east of Denver toward such goals. (There is some evidence of progress. Beginning in 1988, for the first time the basic provisions of the model codes—the Standard Building Code—will specify a basic level of earthquake design criteria for new [not existing] structures. Communities must adopt, use, and enforce such provisions, however, and not all have done so. The step, while hopeful, is merely a beginning.)

4. Not that they haven't been warned. Scientists have tried for years to tell Memphis city fathers and Shelby County officials what will happen to the area the next time the New Madrid Fault lurches violently. Dr. Arch Johnston of Memphis State University, for one, has worked long and hard for years to establish the Tennessee Earthquake Information Center in Memphis, gaining funding from the Federal Emergency Management Agency through the 1977 Earthquake Hazard Reduction Act to start a tiny program of education to teach just this point: that Memphis is in danger. It is information, however, for a population that so far does not seem to want to listen.

5. The Earthquake Hazard Reduction Act of 1977 had envisioned (and provided some funding for) a new type of regional or municipal organization which would spread the word and spur people to action. FEMA had been chosen as lead agency by the bill, and one thing FEMA's people knew they needed to do from the very first was establish a model "project" in one of the California communities most likely to suffer the next great quake. Such a group would be funded partially by its own state, and partially by the federal government, and would work as a communicator without the power to write or enforce any laws. It would, instead, encourage communities to recognize the reality of their seismic exposure; pass new building codes and get rid of the masonry seismic bombs; educate their people on what to expect and what to do when the ground started shaking; coordinate search, rescue, and recovery capabilities; and get better zoning control of hazardous land areas. Most of all, though, such an organization would try to convince people to accept the bad news of impending earthquakes with the good news and vital knowledge that earthquake damage can be minimized if people and cities prepare in advance.

The logical choice, of course, had been Los Angeles, sitting as it was in the shadow of the Palmdale Bulge and the growing tectonic strain on the Fort Tejon section of the southern San Andreas Fault. Following Kerry Sieh's findings at Pallett Creek, there was no longer any question of if, merely a question of when. After Dr. Frank Press had stunned President Jimmy Carter on the flight back from the presidential inspection trip to Mount St. Helens in May of 1980 with that news, and after the President had assigned the National Security Council to look into the threat, the report the NSC issued six months later confirmed that Southern California—and our defense facilities there—were in fact at great risk. The overall conclusion was frightening: No level of government was adequately prepared to handle what was coming. Among the things needed, said the NSC, was "a small, dedicated staff in California to concentrate on Earthquake Preparedness. . . ."

That gave California's state legislators the nucleus of an idea they needed to construct a program for earthquake hazard reduction—something long discussed in the state but never enacted. Within a few months the California Assembly had written and passed Assembly Bill

370

2202 (September 1980) which authorized funding of a pilot project—the beginnings of an organization which would tackle the prodigious job of trying to convince California communities, which were obviously at risk, to do something to prepare.

6. Both SCEPP and its counterpart in Oakland, BAREPP, in just a few years have developed effective methods of educating the public on what to do before, during, and after a major earthquake. And, they have pioneered ingenious methods of involving the business community in earthquake preparedness programs. The accomplishments of both groups on minimal funds have been nothing short of amazing. Both are excellent models for the earthquake hazard reduction organizations which should be in operation in the other thirty-eight high-seismic-risk states of the United States.

Chapter 23

1. Lidia Selkregg was the principal investigator on an excellent and comprehensive study of real-time, realistic hazard mitigation (and what should have been done and was not done in Anchorage) entitled "Earthquake Hazard Mitigation: Planning and Policy Implementation: The Alaska Case," written with six others under a National Science Foundation grant (CEE 8112632) and published in 1984. Selkregg and scores of other scientists and engineers had watched in fascination and frustration during much of this period, but never so intensely as when the Anchorage Municipal Assembly voted against Task Force 9's recommendations for dealing with the ongoing dangers of Turnagain Heights. That abdication of responsibility came in June of 1967, and immediately thereafter the Assembly began considering applications for new houses and apartments in the slide area itself—while never attempting to stop the beach erosion which had begun the winter of 1965, and which would undermine even the geologically temporary stability of the new Turnagain bluff if allowed to continue.

2. In an editorial shortly after the quake, Bob Atwood's paper stated: "Alaskans are learning that there are some things worse than the aftershocks that follow an earthquake. Among them are scientists." (From the *Anchorage Daily Times,* April 27, 1964, as quoted by Lidia Selkregg in the book cited in above).

3. The publication was prepared by William Spangle and Associates, Inc. of Portola Valley, California, in conjunction with Earth Sciences Associates and others, and issued in 1978 (NSF Grant ENV 76-82756). The quotation here comes from p. B-26. The book is an excellent chronicle of why no more has been done, and of precisely what did and did not occur from an engineering and social point of view following the quake.

It is very instructive to understand the assumptions which people made as they decided later to build new, major structures in the L Street area. The authors point out: "[The developers] apparently assumed that any future losses would be covered by insurance or federal disaster assistance. This rationale was further reinforced by the willingness of local financial institutions to fund construction in the area in spite of federal refusal to insure loans [due to the high-risk classification]. Risk from future earthquakes is largely discounted, in part, because of the feeling that, having had a major earthquake, another one is a long way off. As stated by a zoning officer in the Anchorage planning department: 'We look at earthquakes here more as a historical incident than as a recurring danger.'

"This view is in sharp contrast to that held by seismologists . . . that recurrence of earthquakes is a virtual certainty."

4. There have been a few sporadic violations of the land use recommendations, including a series of two-story condominiums built on the mud flats adjacent to the site of the former small-boat harbor. In graphic demonstration of how dangerous such a site can be, a small flood in 1986 easily washed away the silt beneath one corner of those condos, and one entire two-story unit fell off its foundation.

5. Through the donation of land at the mouth of Mineral Creek several miles to the west by local businessman Owen Meals and through the use of federal funds and state funds, the entire community was relocated, and the old town razed. But the process was by no means an exercise in sweetness and light and unlimited cooperation. There were great and bitter

disagreements over the governmental classification of the entire river delta—and thus the entire townsite—as high-risk, and numerous residents did not want to move. The successful relocation could not have succeeded, in fact, if it had not been done rapidly and with courageous decisions made by a host of people in city, state, and federal governmental positions—as well as community leaders—nor would it have succeeded if people had been allowed to keep their titles to the old lots, as with Turnagain Heights, or if the old town had not been strictly rezoned for recreational use only. It should also be noted that the story of the relocation—the valiant efforts of many, the tears, travail, personal hardships, and financial losses coupled with hope for a new start—has not been fully told as yet, and years hence could easily fill the pages of a gripping historical novel.

6. Henry Coulter, a geologist with the USGS, and Ralph Migliaccio, of the Alaska Department of Geology, probed the underwater slide in the weeks of investigation following the earthquake in an effort to find out how far down the docks and debris (and bodies) had descended toward the bottom of the bay. Migliaccio put on a wet suit one afternoon and went over the end of the dropoff to investigate—emerging shaken and somewhat hysterical a short while later. ("He couldn't get out of that water fast enough!" according to Coulter). While Migliaccio never described all he had seen, the fact that the slope dropped off into hundreds of feet of deep water had made no small contribution to his reaction.

A short while before, Migliaccio had been profoundly shocked while viewing one of the 8 mm movies taken by a *Chena* crew member when the faces of several people in one particular vehicle (which had driven safely off the dock moments before the quake) rolled across the screen: They were his wife and children. Ralph Migliaccio had not known they were anywhere near the dock that day—and had not known how close he had come to losing them.

7. A local newspaper article (as quoted in "Land Use Planning After Earthquakes") by Larry Makinson reported the changes, saying that the preliminary draft of the municipality's Comprehensive Development Plan echoed both the warnings of the consultants and of Task Force 9. Among its recommendations for policies to be followed by the local government:

"The portions of the Comprehensive Development Plan which have been identified as being susceptible to earthquake-induced landslides and given a high risk classification by Task Force Nine must be respected. Any development in these areas should conform with the specifications governing the development of such areas.

"That recommendation was deleted in its entirety . . . [as] was any mention of the word 'earthquake.' Privately, the planners say little has been done with the recommendations of the federal task force . . . because of simple political pressure.

"But politicians, after all, often reflect the attitudes of their constituents. And people in Anchorage seem to have largely forgotten the Great Alaskan Earthquake of 1964, except as history."

Chapter 24

1. The first settlers in Parkfield—three brothers who arrived in 1854—had settled down just in time for the 1857 Parkfield quake (which may have been the trigger to the great Fort Tejon earthquake of the same period).

2. In fact, if the trends of movement on all eighteen base lines measured by Duane Hamann's careful work were to be magnified logarithmically and sped up many times over by a computer graphic display, the points surrounding Parkfield that it monitors would be seen to wiggle, undulate, and twitch almost like the surface of a bowl of very cold, very rubbery Jell-O tapped in the middle. The overall trend lines give the seismologists back in Menlo Park a continuous indication of the fault's movements at the surface, and it is those measurements which they hope will detect any slippage which might occur suddenly in the days or weeks before the next quake. In the meantime, the multiyear examination of the undulating surface has provided a wealth of supportive information for other seismic observations. After the 1983 Coalinga quake, for instance, the Pacific plate side of the fault actually began reverse

movement of a few millimeters for a short time. Exactly what that means, however, is still unclear.

3. The reflectors, which he also helped mount, are so optically pure that a two-cell flashlight beam aimed exactly at one causes a highly visible spot of light to shine back, even from the most distant reflector, 9.2 kilometers to the south.

4. Hamann himself, a dedicated teacher and schoolmaster of the one-room (though modern and well-equipped) Parkfield School, has been a familiar fixture in the small community for eighteen years. The mixture of his limitless enthusiasm and the unending trail of television crews and journalists who have made the pilgrimage to Parkfield have also made Duane and his pupils media stars of sorts—and that in turn has made a demanding life a bit more fun.

5. This is called a deterministic forecast, or one in which it is stated that an earthquake either will or won't occur on a given date and at a given time, rather than the current tentative realm of "probabilistic" forecasts, such as stating that there is a one-in-five chance assigned to the possibility of a particular quake's occurring within a given area.

6. In early 1988, Dr. Zoback's drilling project was suspended because of cuts in the National Science Foundation's budget. The tragedy was that the project had only reached 11,420 feet down, and had several thousand feet to go before penetrating the segment of the San Andreas Fault system that the scientists had most wanted to study. While some of the information obtained in the first 11,000 feet showed a contradictory lack of stress parallel to the fault, and considerable stress across the fault (a discovery called "surprising" by those associated with the project), the drill bit would have needed to penetrate below 16,000 feet to provide the hard-core, meaningful information they were really after on whether or not the fault system is under extreme parallel tension as postulated. While one newspaper report labeled the initial findings as putting the prevailing theories of strain-release cycles in some doubt, scientists associated with the project pointed out that the "cross-the-fault" stress field simply meant that Los Angeles is probably in even more danger than previously believed from small fault systems underneath the L.A. basin.

Chapter 25

1. The shaken group would be joined momentarily by the only teacher who had been inside the school, a teacher who had done exactly what she had taught her students to do so many, many times in earthquake preparation classes: duck and cover, get under a desk, and wait. Within a minute after the shaking stopped, she gingerly made her way down the stairs and outside—to the considerable relief of the others, who had just noticed she was missing.

2. Lupe had died instantly, but her death was a horrifying reminder of how many lethal dangers an earthquake can place into motion in the space of a heartbeat—and how much work remains to be done on older structures which incorporate them.

3. Three others died of heart attacks, and many hundreds of minor injuries sent a flood of people to hospitals throughout the area.

Chapter 26

1. The April 13, 1949, earthquake was centered between Olympia and Tacoma and registered M_s 7.1, killing eight, and causing $25 million of damage—most of it confined to marshy, alluvial, or filled ground similar to that underlying the heaviest damage in Mexico City's 1985 quake. Nearly all the tall buildings in Olympia (the state capital) were damaged. On April 29, 1965, a M_s 6.5 quake occurred between Seattle and Tacoma, causing $12.5 million of damage, most of it in Seattle. Four persons were killed, and three died of apparent heart attacks as a result of the quake.

2. The bill would have formed an independent Seismic Safety Commission modeled after the California Seismic Safety Commission. Governor Booth Gardner vetoed the bill on the ground that the Department of Emergency Management already had the authority to carry out the commission's functions. (The Department of Emergency Management has since been reorganized as a division within the Department of Community Development, and earthquake preparedness is predictably a poorly funded, tiny adjunct to that agency's agenda.) While it was clear that the governor agreed with the goals and expected them to be fulfilled by the existing state agency, mixing hazard mitigation with emergency preparedness (or management) has been historically a lost cause. Only a specifically dedicated state function directed to the earthquake preparedness and hazard reduction programs can adequately focus a staff's undivided attention on the essence of the problem. The very same arguments against a new governmental program were raised for five years in a row by the Nixon and Ford administrations against the passage of the national Earthquake Hazard Reduction Act: the justification that the same authority was already in the hands of existing agencies.

Demystifying Earthquake
Magnitude Ratings and Scales

We have all heard the phrase "Richter Scale" applied to measurements of an earthquake's size, usually in the form of a number (such as 6.4, or 7.2). In fact, Dr. Charles Richter of Caltech formulated the original scale that has come to bear his name to measure only California earthquakes by finding a way to standardize the meanings of the various instruments (seismographs) and the various ways they recorded the picture of seismic waves. Before that time, comparing different seismograph readings was difficult because the waves grow less energetic as the miles from the epicenter increase, and thus the very same earthquake could appear much more intense on seismograph drums closer to the epicenter than on drums hundreds of miles away. Richter, along with Dr. Beno Guttenberg, devised a way of adjusting the readings from a specific type of seismograph for distance and other factors to arrive at a standard "apples-to-apples" reading that would describe the strength of a California quake. This became the "Richter Scale." Unhappily, though, the scale can be applied to only one area, and since the seismographs are measuring just one range of the wavelengths (approximately 300 meters to 6 kilometers, or .1 to 2.0 cycle per second waves), the scale represents merely a "snapshot" of a small part of the picture (seismologists call it "spectra") of an earthquake. For one thing, areas outside of California respond differently (the eastern United States, for instance, transmits seismic waves with an efficiency increase one order of magnitude greater than California subterranean real estate). And another major problem with the Richter Scale is that the larger an earthquake becomes, the more energy it transmits through the ground in wavelengths that cannot be registered faithfully by looking at Richter's target wavelengths.

Therefore, additional means of measuring the strength of an earthquake and expressing it in digital, logarithmic terms were needed, and that gave rise to additional scales, the more important of which are listed below. All these scales are logarithmic, so that a 1.0 increase means a ten times increase in the movement of the ground beneath that particular seismometer, and suggests roughly a thirty times increase in energy release.

M_L **Local Magnitude:**   Essentially, this is Dr. Richter's scale, most accurately applied when dealing with California quakes. It is still quite useful today for describing smaller and more moderate earthquakes, but it is not useful in earthquakes classed as "Great."

M_S **Surface-Wave Magnitude:**   This scale was formulated by Dr. Guttenberg to describe quakes at distant locations. The scale principally measures surface waves with a 20-second period, or a wavelength of approximately sixty kilometers.

M_B **Body-Wave Magnitude:**   Also formulated by Dr. Guttenberg, this scale measures the type of waves that pass through the interior—the body—of the planet, and that have a period of between 1 to 10 seconds (although the USGS applies a standard under this heading of measuring only wave periods of 0.1 to 3.0 seconds).

M_W **Moment-Magnitude:**   (Sometimes expressed as M_m): This is today perhaps the most meaningful scale for large and great earthquakes, in that it combines a measurement of total energy release with the magnitude (amplitude) of the earthquake waves themselves. The measurement takes into account the surface area of the fault that moved to cause the quake, plus the average displacement of the fault plane, and the rigidity of the material of the fault. A seismic moment, M_o, is the result, and when that is combined with an energy-magnitude formula, the result is a common means of measuring the greatest earthquakes on the planet, such as Alaska, 1964, and Chile, 1960. This is the work of K. Aki and Hiroo Kanamori, among others, and is very recent—which is why great earthquakes, such as that in Alaska in 1964, which were once related in the M_S 8.5 range have been upgraded to an M_W rating in the low 9's. This is also the magnitude quake that the Pacific Northwest may be facing.

While these scales all have the similarity of being logarithmic and measuring seismic waves, they measure radiation of an earthquake at separate frequency bands. Therefore, while some readings may be equivalent between an M_S and an M_W, for instance, other comparisons may be wildly different for the very same earthquake. Therefore, there has always been a need to find another way to measure the effects on man and his structures that would bypass these technical problems in dealing with different-size

376

quakes, and that is best done with the Modified Mercalli Intensity Scale, which basically measures the results of ground shaking in human and structural terms, assigns a Roman-numeral value, and provides an apples-to-apples comparison of resulting damage not possible with diverse magnitude scales.

Modified Mercalli Intensity Scale of 1931 (Abridged)

(After Wood and Neumann, 1931, as printed in "Earthquake Hazards, Risk, and Mitigation in South Carolina and the Southeastern United States" [see citation under References, Chapter 227]).

I.

Not felt except by a very few under favorable circumstances.

II.

Felt only by a few persons at rest, especially on upper floors of buildings. Delicately suspended objects may swing.

III.

Felt quite noticeably indoors, especially on upper floors of buildings, but many people do not recognize it as an earthquake. Standing motor cars may rock slightly. Vibration like passing of truck. Duration estimated.

IV.

During the day felt indoors by many, outdoors by few. At night some awakened. Dishes, windows, doors disturbed; walls made cracking sound. Sensation like heavy truck striking building; standing motor cars rocked noticeably.

V.

Felt by nearly everyone; many awakened. Some dishes, windows, etc., broken; a few instances of cracked plaster; unstable objects overturned. Disturbance of trees, poles, and other tall objects sometimes noticed. Pendulum clocks may stop.

VI.

Felt by all; many frightened and run outdoors. Some heavy furniture moved; a few instances of fallen plaster or damaged chimneys. Damage slight.

VII.

Everybody runs outdoors. Damage negligible in buildings of good design and construction; slight to moderate in well-built ordinary structures; considerable in poorly built or badly designed structures; some chimneys broken. Noticed by persons driving motor cars.

VIII.

Damage slight in specially designed structures; considerable in ordinary substantial buildings with partial collapse; great in poorly built structures. Panel walls thrown out of frame structures. Fall of chimneys, factory stacks, columns, monuments, walls. Heavy furniture overturned. Sand and mud ejected in small amounts. Changes in well water. Persons driving motor cars disturbed.

IX.

Damage considerable in specially designed structures; well-designed framed structures thrown out of plumb; great in substantial buildings, with partial collapse. Buildings shifted off foundations. Ground cracked conspicuously. Underground pipes broken.

X.

Some well-built wooden structures destroyed; most masonry and frame structures destroyed with foundations; ground badly cracked. Rails bent. Landslides considerable from river banks and steep slopes. Shifted sand and mud. Water splashes (slopped) over banks.

XI.

Few, if any (masonry) structures remain standing. Bridges destroyed. Broad fissures in ground. Underground pipe lines completely out of service. Earth slumps, land slips in soft ground. Rails bent greatly.

XII.

Damage total. Waves seen on ground surfaces. Lines of sight and level distorted. Objects thrown upward into the air.

Appendix 2

"Okay, so what do I do?"

While writing your congressional delegation about additional funding for research and preparedness efforts and a national earthquake insurance bill are urgently needed actions, there are things you and your family can do right now to greatly—and I do mean greatly—enhance your prospects of coming through a great earthquake (or a lesser one) unscathed.

First, understand that most casualties are caused by falling objects and debris:

- Partial building collapse, such as toppling chimneys, falling bricks, ceiling plaster, or light fixtures.
- Flying glass.
- Overturned bookcases, furniture, appliances.
- Fires from broken chimneys, broken gas lines, overturned gas water heaters, and other causes.

Step One

Survey your home for possible hazards:

- Locate all the heavy furniture, bookcases, filing cabinets, and other items that could fall on you or your children if the foundation begins jerking around beneath the structure you call home.
- Identify domestic "seismic bombs"; gas water heaters that can topple, gas lines that have no cutoff wrench permanently placed beside them, or fireplaces without a working fire extinguisher nearby.

379

- Determine which parts of your home would provide the most protection from falling objects and breaking glass in an earthquake.
- Determine whether there are trees, power lines, tile roofs, overhangs, or other hazards that could fall on you if you ran outside during a major earthquake.

Step Two

Hold a Family Preparedness Meeting:

- Decide on a plan if the ground starts shaking.
- Brief everyone—especially children—on where to go and where NOT to go.
- Brief everyone on the necessity to avoid glass windows and doors, which could shatter.
- Determine what can be done to make the home safer.

Step Three

Preventative Steps in the Home:

- Screw or bolt heavy free-standing furniture to the floor and hanging pictures to the wall.
- Remove or secure hanging plants or lamps.
- Remove glass bottles from medicine cabinets and from or around bathtubs. After an earthquake you may need to use the tub for a personal water reservoir, and one full of broken glass would not meet that need.
- Consider replacing kitchen-cabinet latches with a type that will not come open in a major quake.
- Secure your water heater with metal strapping.
- Check brick fireplaces and walls for stability. If falling bricks or masonry blocks could come through the ceiling, use plywood sheathing to provide a protective barrier.
- Keep breakables and heavy objects on low shelves everywhere in the home.

Step Four

Determine How You Are Going to Survive Without Outside Help for Up to Three Days:

In a major earthquake, municipal rescue and emergency facilities will be overwhelmed for miles around. You and your family will very likely be on your own for up to three days without electricity, water, gas, or other services. Hold a family roundtable discussion of what you would need for survival, and spend a few hours on a Saturday afternoon rounding up the items, such as:

- Flashlight and batteries.
- Portable radio and batteries.
- First-aid kit
- Medicines, especially an emergency supply of any prescriptive medicines of life-threatening importance.
- Extra clothing in a safe place, such as a trunk near the front of your garage.
- Sufficient food and water in plastic containers.

Survival is not luck! Even the worst earthquake possible, such as Alaska, 1964, is very survivable, and the wood-frame American home is the most resilient structure possible for riding out such a cataclysm, but not if a tumbled water heater starts a fire, or family members are hit by falling objects, or no first-aid help is available due to lack of planning. No matter where you live in the United States, knowing these basics and doing the brief and relatively easy things each family should do to prepare for something that we hope will never occur (except in Los Angeles, where it is a certainty) is just good sense.

This is not a complete list or a definitive checklist, but simply a general guide to get you thinking about how to utilize the knowledge we have to prevent earthquake tragedies.

For pamphlets and more information, contact any of the following organizations:

FEMA (Federal Emergency Management Agency), Washington, D.C., or your local office in major cities listed under U.S. Government.
SCEPP (Southern California Earthquake Preparedness Project), 600 South Commonwealth Avenue, Suite 1100, Los Angeles, CA 90005; 213-739-6695.

381

BAREPP (Bay Area Earthquake Preparedness Project), Metrocenter, 101 8th Street, Suite 152, Oakland, CA 94607; 415-540-2713.

Tennessee Earthquake Information Center (a function of the Center for Earthquake Research and Information of Memphis States University), 901-454-2007.

Acknowledgments

The senior seismologist sat back thoughtfully in the midst of his crowded office, the desk covered with papers-in-progress, letters, and other pressing matters, his bookshelves laden with the written chronicles from decades of scholarly and precise work.

"Yes, I'll help you. The public needs to know, and we don't have the means to communicate how urgent these things really are."

I have heard essentially the same statement from scores of scientists, professors, government and industrial representatives, and others during the last three years—people who really didn't have the time to help me achieve what one professor laughingly referred to as a "poor man's Ph.D.," the minimum necessary threshold of knowledge required to write this book. Nevertheless, they gave their valuable time to the project to help combat a worrisome by-product of technological and scientific advancement: the decreasing ability of the average American to maintain a basic understanding of the very subjects that will most affect us and change our lives (and society) in the decades to come. If I had not had access to the continuous assistance of such professionals, from first contact through final galley proofs, this work would never have been able to achieve such a degree of accuracy and scientific precision.

Science in general, and the geophysical sciences in particular, are human endeavors—and exciting ones at that. Conveying that central human element to you has been a prime goal. That is why I've presented such individuals as Dr. Kerry Sieh and Dr. Brian Atwater in a narrative style with the pacing (not the fabrication) of a fiction novel. I wanted to place you there with Dr. Sieh in the Mojave Desert on the ragged edge of great discovery, and to take you to that misty Northwest meadow with Dr. Atwater as he spaded into

383

the banks of the Waatch River, equally poised on the brink of a seminal and socially significant discovery. I intended those scenes to convey the mystery and the excitement and the accomplishment of individual effort because all too often science is seen as dry or boring, even though that is exactly the opposite of the truth. I also wanted you to feel the human struggles inherent in such discoveries, the agony and ecstasy and serendipitous aspects that are the same in our common human experience whether we are piloting a spacecraft, cutting a significant corporate deal, or changing the face of the geophysical sciences.

I do not, however, want to leave you with the idea that the men and women whom I have spotlighted worked alone. As they themselves have repeatedly pointed out to me, each paper and probe was an amalgam of their personal and professional efforts in conjunction with scores of equally impressive colleagues. For purposes of telling the story, however, some must be singled out. The fact that those singled out are wholly representative of their colleagues means that this area of science is not just exciting for a few, it is exciting and fraught with opportunity for all who enter with an open and inquisitive mind and a dedication to hard work spiced by the prospect of significant accomplishment.

There are literally hundreds of people who have helped during the years of research, the seventy-five thousand miles of travel, and the 150 hours of taped interviews that underlie this work, but among them is a cadre of men and women to whom I owe an extra vote of thanks and appreciation:

Dr. Brian Atwater of the USGS not only devoted many hours over several interviews to the task of explaining the nuances of his research as well as the major implications, he was gracious enough to invite me along on one of his research trips to the coastal area of Washington State near Willapa Bay. While he and an associate jumped in and out of a canoe through a long day of looking at the banks of the Bear River during an exceptionally low tide, I provided ballast and endless questions. The opportunity to see nose-to-nose the same dark layers of ancient, submerged meadows (and a subsequent trip at his direction to Neah Bay) provided vital elements of research. I also am in his debt for his careful perusal of portions of the book as it progressed.

Dr. Karen McNally of the University of California at Santa

384

Cruz has also been more than generous with her time through several visits to her office and numerous phone calls, not to mention her assistance in reviewing parts of the manuscript for accuracy. Her help, and that of an associate, **Dr. Fredereko Guendel** of Costa Rica, were pivotal in my understanding of the Central American seismicity problems and the subduction zones in southern Mexico.

Dr. Kerry Sieh of Caltech spent hours of his time on a rainy September afternoon in 1986 explaining the mysteries of the San Andreas in great detail, providing much-needed copies of his professional papers and other supporting research, and directions to his research site at Pallett Creek. That plus his fielding of phone calls and his thorough review and correction of the chapters concerned with the San Andreas research were of inestimable value to the precision of this work.

At USGS Western Headquarters in Menlo Park, California, I was given unlimited time and invaluable assistance by a gentleman who has been called "Mr. Alaska" by the geological community for his decades of pioneering research for the survey, **Dr. George Plafker.** I am particularly in his debt for his careful reading and correction of more than half of the manuscript, and all the sections concerning Alaska in 1964, and for his wealth of facts and references that helped guide my understanding of the tectonic processes that erupted beneath the forty-ninth state in that amazing year.

The senior scientist who is generally known with great affection and respect throughout geophysics as the "father" of paleoseismology (though he defers that title to Karl Gilbert), **Dr. Robert Wallace,** spent several hours with me in his Menlo Park office, and in doing so provided many keys to various aspects of the subject. In addition, he too helped significantly in the review process, for which I am very appreciative.

Also at Menlo Park, **Dr. David Hill** spent an early afternoon with me going over the Mammoth Lake, California, situation, and the history of what had transpired when the infamous warning notice was issued in 1982. Dr. Hill was also kind enough to review the chapter on Mammoth Lakes for accuracy, as well as answer numerous telephonic questions.

At Caltech in Pasadena, California, USGS seismologist **Dr. Thomas H. Heaton** provided voluminous information, research material, and assistance, and followed up later by being available to help me fine-tune my understanding of what he and colleague **Dr. Stephen H. Hartzell** had postulated as a potential great subduction-zone earthquake danger for the Pacific Northwest.

At USGS Headquarters in Reston, Virginia, former USGS chief geologist **Dr. Robert Hamilton** and **Dr. Robert Wesson** patiently explained a wide range of subjects, from the research into the strata of the New Madrid Fault, to the events following the 1980 eruption of Mount St. Helens in Washington State. Their time and the reference materials they provided helped immensely.

In Alaska, I was given great assistance by two distinguished Anchorage citizens who often in the past have found themselves on the opposite ends of debates relating to urban progress where it clashes with earthquake preparedness: **Robert Atwood,** publisher of the Anchorage *Times,* and **Dr. Lidia Selkregg,** formerly of the University of Alaska faculty. I very much appreciate the time both these good people gave me, the materials they furnished, and their immensely helpful reviews of the chapters concerning Alaska and Anchorage. The time that Anchorage *Times* editor-in-chief **Bill Tobin** spent with me in an Anchorage coffeeshop relating his frightening encounter with the great earthquake was very helpful—and I particularly appreciate the pieces of J. C. Penney's tile facade and the turn-signal lever from his crushed Buick, which he brought along to give additional substance to a memory in some ways all too visceral, in other ways all too distant and unreal.

I owe, as well, a debt of gratitude to a well-respected senior seismologist who gave me considerable assistance on the subject of New Madrid, Missouri—**Professor Otto Nuttli** of St. Louis University, who died in late spring, 1988, after a long and distinguished career of contribution to geophysics and to his fellow man. Dr. Nuttli will be missed, and remembered.

In addition, I am indebted to the efforts and the time given by the following people:

Charleston, South Carolina: Professor Charles Lindbergh of The Citadel, Professor Joyce Bagwell of the Baptist College at Charleston, and Charleston City Building Inspector Doug Smits.

Memphis, Tennessee: Dr. Arch Johnston, director of the Tennessee Earthquake Information Center at Memphis State University, and his associates.

386

New Madrid, Missouri: Virginia Carlson of the New Madrid Historical Museum, former mayor James Craven, and Don Lloyd.

Palisades, New York: Dr. Roger N. Anderson of the Lamont-Doherty Geological Observatory of Columbia University.

Washington, D.C.: Dr. Frank Press, president, U.S. National Academy of Sciences; Dr. John Filson of the USGS; Dr. Walter Hays of the USGS; Dr. Michael Gaus of the National Science Foundation; Ugo Morelli of the Federal Emergency Management Agency; Dr. Henry W. Coulter, USGS, retired; Gary Aldridge, legislative assistant to Senator Alan Cranston of California; and Dr. Paula Gori of the USGS.

Denver, Colorado: Dr. Waverly Person of the USGS; Joe McGregor and Carol Edwards of the USGS Photo Library.

Anchorage, Alaska: Warren Hines; Dick Reeve (son of Bob Reeve and head of Reeve Aleutian Airlines); Robert and Baxter Rustigan; A. J. Joy (who talked to me briefly under a gentle snowfall on the edge of the new Turnagain bluff, where his house now sits as new and perilous view property); and Dr. Perry Mead.

Seward, Alaska: Lee Poleske, museum curator, who opened up especially for me on a Sunday; Virginia Darling; Bernie Hulm; Jackie Deck, Seward librarian, who also helped me on that same clear and cold Sunday afternoon, opening the library and her excellent files; Bev and Willard Dunham; Dan Seavey; Mr. and Mrs. Doug McRae; and from the Anchorage Pioneer Home, Margaret Hofemeister, former civil defense director.

Valdez, Alaska: City Treasurer Tom Gilson; Valdez Dock Company owner John T. Kelsey; Marion and Red Ferrier; Mrs. Dorothy Clifton, representative of the Valdez Historical Society; Tom McAlester, former fire chief and now port services coordinator; and most especially Joe Leahy, director of the City of Valdez Museum, who spent an entire day showing me around and providing assistance in the teeth of a howling, subzero winter day.

Seattle, Washington: Captain Merrill Stewart, retired skipper of the SS *Chena;* Dr. Steve Malone, observational seismologist at the University of Washington; and Linda Noson, formerly of the University of Washington, now with FEMA.

Menlo Park, California: At USGS Headquarters, Dr. George Gryc and Dr. Arthur Grantz; and with the Parkfield Project, Dr. Bill Bakun, Dr. Al Lindh, Dr. Wayne Thatcher, and Dr. Bob Burford.

Parkfield, California: Teacher Duane Hamann and all the students of the Parkfield School; Mrs. Donalee Thomason; and Martin and Gloria Van Horn of the Cholame Creek Ranch.

Mammoth Lakes, California: Mono County Supervisor Andrea Lawrence; Mammoth Lakes Mayor Gary Flynn; newspaper editor Dave Rocknic; Fire Chief John Sweeny; Mono County Sheriff Martin Strelnick; and the people of Mammoth.

Coalinga, California: Marlene Dakessian, owner of the Kruger Motel; Mayor Keith Scrivner; former city councilwoman Florence Bunker; Public Works Director Alan Jacobson; Assistant City Manager Bob Semple; and newspaper editor Bill Howell.

Pasadena, California: Dr. James Beck, professor of structural and seismic engineering; and Dr. Clarence Allen, both of the California Institute of Technology (Caltech).

Los Angeles, California: Paul Flores, director of the Southern California Earthquake Preparedness Project (SCEPP).

Whittier, California: Father Tony Ross; Mrs. Mary Neyer; Mr. Gary Strait; Mr. Ronald Reader.

Apple Valley, California: Mr. Roy Rogers, perhaps our best-known cowboy and a personal hero of mine, who had flown to Anchorage several weeks following the great quake in 1964, and who was nice enough to recall at length for me the destruction he had seen in Kodiak and elsewhere on that trip; and Francy Williams, general manager of Roy Rogers Enterprises.

Oakland, California: Richard Eisner, director, and Jim Brady, public information officer, both of the Bay Area Regional Earthquake Preparedness Project (BAREPP); and Dr. Charles Thiel, who took time from a busy schedule to meet with me at BAREPP's headquarters.

Sacramento, California: Jim F. Davis, head of the California Division of Mines and Geology; and Richard Andrews, assistant director of emergency services of the Governor's Office, State of California, for a multi-hour interview in Sacramento.

Portola Valley, California: George G. Mader, of William Spangle and Associates, for his help with the Mammoth Lakes story.

Stanford University, California: Dr. Mark Zoback.

Libraries provide the backbone of my research capabilities, and a national asset beyond valuation. In this work you will find the fruits of research done at, and with the help of, the following institutions:

388

Library of Congress, Washington, D.C.
Main Library of the University of Puget Sound, Tacoma, Washington
University of Washington Libraries, Seattle, Washington
Seattle Public Library, Seattle, Washington
Tacoma Public Library, Tacoma, Washington
Pierce County Library System, Tacoma, Washington
Pacific Lutheran University Library, Tacoma, Washington
Columbia Basin Community College Library, Pasco, Washington
Stanford University Library, Palo Alto, California
Caltech Library, Pasadena, California
Main Library, University of California at Santa Cruz, California
UCLA Main Library, Los Angeles, California
Charleston Public Library, Charleston, South Carolina
Main Library, Memphis State University, Memphis, Tennessee
Main Library, University of Alaska, Anchorage, Alaska
Alaska State Library, Juneau, Alaska
Seward Public Library, Seward, Alaska
Valdez Public Library, Valdez, Alaska
U.S. Geological Survey Photo Library, Golden, Colorado

By no means is this a complete list. I owe thanks and appreciation to all who came in contact with the project and helped it along, whether by phone calls, singular kindnesses, books provided, questions answered, or directions given.

Genesis

This book would have never been launched without the efforts of the following people:

My editor at William Morrow, Howard Cady, sparked this entire project with a suggestion he made by phone in 1985, which led to the discovery that we both shared a deep interest in the subject of earthquakes, volcanoes, and the nation's response to natural hazards. His subsequent help throughout, with normal editorial chores as well as constant support and friendship, has been in the very highest tradition of the American book editor.

My heartfelt thanks also to my agents in New York, George and Olga Wieser, for their constant support and friendship.

And a very special vote of appreciation to Adene Corns of William Morrow for her steadfast belief in and dedication to this project from the first, and for service as a Morrow sales representative above and beyond the call of duty!

And as to my editor of first resort—my wife and partner, Bunny Nance—I frankly don't know how she does it. To put up with the slings and arrows of outrageous preoccupation with an all-encompassing subject for so long, and still accomplish so much in keeping the chapters and the prose in far better form than I could ever achieve alone is a Herculean task. It is teamwork that produces such a book, and on that team as well are daughters Dawn and Bridgitte, and son Christopher, all of whom have perfected the art of leaving Dad relatively undisturbed whilst he slaves over a hot word processor in the basement office, only half-jokingly referred to as "the dungeon."

I would also like to spotlight the material contributions of two valued friends who read and reread the developing manuscript in its entirety and functioned as unpaid editors of the highest quality: Patricia Davenport of Kent, Washington, a fellow writer; and Mary Ann Shaffer of San Francisco, a professional editor. Patricia also did extensive field research for this work on the New Madrid earthquakes with much-appreciated precision and depth.

Captain James J. Nance of Republic Airlines, the Reverend Gerald A. Priest of Marshall, Texas, and Mrs. Martha Kanowsky of Dallas, Texas, also spent untold hours going over the book and providing suggestions and changes.

And finally, my deep appreciation to Mr. Harold Simmons of Dallas, Texas, the gentleman to whom this book is dedicated, and whose faith in my vision of what one writer can accomplish has, quite simply, made this work possible.

References

(Narrative Bibliography)

Cold, alphabetical listings of source material seldom get read, but there are numerous sources to which I would like to point the casual reader, the serious student, or the curious scientist alike if further information on any aspect of this story is desired. Therefore, the following is a brief review, by chapter and by chapter groups, of where to find more detailed information. In the case of professional papers and books, each will have a wealth of additional, formal citations that can take you into the deepest levels of the scientific underpinning of each subject.

First, there are a few basic publications available in most libraries that will give you an excellent introduction to this entire subject, and one by Charles Richter that is absolutely required as the starting point in any serious seismological education:

For a thorough layman's overview, the book *Earthquake* by Bryce Walker and the editors of Time-Life Books (Alexandria, VA: Time-Life, 1982) is highly recommended. Frankly, I kept expecting my research to prove the book excessively shallow or out of date, but it withstood the tests very well. If read carefully, it is an outstanding threshold primer, and the excellent photographs and illustrations throughout give a visceral feel for the subject from many angles, including the deep historical.

Second, the bedrock bible of first-year seismology is still Charles F. Richter's *Elementary Seismology* (NY: W. H. Freeman, 1958). Another set of excellent basic books is Dr. Bruce Bolt's *Earthquakes: A Primer* (NY: W. H. Freeman, 1978), and *Earthquakes and Volcanoes* (NY: W. H. Freeman, 1980). These are academically oriented, but if you get the bug to know more than the average layman, dive into them with note pad in hand. You'll be fascinated.

391

Chapter 1

The Great Quake in the Pacific Northwest's Future   This rapidly developing area regarding the seismic potential of the Pacific Northwest and the Cascadia Subduction Zone can be researched in greater detail through the following pivotal papers:

1. Brian Atwater's initial evidence can be sampled in an article published in *Science* in 1987, Vol. 236, pp. 942–944, entitled "Evidence for Great Holocene earthquakes along the outer coast of Washington state."

Also see Atwater, Brian F. (1988). "Geologic studies for seismic zonation of the Puget lowland, in National Earthquake Hazards Reduction Program, Summaries of Technical Reports," Vol. 25: U.S. Geological Survey Open-File Report 88–16, pp. 120–133.

2. The professional papers that sparked Brian Atwater's interest were those of Dr. Thomas Heaton and Dr. Stephen Hartzell, summarized in a *Science* article in 1987, Vol. 236 (same volume as the first Atwater article listed above), pp. 162–168, entitled "Earthquake Hazards on the Cascadia Subduction zone."

Also see:

Heaton, Thomas H., and Hiroo Kanamori, "Seismic Potential Associated with Subduction in the Northwestern United States," *Bulletin of the Seismological Society of America*, Vol. 74, No. 3, pp. 933–941, June 1984.

Hartzell, Stephen H., Thomas H. Heaton, "Teleseismic Time Functions for Large, Shallow Subduction Zone Earthquakes," *Bulletin of the Seismological Society of America*, Vol. 75, No. 4, pp. 965–1004, August 1985.

Chapters 2–8

The Great Alaska Quake of 1964 and Its Consequences   For those who would like to delve further into this momentous event, I would send you first to the library to peruse the copies (no longer in print) of the U.S. Geological Survey's Alaska Earthquake Series, a group of six professional papers with associated maps published in the years following 1964 by the USGS/Government Printing Office.

I would also refer you to the subsequent bound-volume series by the same name published by the National Academy of Sciences, for which the formal citation is: Committee on the Alaska Earthquake of the Division of Earth Sciences, *The Great Alaska Earthquake of 1964,* Vols. 1–8, National Academy of Sciences, 1973.

Also see:

Engle, Eloise, *Earthquake! The Story of Alaska's Good Friday Disaster* (NY: John Day, 1966).

Grantz, Arthur, George Plafker, et al, *Alaska's Good Friday Earthquake, March 27, 1964, a Preliminary Geologic Evaluation* (Government Printing Office, 1964). Note: This was the report that George Plafker, Art Grantz, and Rueben Kachadoorian managed to produce within one month of the quake through nonstop effort.

Wood, Fergus, ed., *The Prince William Sound, Alaska Earthquake of 1964 and Aftershocks* (Government Printing Office, 1966).

The Library of the University of Alaska at Anchorage can assist as well with back newspaper copies from the period, which are always rich in detail that does not percolate down through the years to many of the books and other distilled accounts of a major event. Specifically, the special-edition copy of the Anchorage *Times* that was heroically cranked out on the Sunday following the quake by Bob Atwood, Bill Tobin, et al, is both a collector's piece and a graphic report (Anchorage *Times* Extra, March 29, 1964).

To dig deeper into the history of the Valdez experience, contact the Valdez Museum and the City Library, both of which can guide you to the proper people and source material.

In Seward, librarian Jackie Deck of the Seward Library and Mr. Lee Poleske of the museum are excellent starting points. The library contains a unique file of written accounts of the earthquake by 1964 Seward residents. Some very wise individual rounded up the citizenry in the weeks of grief and disruption following the event and asked them to write out in complete detail what they went through. Facts and experiences, thoughts and observations that would fade into obscurity within years if not months were thusly preserved, and through these accounts I was able to reconstruct rather exacting models of a massively confused sequence of events spanning a mere five minutes. Not only do I commend them to you, I would hope some philanthropically minded individual would consider a grant to the library to organize and reproduce that entire file. I would also recommend anyone caught in a future civic up-heaval follow the same example, collecting written eyewitness accounts within days of the event. Not only is posterity served, the very fabric of human experience depends on the recording of such detail for future understanding.

The situation with respect to earthquake preparedness and the lessons not learned in Anchorage is very well treated by Dr. Lidia Selkregg and Dr. Jane Preuss, et al., in a book previously cited in the text, but worth repetition here: *Seismic Hazard Mitigation: Planning and Policy Implementation,* The Alaska Case, Selkregg and Preuss, et al., printed under a National Science Foundation Grant (CEE 8112632) at the University of Alaska in 1984, and available through the university's library (limited availability).

Chapter 9

En Route to St. Louis   In researching the history of earthquake seismicity in the United States, I wanted to drive home the point that this is under no circumstances just a West Coast problem, as too many uninformed people continue to insist. For late, though technical, treatments of just how serious a problem New York, Boston, Washington, D.C., and the entire Eastern seaboard face, see the U.S. Geological Survey Open-File Services Section reports on the series of earthquake hazard conferences that began in 1978 and continue through this day. Specifically, with respect to Eastern seismicity, see: Open-File Reports on Conferences XV (1982), XVIII (1983), XXI (1983), XXIII (1983), and specifically concerning the threat to New York, XXIX (1985). Contact the Open-File Services Section of the USGS Distribution Branch in Denver (P.O. Box 25425, Federal Center, Denver, CO 80225) for help.

Also see (regarding seismological history):
Davison, Charles, *The Founders of Seismology* (Arno Press, 1978).
Herbert-Gustar, A. L., and P. A. Nott, *John Milne: Father of Modern Seismology* (Tenterden, U.K.: Paul Norbury Publications Ltd., 1980).
Kendrick, T. D., *The Lisbon Earthquake* (London: Methuen and Company Ltd., 1956).
Sullivan, Walter, *Continents in Motion* (NY: McGraw-Hill, 1974).

Chapter 10

The New Madrid Quakes of 1811–1812   The definitive work is that of Dr. James L. Penick, Jr., *The New Madrid Earthquakes of 1811–1812* (Columbia, MO: University of Missouri Press, 1976). Also see my previous citation to the book *Voices on the River* in the notes for Chapter 10. Any serious investigation of that mammoth series of quakes should include a trip to New Madrid and the assistance of the New Madrid Historical Museum. There is a definitive "Essay on Sources" in Penick's book, beginning on page 154, which should be a starting point as well.

For the technical side of the issue—what will New Madrid's fault do in the future, and what were the technical signatures of the 1811–12 events—see an equally definitive report by the late Dr. Otto Nuttli entitled "The Mississippi Valley Earthquakes of 1811 and 1812—Intensities, Ground Motion, and Magnitudes," *Bulletin of the Seismological Society of America,* Vol. 64, pp. 1189–1207, February 1973—including a microfiche of early written reports. And the USGS Professional Paper 1236 edited by F. A. McKeown and L. C. Parker entitled "Investigations of the New Madrid, Missouri, Earthquake Region" (Government Printing Office, 1982) is a must.

Also see Fuller, Myron, *The New Madrid Earthquake* (Government Printing Office, 1912).

Chapter 11

Dr. George Plafker and His Work   Dr. Plafker's contributions to the previously cited USGS and the National Academy of Sciences series on the Great Alaska Earthquake of 1964 were beyond invaluable, but his contributions to geophysics came from a series of seminal papers that are required reading for anyone interested in the evolution of the plate tectonics theory. First of all, the article in *The New York Times* that seemed to pit Plafker and Dr. Frank Press against each other with opposing theories can be found in any library that has the last twenty-five years of *The New York Times* on microfilm. Look for the article "Science: The Earth's Upheavals" by Walter Sullivan, Section E, p. 6, Sunday, July 11, 1965. The pivotal paper that sparked it all was printed in *Science,* Vol. 148, No. 3678, pp. 1675–1687, June 25, 1965, and entitled "Tectonic Deformation Associated with the 1964 Alaska Earthquake" (by George Plafker).

His research on the Chilean earthquake of 1960 and what it meant to the emerging model of plate tectonics was published in the *Bulletin of the Geological Society of America,* Vol. 81, pp. 1001–1030 (plus 14 figures), April 1970, entitled "Mechanism of the Chilean Earthquakes of May 21 and 22, 1960."

And a more energetic and confident presentation of the growing conclusions regarding the veracity of the plate tectonic model as demonstrated by the Chilean and Alaskan quakes was entitled "Alaskan Earthquake of 1964 and Chilean Earthquake of 1960: Implications for Arc Tectonics" (by George Plafker), *Journal of Geophysical Research,* Vol. 77, No. 5, February 10, 1972.

Chapter 12

Dr. Robert Wallace and His Research   Dr. Wallace's name can be found on a myriad of professional papers, and I will not attempt to reproduce a comprehensive list here. But he is the contemporary midwife to (if not father of) the new science of paleoseismology, and those interested in looking over the shoulder of his research should start with a February 1985 article in *Scientific American* (Vol. 252, No. 2, pp. 35–44) entitled "Predicting the Next Great Earthquake in California," by Robert L. Wesson and Robert E. Wallace. In addition, his fascinating paleoseismological detective work on the great quake in China in 1739 should be studied as published in the *Bulletin of the Seismological Society of America,* Vol. 76, No. 5, pp. 1253–1287, October 1986, entitled "Fault Scarps Related to the 1739 Earthquake and Seismicity of the Yinchuan Graben, Ningxia Huizu Zizhiqu, China," by Yuhua, Shunmin, Wallace, Bucknam, and Hanks.

Dr. Wallace's work on earthquake prediction, and his steady support and guidance of other scientists studying the subject, have helped to push the process along at a steady speed. The result of his participation on the Steinbrugge panel of 1970 resulted in his coauthorship of the formal report I cited in the text of this chapter as a breakthrough in diplomacy: "Report of the Task Force on Earthquake Hazard Reduction, Executive Office of the President, Office of Science and Technology" (Government Printing Office, September, 1970). And, of course, there is the report on G. K. Gilbert's research cited in the notes to this chapter.

Chapter 13

The San Fernando Quake of 1971   First you should reread my notes to this chapter for several of the applicable articles and papers. The February 22, 1971, issues of *Newsweek* and *U.S. News & World Report* both contain useful roundups of the available information at that time. So too do the series of articles following the February 9 quake in *The New York Times* and the *Los Angeles Times,* both widely available on microfilm.

Incredible pictures of the Lower Van Norman Dam (in addition to the one in the picture section of this book) may be found at the USGS Photo Library in Denver, Colorado. Mere inches and luck saved the lives of perhaps ten thousand people that morning: Recall that the reservoir was only half full, and after the quake less than three feet of dirt shoulder remained above the waterline on the eastern side. There are other old such hydraulically filled dams of equal fragility in our country today, waiting—just waiting—for a major seismic jolt to fragment their structures and release their contents on the trusting communities often built below.

Chapters 14–15

Dr. Kerry Sieh   In order to properly follow Dr. Sieh's pivotal work, obtaining and reading the following is a minimum requirement:

Sieh, Kerry E., "Prehistoric Large Earthquakes Produced by Slip on the San Andreas Fault at Pallett Creek, California," *Journal of Geophysical Research,* Vol. 83, No. B8, August 10, 1978.

Sieh, Kerry E., and Richard H. Jahns, "Holocene Activity of the San Andreas Fault at Wallace Creek, California," *Geological Society of America Bulletin,* Vol. 95, pp. 883–896, 11 figures, 3 tables, August 1984.

Sieh, Kerry E., "Lateral Offsets and Revised Dates of Large Pre-historic Earthquakes at Pallett Creek, Southern California," *Journal of Geophysical Research,* Vol. 89, No. B9, September 10, 1984.

Weldon, Ray J., and Kerry E. Sieh, "Holocene Rate of Slip and Tenta-tive Recurrence Interval for Large Earthquakes on the San Andreas Fault, Cajon Pass, Southern California," *Geological Society of America Bulletin,* Vol. 96, pp. 793–812, June 1985. (This one is especially important to anyone following Dr. Mark Zoback's project at Cajon Pass.)

In addition, Kerry Sieh's work on the 1857 great quake (called the Ft. Tejon quake because of the epicenter's location near Ft. Tejon) can be found in the following:

Sieh, Kerry E., "Central California Foreshocks of the Great 1857 Earthquake," *Bulletin of the Seismological Society of America,* Vol. 68, No. 6, pp. 1731–1749, December 1978.

Agnew, Duncan Carr, and Kerry E. Sieh, "A Documentary Study of the Felt Effects of the Great California Earthquake of 1857," *Bulletin of the Seismological Society of America,* Vol. 68, No. 6, pp. 1717–1729, December 1978 (same issue as previous citation).

Chapter 16

China   Officially China has never announced the true death toll in Tangshan, and it is still difficult to piece together that and other stories regarding the Chinese experience during the past twenty years. The previously cited Bryce Walker book *Earthquake* contains five citations that are good starting points:

"China Discloses 1976 Quake Deadliest in Four Centuries," *The New York Times,* June 2, 1977.

"China, in effort to Modernize, Puts New Stress on Science and Technology," *The New York Times,* July 14, 1977.

"China Predicts a Major Earthquake," *Unesco Courier,* May 1976.

"China's Killer Quake," *Newsweek,* August 9, 1976.

"China's Secret Earthquake," *New Scientist,* October 4, 1979.

As to the Earthquake Hazards Reduction Act of 1977, I would point any interested researcher to the full *Congressional Record* beginning with the appropriate House and Senate hearings of 1973, and focusing on the hearings before the Senate Subcommittee on Science, Technology, and Space of the Committee on Commerce, Science, and Transportation of the 95th Contress (Bill S-126) and the equivalent hearings in the House. Be prepared for a lot of pontificating, but there is a wealth of information there that lays the foundation for all that has come since. The reauthorization hearings that have occurred since then are also important sources of additional, updated information—especially the series in 1985 and 1987.

Chapter 17

Dr. Karen McNally and the Mexican Quakes   Please examine the notes to this chapter to review several key elements of source material concerning the Mexican earthquake "trapped" by Dr. McNally.

For a definitive look at the problem of labels in earthquake prediction, I highly recommend the following paper written by Dr. McNally in conjunction with Dr. Robert Wallace and Dr. James F. Davis (who, you may recall, is director of the California Division of Mines and Geology in Sacramento): Wallace, R. E., J. F. Davis, K. C. McNally, "Terms for Expressing Earthquake Potential, Prediction, and Probability," *Bulletin of the Seismological Society of America*, Vol. 74, No. 5, pp. 1819–1825, October 1984.

Chapter 18

St. Helens   Frankly, this is such a current event that research into the subject in any well-equipped library will yield a rich lode of resource material. I would also recommend you check the current USGS *Publications of the U.S. Geological Survey* book for late papers and circulars on the subject. Descriptions of the days surrounding the eruption of 1980 should be sought in the *Seattle Times, The New York Times,* and the *Los Angeles Times,* and summations in various magazines.

Chapter 19

Mammoth Lake's Volcanic Confrontation   I urge any interested person to obtain a copy of George Mader and Martha Blair's study, *Living with a Volcanic Threat* (Portola Valley, CA: William Spangle and Associates, 1987). I have independently researched in Mammoth Lakes the entire scope of events described in the book, and find it to be highly accurate and an excellent work on the subject (though perhaps a bit strident in placing blame, which is understandable when you consider the innate frustration of urban planners who watch local populations repeatedly refusing to listen to the facts). The book is not available in unlimited quantity, but the authors may be contacted through their publisher at 3240 Alpine Road, Portola Valley, CA 94025. The report was prepared pursuant to a National Science Foundation Grant (ECE-8302302).

For the latest volcanological information, consult the U.S. Geological Survey's publication catalog *(Publications of the U.S. Geological Survey)* for the current year under Long Valley Caldera.

Chapter 20

Coalinga   There is no single source on Coalinga's 1983 earthquake. Newspaper and magazine accounts provide a good starting point, but the story here is a human tragedy—the misguided reliance on the government and on private insurance (unbuttressed by a national earthquake or natural hazards reinsurance program) to put Humpty Dumpty back together again. Coalinga has never recovered, and while the depressed oil industry is part of the reason, the earthquake of 1983 bears the lion's share of the blame. To follow my research, one would need to spend time in the town of Coalinga getting to know the story from the residents' point of view. There is a study available through the California Office of Emergency Services, which was produced after hearings were held to examine what went wrong during the recovery period, but the root cause of the postrecovery malaise is not adequately addressed there.

400

Chapter 21

Mexico City   For David Smollar's article regarding Karen McNally's hurried expedition to the Mexican coast, see the Wednesday, September 25, 1985, edition of the *Los Angeles Times,* Part 1, p. 11.

An excellent source of information comes from the cited hearing before the Subcommittee on Science, Technology, and Space of the Committee on Commerce, Science, and Transportation of the U.S. Senate, 99th Congress, "First Session on the Earthquake in Mexico," October 3, 1985, available in the Library of Congress, or from the Government Printing Office.

National Geographic also presented an excellent summation in an article printed in its May 1986 edition (Vol. 169, No. 5, p. 655), "Earthquake in Mexico," which goes on to treat a variety of related subjects from Dr. McNally's work to the Parkfield project. (The Dr. José Hernández Cabañas mentioned in the article, by the way, is not the same physician as that mentioned in this chapter, Dr. José Hernández Cruz.)

Also see:

"The Catastrophe in Mexico," *Newsweek,* September 30, 1985, p. 16.

Fairweather, Virginia, "Rebuilding Mexico City, How Mexican Officials and Engineers Are Coping with the Earthquake Aftermath," *Civil Engineering/American Society of Civil Engineers,* January 1986, p. 36.

Rosenblueth, Emilio, "The Mexican Earthquake: A Firsthand Report," *Civil Engineering//American Society of Civil Engineers,* January 1986, p. 38.

"Damage in Mexico: A Double Quake," *Science News* (Earth Sciences Section), January 11, 1986, p. 25.

Eisner, Richard (director of BAREPP), "The Mexico City Earthquake of September 19, 1985: Lessons for the Bay Area," *Networks: Earthquake Preparedness News,* February 1986 (a publication of BAREPP, available through their offices at Metrocenter, 101 8th Street, Suite 152, Oakland, CA 94607).

Martinez, L., J. L. Albarran, and J. Fuentes, "Lessons in Welding from the 1985 Mexico City Earthquake," *Welding Journal,* March 1987, p. 23–31.

Stockton, William, "Lessons Emerge from Mexican Quake," *The New York Times,* November 5, 1985, Section C, p. 1.

Beck, James L., and John F. Hall, "Engineering Features of the Recent Mexican Earthquake," *Engineering and Science Magazine* (a publication of Caltech), Vol. XLIX, No. 3, p. 2, January 1986.

NOTE: These represent just a good starting sample. There are voluminous citations in the years following the 1985 quake, and I would caution that a full review requires examination of a broad range of disciplines.

Chapter 22

Charleston, SCEPP, and BAREPP   For further research into the great Charleston quake of 1886, start with the historical document *The Charleston Earthquake* (Government Printing Office, 1890).

For an excellent and comprehensive look at the emerging struggles to effect technology transfer of seismic engineering information in the southeastern United States, and to educate the population to the seismic risks, see *Earthquakes Hazards, Risk, and Mitigation in South Carolina, and the Southeastern United States,* prepared by the South Carolina Seismic Safety Consortium in participation with the Southeastern United States Seismic Safety Consortium, Dr. Charles Lindbergh of The Citadel, contributing editor (The Citadel Print Shop, Charleston, August 1986).

An interesting book of stories about the 1886 quake principally aimed at children has been compiled by Professor Joyce B. Bagwell, of the Baptist College at Charleston, entitled *Low Country Quake Tales* (Southern Historical Press, Inc., P.O. Box 738, Easley, SC 29641, 1986).

SCEPP, the Southern California Earthquake Preparedness Project, and BAREPP, the Bay Area Earthquake Preparedness Project, are both pace-setting organizations with highly developed methodologies and information resources that manage to do an amazing amount of good with minuscule funding. The address and phone number of each organization are reproduced here in the hope that anyone interested in beginning a community or area approach to earthquake preparedness will study the pioneering work already accomplished by these two organizations in public motivation, information dissemination, and the effective advocacy of community action and intergovernmental coordination.

SCEPP

(A cooperative state/federal action-planning project under the Governor's Office of Emergency Services and the Federal Emergency Management Agency)

    600 S. Commonwealth Ave., Suite 1100
    Los Angeles, CA 90005
    213-739-6696

BAREPP

(A project of the California Seismic Safety Commission funded jointly by the State of California and the Federal Emergency Management Agency)

    Metrocenter
    101 8th Street, Suite 152
    Oakland, CA 94607
    415-540-2713

Chapter 23

Anchorage—Current Status   Please see this chapter's notes for the applicable citations.

Chapter 24

The Parkfield Project   There have been many articles written during the past few years on this spotlighted project, and a perusal of the popular-magazine article listings in your library under "Earthquakes" as a gross subject heading will yield a wide variety of information sources.

For a comprehensive technical view, however, see Bakun, W. H., and A. G. Lindh (of the USGS), "The Parkfield, California, Earthquake Prediction Experiment," *Science,* Vol. 229, pp. 619–624, August 16, 1985.

There is a good overview article covering Parkfield and many of the other current subjects involving California in Brownlee, Shannon, "Waiting for the Big One," *Discover,* July 1986, p. 52. This touches on New Madrid, Charleston, Dr. McNally's work in Mexico, the Mexico City quake, and numerous other aspects.

For information on the history of the tiny Parkfield community, I would refer you to Mrs. Donalee Thomason, who is the de facto historian of the area, and who is working on a book concerning the past century in the Cholame Valley. (She may be reached at P.O. Box 3565, San Miguel, CA 93451.)

Chapter 25

The Whittier, California, Quake of 1987   Studies and technical papers are emerging as this book goes to press, so a deeper investigation of the seismological details requires a search of the latest scientific publications, and especially the *Bulletin of the Seismological Society of America.*

The story of the quake itself requires first a perusal of the *Los Angeles Times,* October 1–6, 1987.

From my on-site research in Whittier the Sunday and Monday following the quake, there is one point I want to drive home in no uncertain terms: All the frightening destruction of average masonry homes and buildings was caused by what was, essentially, a tiny earthquake and its aftershocks. The quake that will occur at any time on the San Andreas near Ft. Tejon will radiate a magnitude 100 times greater, and release energy over 900 times greater than the tiny seismological "love pat" that killed three people and did $100 million damage in Whittier. Please think about that, wherever you live. The $60 billion loss (not to mention the loss of fellow citizens) that WILL eventually occur in the L.A. basin will cause insurance companies alone to frantically liquidate assets in the hundreds of millions, threatening our financial system, and posing the possibility of a national economic disaster and stock market collapse. If you think this is exaggeration, work the numbers out yourself—then try to tell yourself this is only a "West Coast problem"!

Chapter 26

Great Quakes and the Pacific Northwest—National Recommendations and Conclusions   When it is published

404

early in 1989, the U.S. Geological Survey's Open-File Report on the April workshop held in Olympia, Washington, on the earthquake hazard to the Pacific Northwest will be a prime source of late information. Having participated in that conference and watched jaws drop all over the room at the revelation of the latest evidence uncovered by Dr. Brian Atwater, et al., I can assure you that this is, indeed, an emerging, cutting-edge story.

In that regard I would refer you to any of the accounts of the USGS Workshop published in the *Seattle Times* or the *Tacoma News Tribune* for the week of April 13, 1988.

The pivotal research done by Brian Atwater can be found in Atwater, Brian, "Evidence for Great Holocene Earthquakes Along the Outer Coast of Washington State," *Science*, Vol. 236, pp. 942–944, May 22, 1987.

Also see:

Heaton, Thomas H., and Stephen H. Hartzell, "Earthquake Hazards on the Cascadia Subduction Zone," *Science*, Vol. 236, pp. 162–168, April 10, 1987.

Sullivan, Walter, "Earthquake Threat Is Posed in Pacific Northwest," *The New York Times*, Monday, April 27, 1987, p. 8.

Monastersky, Richard, "The Juan de Fuca Plate: A Sticky Situation" (reaction to Atwater's May 22, 1987, paper in *Science*), *Science News*, July 18, 1987, p. 42.

A FINAL NOTE: The essence of the scientific method is to constantly examine all viewpoints and theories retaining any credibility until the preponderance of evidence favors one. Therefore, seismology, geology, geophysics, and paleoseismology are always in a state of dynamic theoretical flux. This book is not about an adventure concluded, but one just begun. Please don't hesitate to explore further, whether in the role of an armchair enthusiast or of a budding geophysicist.

Index

408

411

Newhall, California, 181
Newington, New Hampshire, 132
Newport Beach, California, 190
Nixon, President Richard, 173
   administration of, 374n
Noble, Levi, 165, 208
Nome, Alaska, 31
North American craton, 129
North American plate, 20, 152, 204, 240, 292,
   324, 326, 344, 353n, 362n, 366n
North Pole, 117
North Star Terminal Stevedoring Company. See
   also: Valdez Dock Company, 38
Northwestern Indians, 23
   Makah tribe, 15
Norwalk, California, 339
Norway, 118
Noson, Dr. Linda, 301, 344–346
Nuevo León apartment complex, Mexico City,
   Mexico, 295
Nuttli, Dr. Otto, 116, 118, 129–135, 298, 299,
   356n

Oakland, California, 308
Oaxaca, Mexico, 239–243, 250, 300
oceanic plates, 17
Office of Science and Technology. See:
   President's Office of Science and
   Technology.
Olive View Medical Center, 181–183, 185
Olmstead, USS, 38
Olympia, Washington
   USGS earthquake preparedness workshop,
   April 1988, 344
Olympic Peninsula, Washington, 22
Oregon, 21, 258, 259, 300, 342–344, 346
   earthquake potential, 15–25
Ottawa, Canada, 118
Owens Valley, California, 177, 250, 259, 264
   1872 earthquake in, 264

P waves (primary or compression waves
      generated by earthquakes), 53, 57, 67, 70,
      80, 83, 134, 140, 180, 228, 230, 233–235,
      245, 250, 292, 304, 324, 346
Pacific Northwest
   earthquake potential, 15–25
Pacific plate, 204, 324, 326, 362n, 366n, 372n
Pacific Rim of Fire, 133
Pacoima Dam, 180, 186
paleoseismology, 152, 223, 237, 344, 359n,
   363n, 365n
   definition, 152
   study of sedimentary deposits of the recent
   geological past, 167
Pallett, George, 205
Pallett Creek, California (Mojave Desert),
   203–223, 370n
Palmdale, California, 165, 206, 235
Palmdale Bulge, 235–237, 364n, 370n
Palo Alto, California, 189
Panshan, Manchuria, 227
Paris, Texas, 48
Parkfield, California, 165, 201, 210, 279,
   323–329, 362n, 372–373n
   Community Hall, 324, 325
   Donalee Site, 323
   earthquakes, 1857, 1881, 1901, 1922, 1934,
   1966, 324, 325

1857 earthquake as cause of Fort Tejon 1857
   quake, 372n
School, 373n
Pasadena, California, 119, 179, 210, 239, 240,
   246, 247, 332, 335, 339
Pearblossom, California (closest community to
   Pallett Creek), 208, 209
Peck, Dr. Dallas, 267, 367n
Pedersen, Ted (mate on *Alaska Standard*,
   Seward), 87, 88, 107, 108
Pemex headquarters, 298
Penick, James L., Jr. (author of *The New Madrid
   Earthquake*), 356n
Penney's, J. C., Anchorage store, 48, 49, 66, 67,
   71–75, 109, 110, 334
Pennsylvania, 370n
Petropavlovsk, Siberia, USSR, 117
Philadelphia, Pennsylvania, 130, 131, 370n
piedmont scarps, 169
Pierce County, Washington, 255
Pike, Zebulon M., 137
Pittsburgh, Pennsylvania, 130, 353n
Plafker, Dr. George, 24, 25, 117–118, 123–127,
   149–154, 160, 163, 167, 169, 223, 357n
plate tectonics theory, 24, 152, 197, 235, 248,
   257, 362n, 364n
   final validation of, 163
plutons, 259
Point Reyes, California, 165
Port Alberni, British Columbia, Canada, 118
Port of Seattle, Washington, 347
Port of Tacoma, Washington, 347
Port Valdez, 38
Portland, Oregon, 20, 117, 133, 252, 309, 346,
   347
President's Office of Science and Technology,
   173, 186–187, 360n
   ad hoc panel on earthquake prediction, 359n
   task force report (1965) on earthquake
   prediction (Dr. Press), 172, 186
Presley, Elvis
   Graceland home in Memphis, Tennessee
Press, Dr. Frank, 154, 160, 172, 251, 252, 255,
   256, 357n, 359n, 364n, 370n
   report of 1965, 186
Prince William Sound, Alaska, 51–53, 65, 70, 86,
   117, 126, 164
Prince, Reverend Thomas, 355n
Princeton University, 159
Providence Hospital, Anchorage, Alaska, 120
Providence, Rhode Island, 49
Puget Sound, 20
   1949 earthquake, 21
   1965 earthquake, 21, 346, 347
Puyallup River, Washington, 347

Queen Anne Hill (Seattle), 116

Rancho La Brea, 362n
Ray, Dixie Lee (governor of Washington), 253,
   254
Reader, Ron, 339, 340
Reagan, President Ronald W., 283, 284, 300
recommendations for National Earthquake
   Hazards Insurance Program, 349
Red Wing shoe oil, 80
Redwood City, California, 307
Reelfoot Lake, Tennessee, 144
Reeve, Robert (Bob), 43, 46, 66, 67, 77, 109

413

415